for Tom Burns

Reconstructions of Secondary Education

Routledge Education Books

Advisory editor: John Eggleston
*Professor of Education
University of Keele*

Reconstructions of Secondary Education

Theory, Myth and Practice Since the War

J. Gray, A. F. McPherson and D. Raffe

Routledge & Kegan Paul

London, Boston, Melbourne and Henley

First published in 1983
by Routledge & Kegan Paul Plc
39 Store Street, London WC1E 7DD,
9 Park Street, Boston, Mass. 02108, USA,
296 Beaconsfield Parade, Middle Park,
Melbourne, 3206, Australia, and
Broadway House, Newtown Road,
Henley-on-Thames, Oxon RG9 1EN
Set in Press Roman 10 on 11 pt by
Hope Services, Abingdon
and printed in Great Britain by
St Edmundsbury Press
Bury St Edmunds, Suffolk

Library of Congress Cataloging in Publication Data
Gray, J. (John)
Reconstructions of secondary education.
(Routledge education books)
Includes bibliographical references and index.
1. Education, Secondary – Scotland – History –
20th century.   I. McPherson, Andrew (Andrew F.)   II. Raffe,
David.   III. Title.   IV. Series.
LA656.M29 1982   373.411   82-13233
ISBN 0-7100-9265-2
ISBN 0-7100-9268-7 (pbk.)

Contents

Contents

Acknowledgments

This book draws on research conducted by ourselves over ten years and by others over a longer period. Our debts are therefore considerable, more especially since a number of the surveys we report have been carried out on a collaborative basis and have been made possible only by the work and support of teachers in nearly every Scottish secondary school, careers officers, local authority officials, school inspectors and administrators in central government. Some of these persons are known individually to us, but we must thank them collectively, along with the many others whom we know only through their efforts on behalf of the research; and this thanks extends also to the school-leavers who have replied to the surveys over the years.

For comments on drafts of some of the chapters we are grateful to Bill Gatherer, Dougal Hutchison, Ian Morris, Bill Nicol, David Robertson, John Westergaard, Roger Williams and our colleagues in the Centre for Educational Sociology: Peter Burnhill, Peter Cuttance, Charles Raab, Adam Redpath and Penelope Weston. Joanne Lamb gave indispensable computing support, assisted by Cathy Garner. Other help has been given generously by Liz Atkins, James Douglas, Lesley Gow, Keith Hope, Hugh Kernohan, David Pike and David Walker. Margaret MacDougall and Carole Holliday processed the various drafts of the manuscript and we should have been lost without their skill and unstinting patience. Amanda McWilliam helped with the processing and Fiona Boyd with the artwork. Joan Hughes as administrator of the Centre gave valuable support and helped in particular with the proofing. The surveys also owe much to her predecessor, Lillias Wylie, and to Eve Scougall. The Scottish Education Data Archive, on which we draw, has been considerably strengthened by the contributions of former members of the Centre, among them Christine Armstrong, Dougal Hutchison, Charles Jones and Guy Neave. Edith Cope made a considerable contribution to the 1977 school-leavers' survey and also greatly influenced our understanding of schooling and of research during her years in Edinburgh.

Acknowledgments

Financial support for the Centre's research has been given principally by the Social Science Research Council (SSRC) and the Scottish Education Department (SED). We have also been helped by the advice of the officials and members of the Educational Research Board of the SSRC and especially by two of its former chairmen, John Nisbet and his successor Jack Wrigley. Other financial support has come from the Manpower Services Commission, Grampian Regional Council, the Department of Health and Social Security, the Sports Council, and, in earlier years, from the W. A. Cadbury and Oakdale Trust and the Scottish Council for Research in Education. Edinburgh University has given continuous and valuable support in kind.

Thanks are also due to three facilitators of the surveys: the Research and Intelligence Unit of the SED, the Statistics Branch of the SED and the Working Party of representatives of the Scottish regional education authorities that meets periodically at the Centre; the support of the Edinburgh Regional Computing Centre, directed by Dr Thomas, has also been invaluable. We are grateful to the Scottish Council for Research in Education for giving us permission to use data from the 1947 Mental Survey and from the Assessment for Higher Education project.

We are solely responsible for the views and claims expressed in this book, although our co-authorship is a small reflection of the contributions that many, many people have generously made to an undertaking that bears our names alone.

The authors and publishers are grateful to the following for permission to reproduce copyright material: HMSO: for figure 4.1, reproduced from *Assessment for All: Report of the Committee to Review Assessment in the Third and Fourth Years of Secondary Education in Scotland*, Edinburgh, HMSO; for figures 5.1 and 5.2 from Wishart, D. (1980), 'Scotland's schools', *Social Trends*, no. 10, pp. 52–60; for material from His Majesty's Chief Inspectors of Schools in Scotland (1922), *General Reports for the Year 1921*, London, HMSO; for material from Council for Scientific Policy (CSP) (1968), *Enquiry into the Flow of Candidates in Science and Technology into Higher Education*, London, HMSO, Cmnd 3541; for material from SED (1965b), *Education in Scotland in 1964*, Edinburgh, HMSO, Cmnd 2600; for material from SED (1969), *Education in Scotland in 1968*, Edinburgh, HMSO, Cmnd 3949; for material reproduced from SED (1921), *Circular 44* (no title); for material from SED (1947), *Secondary Education, a Report of the Advisory Council on Education*, Cmnd 7005; for material from SED (1958), *Education in Scotland: the next step*, Cmnd 603; for material from SED (1966), *Circular 614*; for material from SED (1977), *Truancy and Indiscipline in Schools in Scotland* (The Pack Report); for material from House of Commons Debates (1966), Scottish Grand Committee: Scottish Estimates, First

Sitting, 24th May; for material from House of Commons Debates (1967), Scottish Grand Committee: Scottish Estimates, Third Sitting, 4th July; all reproduced by permission of the Controller of Her Majesty's Stationery Office; The Aberdeen University Press for material from *Tell Them From Me* (ed. L. Gow and A.F. McPherson, 1980).

Finally, this book is dedicated with gratitude to Tom Burns, Emeritus Professor of Sociology at Edinburgh University. Without his example and support during the early years of the Centre's work, literally none of this research would have been conducted. Whatever the merit of this book it can only be, at most, a small return.

Preface

The 'reconstructions' of our title refers both to major changes that have been made since the Second World War in the organisation and practices of secondary education, and also to attempts to understand, or to construe, secondary education in new or better ways. The intellectual construction of education by governments, local authorities and others has itself affected organisation and practice. But it has never wholly determined them, and sometimes, indeed, its effects have been unexpected or only marginal. How, then, is the whole enterprise of secondary education to be understood? This book addresses two sorts of answer to this question. The greater part of it contains our own attempt to describe, understand and evaluate certain substantive post-war developments. But out of this construction of ours there also comes a methodological argument about the way in which the enterprise of understanding education is itself managed, and might be better managed.

Our substantive discussion deals with, among other things, questions arising from the hopes and expectations for post-war reconstruction, as it was called, the reconstruction that finally made a fact of compulsory secondary education. We explore whether social-class inequalities in secondary education have changed since the 1940s and we examine the effects of educational expansion on opportunity in the post-war era. We also discuss the rejection in the 1960s of selection for secondary education, and we assess the impact of comprehensive reorganisation on academic performance and on other outcomes of schooling. From these reforms, and from discussion and criticism of them, has arisen the question: how much difference do individual schools, and the school system, make to pupils' learning and other experiences of education? How much of a difference could they make? We offer answers to these questions too, and discuss some of their implications for school accountability and for the publication of school examination results.

Preface

The consequences of education for an individual's subsequent employment are also important. Parents', pupils' and teachers' expectations about such consequences both facilitate and constrain what schools can do; and questions of fairness are also involved. Over the last two decades the large majority of pupils have become involved in the certification race. Has this made the links between education and employment tighter or more pervasive? In answering this question we discuss, too, how employers select for jobs and how they might influence the school curriculum. We also explore the implications of the selective function of schooling for what is now the non-certificate minority of pupils who are obliged to remain at school until 16 with little prospect of finding immediate employment on leaving. How do they themselves construe their schooling and what attention should one pay to their understandings, especially in relation to the truancy and rejection of school that has been common among them? How far has an innovation like the Youth Opportunities Programme changed the employment prospects of such pupils and does it offer guidelines for a wider reconstruction of later education and of its links with employment?

We try to answer these and similar questions, partly because we think most people would agree that they are important in their own right, and partly because their currency is symptomatic of deeper uncertainty about the state of the secondary-education system, about how it works and is working, and about what might be expected from it for the future. We try to analyse the sources of this uncertainty both in Britain as a whole and in Scotland in particular. In its own special way, the Scottish experience exemplifies a situation that we think is more widespread. It can be described as a situation of simultaneous and related disturbance in the moral and explanatory orders (terms which we explain more fully in chapter 1). This disturbance is not confined to education, but is a feature of several of the areas of human experience that people have tried to change, since the early nineteenth century, using ideas and institutions, many of which came to be incorporated in the post-war welfare state. It is a situation that has been aptly characterised as the fading afterglow of the Victorian love-affair with the idea of the perfectibility of mankind through public institutions. The fading of the dream of progress has left not only conflict and doubt about what can be achieved for people through public intervention in their lives, but also uncertainty about the human qualities that it is right and possible to realise in all members of the moral community. In other words, it has left uncertainty about collective identity.

Because of Scotland's historic commitment to a national identity in which generous public educational provision has figured prominently, the challenge posed by this situation to received ideas about Scottish education is particularly acute; and in the national response to this challenge, myth, in the anthropological sense of the term, has had an important part to play. The continued retailing of Scottish educational myth has been important as a means of expressing the enduring identity and values through which Scots have made sense of their education system and have interpreted the need for change. But it has also been important as a means of managing, filtering and excluding from public awareness the human experiences that might disquiet the public conscience or dismay the public mind. Myth has also, therefore, offered an explanation of the world, but an explanation that has been less than fully scientific.

Values and explanations are similarly embedded in all accounts of education. Underlying public discussion of equality of opportunity, for example, are ideas of what it means to be a member of a moral community (of the values that are recognised as common) and also explanations of how such ideas might be realised. Values and explanations, however, tend to remain implicit. In day-to-day discourse they usually appear in unproblematic and symbolic form: in the ideas and feelings that are evoked, for example, by symbols such as 'the grammar school' or the 'comprehensive school'. But, if the underlying ideas are made more explicit in the course of argument and persuasion, they may well turn out to be more ambiguous, problematic and incomplete than the familiar symbols might initially have led one to assume. Subsequent argument, then, often concerns what is meant by the underlying concepts and whether, if they have not been adequately understood or agreed, their merits can possibly be assessed from the actions that have been undertaken in their name: 'Does comprehensive education work?' someone might ask; 'Has "true" comprehensive education honestly been tried?' another might reply.

The relation of science to educational theory and practice cannot, therefore, be the same as the relation of science to the inanimate world. A social science of education must try to understand the understandings that have guided action. Myths, and other ideas, must be treated seriously as expressions of what people think they are doing and therefore as partial explanations of their actions; they must be regarded as accounts, or explanations of the world, which *may* wholly correspond to it, but which may also be inaccurate or incomplete. Logically, our own explanations of the myths, theories, perceptions and expectations that have guided practice must also be treated in this way. Such a regress is often taken to mean that a science of the social world is impossible; and one implication of this would be that the answers to the substantive questions we pose depend less on the way the educational world is than on the way we ourselves have chosen to describe it.

There is much in this position, and the final sort of reconstruction which we wish to discuss, mainly in our last chapter, concerns the relation between social science and practice that is entailed in the attempt to establish a persuasive account of the world. Clearly we do not think that all explanations are sealed within a hermetic subjectivity that leaves one with no means of choosing among them or of acting on them. If we did, we would not have offered so much empirical evidence to illustrate and support our arguments. But we do think that our arguments should themselves be called effectively to account; and that this implies a rather different relationship between research and practice to that which commonly obtains.

Our methodological argument is framed in general terms, but our empirical evidence is drawn almost exclusively from Scotland, and this requires a comment. Where evidence from elsewhere in the United Kingdom is relevant to the immediate argument we have quoted it. We have not, however, been concerned to conduct an extensive comparative study of different education systems. Some features of the Scottish system are, indeed, unique, and are celebrated as such. But, in general, we discern similar pressures and developments across education systems, when such systems are analysed using the concepts offered in chapter 1. We believe our readers may readily make the appropriate transformations, where these are necessary, but we have not, for the most part, chosen to lengthen our account with comparative details. On many of the topics we discuss, moreover, there is no comparable English or Welsh evidence. This is regrettable and we hope that one consequence of our own attempts will be to persuade people that it may be both possible, and worthwhile, to say much more about the functioning of the secondary-education system south of the Border than is currently the case.

We do not think that any special interest in, or knowledge of, the substantive detail of Scottish education is required to make sense of part 1 or of parts 3-6 (except perhaps for a familiarity with certain terms that are explained in chapter 2). Scottish concerns are more salient in part 2 and especially in the discussion of post-war policy for certification in chapter 4. Readers who skip part 2, however, will miss a grounded discussion of the functions of myth in educational theory and practice, a discussion which has implications for our general methodological argument. They will also miss an account of the spread of certification in the last two decades to the majority of secondary-school pupils. This account has an obvious application to the situation that must be faced in England and Wales, no less than in Scotland, not only with respect to the system of public examination, but to the school curriculum as well.

Part 1

Problems and Methods

Chapter 1

Overview

Introduction

The first and major purpose of this book is to give an empirical account of various developments in secondary education since the Second World War, and to describe and analyse its present state as it is reflected in the experience and views of recent school-leavers. The second and minor purpose is to attempt a modest contribution to current thinking about some social and political aspects of the organisation of educational research and about related questions to do with the philosophical basis of arguments over education. The two purposes are connected in that our empirical analysis is, in part, an example and a product of our views about the nature and possibilities of social research in education, and about the relationship between research and action. But it is with the empirical analysis itself that we are mainly concerned.

Our study is based upon data from a number of sources, of which the main one is a postal survey that we conducted in 1977 of a sample of young people who had left Scottish secondary schools during or at the end of the 1975–6 academic session. The data from this survey, one of a series that we are conducting, have several strengths. In the first place, they are, with a few exceptions described in chapter 2, representative of an entire system of secondary education. Second, the sample was large, numbering more than 20,000 and based on a sampling fraction of nearly 40 per cent. Its size has allowed us to provide detailed descriptions of even quite small sub-groups as well as reliable accounts of the age-group as a whole. The large sample also enabled us to send out different versions of the questionnaires and thereby ask questions on a larger number of topics. Third, unlike many surveys which focus on a restricted set of topics, ours deliberately covered a variety of separate but connected issues in secondary education, ranging chronologically from the subjects pupils had chosen at the age of 14 to their

3

further education, jobs or unemployment in the year after they left school. Fourth, the quality of the data appears to be good. The level of response to the survey was 86 per cent, averaged over the different questionnaires and, as far as we have been able to judge, the reliability and validity of most of the analysed items were satisfactory. Finally, the way in which we designed the survey and processed and stored the data reflected our belief that research should be a process of dialogue. Through a programme of collaborative research based upon the Scottish Education Data Archive (SEDA), we have made the data publicly available for analysis and reanalysis, and we have tried to do so in a way that allows people to challenge our own assumptions and concepts and to use their own if they wish.

We therefore believe that we have a reliable and versatile source of data on an entire secondary-school system, data which cover a range of themes such as certification, curriculum, truancy, unemployment and inequality, and which offer to us and others a rare opportunity to explore the interrelatedness of such topics. Our book is partly an attempt to construct a view of a whole system of secondary education in many of its aspects; but it is also an invitation to the reader to put his or her own construction on the phenomenon of secondary schooling, assisted by the SEDA. As with any such study, we ourselves make some judgments which go beyond what the data in their narrowest interpretation can sustain, but we do this in the knowledge that the same data are available to the sceptical reader who wishes to test these judgments or to apply his or her alternative interpretation to them. In the longer term, the reader may also influence the content of the school-leavers' surveys and the problems they address provided, that is, that we can continue to secure support for the collaborative element in our work.

The young people in the sample attended secondary school between 1970 and 1976. Our survey therefore offers a snapshot of an education system at a unique stage in its development, when the move to comprehensive education was more than half-completed and when the system was learning to cope with problems created by the raising of the school-leaving age (ROSLA), rising youth unemployment and the end of post-war expansion in education. It was also a time of questioning and self-doubt. In the year of our survey (1977) three official reports were published, evaluating and proposing reforms in secondary schools' certification, curriculum and disciplinary procedures respectively (Scottish Education Department, 1977a, b and c).

To achieve a perspective on these themes we have thought it important to place our analysis of the 1977 survey in a wider historical context. We have therefore analysed documentary information and also survey data from other sources, where appropriate, in order to describe the development of Scottish secondary education since the Second

4

World War. We describe the data sources, and give further details of our own 1977 survey, on which the bulk of the empirical analyses rests, in chapter 2. In the remainder of this introductory chapter we first summarise this historical development and, in particular, the ideas and beliefs that inspired it. We then analyse some of the interrelated problems that faced secondary education in Scotland and elsewhere by the end of the 1970s. We give a brief indication of the contents of the chapters that follow and, finally, we mention some of the problems of research and learning that have run parallel to the substantive educational problems we discuss. But only in our last chapter do we discuss at length how this book relates to them.

The expansionist perspective

We will begin with some assertions: most public arguments about education contain two strands, an evaluative strand to do with the sorts of people or things that are held to be valuable, and an explanatory strand to do with how individuals or groups might act to achieve that which is valued. A prerequisite for the sustained generation, implementation and further development of educational ideas is some general level of consensus, of agreed values and shared explanatory beliefs. However centralised and arbitrary initial decisions may be, their implementation and their modification to suit local conditions depend ultimately on what people do in the scattered and less controlled areas of a public system. Consensual policies become possible in two sets of circumstances: either when people agree both on what they value and on an explanation of how it might be achieved; or when people do not completely agree on what they value but, nevertheless, share an explanation of the world in terms of which collective action will simultaneously serve their different purposes.

Maurice Kogan has described the years from 1945 to 1964 as a period of consensus in the politics of education in Britain (Kogan, 1978). At first, we think, this consensus was founded both on shared values and on shared explanatory beliefs. In the early years of post-war reconstruction, universal compulsory secondary education was widely supported both as an expression of the purposes of a nation united by war and also as a means of reproducing that social solidarity in times of peace, of preserving the moral principles of the nation. To increase participation in education was to recognise an individual right that young citizens were believed to enjoy simply by virtue of their citizenship; it was to make a statement that, in certain new respects, all citizens were universally valued and that neither individual nor society could be regarded as morally complete until these new conditions of citizenship were met. The policy for universal compulsory secondary education was, in this sense, an expression of shared identity.

Nevertheless, the policy also rested on an explanation of how the world of education worked and of how education could be made to work in the world. At a collective level, increased participation would promote economic growth and social and cultural progress. At an individual level, a lengthened education would help the school-leavers to better themselves materially and in other ways. Public and private purposes could thus sustain each other, and thereby supplement the political will to realise new conceptions of value and identity. A wide spectrum of opinion subscribed, albeit with differences of emphasis, to this happy conjunction of purpose and explanation.

In summarising the expansionist perspective (as we shall term it) in this way, we are not suggesting that there was a single monolithic view. Increased participation was variously valued as a consumer or citizen right, as conferring individual or collective advantages, or as combinations of these. But most of these views shared the explanatory belief that education worked as a potent force in the lives of individuals and groups; and, as time passed, the plausibility of expansionist policies came to rest, we think, more on the assumed truth of this belief and less on the shared moral purpose that had accompanied the introduction of compulsory secondary education.

Over the last three or four decades this shared belief in the potency of education has led people to expect it to do a variety of things for them. They have tried, for example, to use it to increase the wealth of the nation; to redistribute opportunity among the sexes, classes and races; to fine-tune the supply of highly trained manpower to the economy; to reproduce an ideal version of society in succeeding generations; to act as a proxy parent; and to undertake the moral, social and emotional education of young people in a changing world. They have expected education to do much of the work of making a wealthier, more efficient, just and adaptive society, while also meeting the great range of backgrounds, interests, needs and abilities that individual pupils, and others, bring to it.

The expansionist perspective, in a phrase, has asked education to do more things for more people. It has looked to education to reconcile and fulfil a variety of possibly conflicting purposes in our economic, political and social life. In the event, the education system has often been unable to reconcile and fulfil all of these purposes and the explanatory belief in the potency of education has been found wanting. As this has happened, the education system itself has had to manage or control the resulting conflicts of value.

We may trace the 'onset of doubt', as Kogan calls it (1978), to a variety of events and considerations that had implications for the expansionist perspective. The slow or non-existent economic growth of the late 1960s and of the 1970s, combined with recurrent restrictions on public spending, appeared to contradict one of the main assumptions and predictions of the expansionist perspective, namely that educational expansion would foster economic growth. Moreover, a succession of empirical reviews in the 1950s and 1960s showed that growing public provision had hitherto failed to achieve the expected redistribution of access and opportunity. More recently, unemployment and under-employment among young people leaving secondary and tertiary education have cast further doubts on the economic functions of education; and high and visible levels of truancy and disruption have also challenged the expansionist perspective and indicated that it does not command universal assent, either from pupils staying on because of the raising of the school-leaving age, or from all of their teachers.

These events have unravelled and frayed the two strands of the perspective, the evaluative and the explanatory, in such a way that they cannot easily strengthen each other or separately remain intact. As with other areas of social policy, conflicts of value and explanation are now much more explicit in education than in the two decades following the Second World War.

Expansion and its dilemmas

In the previous section we described the perspective underlying the post-war expansion in secondary education. The facts of expansion can be more briefly stated.

The most visible forms of expansion concerned the numbers of pupils respectively staying on at school and obtaining external qualifications (certification). In 1952 only 21 per cent of Scottish school-leavers had stayed on beyond the school-leaving age (Scottish Education Department, 1953, p. 87). By 1977 the school-leaving age had been raised to 16 and 40 per cent of 16-year-olds stayed on voluntarily (Scottish Education Department, 1978, p. 1). Broadly comparable figures for England and Wales are, respectively, 20 per cent (from Department of Education and Science, 1974, pp. 2–3) and 48 per cent (from Department of Education and Science, 1978, p. 11); the arrangements for leaving at the minimum age in Scotland in the mid-1970s differed somewhat from those in England and Wales. As for qualifications, in 1952 only 8 per cent of pupils leaving Scottish schools possessed an external qualification in the School Leaving Certificate (Scottish Education Department, 1952, p. 89). By 1964, 27 per cent had an external qualification and by 1976 the proportion was 65 per cent (Scottish Education Department, 1977a, p. 131). The growth over this period in the proportions of school-leavers gaining external qualifications was even larger in England and Wales, and by the mid-1970s, over 80 per cent of the leaving group held some type of award. Both education systems also saw considerable expansion in provision for tertiary education in the 1960s.

There have also been more qualitative changes. The post-war reforms in England and Scotland gave expression to the idea that *some* form of secondary education should be provided for all children; the comprehensive reorganisation initiated in 1965 by Circular 600 (equivalent to the English Circular 10/65) was based on the principle that the *same* form of secondary education should be provided for all children, regardless of their ability or other circumstances. From having the relatively specialised task of preparing the ablest young people primarily for higher education, secondary education came to acquire responsibility for a whole age-group and was expected to perform a variety of social, economic and political functions. Employers' organisations took a renewed interest in the performance of the secondary system, along with such groups as subject associations, other groups that wished to influence the curriculum, new examination boards, a new range of further education institutions and, belatedly and in small measure, groups representing the community and parents themselves.

In Scotland as in England this process of expansion has given rise to three related problems, which we shall term respectively the problems of difficulty, selection and motivation.

Difficulty

The problem of difficulty concerns the adoption of standards that are appropriate to pupils of widely varying abilities. It has several facets. In relation to a single subject or course, the main question is whether a standard that is easy enough for some might be too difficult for others. In relation to a curriculum, or groups of subjects or courses, the main question concerns the lower and upper limits to the number of courses that pupils of varying ability might take. If these courses are each of a moderate or average difficulty, then, at one extreme, very able pupils might take many of them whereas, at the other extreme, less able pupils might take only one or two. To the extent that the level of difficulty in an individual subject or course is 'wrong', a 'solution' may be found in the number and manner in which courses are combined. But the availability of this solution is, in its turn, constrained by ideas to do with over- or under-examination, and with the content and balance of the curriculum.

The problem of difficulty has been exacerbated by expansion and by the extension of courses to larger and larger proportions of the ability range. The Scottish O-grade examination, for example, was introduced in 1962. It was designed for no more than the top third of the ability range and with the intention that, in most subjects, it would be bypassed by a substantial proportion of the pupils who were certain to go on to take the Highers examination in those subjects. (The Scottish system of public examinations is described in chapter 4.) By 1976, however, the Scottish O-grade was attempted by 70 per cent of pupils with virtually no bypassing. The examination cannot discriminate satisfactorily across the whole of this ability range. Expansion led, in this instance, to a situation in which many pupils have prepared for an examination that was insufficiently demanding for them, and even more have prepared for an examination in which they had little chance of significant success.

Selection

Sociologists have frequently analysed education in terms of its function of social selection. They have viewed the differentiations imposed by education systems on their students as determining, or at any rate legitimating, their subsequent allocation to positions of differing power and advantage. There are two main problems of selection.

The first problem of selection concerns when to select, and how many to select. Formally, comprehensive reorganisation removed selection at the age of 12 (11 in England) and was somewhat equivocal over selection at 16. In practice, the first formal stage of selection in Scotland now occurs at 14, when pupils choose (or are chosen for) certificate or non-certificate courses. And, among the majority of pupils who are selected for certificate courses, more subtle forms of differentiation persist, in the guidance of more and less able pupils towards more and less 'difficult' subjects, in streaming and setting, and in the tests, internal examinations and 'prelims' that are used to judge whether 15- and 16-year-old pupils should continue with certificate-course work in particular subjects.

The longer that selection is deferred, and the fewer (and, therefore, the larger and the more heterogeneous) the groups into which pupils are initially sorted, the more acutely the school system faces the problem of difficulty, that is, of finding a curriculum and examination system suitable for a wide range of ability and interest. Even selection at an earlier age, however, must still achieve a compromise between, on the one hand, a solution to the problem of difficulty and, on the other hand, problems concerned with the fairness of selection and the risk of 'wasting' potential talent. Suppose that a qualification is set at a level of difficulty at which only 10 per cent of the age-group would be expected to obtain it; a school system might decide to admit on to courses leading to the qualification only pupils with a reasonable chance of success. But such pupils can only be identified through tests which are imperfectly correlated with success in the examination. So, at one extreme, the admission of only 10 per cent of pupils to the course would involve rejecting many pupils who might have been successful. At the other extreme, the admission of all pupils, that is, the abolition of selection, would be to build high rates of wastage and failure into the system and thus to reintroduce the problem of difficulty. In practice, selection in comprehensive schools in Scotland has veered towards the second extreme; a large majority of pupils are now admitted to courses designed for the minority.

In part 2 of this book we examine policy and practice since the war in relation to certification and curriculum. We argue that policy has advanced through a process of 'downward incrementalism': the kind of education formerly offered to the academic elite of pupils, and the assumptions which sustained this education, have been extended to larger and larger proportions of the age-group through a sequence of piecemeal, incremental changes. As a result, the education system has experienced the problems of difficulty and selection which we have outlined above. There have been tensions between the solutions that schools have adopted to each of these problems, and the solutions themselves have sometimes conflicted with ideals, both old and new. For example, it has not proved possible to sustain in practice older Scottish ideas of a 'general' secondary education as secondary education itself became more general to the age-group. Nor has anyone yet devised a common, core curriculum for 12 to 16-year-olds that does not rest heavily, though implicitly, on an early selection of pupils to appropriate levels of study.

In the context of 'downward incrementalism' we turn, in part 3, to the second problem of selection. Are the criteria which the school system uses to differentiate its pupils appropriate to the selective purposes which education is asked to play in society? The public examination system has grown out of a system which was originally designed to select a small minority of able pupils for university, on the grounds of their academic prowess. Is it suitable for selecting the large majority of school-leavers to different kinds and levels of employment in which purely academic skills may be less highly rated? In chapter 7 we review the so-called tightening bond between education and employment. In Britain this has typically been discussed in terms of the occupational achievements of the academically successful minority, those who entered selective secondary schools or higher education. Now however, the expansion of certification has introduced formal differentiations into all but the lowest parts of the attainment range. Are these newer and lower levels of educational qualification associated with placement in occupations, training and education?

We have posed the second problem of selection in apparently functional terms: does education serve the needs of society? Yet underneath it there are continuing issues of conflict and power. One consequence of comprehensive reorganisation has been to increase the one-dimensionality of secondary education: that is, its reliance upon a single criterion of value by which to judge most, if not all, pupils. This dimension has increasingly been represented by the certification system. Public examinations have long been an important means through which the school system has been controlled or influenced by those outside it. In the past this influence has mainly been exercised, first, by central government, which has had ultimate responsibility for the examinations in England and Wales and, until 1965, direct responsibility in Scotland. Second, the universities have always been involved in public examining, indirectly in Scotland, but often directly in England and Wales; and they have also been able to use their position as a principal 'consumer' of certificates to determine the relative value of different subjects and qualifications. If employers are beginning to rival universities as consumers of certificates, to what extent have they imposed an alternative set of values on education?

Our discussion in part 3 suggests that, to a significant degree, they have not; that the reliance upon credentials in the selection to jobs is to some extent arbitrary; and that the development of new quasi-educational forms outside the one-dimensional education system (in particular the Youth Opportunities Programme) may pose a threat to the function of secondary education as an agency for selection.

Motivation

The third problem, motivation, is closely bound up with the other two. It is connected with the problem of difficulty, since pupils on a course in which success is either assured or virtually unattainable will, in either case, tend to lose motivation unless the course has compensating intrinsic attractions. It is even more closely bound up with the problem of selection. Selection has, in recent years, been defined increasingly in terms of certification. We no longer have junior and senior secondary-school pupils (respectively equivalent to secondary modern and grammar-school pupils in England) but we do have certificate and non-certificate pupils, and also O-grade, Highers and (more recently) CSE pupils. Yet certification has also been used increasingly as an instrument for motivating pupils. In 1963 a government report proposed the construction of courses around the 'vocational impulse' for pupils of average and lower ability, in the belief that this would sustain and enhance an *intrinsic* motivation to learn (Scottish Education Department, 1963). In practice, this proposal has been largely neglected; instead the strategy to secure the compliance of such pupils has rested upon the *extrinsic* sanctions and incentives of national academic certificates. The incremental extension of these certificates to the majority of the age-group has, in its turn, involved a majority of pupils in work for an attenuated form of the academic curriculum that had previously been regarded as suitable only for university entrants.

This strategy has not been wholly successful, and in part 4 we explore the limits to its success. The one-dimensional nature of the values incorporated in the certification system discourages pupils who do not share them, and also discourages pupils who have resigned themselves to failure in terms of this criterion of attainment and who lack any alternative avenues through which to seek success. The effectiveness of certificates as incentives also depends on their perceived value. For the majority of pupils this means their value in obtaining a job, although the perceived value of certificates depends not only upon the actual importance which employers attach to qualifications, but also upon the readiness of employers to make explicit to applicants and pupils the importance which they do attach to them.

If certificates are valued for their extrinsic worth, for their value in the employment market, then a policy which aims to increase motivation by increasing the number of certificates will create an inflationary situation in which the value of the certificates declines. A policy of offering 'prizes for everyone' is likely to encounter diminishing returns. The most acute problems of all, however, concern the non-certificate pupils, those who have been excluded from the certification system. As certification expands, their position as a shrinking minority at the bottom becomes more and more invidious. Chapters 10 and 11 examine how these pupils, in particular, responded to their situation. We reproduce a selection of their accounts of their schooling and we discuss the phenomenon of truancy. We suggest that the present incidence of truancy should be seen not so much as part of an individual or family pathology, but as a reasonable response to the pupils' situation at school and to the breakdown of the system of incentives. High levels of truancy challenge both the evaluative and the explanatory components of the expansionist perspective. They are an indication of prevailing uncertainties over whether and how the methods and purpose of elite education might be extended to all, and of uncertainties over the membership and boundaries of the moral community.

Inequality, the school system and individual schools

In part 5 we examine policy and practice in relation to selected aspects of expansion. Both the expansionist perspective and the indigenous Scottish perspective on education (described in chapters 3-6) place a value on equality of opportunity. In chapter 12 we present evidence assembled from a variety of sources to estimate the level and trend of social-class differences in educational attainment in Scotland since the war. In chapter 13 we outline the pattern of comprehensive reorganis- ation in Scotland, and the interaction of local and national circum- stances which affected its progress in different areas. Our 1977 survey of school-leavers represented, as it were, a snapshot of the school system at a particular point in the transition to comprehensive edu- cation, and in chapter 14 we offer a quantitative comparison of the school experience of pupils from the fully comprehensive and selective sectors of this system. This comparison leads in chapter 15 to a more detailed examination of schools and attainment in the context of an issue which has aroused growing interest in recent years: what causes differences between schools and what goes to make a 'good' school? Is it possible to improve educational practice by comparing 'good' and 'bad' schools?

People often wish to make such comparisons in order that the practice of the good schools should prevail. This might happen either through deliberate imitation, once the practices of the good schools have been identified, or through a competitive process in which the bad schools fail to survive for lack of pupils. Either way, a process of public learning and action is involved.

It might seem that a first step is simply to obtain the detailed information about each school that is needed to identify the good and the bad. Not surprisingly, against a background of falling rolls and cuts in public spending, schools feel threatened by such proposals and resist attempts to make such information public. With some reason they fear that the ensuing comparisons would be unfair. Comparisons based on a common yardstick, such as external examinations, would not respect the variety of goals and priorities which different schools set out to achieve. Thus evaluative differences of opinion over the purposes of education can inhibit public learning. Moreover, any simple comparisons that might be made on the basis of a single, agreed criterion of evaluation would still ignore the great variation between schools in the social and intellectual composition of their intakes, and in their history and other circumstances.

This problem, of how one isolates from all the interconnected differences between schools, those aspects of school provision that lie within the power of the school itself to change, is not easily solved.

13

It is not simply a matter of obtaining all the detailed information about each school, for, in the absence of generally accepted and true explanations of how school provision interacts with pupil intake to produce different outcomes, we cannot know to which aspects of school intake and practice we should direct our attention. Thus uncertainty of theory and explanation can also inhibit public learning, for schools may understandably argue that they see no reason to open their activities to the public until the public can authoritatively indicate what data are relevant, and why. 'Why', schools may argue, 'should we submit ourselves to final judgments that are based on spurious and incomplete measurement or on the seat-of-the-pants intuitions of parents, politicians or other professionals?'

All these considerations help to explain why it has been difficult to conduct studies of the strategies and effectiveness of schools at the very time that such studies would otherwise seem to be most necessary. As a result, public knowledge of schools is, at best, fragmentary. It is not known, for instance, whether the choice of yardstick does make much difference to conclusions about which schools are doing well; whether, for example, schools that do well by their pupils in the cognitive domain, also do well by them in non-cognitive areas. Many of the studies of school effectiveness in attainment are based on standardised attainment tests. Are their results applicable to performance in public examinations which more accurately reflect school curriculum? Other studies have been based on small and unrepresentative samples of schools and it is not known how far their results can be generalised to other kinds of schools. There is no systematic description of the range of differences between schools, either in terms of outcomes, such as examination performance, or in terms of the characteristics of the intakes with which they must work. And, more generally, there is a lack of procedure for systematically observing similarities and differences between schools, and for thereby developing public understanding of what, and how much, one can expect a school system to achieve for its pupils.

Chapter 15 discusses, with examples, how one might set about rectifying these deficiencies and how, to a limited extent, they *are* rectified in the procedures of the Scottish Education Data Archive and the associated programme of collaborative research. As we have indicated, this approach has tried to eschew the use of data to impose authoritative and final judgments on the public (who may not consent to the assumptions and practices underlying the production of the data), in favour of a model in which data inform a more open-ended dialogue between practitioners and others and are produced and reproduced in a less centralised and more pluralist manner.

Theory, myth and practice

Our discussion of specific examples of policy and practice is therefore also part of a more general discussion of our second theme concerning the nature and possibilities of social research in education. As the schools example has just illustrated, inadequacies in the state of public knowledge about the limits and possibilities of schooling are partly a cause and partly a consequence of the state of political life. Evaluative disagreements over the purposes of schooling create situations in which it is difficult to observe and learn from examples of practice; explanatory uncertainties are also a cause and a consequence of this situation.

To understand how we might break out of this impasse we also need to understand how it is that we have been able to live in and with this situation. In one sense the empirical and descriptive analyses of the first four parts of this book, and especially part 2, are directly concerned with this issue, for they can be read, not just as descriptions, but also as explorations of how people have, wittingly and unwittingly, adjusted their understandings of the world of education and their purposes for it, in order to maintain an evaluative and explanatory view of the world in which purpose, understanding, action and evidence were coherently related. We enter this discussion in chapter 3, where we describe and analyse a unique historic configuration of values and beliefs concerning the importance of expanded educational provision, a configuration that we shall call 'the Scottish myth'. We hope that most, if not all, of the chapters that follow can be read both as separate empirical investigations in their own right and also as a developing argument about values, beliefs and actions in education. But only in our final chapter do we move from an essentially historical analysis of events and ideas to an explicit and prescriptive discussion of the relationship between social research and political practice.

Chapter 2

Data, Methods and Collaborative Research

Introduction

The main source of the quantitative data used in this book is a survey, conducted in 1977, of young people who had left school in the previous academic session (1975-6). The survey was carried out on a large scale, with more than 20,000 sample members, and it covered former pupils from nearly all of Scotland's secondary schools.

The young people in the sample were sent questionnaires by post, and a very large proportion, over 80 per cent, returned them. The questionnaires asked about a wide variety of aspects of their secondary schooling, including their curriculum and public examinations, their experience of truancy and corporal punishment, their relationships with teachers and their current views on the value of what they had experienced at school. A further set of questions asked about their experiences since school of further education, employment and unemployment, about the processes by which they had arrived at their current destinations, and about their opinions on them. We also asked for some details of family background.

Much of this information has been used in this book, along with data from other surveys of Scottish school-leavers: surveys of 'qualified' leavers conducted in 1962-3, 1971 and 1973 respectively; and a survey conducted in 1979 which (like the 1977 survey) covered both 'qualified' and 'unqualified' leavers, but which was based on a smaller sample than in 1977. We have also analysed data from three large longitudinal surveys: the Scottish Mental Survey of Scots born in 1936, the National Survey of Health and Development which was based on a sample born in 1946, and the National Child Development Study of a sample born in 1958.

In this chapter we provide some of the more technical details of the data used in our statistical analyses. We describe the kinds of data, how they were collected and from whom, and we provide other information necessary for an appraisal of our evidence. However, in telling the story of the data, we must also say something about the Centre for Educational Sociology which collected them, the Scottish Education Data Archive in which they are housed, and the programme of collaborative research under whose auspices many of the data were collected. We pick up the story in 1975.

The Scottish Education Data Archive and collaborative research

At that time the Centre for Educational Sociology (CES) at the University of Edinburgh held, on computer, data that had been collected in three surveys of 'qualified' Scottish school-leavers, conducted in 1962–3, 1971 and 1973 respectively. The first of these, the *1962 survey*, covered all pupils in Scottish education-authority (EA) and grant-aided (GA) schools who took at least one SCE Higher examination in their fifth year in 1962 and who had passed at least one Higher by the time they left school. (Details of the Scottish examination system are given later in this chapter.) The modal date at which the population left school was the summer of 1963, when its modal age was 17 years. (Pupils in Scotland transfer to secondary school at 12 years of age.) In terms of attainment, the population comprised roughly the top 15 per cent of the age-group. The sampling fraction was 100 per cent; in other words, all pupils who fell within the population definition were surveyed. The survey was carried out by the Scottish Council for Research in Education (SCRE). We use data from this survey on pupils' school courses, their public examination attempts and results, the type of school they attended and their fathers' occupations.[1] Most of the information was collected from the pupils, or their teachers, in the school setting.

The *1971 and 1973 surveys* were carried out by the CES itself. Each attempted to survey a 20 per cent target sample of the population of Highers-qualified pupils from all Scottish schools who left during or at the end of a single school year, 1969–70 and 1971–2 respectively. As in the 1962 survey, the populations only covered leavers with Highers passes, although by 1970 such pupils accounted for about a quarter of all leavers. Unlike the 1962 survey, subsequent leavers' surveys also covered leavers from independent schools, comprising about 1 per cent of all Scottish secondary-school leavers; and whereas the 1962 population was identified in terms of school stage, the populations for the later surveys were identified by the academic year of leaving school. The surveys of 1971 and later therefore included leavers who had only first attempted Highers in their sixth year. Such persons have been excluded from our comparisons between the later surveys and that of 1962–3. The data-collection methods of the later surveys were also different; school-leavers received questionnaires through the post early in the year after they had left school (1971 and 1973 respectively). The response rate for the 1971 survey was 92 per cent. However, the CES sample was obtained from respondents to an earlier survey of the same target sample run by the Scottish Education Department (SED). Respondents to the SED survey were asked to consent to their names being passed to the CES. Since some leavers did not respond to the SED survey, and others did not give their consent, the overall response rate to the CES survey (the rate that allows for non-respondents to either survey and for those who did not give their consent) was lower, at 68 per cent. The sampling arrangements and response rates for the 1973 survey were similar.[2] The questionnaires produced data on a variety of topics. Data on school courses, examination attempts and results, fathers' occupations and type of school are used here.

In 1975 the CES combined the data-sets from the SCRE survey of 1962–3 and the CES surveys of 1971 and 1973 into the first data-set of the Scottish Education Data Archive.[3] Selected variables were made as consistent and comparable as possible across the three surveys and, subject to confidentiality restrictions, the data were made available on computer to all with an interest in their analysis. In the same year the CES also began a programme of collaborative research. This aimed to extend the sequence of surveys in the archive with a fourth, larger-scale survey of an approximately 40 per cent sample to be carried out in 1977. The 1977 survey is the main source for the data which we use in this book, and we describe it below. Since 1977 there have been two further surveys of leavers from all schools in Scotland, one of a smaller sample conducted in 1979 and one of a sample almost as large as that in 1977, conducted in 1981.[4]

The size of these samples is directly related to the collaborative mode of research we have pursued. We have actually involved practising educationists and others in the planning of surveys and in the analysis, interpretation and discussion of the data that have been collected. Our programme has attempted a substantial decentralisation of the use of the 'big science' of surveys to pose problems about local and national situations and to invoke quantitative data in publicly addressing those problems. Involvement in the programme and access to the data have been open to any person interested in the topics concerned. Participants so far have included schoolteachers, college and university lecturers, officials of central and local government, inspectors, careers officers and, less successfully, a few pupils and parents too. Participants proposed items for inclusion in the 1977 survey; they also suggested substantial improvements to the wording and presentation of the questionnaires. From the start, therefore, the survey was designed to reflect and accommodate a variety of interests and perspectives in Scottish education, and to permit analysis and reanalysis from different points of view. Through the use of different versions of the question-naire, described below, the large samples allowed us to incorporate in the data a wider range of perspectives than is normally the case with a national survey.

When the survey data became available on computer, participants, working individually, in informal groups or in working parties, pursued their various interests through the direct analysis of the data. Members of the CES offered technical help but, as far as possible, decisions on how to conduct these analyses were made by the participants them-selves. Many of the products of this collaboration have been published periodically in the *Collaborative Research Newsletter*, and we refer to some of these in later chapters. Other products of collaboration fed into study groups, committees and individual concerns and have not ap-peared in published form.[5] At the time of writing (summer 1981) collaborative research, then in its second phase, continued; questions for the 1981 survey had been determined through a process of consul-tation with participants, many of whom could play by then a more extensive role in the process, as they had gained familiarity with the 1977 survey (Weston, 1980). The use of the archive is governed by a Code of Practice, published in the sixth issue of the *Newsletter* (CES, 1979), and available on request from the CES. Among other things, the code of practice guarantees the anonymity of individual sample members at all times, and of individual schools except under specifically defined circumstances.

The archive therefore allows the ordinary user to reproduce one aspect of the official account of pupils, schools and leavers that is contained in the school-leaver statistics produced by the SED.[6] But it also allows one to go beyond the official account, by presenting the data in different ways, by examining them in relation to other variables and explanations, and by localising them to the arena of one's own knowledge or practice in a geographical area, an institution, an area of the curriculum, or whatever. This sort of facility is, we think, import-ant in the development both of a public awareness of education and also of a means to adjudicate disputes over situations, definitions and explanations.

The archive can also be used in a more conventional mode to provide academics or professional researchers with data to be written up into research reports. In one sense the present book is one such report. The three authors are all professional researchers, past or present members of the CES, who played a part in the design and administration of the

1977 survey. However, we also intend this book to be part of a continuing collaborative dialogue. Within the code of practice, most of the survey data are available for reanalysis. Thus opportunities to criticise our arguments, to elaborate them, or to explore them in local contexts are perhaps more effective than is often the case with conventional social research.[7]

In our concluding chapter we attempt to relate collaborative research and this book to our views on the relation of research to practice; by practice we refer to the formulation of policy at a national level, to the activities of teachers and pupils in classrooms and to intermediate activities as well. Here, however, our main concern is to describe the surveys that underpin the account that we have to offer.

The 1977 survey

The 1977 survey covered Scottish school-leavers who had left school during or at the end of the 1975–6 academic session. It broke new ground with respect to some aspects of postal-survey research on young people. In the first place, it covered school-leavers at all attainment levels. The 1962, 1971 and 1973 surveys covered only Highers-qualified leavers, less than one-third of the age-group. In 1973 an additional survey of O-grade-qualified leavers was carried out, but it was limited in scope. Initially the 1977 survey aimed only to cover leavers with Highers or O-grade awards (who by then made up about two-thirds of the age-group). We were encouraged in this limited strategy by our previous survey experience and also by the conventional wisdom of survey methodology. Both indicated that postal surveys of educationally 'unqualified' samples would meet with unacceptably low response rates. We therefore had envisaged conducting only exploratory (and, in view of the costs involved, very small scale) interview studies of unqualified leavers. But we did not consider that a postal survey of such leavers could realistically be a key part of our data-collection.

However, mindful of the interest of many participants in the academically least successful school-leavers, and under pressure from one local authority in particular, we designed questionnaires for the unqualified. We piloted these on three different samples of such leavers, one of which was restricted to schools designated by their local authority as serving socially deprived areas. In each of these pilot surveys the response rate was over 80 per cent. Buoyed by this unexpected success, we made belated plans to extend the postal survey generally to unqualified leavers, or 'non-certificate' leavers as we shall more correctly term them.

The sample for the survey came from two sources. As in the 1971 and 1973 surveys, we obtained names and addresses of co-operating respondents to the SED's own 20 per cent survey of 'qualified' school-leavers. Leavers from all three sectors — EA, GA and independent — were included in this part of the sample. We supplemented these with further names and addresses collected from all the 400 or so maintained (EA) secondary schools in Scotland from which eligible population members had left. This was done with the co-operation of the regional authorities and schools. The overall sampling fraction was nearly 40 per cent. (Under local government reorganisation in 1975, nine mainland regional authorities in Scotland, together with three island area authorities, assumed local responsibility for education.)

The two parts of the sample are not precisely comparable. First, the sample coverage differed between the two sources: only the SED source included leavers from grant-aided and independent schools, and only the regions' source included leavers who had not gained any SCE awards. Second, even before we surveyed its members, the SED-derived sample was affected by non-response to the SED's survey and by non-co-operation (see above). The two parts of the sample are therefore subject to differing biases, some of which have been investigated and documented elsewhere (McPherson and Raffe, 1978). We have therefore weighted the sample data to compensate for some of these differences and also to compensate for differences in non-response associated with sex and SCE attainment. The weights mean that the distribution of the weighted sample in terms of sex, attainment and school type corresponds to the distribution of the population of 1975–6 school-leavers as a whole.[8] We have accordingly used weighted data in all tables other than those relating to the 1962 Highers-qualified population; we have used unweighted data to estimate statistical significance. The reported '*ns*', that is, the sample number on which table percentages or other estimates are based, are all unweighted. For this reason readers should not rely upon reported '*ns*' for an estimate of the composition of the population, or of the marginal frequencies of the tables we report. (Such estimates would be additionally misleading where tables are based on survey data collected from different fractions of different sub-groups of the sample, as described below.)

The target population in 1977 itself had one noteworthy gap: because of our belated discovery of the possibility of including non-certificate leavers in a postal survey, we managed in 1977 to survey non-certificate leavers only in Fife, Lothian, Tayside and Strathclyde.[9] These four regions contain three-quarters of the population of Scotland, so there is a fairly immediate logical limit to the extent to which they can be unrepresentative of the whole of Scotland. They exclude, however, much of the geographical periphery (in population terms) of Scotland, namely the south-west, Borders, Highlands and Islands, and also the north-east. Where we have wished to make generalisations or comparisons across the whole range of school-leavers, including the non-certificate leavers, we have confined our analyses to the four regions where all attainment levels were covered.

The overall response rate to the 1977 survey was 82 per cent. Some of the non-respondents were leavers who could not be contacted at the known addresses; among the sample members who were contacted the response rate was 86 per cent. This rate varied according to the source and attainment level of the sample, but even among the non-certificate leavers, the most difficult group for a postal survey, 79 per cent of those contacted eventually responded. To the biases associated with non-response must be added further biases associated with the deficiencies in the sampling frame, a problem experienced by most surveys. These deficiencies are difficult to quantify, although an attempt to do so by two of the authors suggests that there was a shortfall in the number of names and addresses of potential sample members made available to the CES and that this shortfall was greatest among non-certificate leavers (McPherson and Raffe, 1978). All the biases in the achieved sample are corrected by weighting to the extent that they are associated with sex and SCE-attainment level; biases in sample coverage that are independent of sex and attainment cannot be compensated for. The net effect of these independent biases is likely to have nudged our account, in a phrase, towards optimism; the less successful and the more alienated school-leaver was more likely to slip through the net of the survey (McPherson and Raffe, 1978).

In order to increase the range of topics covered by the survey, the questionnaires were administered in 21 overlapping versions to random subsets of the sample. Some questions, however, were asked in all 21 versions. From information collected during sampling we knew the examination level of each sample member, and we designed separate questionnaires for each level. Highers leavers (terms are defined below) received a 16-page questionnaire; O-grade leavers received a 12-page questionnaire; and non-certificate leavers received one of six pages. The longer the questionnaire the greater also was its verbal and organisational complexity.

Some of our tables are based upon items which were only included in some versions of the questionnaires, and sometimes the fraction of the sample covered varied between the different examination levels. In all such cases we have adjusted our weighting coefficients to compensate for the differential coverage, and we continue to report unweighted numbers, where numbers are given.

The archive is intended to allow a versatile and flexible range of analyses. Information has been stored in detailed, disaggregated form, thereby permitting users to implement a variety of alternative classifications of, for example, curricula or jobs. However, a large number of aggregated 'summary' or 'derived' variables have also been incorporated in the archive. This makes it easier for the beginner in computing to find his or her way into the data using a distance-learning manual (Gray and McPherson, 1979) and a 'Dictionary' of documentation (Raffe, Lamb *et al.*, 1978 and 1981). It also allows access to, and the reproduction of, other persons' constructions of the world through aggregations of the data into 'derived variables'. In this book we have limited ourselves to only a few of the 1,200 variables that are documented for the 1977 survey.

For the most part we describe the variables, their constituent categories and the populations on which analyses are based as they are introduced in the course of our discussion. A few terms and concepts, however, may usefully be spelt out in advance.

Some definitions

Highers leavers, O-grade leavers and non-certificate leavers

These three terms are always used to describe leavers who had *attempted*, respectively, Highers examinations, O-grade (but not Highers) examinations, and no SCE examinations while they were still at school. The terms refer to examination attempts (or 'presentations') and must be distinguished from terms such as 'Highers-qualifed leavers', which refers to passes. Chapter 4 describes the evolution of the SCE Highers (H-grade) examination and of the SCE O-grade examination (not 'O-level', though many Scots know it as such). Since 1965 the examinations have been administered by the Scottish Certificate of Education Examination Board (SCEEB) and there is no formal connection with the English GCE. In the mid-1970s roughly 30 per cent of an age-group attempted at least one Higher; and a further 40 per cent, roughly, attempted at least one O-grade, but no Higher. At that time few Scottish pupils attempted CSE examinations, perhaps 1 or 2 per cent. In the mid-1970s about 2 per cent of the Scottish age-group attempted English GCE examinations, the proportions doing so being highest in the independent sector; and for most Scottish pupils attempting the GCE, it was marginal and additional to their main, SCE-based, course. The GCE and the CSE have therefore been ignored in classifications of leavers and of their attainments.

Table 2.1 compares the proportions of the 1975–6 school-leaving groups in Scotland and in England and Wales respectively gaining SCE awards and GCE/CSE awards. It indicates that the Scottish Highers examination served a higher proportion of the age-group than did the

TABLE 2.1 Percentages of school-leavers during the academic year 1975–6 at various levels of qualification in Scotland and in England and Wales: leavers from all types of schools

	Percentages of school-leavers in 1975–6		
	Scotland	England and Wales	
3 or more SCE H-grade passes	17	9	3 or more GCE A-level passes
1–2 SCE H-grade passes	9	7	1–2 GCE A-level passes
5 or more SCE O-grades (A–C), no H-grade passes	7	9	5 or more good GCE O-level or CSE results, no A-level passes[1]
1–4 SCE O-grades (A–C), no H-grade passes	24	26	1–4 good GCE O-level or CSE results, no A-level passes
D or E awards at SCE O-grade only	9	33	1 or more GCE O-level or CSE, but no good results and no A-level passes
No qualification	35	17	No qualification[2]
Total percentage	101	101	
n	(91,100)	(707,440)	

Notes: 1 'Good' indicates an O-level result at A–C or a CSE result at Grade 1.
2 The figure includes 1.4 per cent of 'others'.
Sources: Department of Education and Science (1978, p. 7) and Scottish Education Department (1977a, p. 131).

GCE A-level examination in England and Wales. But the proportion in Scotland that left school with no qualifications was also considerably higher. This was due to the more widespread development of the CSE in England and Wales.

SCE attainment

We have constructed a scale of SCE attainment as follows: 18: 6 or more Highers passes. 17: 5 Highers passes. 16: 4 Highers passes. 15: 3

Highers passes. 14: 2 Highers passes. 13: 1 Highers pass. 12: 6 or more O-grade awards at A–C, no Highers. 11: 5 O-grades (A–C). 10: 4 O-grades (A–C). 9: 3 O-grades (A–C). 8: 2 O-grades (A–C). 7: 1 O-grade (A–C). 4: D or E awards only at O-grade. 1: no SCE awards.

We have somewhat arbitrarily assumed that one Higher-grade pass is 'better' than any number of O-grades and we have not distinguished between subjects. The issue of the different value of different subjects is discussed elsewhere, especially in parts 2 and 3. When using this variable in regression-type analysis, we adopt the scaling shown above. The scaling prevents the higher reaches of attainment from becoming excessively influential (a tendency of many educational scales) by increasing the differential between the three lowest levels of attainment. In cross-tabulations a more aggregated form of the variable is usually used.

School type

In the 1977 survey we distinguish three types of schools: independent schools, which comprised a mere 1 per cent of leavers in Scotland (fewer than in England); grant-aided (GA) schools (equivalent to English direct-grant schools), which accounted for about 3 per cent of leavers; and maintained (EA) schools. (Most grant-aided schools have become independent since 1977.) Because of the small sample numbers in non-EA schools, and because of the differential sample bias associated with these schools (see above), most of our analyses are based on leavers from EA schools only. The exceptions are in parts 2 and 5, where the substantive importance of including grant-aided (but not independent) schools outweighs the technical disadvantages. Within the EA sector, other types of school are distinguished, mainly in chapters 13, 14 and 15, according to the history of their organisation and the part they played in arrangements for selective transfer to secondary education. Most EA schools in Scotland had become comprehensive by the time the 1977 sample members left them (see chapters 13 and 14).

The four regions

This phrase identifies Fife, Lothian, Strathclyde and Tayside, for which (as described above) the 1977 survey covered EA leavers at all levels, including non-certificate leavers. The four regions contain three-quarters of the population of Scotland. The 1979 survey, which covered leavers at all attainment levels and from all regions, provided information on the extent to which certain generalisations about 'Scotland' could be made from the four regions alone (see 'Other sources of survey data', below).

Social class

This is defined in terms of father's occupation, classified according to the Registrar-General's five classes, with class III subdivided between non-manual and manual. In regression analyses this is used as a six-point scale. Often we employ a simple dichotomy, with classes I, II and IIIN grouped as 'middle class', and classes IIIM, IV and V grouped as 'working class'. A third, unclassified, category includes occupations (such as the Armed Forces) which are not classified, occupations described in inadequate detail to be classified, and those on which sample members were unable or unwilling to supply the required information. A large number of sample members in this category were probably from single parent families, although the data do not permit us to verify this directly. The original classification of father's occupation used by the Scottish Council for Research in Education in the 1962 survey was incompatible with that of the Registrar-General. Resources did not permit a reclassification of the entire sample, but approximately 6,200 of the 9,285 were reclassified (Armstrong and McPherson, 1975). The data from the 1962, 1971 and 1973 surveys were classified according to the 1966 version of the Registrar-General's classification (General Register Office, 1966); the 1977 survey used the 1970 version (Office of Population Censuses and Surveys, 1970). At the highly aggregated level of the social classes the difference between the two versions is negligible.

Other sources of survey data

The 1979 survey

This covered a sample of 1977–8 leavers that was equivalent to the sample of the 1975–6 leavers surveyed in 1977 except that non-certificate leavers were covered in all regions and the sample was much smaller, at 10 per cent for Highers leavers and O-grade leavers with one or more A–C award at O-grade, and 20 per cent for non-certificate leavers and those with only D or E awards at O-grade. These fractions compare with one of nearly 40 per cent in 1977. This book was already in preparation when the 1979 survey was being carried out and, in any case, the smaller sample would have made it inappropriate for most purposes. However, in chapter 9 we have referred to provisional data from this survey on the Youth Opportunities Programme, a programme that did not exist at the time of the 1977 survey; we have used some information relating to employment in chapters 9 and 11; and some of the leavers' accounts of their schooling reproduced in chapter 10 were also returned in 1979.

A second use for the 1979 survey was to confirm the extent to which the four regions were typical of all of Scotland with respect to certain variables that we use later in the book. These concern unemployment, truancy, the use of the belt and leavers' satisfaction with their education. The incidence of each of these four variables in the 1979 survey was estimated first from the four regions and, second, from all regions. The two estimates were then compared. Comparisons were made within each of the three presentation levels (Highers, O-grade and non-certificate) yielding twelve comparisons in all. Of these six were identical and six differed by only 1 percentage point. This is not to say that localities may not vary in these or other respects; the incidence of truancy, for example, may be lower in the islands (Cope and Gray, 1978). The comparisons merely indicate that the regions outside the four that we studied in 1977 were neither sufficiently populous, nor sufficiently different, to invalidate generalisations made about Scotland as a whole from the four regions that contained three-quarters of the population. The archive has, on occasion, been used to analyse local variations in education in the geographical periphery of Scotland, but this is not a theme in our present study.[10]

The Scottish Mental Survey

In 1947 the Scottish Council for Research in Education administered intelligence tests to all Scottish pupils born in 1936. A sample of 1,208 of these pupils, born on six days spread across 1936, was selected for further study and was followed up for the rest of their school careers. The results of this study have been published in a number of reports (Scottish Council for Research in Education, 1953; Macpherson, 1958; Maxwell, 1969). From the last of these we have extracted data on the social-class distribution of verbal-reasoning ability which we have used in our study of trends in the social-class differences in educational attainment. The data are used to describe what we term 'the 1948 cohort' in chapter 12. However, the categories of social class used by Maxwell differed from our own (see 'Addendum' at the end of chapter 12). We have therefore carried out our own reanalyses of the data from this sample, using records held by Keith Hope of Nuffield College.[11] Since the data available for reanalysis covered only male sample members we do not, for the most part, include them directly in our comparisons in chapter 12. However, we were able to use the data to investigate the effects of using Maxwell's class categories compared with our own and thus to make appropriate allowances when evaluating trends.

The National Survey of Health and Development

This is a longitudinal study of more than 5,000 people born in Great Britain in the first week of March 1946. Illegitimate and twin births were excluded, and the remaining sample was stratified. All of the non-manual and agricultural workers' children, but only a quarter of children of manual workers were followed up. This stratification is corrected by appropriate weights in all analyses (except when computing confidence intervals). The sample was followed through its school career and beyond. Its experiences of primary and secondary school respectively were reported in Douglas (1964), in Douglas, Ross and Simpson (1968), and in many other reports. For chapter 12 we have used reanalyses of the 500 Scots in the sample conducted for us by James Douglas to provide one source of data for the 1957-8 cohort in our study of trends in educational inequality since the war.[12]

The National Child Development Study

A similar longitudinal study conducted by the National Children's Bureau (NCB) has been based on a sample of all the British children born in one week in March 1958 (Davie, Butler and Goldstein, 1972). A former member of the CES, Dougal Hutchison, now at the NCB, has reanalysed on our behalf data on the 1,386 members of this sample who were born in Scotland.[13] These have been used mainly to validate the data on our own 1977 sample, most of whom were born in 1958, 1959 or 1960, and to compare the four regions with the rest of Scotland using data for a sample of the entire age-group.

Part 2

Policy and Myth

Introduction[1]

In 1947 the Advisory Council on Education in Scotland published its blueprint for the reconstruction of secondary education in the post-war world. The Council's report is remarkable in several respects, and not least because it proposed a model towards which many people have since been moving again in their search for a rationale for secondary education in the 1980s. The Council recommended, for example, that there should be a national examination for all 16-year-olds at school incorporating elements of both internal and external assessment, and it argued for what was, in effect, to be a core curriculum for all pupils during the greater part of the first four years of their secondary education between ages 12 and 16. This was to have permitted relatively little choice and was to have covered seven areas: English, mathematics, general science, social studies, technical and aesthetic work, physical education and religious education. The Council also favoured the omnibus school providing for all pupils from a fixed area throughout their compulsory secondary education, seeing this as 'the natural way for a democracy to order the post-primary schooling of a given area' (Scottish Education Department, 1947, para. 164). In the mid-1960s the Secretary of State for Scotland adopted the all-through comprehensive school as the preferred form of secondary provision and, in the mid-1970s, the Dunning and Munn Committees substantially restated the Council's main recommendations for assessment and curriculum (Scottish Education Department, 1965a, 1977a, 1977b).

It might therefore seem that post-war secondary education in Scotland has developed in a manner that has been linear and con-sensual, if somewhat slow. But this would be to ignore the fact that the line of development that was actually followed in Scotland for the first twenty years of compulsory secondary education departed in several major respects from that envisaged by the Advisory Council in 1947. In particular, the form of comprehensive organisation that was urged afresh by the Labour government's Circulars of 1965 cut swiftly and unexpectedly across the bipartite policy for secondary-school organisation that had been followed in England and Wales since the war and in Scotland, too, especially in the larger urban areas. This 'extraneous' political intervention, as it seemed to many educationists in the mid-1960s, is discussed mainly in part 5. But the abolition of selective transfer to secondary education is also relevant to the chapters that follow, for it has left a long agenda of unanswered questions concerning what should happen within secondary schools now that formal selection is deferred.

Until the mid-1960s in Scotland, post-war national policy-making for certification, and also largely for curriculum, disregarded the views of the Advisory Council's 1947 report and concerned itself mainly with the children who were taken to be in the most able third of the age-group. The main exception was the Memorandum by a group of HM Inspectors in 1955 on *Junior Secondary Education* (Scottish Education Department, 1955). This supported many of the Advisory Council's 1947 recommendations on curriculum and pedagogy, but only for pupils allocated to junior secondary courses (equivalent to the courses offered by secondary modern schools in England and Wales). National certification was thought to be inappropriate to such pupils; local or school-based certification would suffice. In a similar fashion, the Dunning Committee's more recent proposals (Scottish Education Department, 1977a) for certification for most 16-year-olds, combining internal and external elements in both curriculum and assessment, are being explored again mainly in relation to those who are currently 'non-certificate' pupils and excluded from the national system of external certification. It is not planned to include substantial internal elements in the courses or examinations taken by the (approximately) 70 per cent of pupils who are already covered by the existing system of certification.

The Dunning Committee's recommendations were a Scottish response to a situation in which comprehensive reorganisation since 1965, together with the raising of the minimum school-leaving age in 1973 (ROSLA), have obliged us to take more seriously the problem of how to provide a rounded education for all children up to the age of 16 years. Youth unemployment in the 1970s has, if anything, extended that period towards 18 years. In this respect it has taken some thirty years for the wheel to turn full circle. The provision of a rounded education for all children to 18 years was precisely the task adopted by the Advisory Council which reported in 1947. It had done so in the light of the wartime Secretary of State's intention to create a compulsory secondary system that would promote common citizenship in a reconstructed post-war world. The Council had recognised the 'deep-felt desire to preserve in peace the unity realised in war', postulating 'equal care for the education of all boys and girls up to eighteen years of age'. It argued that: 'our nation is facing for the first time . . . the . . . task of providing *general* secondary education for all its children in all their variety' and that: 'it is possible to see in all secondary education from twelve to sixteen a unity which is not illusory or merely sentimental but real; for underlying every difference in class or taste or talent is an identity of childish and adolescent need and response which is best met by the formulation of a curriculum broadly uniform in content and purpose' (Scottish Education Department, 1947, paras. 18, 24, 268 and 261).

Inspired by such sentiments, the Scottish Advisory Council rejected what was then the English preference for tripartite secondary provision in grammar, technical and modern schools. Instead it tried to respond in contemporary terms to what it took to be an inherited Scottish preference for education that was liberal, general and democratic. The post-1965 policy of comprehensive education, and ROSLA in 1973, were policies common to both England and Scotland. Both can be understood as fresh attempts to realise the goals of post-war reconstruction, but in the context of a weakening political consensus.

However, where recent thinking has differed markedly from that of the Advisory Council's 1947 report is over the status of the subject as the basic unit of the curriculum during compulsory education. In 1977 the Munn Committee reported on the curriculum in the third and fourth years of the Scottish secondary school (Scottish Education Department, 1977b). Its proposals accepted the subject as the fundamental unit of the curriculum. By contrast the Advisory Council in 1947 had advocated a form of pedagogy that owed much to an essentially learner-centred philosophy of liberal education. Based on what it took to be the young adolescent's natural curiosity, this philosophy aimed to bring concentrically widening areas of social and intellectual experience under the mastery of the pupil's understanding; if necessary, the abstractions and reifications of experience contained in institutionalised 'subjects' should be subordinated to the creation of a predisposition to lifelong inquiry. For the Advisory Council, the practical consequences of this philosophy included an integrated approach to school subjects (recommended afresh for social subjects in a dissenting note by a member of the Munn Committee); project work; what have come to be known as 'link' and 'taster' courses; the development of further education for all young entrants to employment; and, above all, methods which decentralised to the teacher, and thence to the pupil, a degree of control over the content, pacing and assessment of learning. Closely allied to this perspective was the recognition of good teaching as an essentially experimental activity that required the teacher to moderate his or her actions and beliefs in the light of feedback on their consequences; and allied also was the view that the teaching profession had 'come of age' and could be trusted to develop a general education for the new era, freed from what the Advisory Council saw as the adverse consequences of control by the Scottish Education Department (SED) through its conduct of the national, external school examination (Scottish Education Department, 1947, chapters V and VI and appendix III).

The 1947 report can, indeed, be understood as a heroic attempt to adapt a philosophy of liberal education, conceived originally for the higher education of a small elite, to the requirements of mass secondary education. With comprehensive reorganisation and ROSLA these requirements are now more pressing. But, in coping with the curricular question anew in 1977, the Munn Committee had to reckon with the developments of a further thirty years. Throughout much of the post-war period, the SED had used the system of external examinations as its main agent of control and change in matters of standards, school organisation and curriculum; and these external examinations were based on individual subjects and were restricted to an able minority of pupils. The individual subject, external assessment and associated pupil-teacher relationships had, if anything, become even more deeply entrenched in Scottish educational life than they had been in the 1930s when William McClelland, a member of the Advisory Council of 1942-7, wrote that '[a] tendency to mechanical methods of class-teaching is one of the educational weeds that seem to thrive under the shadow of external examinations' (McClelland, 1935, p. 174).

This was no idiosyncratic view of McClelland's but an expression of a sustained and considered philosophy of liberal education that many Victorian Scottish university teachers had fought long and hard to preserve in the face of Westminster's insistence that they and their institutions become accountable through the medium of written examinations. Indeed, in the Scottish humanist vocabulary, the word 'examination' had a quite different meaning, referring to that process of teaching and learning wherein teacher and pupil alike explored each other's minds without reference either to narrowly instrumental benefits that might be attached to merit, or to extraneous criteria of value that external examiners or selectors might impose. It was in order to realise a humanist conception of secondary education, that allowed scope for teachers to engage and widen the curiosity of their pupils, that the Advisory Council called in 1947 for what we now call internal assessment. The Council argued that national assessment at 16 years of age, whatever its form, should be framed in terms that could comprehend

34

all children and not simply the small minority that might go to university: 'the surest way to distort a School Certificate', it wrote, 'is to peg it to university matriculation requirements' (Scottish Education Department, 1947, para. 253). We can only appreciate the magnitude of this heresy if we understand how far it departed from the policy that the SED had hitherto followed and was, thereafter, still to follow, in linking school certification to the prospect of favoured access to university (and, later, to employment).

Nevertheless, there was one important similarity between the approaches of the Advisory Council and of the SED to policy for certification and for secondary education more generally. Both were deeply influenced by Scotland's educational history and by a sense of national identity and purpose expressed in and through that history. That said, the Council and the SED nevertheless differed in the way in which they selectively interpreted this history when framing and justifying advice and policy. Some understanding of the uses that have been made of history is essential to the two main purposes of this book, both to our description of how and why the post-war secondary-education system developed as it did, and to our argument about the relationships between social science and social practice.

In the next chapter we describe and analyse Scotland's treatment of its educational history in terms of the concept of 'myth', understood as a story that interprets the past and present, expresses shared purposes and thereby facilitates action. Then, in chapter 4, we explore the use of myth in the purposes and justifications offered by the SED for post-war policy for certification; the limits and assumptions within which the policy was intended to apply; and the forces that have loosened these limits since the early 1960s. This is followed by two chapters in which we discuss how far the official account of secondary education in fact corresponded to various empirical representations of the curriculum and of the certification system that we are now able to make. In particular we draw attention to the way in which the dilemmas of selection, difficulty and motivation were experienced more acutely as the logical limits to the post-war policy were reached. Intentions for curriculum and pedagogy were distorted and the scope for innovation or remedy was restricted. Later in the book we take up the main political and methodological question raised by our discussion: what do we do when two public accounts disagree or when an account that sustains current practice does not correspond to empirical representations of the world it purports to describe?

Chapter 3

Scottish Education and the Scottish Myth

Introduction

A discussion of Scotland's educational inheritance can advance our inquiry in two ways. First, a distinctive understanding of the nature and importance of Scottish education has often figured prominently in the national consciousness and has, on occasion, influenced efforts to change or preserve educational practice. Most of this chapter is devoted to a discussion of this consciousness, partly because of its material influence on many of the events and situations we analyse later, and partly because our general argument concerning theory and practice in social research makes reference to the nature and state of public awareness. Before this, however, it may be useful to make a brief comparison between Scotland and England with respect to the forms that education takes and to the phasing and pattern of post-war expansion. Both education systems have experienced the dilemmas of expansion that we described in chapter 1 and it may be that some of the features of provision and response that characterise the Scottish education system in other respects – its distinctive curriculum, certification system and history of school organisation – will provide a helpful contrast with systems elsewhere.

Some reasons for studying Scotland

Secondary education in Scotland has always been administered separately from secondary education in England and Wales, and Scottish culture and institutions have always had a character of their own. Nevertheless, the broad outlines of the Scottish system, and of the population that it serves, are sufficiently similar to those further south for an analysis of it to be relevant to England and Wales, and to other systems as well.

It is also the case that the timing and general drift of major changes in educational policy have been remarkably similar north and south of the Border. The main features of the 1944 Education Act were applied to Scotland in a separate statute of 1945. Both countries abandoned a group leavers' certificate in 1951 (see chapter 4) and thereafter extended the prospect of certification to a growing proportion of the age-group. Both countries ultimately implemented a largely bipartite system of compulsory secondary education that depended heavily on selective transfer from primary school. Twenty years later separate government Circulars were issued, but both in the same year (1965), to urge local authorities in both countries to adopt a comprehensive secondary-school system; and the timing of the deferment, and eventual implementation, of the raising of the minimum school-leaving age to 16 years also coincided. In both countries these policies were applied, moreover, to largely urban populations sharing similar, though not identical, family and occupational structures. In both systems schools were staffed to broadly similar standards and in the urban areas of both countries the schools served catchments that were strongly differentiated one from another in terms of parental occupation and related social and economic factors.[1]

To the extent that the features which distinguish the Scottish system have mediated the application of expansionist policies at a local level, they give us some insight into how expansion has worked. For example, we show in chapter 5 how the different structure of school examinations in Scotland has been associated with differences in rates of staying on for successive stages of post-compulsory secondary education. On a slightly different tack, it happens that some aspects of existing Scottish provision resemble forms that have, on occasion, been canvassed for England and Wales. Scotland already has, for example, a five-subject terminal school examination, the Scottish Certificate of Education Higher grade (SCE H-grade), the breadth of which has impressed some who have wished to replace the GCE A-level with a less specialised examination. Our discussion in chapters 5 and 6 of some of the preconditions for this broad curriculum, and of its survival during the period of expansion, is relevant to any educational system in which selection operates.

A further advantage in a Scottish study is that, compared with England and Wales, the country has had, at least for the last hundred years, a more centralised and less pluralist pattern of administration and control in education. This often makes it easier to discern relationships between various elements of policy and practice. Until 1964, for example, the school certificate examinations were conducted by the Scottish Inspectorate. Thereafter they were conducted by a single board, the Scottish Certificate of Education Examination Board

(SCEEB) on which the Scottish Education Department (SED) is well represented. At a mundane level, this arrangement disposes of the tiresome technical problem for the researcher of the comparability of standards between the examinations of different boards, and also of the tiresome possibility that different types of pupils select themselves to present to different boards. These problems may sometimes cloud discussion of examinations and certification in England and Wales. More important, the Scottish arrangements have produced tighter connections between policy and practice and better opportunities to test the assumptions and intentions behind policies against the way in which practice has unfolded. In some respects, the Scottish Education Data Archive (see chapter 2) is itself an indirect product of this situation. We must add, however, that such differences in form and process result also in differences in substance. For example, the closer control exercised by the SED over the certification system helps to explain why Scotland has until recently lacked an alternative, school-based, form of assessment corresponding to the English CSE Mode 3; and it also explains how Scotland was able to modernise its school science syllabuses so quickly in the 1960s.

Finally, and this brings us to the main theme of the chapter, Scots have, over the centuries, attached a particular importance to the generous public provision of educational opportunity, and they have, on occasion, framed and revised policies and practice in the light of a certain historical understanding of the place of public educational provision in the life of the nation. The expansionist perspective on education that has dominated post-war educational provision in Britain has been a continuing and explicit preoccupation in Scotland for a much longer period.

But the very longevity of this Scottish preoccupation poses a problem. Scottish secondary provision has changed in many respects since the war and has undertaken new commitments. But Scotland's account of its public education system (both as a statement of aims and as a description of achievements) remains rooted in the practices and conditions of the past. How is this possible? How is it that large numbers of people continue to subscribe to a particular account of the purposes, workings and achievements of their educational world, despite the fact that this world has manifestly changed? Have events in the post-war world increased or reduced the correspondence of the education system to the received account; or has this account maintained public credibility without reference to the changing course of events? More generally, how might one compare the way in which people describe their purposes and actions with possible alternative accounts? These are important questions both for educational practice and for social research. We may enter them through an analysis of the role of myth.

Educational myth and national sentiment

We do not mean by 'myth' things that are thought to be true but that are, in fact, always false; nor do we mean things that are thought to be valuable but that are, in fact, beyond human attainment or consent. Instead, we use the term myth to refer to a story that people tell about themselves, and tell for two purposes. These purposes are, first, to explain the world and, second, to celebrate identity and to express values. To what extent these explanations are true, and to what extent expressed values are realised in practice, are questions that we shall for the moment leave open.

Myths are historically grounded and we must introduce the Scottish myth with the caveat that it has a long history, in the course of which it has undergone changes of emphasis, has jettisoned some elements, has acquired others, has been stretched in some places to account for new phenomena, and has contracted in others in order to disregard external phenomena that embarrassed its internal consistency.

Nevertheless, it is possible to identify an enduring set of ideas, many of which cluster around a view of the history of Scottish society in relation to its larger metropolitan neighbour in the south. We may summarise this set of ideas as follows: to be Scottish is to subscribe to a certain style of individual behaviour and to certain forms of collective, public behaviour that sustain and reproduce the identity of individual Scots. Scottish society, so the story runs, is more egalitarian and more meritocratic than English society.[2] To be Scottish in individual relationships is to set less store by differences of rank in one's behaviour towards, and judgments of, other individuals. To the extent that one does differentiate, it is to do so on the basis of merit; that is, on the basis of the extent to which universal human qualities are realised in a person's behaviour, rather than on the basis of inherited position or of claims to eminence based on attributes that are not common to all people. For example, claims to esteem based on superior intelligence, which all people in some degree possess, may be legitimate, but claims based on race or locality are not; and the scope and span of differences in esteem are smaller. To be Scottish in collective or public behaviour is thus to give greater support (than the English – the comparison is usually there implicitly and is often explicit) to public institutions that realise this conception of the person in society.

To be Scottish, therefore, is to support, among other things, generous public provision in education and to be committed by implication to the explanatory belief that the generous provision of public education can make it a potent force in the lives of individuals and groups. It is to eschew private education, private endowments, and forms of institutional organisation, such as the collegiate or the residential, that aim to create or reproduce differences between peoples' identities by socialising groups of them, from an early age, in exclusive environments directed towards the acquisition of specialised adult identities. It is to be more committed, therefore, to the explanatory belief that what happens in the classroom or lecture hall can itself be enough to engage and develop the interests and talents of pupils and students; that the extra-curricular is, simply, extra. It is to believe more strongly that the curriculum itself should be framed to cater for all sorts and conditions of person; that pupils should share for longer a common curricular experience which inducts them into a common culture; and that they should not be sorted early into courses which are wholly restricted to the specialised areas of knowledge within which the division of labour in adult life may later oblige them to work.

To be Scottish, therefore, is to have and to share in what has come to be called 'the democratic intellect'; democratic because membership of the society was acknowledged to entail a right to a certain level and type of education; because the educational institutions gave wide access to it; because those with access were inducted into a shared intellectual discourse; because individual merit therein could therefore be commonly acknowledged and would not depend on taking the authority of argument on trust; and, finally, because, however great the differences in individual merit, they could only set people apart from their fellows in certain limited respects, for the universal esteem of true individual distinction also implied merit in all who could recognise it.

Some illustrations of the myth

A full account of the Scottish myth would describe its origins in the Knoxian plan for a godly Scottish commonwealth served by a developed state system of primary, secondary and tertiary education; its secularisation and adaptation in the currents of Victorian thinking on state intervention, *laissez-faire* and social Darwinism; the influence on its curricular and pedagogic ideas of the phenomenologically based Scottish philosophy of common sense; and how the perspective has been recurrently articulated in the last two centuries in the context of political debates with Westminster and Whitehall over the funding of Scotland's peculiar institutions and over the implementation of UK social, educational and economic policies in North Britain. For the present, we can only assert, and briefly illustrate, the continuity and living force of this perspective as a factor in people's understandings and actions.

Here, first, is an extract from the Report of the Commission on the Scottish universities (Education Commission (Scotland), 1868, p. x):

The theory of our School system, as originally conceived [by Knox] was to supply every member of the community with the means of obtaining for his children not only the elements of education, but such instruction as would fit him to pass to the Burgh school, and thence to university, or directly to the university from the parish school. The connexion between the Parochial and Burgh schools and the university is therefore an essential element in our scheme of National Education. . . . 'So far' it has been truly said, 'as an industrial culture has an industrial value, makes a man's business work better, and helps him to get on in the world, the Scotch middle class has thoroughly appreciated it, and sedulously employed it, both for itself and for the class whose labour it uses; and here is their superiority to the English, and the reason of the success of Scotch skilled labourers and Scotsmen of business everywhere. . . .' Therefore. . . the ancient theory of Scottish National Education should be scrupulously respected.

Moving on some fifty years, this is J. A. Macdonald, a Chief Inspector of Schools, writing in 1921 about the north-east of Scotland (His Majesty's Chief Inspector of Schools in Scotland, 1922, p. 79):

The fact that everywhere else in the Division, in spite of a decreasing population, larger advantage is being taken of the facilities offered for secondary education is very gratifying; and, for this Division at least, there seems good ground for the belief that, in so far as the contribution made by education is concerned, there is not likely to be any abatement of what has recently been described as the 'unpleasant pre-eminence of Scotsmen' in the affairs of the empire and of the world. From the point of view of social solidarity and social progress, a highly important consideration is the extent to which the opportunities of secondary education are effectively extended to all classes and sections of the community, and particularly to the lowest. The importance of this consideration is two-fold. In the first place, the contribution to social solidarity made by the advancement of capacity through education is peculiarly valuable. Not only do the individual and his family benefit, but there is also an enlargement of the horizon of life's possibilities for a number of other individuals and families whose connection is less intimate. In the second place, capacity much above the average, while rare in any class, seems to be fairly equally distributed among all classes; and it is clearly to the interest of society as a whole that, when occurring, it be given such opportunity for development as shall enable it to render to society the special service that it is specially capable of rendering. Indeed it is hardly too much to say that one of the tests of the sufficiency of modern civilisation is the measure in which this opportunity is everywhere made effectively available.

The theory of the functions of education respectively for the group and for the individual, and of the connection between these two functions, is quite explicit here; so, too, are the proposed limits to the application of the theory (the limits set by 'capacity'); and so are the further beliefs (about the nature of 'capacity' and its distribution among the social classes) that are entailed. The celebration of nationality is to be found in the muted and invidious comparison of Scotland's record of secondary provision with that of England and elsewhere.

Here now are two illustrations of the power and penetration of such ideas and of the way in which they were reproduced, first through the curriculum: '"The Scot abroad"; discuss and illustrate the qualities which have made Scotsmen successful abroad.' This was asked in the Higher-grade English examination, taken by virtually all Highers candidates in 1921. 'Unpleasant pre-eminence' to outsiders, perhaps, but to Scots themselves a matter for some quiet celebration in which the younger members of the tribe should join. Second, an extract from Circular 44 with which the SED conveyed to the local authorities its recommendations for the development of secondary education under the 1918 Act (Scottish Education Department, 1921):

> Despite defects and imperfections which experience is gradually remedying, the present organization of Secondary education in Scotland may be regarded as fairly satisfactory. Moreover, the force of public opinion is strong enough to ensure the maintenance of the immemorial Scottish tradition that, subject to the overriding condition of intellectual fitness, no child, whatever his home circumstances, shall be debarred access to the Secondary School and the University by lack of opportunity. There is abundant evidence that, so far as this particular obligation is concerned, the liberality of Education Authorities has brought Scotland nearer to the ideal than she has been at any previous period in her educational history.

And in the 1930s, before he became a member of the Advisory Council on Education in 1942, William McClelland summarised the Scottish perspective as follows (McClelland, 1935, p. 174):

> The reader will have the key to the understanding of most of the features of our system if he bears in mind that the Scottish people value education, and that the central and unbroken strand in our long educational tradition is the recognition of the right of the clever child, from whatever social class he may come, to the highest and best education the country has to offer.

Notice again the correlation of the explanatory and celebratory elements, and also of past and present, a present that is to be explained as an inheritance that has been adapted in the light of an enduring value that is made potent through the consent it commands.

The following chapters will illustrate at greater length how this story extends into post-war Scotland, but here are three brief examples. First, we have a Director of Education arguing in 1965 against comprehensive reorganisation: 'although considerations of class-consciousness and social apartheid may be a major issue in England, especially in the context of secondary education, they are much less important in Scotland' (see chapter 13). And here is a Senior Chief Inspector of Schools in Scotland telling the Kilbrandon Commission on the Constitution in 1969 that the distinctive institutional features of the Scottish education system were 'reflections of our national characteristics. We have an interest in the common man, therefore we have an interest in a broad education. Our education is not nearly so specialised' (Royal Commission on the Constitution 1969–1973, 1973-4, para. 733). Finally, here is a government White Paper of 1972: 'Scottish universities . . . have by tradition provided a broadly based higher education through the ordinary degree course in Arts. The Scottish ordinary degree course represents a natural extension into university education of the secondary school curriculum' (Cmnd 5175, para. 11).

Some functions of myth

We may use these few examples to make some more general points about this public awareness of education in Scotland. It has continuity. It is widely shared (though our examples have not, of course, shown how widely). Influential people subscribe to it; it is invoked in the run-up to decisions and may, therefore, influence change. Also it commonly contains elements that are simultaneously descriptive of present and past states of affairs and prescriptive of their ideal and future state. The practical and normative guide that it offers to future action is offered in the name of a certain interpretation of the past. It is, in other words, the language of living tradition, a language that is not peculiar to the public system of education, but that is surely familiar to all who have interested themselves in the affairs of schools, colleges, universities and the educational provision of neighbourhoods, regions or whole systems.

What perhaps distinguishes the Scottish account is, first, the fact that, describing a small and relatively centralised country, with a long history of public provision for education, the story has a special place within it for the public (state) system itself. In more pluralist systems, such as that of England, many of the myths or stories are themselves more fragmented and diffuse, gathering around particular schools or the sub-system formed by certain 'public' schools, certain Oxford and Cambridge colleges and the governing institutions of the country.[3] Second, the story of Scottish education has acted as a stronger focus for Scottish sentiment and has been told more clearly and, it must be reluctantly admitted, more insistently, than many others. Arguably this is because of the peculiar situation whereby Scotland has some of the institutions of a sovereign democratic state, such as a church, judiciary, education system and parts of an administration, but not the central one of a deliberative and legislative body through which the aspirations of its people might be expressed and the public actions of its representatives or their agents called to account. But in other respects we think that an analysis of the Scottish account or belief system has a wider application.

When we talk of such an account as widely shared, as a collective sentiment, we do not mean that all persons have agreed on it; and, in what follows, we do not attempt a complete sociological account of how assent to it might vary according to persons' social situations, important though such a study would be. Nor do we mean that persons who subscribe to some part of the account subscribe to, or are even aware of, all parts of the account. Indeed, it is an important part of our argument that people may often not be fully aware of its totality, although, in certain circumstances of political discourse or of detached reflection, they may become more aware of the nature and extent of the network of beliefs and feelings to part of which they hold. Nor do we mean that when individuals embrace the values and share in the feelings that are associated with one element of the story (when, so to speak, they applaud one of the characters, episodes or settings), they necessarily subscribe to, or are even aware of, the part played by that element in the larger cognitive scheme.

Thus, in everyday usage, only parts of the account are apparent, and then sometimes only implicitly. Nevertheless, one may glimpse it in the strength of feeling with which people might oppose, for example, changes in the institutional structure of the Scottish Ordinary MA or general degree, or, on a wider front, changes in a particular comprehensive school or comprehensive-school system. Particular institutions and practices acquire symbolic meaning and values — 'the parochial school', 'the grammar school', 'the secondary modern school', 'the public school', 'the Ordinary MA degree', 'the GCE A-level', 'the SCE H-grade', 'a general education', 'equality of opportunity' — and they tend to attract their supporters and opponents in a totemic fashion; that is, as elements of a larger system of feeling and understanding that, for everyday purposes, may be adequately understood, and felt about, as discrete symbolic elements.

Durkheim (1915, p. 230) stressed that the totem 'is not merely a convenient process for clarifying the sentiment society has of itself: it also serves to create this sentiment; it is one of its constituent elements'. In the same way, we regard these shared sentiments about Scottish education in two lights: first, as a set of proto-scientific statements which are amenable to explication and some to empirical test; and, second, as a set of totems which have guided people's actions and have thus helped to reproduce the very social structure that they profess to describe.

In the three chapters that follow, we mainly limit our exploration of the totemic belief system to the way it has guided one very special sort of action, namely the framing and execution of policy by central government. One reason for this is that the circumstances that some-times require government to ground its actions in public statements of its beliefs also make it easier for us to provide documentary evidence about such beliefs. However, although we would argue that the Scottish myth has been more widely shared than our documentary evidence shows, we do not imply, to repeat, that it has been universally shared.

The Scottish myth and the challenge of expansion

One of the main totemic figures in the pre-war Scottish account, the personification whose story celebrated and explained the Scottish system, was the 'lad o' pairts', a vernacular and folk description for a vernacular and folk character: the young man of attributes, from whatever social background; a lad, not a young master, who had made his way to one of the four Scottish universities from the omnibus parish or burgh school and would return as the dominie (teacher), or else master a profession, or serve the Empire in an elevated position. If this account is to be maintained in the post-war world, it must accommodate to at least three changes of circumstance. The story had its origins in pre-industrial Scotland and especially in the country and burgh communities of the east and north. Can it be told meaningfully in relation to the educational and social forms of the cities and of the western conurbation, in which areas the majority of the population now lives? Can it, second, be maintained despite the loss of employment opportunities for the educated minority arising from the decline of an Empire, from the improvement of English secondary and tertiary education, and from the present 'staffing-up' to capacity of an edu-cation system that had, for a hundred years, offered expanding employ-ment opportunities to teachers, and especially to educated women? Third, and most important, there is the need to reinterpret, and to extend to all children, a generalist educational and social philosophy that had earlier been framed for a meritocratic elite. One might talk of the child 'of parts' but can one now talk of the child 'of intelligence', 'of capacity' or 'of ability'? If not, if ability, for example, is acknowledged as a continuum, or several continua, how can one now frame and justify educational provision that rests on the assumption that children can be dichotomised, or that any of their parts can be disregarded?

Scotland has, in other words, experienced the dilemmas of expansion, selection and diminishing employment opportunity in a particularly acute form. Its public system expanded earlier than that of England. At first it could avoid some of the pain of necessary decisions about aims and selection because it was parasitic upon a metropolitan neighbour (which, nevertheless, took much advantage from the arrangement). With the mid-nineteenth-century Whig and Liberal reforms of government and administration England had been quicker to lay the basis of a more meritocratic state than it had been to educate for it. But the advantage that this and the Empire gave to the Scottish education system has passed away in the post-war world. Moreover, the inner logic and values of the Scottish perspective on education have less defence than the English against arguments that would universalise access to a full secondary education as a right and obligation of citizenship. The Scottish Advisory Council Report of 1947 did not look for such defences and addressed itself directly to the resultant question which, briefly stated, was this: what does it mean to provide an education for all 12 to 18-year-olds which places more emphasis on their common humanity than it does on the differences between them; and to what extent might this conception be realised, given the state of public knowledge, the reserves of political will, and the possibility that both of these might be interdependent and also open to change?

With moves towards comprehensive reorganisation in the 1960s, politicians and others were to return to this issue; and with the raising of the school-leaving age, growing evidence of pupil dissatisfaction and an increasing problem of youth unemployment, it became even more pertinent in the 1970s. However, for two decades after the war this was not the overriding concern of those who made educational policy in Scotland. Theirs was a different preoccupation: the problem of the 'wastage' of able pupils. It is to this problem that we now turn, for the attempts between 1945 and 1965 to solve the problem of wastage have helped to frame the context in which the more recent problems, of the years since 1965, must be addressed.

Chapter 4

Policy for Certification since the War

Introduction

The Scottish Education Department (SED) faced many problems in the immediate post-war period arising both from the legacy of the war itself and from the requirements of the 1945 Act. 'Roofs over heads' was one pressing concern and the modernisation of the secondary-school curriculum came, in the early 1950s, to be acknowledged as another. But the problem to which the department attached particular importance was that of the 'wastage' of able pupils. High proportions of pupils were leaving school at the minimum age of 15, as it became in 1947, despite the fact that they had been allocated at 12 years of age to a course that could have led to certificate presentation at 17 years. A departmental survey of pupils who transferred to secondary school in 1949 found, for example, that among pupils originally allocated to selective secondary schools, two-thirds (67 per cent) had left school by the beginning of what would have been their fifth year of secondary schooling (Scottish Office, 1954). (Here and elsewhere we use the term 'selective' in relation to a course or a type of school to designate the entity *into* which abler pupils were selected.) The publication of the results of this survey coincided with, and in the accompanying press release were explicitly linked to, the publication of the report on *Early Leaving* in England and Wales (Central Advisory Council for Education (England), 1954). From the outset, therefore, the SED's approach was dominated by a UK concern to identify and retain in secondary education future sources of trained manpower.

Unlike their immediate predecessors, the men who in the early 1950s came to shape the department's policy for curriculum and certification had been favourably impressed by the 1947 Scottish Advisory Council Report on *Secondary Education*. However, the main justification that was offered for changes in certification was the need to reduce this wastage from certificate courses. Although some of their reforms arguably tended in the direction that had been indicated by the Advisory Council, they were always consistent with a general strategy to reduce wastage through modifications in, and additions to, the (existing) system of national certification. This essentially incrementalist policy never questioned the subject as the basic unit of the curriculum; it never advocated a place for internal assessment in the procedures for national certification; and it never attempted to displace the fifth-year examination for Highers in favour of a 'four years plus two years' structure more like that of England. (Scottish pupils transfer to secondary school at 12 years.) Yet all of these had been important planks in the Advisory Council's proposals for secondary schooling. That they were disregarded is indicative of the essentially conservative nature of official policy for certification in this period. Where they conflicted, the reduction of wastage took precedence over the implementation of the Council's recommendations in the formulation of departmental policy.

If one is to understand the workings of certification today, particularly with respect to current proposals that in many respects resemble the disregarded 1947 recommendations of the Advisory Council, one must try to understand what it was that the SED was attempting to conserve as it grappled with the wastage problem; and one must also understand how the incrementalist policy of the last thirty years has influenced present provision. This chapter describes how this policy has unfolded over a period of three decades, identifies the assumptions on which it was originally based, and begins to explore the consequences of an expansionist trend which has seen certification grow from being an elite reward to a point at which it is now applied to the large majority of pupils, and is recommended for application to all.

The university inheritance

The key to understanding the post-war system of certification in Scotland lies in the continuing influence on educational belief and practice of the Scottish idea of the university. Derived originally from the Knoxian plan for a godly commonwealth, and successfully secularised and adapted in the centuries that followed, one distinguishing feature of the Scottish concept of the university, as it came to be articulated in the nineteenth century, was an emphasis on accessibility; university education should be accessible to able Scots wherever they lived, whatever their religion, however poor their secondary education, however slender their means, and in whatever numbers they presented themselves. In the light of this ideal, Scotland had a form of university education in the nineteenth century which, despite the relative poverty of the country and the uncomprehending antipathy of the Westminster Parliament, nevertheless succeeded in making university education more widely accessible, in all of these senses, than it was at the time in England, and possibly anywhere else in the world with the exception of the USA (McPherson, 1973a).

The form of this provision has influenced more recent thought and practice in several ways that are important to the present argument. First, the Higher level of the School Leaving Certificate, introduced in 1888, was strictly related to university entrance requirements until 1924 and, until the early 1960s, Highers courses were 'still largely framed for pupils aiming at a university entrance qualification' (Scottish Education Department, 1965b, p. 32). The belief in the accessibility of the Scottish university had legitimated the monotechnic function of the Higher for some eighty years; and it may well have continued to exercise an influence thereafter.

It was this link that the Advisory Council had tried to break with its 1947 proposal for national certification for 16-year-olds. It recommended that the function of selection, or 'attestation of fitness', for university entry should be met not by a school-leaving certificate but by a separate examination conducted by the universities. The Council argued that 'experience on both sides of the Border has shown that the surest way to distort a School Certificate from its proper function is to peg it to university matriculation requirements' (Scottish Education Department, 1947, para. 253). However, four years later, the SED countered in a long *apologia* for its conduct of the certificate examination that, although its first aim in instituting the Leaving Certificate examination had been 'to develop a more uniform level of secondary education throughout the country', the second aim had been, and still was, 'to provide, under a national guarantee of integrity and standard, a common school leaving examination which would be accepted by university and other examining or professional bodies for admission or registration purposes'. It added that 'the chief care of the Department in this field has been to ensure that pupils from schools under their inspection before entering the Scottish universities should have undergone successfully a full course of secondary education' (Scottish Education Department, 1952, pp. 19, 21). Remarkably, no mention was made of the Scottish central institutions (now broadly equivalent to polytechnics in England) which had been administered by the department since about 1900 and which provided non-university courses of higher education.

Through its influence on the Leaving Certificate examination, the belief that Scottish university education ought to be, and as a matter of fact was, widely accessible, came also to influence the phasing, length and structure of secondary provision. A common view was that a secondary course leading to the attainment of qualifications for university entry should be as short as was compatible with the prevailing standard for entry to university; to lengthen it compulsorily beyond that minimum might unfairly deter the potential student from the poorer family that could well find additional education burdensome. Hence, for most of its existence, the Higher has been open to those presenting at 17 years after a five-year secondary course, though further subjects could also be taken at 18 years, especially once the 'group' requirement had been discontinued in 1951.

We have already mentioned McClelland's (1935) comment 'that the Scottish people value education, and that the central and unbroken strand in our long tradition is the recognition of the right of the clever child, from whatever social class he may come, to the highest and best education the country has to offer'. McClelland himself lengthened this strand in 1942 when his research-based recommendations for a system of selection for compulsory secondary education adopted as the criterion for admission to a certificate course at 12 years of age (known at that time as a senior secondary course), that the pupil should have at least an 'evens' chance of attaining the minimum requirements for a group certificate five years later. This, in turn, would secure entry to advanced education, and probably admission to a Scottish university, though not necessarily in the course of the student's choice. By this criterion about 30 per cent of an age-group were considered fit for a selective secondary course (McClelland 1942, pp. 211–21). The proportions of the age-group admitted by the Scottish local authorities to selective courses came, by the late 1950s, to approach a national average of 40 per cent, this figure being markedly higher than that for England and Wales.[1]

It is against this background of a concern for, and a belief in, the accessibility of the Scottish university and of the route towards it, that we may try to understand the purposes and the legacy of post-war policy for certification.

The 'holy of holies'

The central, unchanging feature of Scottish secondary education since the war has been the terminal Higher-grade examination, first taken after only five years of secondary education, at the age of 17. In the late 1940s less than 10 per cent of the age-group attempted the Higher-grade. By 1962 this proportion had increased slowly but steadily to around 15 per cent. In the next ten years it doubled to around 30 per cent, at which level it remained more or less constant through the

1970s. Scottish secondary education is thus distinguished both by its later start (at 12 years) and its earlier termination (at 17 years, in principle). A further feature, which many Scots believe also expresses and sustains an important element of the Scottish tradition, is its generality or dislike of early subject specialisation. Early specialisation has been regarded as a product of a typically English elitism in education, a *vice anglais*. Where it occurred in England, Scots regarded it as a product of excessive competition for a restricted number of university places and of the influence of the Oxford and Cambridge scholarship examinations (Scottish Education Department, 1960, para. 23).

Whereas, after 1951, the English A-level might normally first be taken at 18 years of age, and usually in not more than two or three subjects, the Scottish Higher could be taken at 17 years in four, five or even six subjects; and English, mathematics, a science and a language were at one stage commonly included in a Highers course. This greater potential for breadth in the Scottish Highers course has been valued and maintained partly in the light of the Scottish universities' degree structure. From 1892 they provided for an undergraduate Ordinary MA, which, after 1908, consisted of seven year-long classes in five subjects, to be completed in three years. Also, the first half of the more specialised four-year Honours-degree course normally required the student to study several subjects other than the intended specialism. As long as the main job of the schools was regarded as the preparation of pupils for university, the availability of such degree courses argued against any pressure that there might have been on schools to award certificates on completion of each of two stages of secondary education, a general stage corresponding to the English O-level, and a more specialised stage corresponding to the A-level. Furthermore, as we indicated in the last chapter, some commentators have also linked the generality of the curriculum directly to what they believed to be the wider social catchment of Scottish selective secondary schools and universities, a view that has been shared by academics and politicians alike and that has achieved its most articulate expression in the title and arguments of George Davie's book, *The Democratic Intellect* (1961).

In all these ways, then, a characteristically Scottish form of society was thought to be symbolised in, and reproduced through, the Higher; and it is indicative of the strength of feeling and identity centred in the Higher that, on the two occasions since the war that the SED has sounded out the possibility of introducing an A-level – once in the 1940s to replace the Higher, and once in the early 1960s to supplement it – the proposals have been roundly dismissed by the Scottish educational world (Cmnd 603, para. 15; and chapter 6 below). Speaking in 1978 to a conference attended by persons from nearly all walks of

Scottish educational life, the Principal of the largest teacher-training college in Scotland reviewed the arguments that had led to the rejection of the proposal for an A-grade in the early 1960s and concluded that any displacement of the Higher 'would be just as clearly rejected today' (Scottish Certificate of Education Examination Board, 1979, pp. 14–15). In the words of John Brunton, Senior Chief Inspector of Schools (1955–66) (Brunton, 1977, pp. 21–2):

> The Leaving Certificate was traditionally the holy of holies of Scottish education. Teachers, and indeed the public at large, understood this examination, and changes in it were a matter of public interest and understanding and could meet with fairly ready acceptance. Consequent changes in the curriculum could also be accepted, provided they did not fundamentally alter the examination, regarded as the gateway to the Universities and to success in the professions.

Controlled incrementalism: changes in national certification before the mid-1960s

Conditions for the award of the Higher were modified in 1951. Until that date it had been awarded on a 'group' basis, the candidate being required in the years immediately prior to 1951 to pass at least two subjects at the Higher grade (one of which had to be English) and three at the Lower grade. In 1951 and thereafter, certificates were awarded for passes in individual subjects, at both Higher and Lower grades; the Lower was still normally taken for the first time in fifth year, the same year as the Higher. There was no minimum requirement for the number or level of subjects a candidate had to sit; it was therefore possible for a pupil to leave school with a pass in a single subject at the Lower grade. More research is required into the thinking behind the reform of 1951, but it seems likely that it owed a lot to the concurrent changes in England and Wales. Nevertheless, it is indicative of the Scottish belief that the overriding purpose of secondary education was to provide a route to the accessible university that no Scottish provision was made in 1951 for an examination at 16 years corresponding to the O-level that was introduced south of the Border in that year for the most able 20 per cent of the age-group.[2] By 1955, however, the SED had decided that the problem of wastage was sufficiently serious to justify the eventual introduction of an examination on English lines for 16-year-olds. Details of the changes were considered by a Working Party that reported in 1959 (Scottish Education Department, 1959a). These were accepted almost immediately, and with few modifications, in Circular 412 of 1959, and were implemented in 1962. The Scottish Leaving Certificate was replaced by the Scottish Certificate of Education; the Higher grade was retained and the Lower grade was replaced by the Ordinary grade to be taken a year earlier, in the fourth year. The hope was that the possibility of presentation for a national examination after only one year of post-compulsory schooling, and not two as hitherto, would encourage more pupils to stay on.

The evidence and arguments presented by the 1959 Working Party clearly indicated that, despite the reforms of 1951, thinking and practice in the schools were still dictated by the view that it was the main job of selective secondary education in Scotland to set the pupil on the (relatively) wide road leading to university. The 1959 Working Party found that 'for the most part the present practice is to treat all entrants to Certificate courses as potential *Higher* grade candidates in all or most of their subjects. . . . The intention has undoubtedly been to give as many pupils as possible the chance of obtaining Higher grade passes' (ibid., paras. 16 and 23). It also found that 'all our evidence goes to show that most Scottish Leaving Certificate courses are still being planned in accordance with the standard traditionally associated with the former "Group" certificate', and this despite the fact, said the Committee, that 'rather less than ten per cent of the pupils in any age-group are in fact capable of obtaining what would have constituted a "Group" certificate' (ibid., para. 4). The Secretary of State, in his turn, responded that 'one of the most urgent tasks facing all those responsible for education in Scotland is to do more for the large group of pupils who have the ability to profit from a senior secondary course but whose bent is not sufficiently academic for them to aspire to university study' (Scottish Education Department, 1959b, para. 13).

The 1959 Working Party recommended that pupils be allowed to take the O-grade examination in their fourth, fifth or sixth year, at the age of 16, 17 or 18. The examination was therefore to serve several functions for several constituencies. It would be a terminal examination for the fourth-year leaver; it would act as an intermediate incentive to a pupil who might then present at the Higher grade in sixth year after a further two years of study; and it would allow an able sixth-year pupil who had already achieved an adequate number of Higher passes in fifth year to broaden his or her learning with a one-year course in sixth year. It was anticipated that such a pupil would have 'bypassed' in fourth year presentation at O-grade in most, if not all, subjects that he or she planned to present at the Higher grade in fifth year. As to standard, this was to be such that the least able presenting pupil, at the lower end of the top 30 per cent of the age-group, would 'have a reasonable prospect of securing passes on the Ordinary grade in at least three subjects in the fourth year' (Scottish Education Department,

1959a, para. 165). It was also made clear that, although the Secretary of State was still concerned that the curriculum should remain 'general', certificate courses would no longer require the study of specified subjects at certain stages (Scottish Education Department, 1959b, paras. 18 and 19). This move was again quite explicitly aimed at giving schools greater flexibility in the provision of courses that would attract more pupils to post-compulsory schooling. In other words, the reduction of wastage took precedence over the maintenance of a compulsorily broad curriculum.

With hindsight, one can understand these changes as clearing many of the obstacles from a path that was to lead, by the mid-1970s, to the award to the large majority of pupils of certification at a variety of levels or grades (as seen already in table 2.1), and in a variety of subjects or combinations thereof. However, the incrementalist policy of the late 1950s and early 1960s viewed matters differently. The policy was still aimed only at the most able 30 per cent of pupils; admission to certificate courses at 12 years of age was to be restricted uniformly to 30 or 35 per cent of the age-group by the local authorities (Scottish Education Department, 1961, para. 85; 1962, para. 15); and it was urged that a minimum of three subjects should be presented for the O-grade examination (Scottish Education Department, 1959a, para. 165). Nevertheless, the introduction of the SCE in 1962 brought with it several new assumptions and practices whose significance was thereafter to grow. Most important was the recognition that schools might legitimately provide for several levels of outcome or attainment, and that pupils should accordingly be allocated to different streams early in their secondary-school career, in order to receive the kind of curricular provision appropriate to their expected future level of attainment. In particular, future Highers pupils and future O-grade pupils should receive separate provision. The Secretary of State agreed 'with the Working Party's view that pupils taking the Ordinary grade in the fourth year and pupils taking the Higher grade in the fifth year should as far as practicable follow separate syllabuses and that the syllabuses should be separated at as early a stage in the course as possible'. This was to be no later than at the end of the second year, at 14 years, for the large majority (Scottish Education Department, 1959b, para. 17). Indeed, the Working Party had also argued that the bottom one in six children transferred to certificate courses should, from the outset, be given only minimal O-grade courses and that others should transfer down thereafter (Scottish Education Department, 1959a, para. 32).

For the first time, in other words, educational outcomes other than the achievement of a qualification for entry to university or higher education were recognised as legitimate in their own right and were, in their turn, held to legitimate more differentiated provision than had previously been made, and earlier differentiation as well.

A year later a Committee of the Advisory Council that had been appointed to make further recommendations for the post-fourth-year examination structure, and that shared several members with the 1959 Working Party, affirmed this legitimation of new educational outcomes in relation to a further group of pupils. It stated (Scottish Education Department, 1960, para. 14) that the 1959 Working Party had:

> clearly envisaged a situation wherein a small number of passes on the new Ordinary grade . . . would prove to be the limited but legitimate objective of a substantial number of pupils in our secondary schools. It is no less true, however, that for a consider-able further number of pupils in our senior secondary schools a somewhat more ambitious, but equally legitimate, objective will continue to be found in (quite literally) one or two passes on the Higher Grade, attainable one year later in the fifth year.

Closely related to the increased public recognition that was urged for certified levels of educational attainment that had hitherto been regarded as inconsequential or valueless, were moves to encourage employers to treat certification 'as an indication of whether a prospective employee has the particular qualifications necessary for a specific post' (Scottish Education Department, 1959a, para. 161). In other words, in addition to the value that certificates derived from their links with higher edu-cation, it was hoped to create further value through the use of certificates to select for the labour market and for the developing system of non-advanced further education attached to it (ibid., paras. 123–38).

At this stage in the late 1950s there was no intention that certification for the labour market should be made available to the 65 per cent of pupils who were not transferred to selective secondary courses; nor was it envisaged that the O-grade examination should also serve pupils who planned to present the same subject at the Higher grade. Thus, although the new provision for certification was designed to serve a wider range of purposes than before, these purposes were to be realised for largely non-overlapping constituencies of pupils within what was still a relatively narrow range of ability and interest.

The envisaged development may be contrasted with the situation that actually obtained in the later 1970s, by which time the SCE exam-ination at 16 years served some 70 per cent of the age-group and was no longer preceded by selection for differentiated secondary courses at 12 years of age. Changes since the late 1950s thereby accentuated problems concerning the level of difficulty and the criteria of attain-ment that were appropriate to an examination that had come to serve the majority of the age group.

Although the reforms of the late 1950s aimed to conserve the old moral order by reserving the allocation of status through certification to an elect minority of the age-group, they nevertheless opened the way to more recent changes by loosening the fabric of evaluative and explanatory beliefs that had legitimated previous practice. In particular, the central organising idea and symbol of the lad o' pairts, the 'finest product of our educational system' as the Advisory Council still put it in the early 1960s, began to lose its definition and identity. When university entry had been the dominant objective of secondary education, the proportion of the age-group admitted to 'academic' courses was decided by an 'evens-chance' principle. The marginal pupil gaining entry to an academic course should be one whose measured ability or attainment at 12 years gave him or her an estimated evens chance of qualifying for entry to university on completion of a secondary course of five, or possibly six, years. However, once a fourth-year examination (O-grades) was introduced, and not solely as a fourth-year rung in the ladder leading to Highers in fifth year, and once Highers was no longer intended solely as a means of qualifying for entry to university or higher education, the evens-chance principle for academic selection at 12 years and thereafter became problematic. If, after 1962, the attainment of three O-grade passes were to be as legitimate an objective in its own right as the attainment of entry qualifications to university, why should the thinking behind the evens-chance principle not also be applied to entry to courses leading to the newly legitimated, but modest, O-grade outcomes? The evens chance had been adopted partly for its intuitive appearance of fairness and partly because it supposedly minimised the number of 'misfits' or 'mistakes' made in allocations to selective secondary courses, as judged by pupils' eventual success or failure in the Leaving Certificate examination (McClelland, 1942, pp. 108-9). The same reasoning could be applied to success or failure in achieving a minimum of three O-grade passes; and, if it were, it would increase the proportion of the age-group that had a right to start an O-grade course far beyond the 35 per cent at which the official policy wished to hold it.

In the event, an expansion in the proportions starting an O-grade course was precisely what happened. But it was to happen without there being any clear understanding of what the schools should aim to achieve for the larger proportion of pupils now admitted to certificate courses. Pupils might now 'legitimately' emerge with three or four O-grades, or with one or two Highers. But what did this make them? Legitimate though they were, they were not 'the finest products' of the system. Ultimately, the lad o' pairts established and fulfilled himself as such through his attendance at university. But what was the moral identity of these new sorts of pupils? How was it to be realised and how, therefore, might one decide what would constitute for them a completed education?

Additions to the national certification system since the mid-1960s

The year 1965 marks a convenient watershed in our analysis. It was the first year in which the Scottish Certificate of Education Examination Board conducted the SCE examination and also the year in which Circular 600 (concurrently with Circular 10/65 in England and Wales) announced the proposals for comprehensive reorganisation. Both merit some comment as a preliminary to our discussion of subsequent changes in the SCE examination.

First, it is worth noting that the problems of certification policy that were thrown into sharper relief by comprehensive reorganisation and the raising of the school-leaving age were already logically entailed by the reforms of the early 1960s. The blurring of the boundaries of the concept of the academic child which underpinned the system of selective transfer; the potential for plural values in the curriculum; the problem of locating a pass mark that would be neither too easy for the able nor too difficult for the less able; all of these arose from the legitimacy that had now been given to more modest levels of achievement than that required for entry to higher education. These problems would have become more acute whether or not Circular 600 and the raising of the school-leaving age occurred.

In figure 4.1 we show trend data taken from the Dunning Report on the expansion of O-grade presentations and awards between 1964 and 1976. By 1968, one or two years before any effect of reorganisation would be expected to show in fourth-year presentations, the percentage of the year-group achieving a minimum of three O-grade passes was already 29 per cent, only 1 per cent below the percentage that the 1959 Working Party had thought eligible for national certification. Already by that date 38 per cent of the age-group were being presented for at least one O-grade, with 36 per cent achieving an award. Any policy for admitting no more than 35 per cent of the age-group to certificate courses had already been breached. What, however, can be attributed to comprehensive reorganisation and more especially to the raising of the school-leaving age is an increase in the proportion of pupils unsuccessfully presented. The proportions achieving A–C awards (formerly 'pass' grades) levelled out in the 1970s at around 60 per cent, whereas the proportions presented increased steadily to 75 per cent in 1976. A glance at figure 4.1 shows that the ratio of passes to presentations in the 1970s was lower than in the 1960s. Schools were increasingly allowing the examination at 16 years to do much of the work of

Percentages are of first-year pupils 3 years earlier

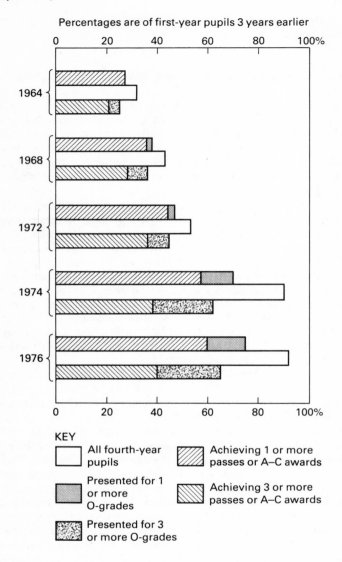

Figure 4.1 Fourth-year pupils presented for and achieving passes (to 1972) and A–C awards (from 1973) in O-grade

selection that had previously been done by the transfer examination at 12 years. We return to the consequences of this later in the chapter.

After 1965 it becomes more difficult to talk of a planned government policy for achieving educational change through changes in certification. One reason for this is purely administrative. In 1965 the SED handed responsibility for the certificate examination to the Examination Board (SCEEB) which had been created by a statute of 1963 and subsequent regulations. However, the Secretary of State retained substantial formal powers over the Board; and he has continued to exercise an influence through the presence of departmental Assessors on the Board, and on its committees and subject panels. This influence has been used to support a strategy of further 'downward incrementalism', extending the prospect of certification to pupils in yet lower reaches of the ability range.

But to talk of this influence as 'government policy' in the sense that obtained until 1965 is also problematic for several other reasons. It had never been intended to extend certification to the majority of pupils. Moreover, before 1965 the incrementalist policy was planned to initiate change (in staying on and certificate presentations); after 1965 it became, in part, a response to changes initiated informally by the schools as they presented increasing proportions of the age-group for public examination, including pupils below the threshold of three O-grade presentations. Also, there is evidence to suggest that, after 1965, ministers themselves took more of an initiative in shaping policy for certification, mainly in the light of comprehensive reorganisation and the raising of the school-leaving age, and under some pressure from Scotland's largest teachers' union, the Educational Institute of Scotland. Before that date, policy for certification had largely originated within the SED and had aimed to realise the full potential of, rather than to challenge, the status quo of the bipartite system for which the 1945 Act had legislated; ministers were there to be convinced, but the policy was the department's in the sense that ministers rarely initiated. However, there are indications that, in the later 1960s, ministers were actively involved when the SED urged the schools and the Examination Board to relax the informal threshold for admission to certificate examinations of a minimum of three subjects; and, in 1970, Chief Inspector Fullwood said to a conference, organised by the Examination Board and attended by nominees who had been invited to 'represent' all walks of Scottish educational life (Scottish Certificate of Education Examination Board, 1970, p. 15):

> by and large the schools have not yet been convinced of the value
> of organising minimal certificate courses. . . . I suspect that the
> truth is that we have become quite conditioned to thinking of three

Ordinary grades as the minimum in school qualifications and I would very much hope that we shall be able to emancipate ourselves from this idea in time for the raising of the school leaving age because if so, this will again tend to increase the proportion of pupils who are involved in certificate presentation.

Fullwood had seen the O-grade 'quietly evolving under its own momentum until it takes in something approaching half the age-group' (ibid.). Such was the momentum, however, that this level of presentation was virtually to be achieved by the time the school-leaving age was raised in 1973. In 1972, 47 per cent of the age-group were presented for at least one O-grade and 45 per cent for at least three. The schools' response to the raising of the school-leaving age was immediate and dramatic. A year later, in 1974, the proportion of pupils presented for at least one O-grade had risen sharply to 70 per cent and the proportion presenting for at least three O-grades had risen to 62 per cent (Scottish Education Department, 1977a, p. 124). Although for individual schools the recourse to certification may have been a logical response to the raising of the leaving age, for the system as a whole it can be regarded more as a reflex action than as a reflective one.

That reflex was, no doubt, conditioned by a further change in policy for the O-grade urged by the department or the minister. In 1973 the pass/fail distinction was abandoned. Thereafter virtually all those who presented were guaranteed an award at one of five grades A, B, C (hitherto the pass grades) or D or E. A sixth category, of 'no award', was retained, but not as a 'fail' designation. The announcement of this change, which had been strongly resisted by several members of the Board, including the Chairman of its Examinations Committee, made it plain that the initiative had come from the Secretary of State and was not without its disadvantages. Indeed, it was as a consequence of these events that the Board made a proposal to the Secretary of State for a general and public review of policy for assessment.[3] The proposal led to the appointment of the committee chaired by Jo Dunning, which in 1977 was to publish its report, *Assessment for All* (Scottish Education Department, 1977a).

This was the first major occasion on which the Board publicly advised the Secretary of State on its own initiative. The title of the report can be seen, in one sense, as the final, logical extension of the incremental policy for certification that Scotland had followed since the war. The committee proposed a national examination for all 16-year-olds, to be taken at one of three overlapping levels: Credit, General and Foundation. The Credit level was intended for the most able 15–25 per cent. Its standard would therefore broadly correspond to the standard of fourth-year work undertaken by pupils who would eventually achieve a Highers qualification, since in 1976 about one-quarter (27 per cent) of leavers had gained at least one Higher. The standard of the General level was to correspond to the level achieved by pupils who presented for O-grade but not for Highers. Finally, in 1976, 35 per cent of leavers had either achieved 'no award' in the O-grade or had not been presented for it; it was for the majority of these pupils that the Foundation certificate was intended.

The Secretary of State's response to the committee's proposals was to postpone any change in certification arrangements for the most able 65 or 70 per cent taking either Highers or O-grades, observing that 'the O grade examination . . . still serves a large number of pupils reasonably well and will continue to do so for some time' (Scottish Education Department (no date), 1979, para. 25). Proposals for Foundation courses were, however, to become a matter for further urgent investigation. In other words, if anything were to happen, it was to be the final increment to a universal system of certification that had established itself, stage by stage, over the previous three decades, fast outstripping the values and intentions that had launched expansion.

Summary and discussion

Some post-war trends in the national system of certification are summarised in figure 4.2, which depicts the situation at three dates: around 1950, before the group award ended; in the early 1960s, when the first effects of the reforms of the later 1950s were beginning to show; and in the middle and later 1970s, when the intervening growth in the proportion of the age-group presenting for Highers and O-grades had levelled off. Briefly, the immediate post-war policy for certification had modest aims, in several senses. First, it was concerned with only a minority of pupils. Second, within this limitation, it labelled achievement in terms of only one criterion or set of values concerning fitness for entry to university or higher education. Thirty years later, actual and mooted policy was much more ambitious. It was addressed to a wide range of pupils, about seven out of ten. It had also developed many more categories, in terms of which differentiation might occur: for example, a simple count of the number of Highers passes, or of O-grade awards if no Highers were passed, could generate a more finely differentiated hierarchy. Third, to a greater degree than hitherto, examination presentation and performance at 16 years, during the period of compulsory schooling, was doing much of the work of differentiation that had previously been done at 12 and 15 years by formal selection and early leaving respectively. Finally, to the extent that national certification was now applied to a wider range of pupils

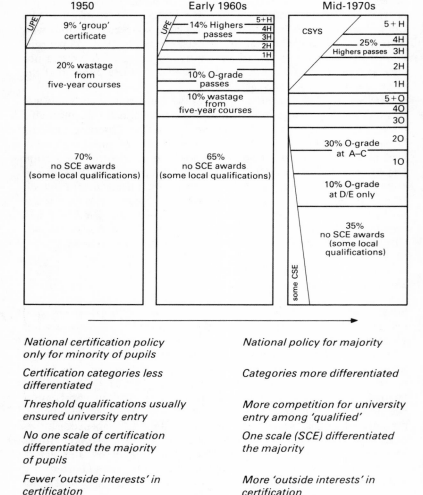

Figure 4.2 Post-war changes in the national system of certification

presenting in a greater range of subjects, and to the extent that attempts to solicit the use of lower levels of certification by employers and other selectors had met with some response, there was now a potential for competition between a plurality of interests and values over the control of the examination system.

However, we can only identify the full implications of these trends and of the continuous application of the incrementalist policy, if we also emphasise the discontinuity of the circumstances in which the policy has been applied. The original policy was based on the view that something of value had been inherited in the Higher; something that was essentially Scottish, that drew its strength from the historical circumstances in which it had been created, and whose value could be tapped, with some circumspection, to tempt more pupils to value education. What it offered, ultimately, was access to a university education and thence to professional status in life. It was not concerned with sorting pupils for any gradations of rank or status that the world might recognise in the non-university and non-professional world. Nor was it much concerned with the possibility that the university and professional world were themselves stratified.[4] The assumed world was morally unproblematic: what was on offer was the undifferentiated best and was available to all who were eligible. Policy for certification was not yet caught up in uncertainties over the extent to which it should reproduce a finely graduated hierarchy of achievement that was analogous to the hierarchy of positions in the world that awaited the school-leaver.

The problem of wastage had therefore both an explanatory (or proto-scientific) and an evaluative (or moral) dimension. The former concerned the extent to which it was believed possible to solve the problem of wastage, and the extent to which a solution was thought to be a matter for the school system. Although the incrementalist changes of the late 1950s were based on the belief that a solution was possible, and was within the means of the school system, the underpinning assumption about the limits to the effectiveness of school policy was still cautious: the formal opportunity for certification was to be extended only to the top 35 per cent of the age-group.

The evaluative or moral dimension concerned whether the world implied by the accessible Scottish university and its educational infrastructure was a good world, and whether the able pupils who rejected this world by leaving the education system at an earlier stage were in some sense morally deficient. (For an example of the 'moral deficiency' argument in action in the 1950s, see chapter 16, note 1, and the related discussion in the text.) We have argued that an attempt was made in the late 1950s and early 1960s to legitimate new 'products' of the school system, namely pupils with a handful of O-grade passes, or with one or two Highers. But, inevitably, the identity of these new figures was more hazy than that of the lad o' pairts and there was no basis, either inherited or attempted, for prescribing the elements of a completed education for such pupils. In the event, there was a continuing recourse to the practice and to the idea of an academic general education. But this was to become increasingly difficult to interpret and apply under conditions of expansion; and where it was applied, it was to leave an increasing proportion of pupils with the sense that their moral position was that of being a lad o' pairts in some part only.

Chapters 10 and 11 examine aspects of this 'demoralisation', the next two chapters explore in greater detail the concept and practice of general education since the 1950s.

Chapter 5

Certification, Selection and General Education

The traditional Scottish secondary school course was one designed to provide a broad general education . . . and this tradition was to a large extent continued in the expanded secondary education of the years after the war. (Brunton Report, 1963)[1]

A 'good general education' remains the traditional Scottish aim. (Scottish Information Office, 1970s)[2]

Introduction

For a long time now Scots have been committed to a belief in the breadth and generality of their education; and, consistent with this, a respect for the 'traditional aim' of a general or broad education has frequently been rehearsed in official accounts of the curriculum. At the same time, however, post-war expansion has radically altered one of the material and conceptual preconditions on which the traditional account had previously rested. The Scottish myth had originally been told, and acted out, in relation to a small and allegedly able proportion of the age-group. Could it be adapted and extended to the circumstances of post-war expansion without sacrificing the notions of identity that were bound up in it, or its inner coherence, or its correspondence with the actual world of secondary education? 'We have an interest in the common man, therefore we have an interest in a broad education' (chapter 3): could these ideals of the broad curriculum and the common man, and the claimed link between these ideals, be sustained when expansion, the raising of the school-leaving age and comprehensive reorganisation put them more seriously to the test? Could a broad curriculum be realised in a system which had also to cope with the problems of difficulty, selection and motivation that were posed anew by expansion (see chapter 1)?

65

One purpose of this chapter is to illustrate some of the explicit and implicit strategies that were proposed or used to manage potential conflicts between, on the one hand, solutions to the problems of difficulty, selection and motivation and, on the other, a continuing commitment to the broad curriculum and to the traditional account of how it might be realised. Briefly, the explicit management strategies were those that were publicly acknowledged as legitimate options within the advisory and policy-making process. The implicit management strategies (we shall say more about this term later in the chapter) had mainly to do with the continued operation of selection on and within the expanding education system. Selection restricted the areas of human experience, and the proportions of pupils, to which terms such as 'broad' and 'common' were in practice applied; and by influencing what was taught, and to which pupils, selection thereby entailed implicit judgments of who and what was of value. However, although such judgments, and the processes by which they were made, were not publicly acknowledged in full, they were often made wholly explicit, and were often keenly felt, in the day-to-day relations between teachers and pupils. Chapter 10 illustrates aspects of these relationships in more detail.

An adequate account of curriculum must go beyond official accounts of the provision that has been made to include some assessment of how pupils have experienced and reacted to their schooling. Such an assessment reveals grave inadequacies in the traditional Scottish account, both as a description of what has happened in the schools and as a basis for deciding how to change pupils' schooling; that is, actions or attempted reforms that have been predicated on the truth of the received account have tended to go wrong, and to go wrong in statistically and logically predictable ways. An improved account would seek to incorporate a description of the tacit and informal processes of selection that have diverted actions in this way and that have weakened both the inner coherence of the received account and its correspondence with the world.

The structure of this chapter is as follows: having first explained the various management strategies that we have in mind, we go on to examine how effective the Highers course has been in facilitating the expansion of post-compulsory schooling. Then we explore evidence on the consequences of expansion for the phasing and number of examination courses taken by able pupils, for the length of their secondary course, and for their experience of success or failure. These aspects of selection influence the scope that is available for the realisation of a broad curriculum as it has commonly been understood. We then examine the new functions of the O-grade examination with respect both to Highers pupils and to the pupils in the middle range of attainment (between the 30th and 70th percentiles) whom it has come to serve in the last fifteen years. We comment both on its general level of difficulty and on the relative difficulty of the examination in individual subjects. In the final section we summarise the constraints that selection and certification have placed upon policy for the curriculum and speculate on some consequences of these constraints for pupils' approaches to learning. Then, in the following chapter, we examine a number of specific examples of how curriculum and pedagogy have been shaped by the processes that this chapter describes.

As in the last two chapters, our account is presented in terms of Scottish ideas and circumstances. But we believe that our general conclusions have relevance both to any education system which faces the problems posed by educational expansion, and also to more general problems concerned with the relations between belief and practice.

Managing expansion

We may identify five strategies which have been proposed or adopted in Scotland's management of the problems that post-war expansion posed for the curriculum. First, as we have suggested, the problem was explicitly and publicly recognised in the thinking that culminated in the Advisory Council's report on *Secondary Education* in 1947. Its suggested solution relied heavily on the social and economic acceptability of providing a common course for all pupils, until 16 years, relatively undifferentiated by ability and freed from the influence of university entry requirements. Also, the Council's understanding of a broad or general education was framed as much in terms of the attitudes and approach of pupils to areas of knowledge and experience, analytically conceived, as it was in terms of pupils' coverage of extant school subjects (see 'Introduction to part 2'). Its recommendations were largely disregarded.

Second, the strategy that was actually followed until the mid-1960s was, again, to recognise the dilemmas of expansion publicly and explicitly, but to try to contain them, first by differentiating certifiable provision to some extent and, second, by limiting it to the most able 30 or 40 per cent of pupils, mainly in senior secondary (grammar) schools and courses. In other words, the traditional account was only required to correspond to the experience of a minority of pupils. (At the same time, interestingly, the otherwise disregarded child-centred approach of the Advisory Council's 1947 report was used to guide and legitimate the education that was recommended for the remaining 60 or 70 per cent of 'non-academic' children.)

During this period the Scottish Education Department (SED) recommended that, where a traditionally broad curriculum proved

67

unduly demanding for certificate pupils, the principle of breadth should be subordinated to the need to suit courses to pupils' interests and abilities (chapter 4). The department also hinted that such subordination did not really compromise the principle of breadth, if this were judged by a less demanding standard that required only that a secondary pupil should have *some* exposure to recommended subjects or areas, and not that he or she should necessarily present them for certification.[3] But such hints were not, and could not be, too explicit about the amount of differentiation there was in the provision that the schools were actually making; or about the level and amount of exposure to each subject that would maintain the minimal conditions for breadth; or about the level of difficulty of subjects and the related presentation and pass rates in certificate examinations.

Third, between the mid-1960s and mid-1970s containment failed, and the proportions presenting for certificate examinations rose to 70 per cent. The 'strategy' that was adopted during this period was largely implicit and consisted of a variety of tactics, listed later in this section, for coping with the problems of difficulty, selection and motivation. At the level of national policy-making and advice there was considerable uncertainty and disagreement over the proportion of the age-group at which national policies for curriculum and certification should be directed.[4]

Fourth, with the publication of the Dunning and Munn Reports (Scottish Education Department, 1977a, 1977b), an explicit attempt was again made to argue for the provision of a common curriculum in relation to (nearly) all pupils. Features of the proposals contained in these reports were the continued recourse to the subject as the basic unit of the curriculum; the prescription of eight areas of modes of study; the formal recognition of three levels of difficulty (in descending order: Credit, General and Foundation) at which presentation might be made; and the incorporation of 'internal' or 'school-based' elements in the curriculum and assessment procedures at all three levels.

Fifth, successive governments have responded to these reports by giving priority to developments at the Foundation level. For reasons which we discuss at the end of chapter 6 we think that this strategy is likely to have to rely, like the third strategy, on a variety of implicit, or publicly unacknowledged, tactics.

The tactics that were used during the period of the third (implicit) strategy, between the mid-1960s and the mid-1970s, all followed from what was left unsaid, or undone, in the explicit attempts to reduce the demands made on less able pupils by a common curriculum. They included the tacit acceptance of a standard of difficulty across most subjects that was unduly high for some pupils, and unduly low for others (the situation which the Dunning Report finally addressed explicitly with its recommendation for three levels of examination). There was a tacit acceptance of the fact that one response to an unduly high level of difficulty was for some pupils to discontinue the serious study of certain subjects before the prescribed time; and this had consequences for their coverage of the curriculum in the later stages of secondary education. There was a tacit acceptance of the fact that one response to an unduly low level of difficulty was for other pupils to take too many examinations; and this had consequences for, among other things, their methods of study. Finally, within the two SCE levels of H- and O-grade, there were consistent and substantial variations between subjects in their level of difficulty. This allowed more pupils to acquire more certificates than would otherwise have been the case and, to some extent, moderated these other dilemmas; but it also raised new problems, of which the most obvious is that of fairness.

Highers, expansion and the five-year course

Relative to the GCE A-level course, the shorter Scottish course for Highers has, in some respects, been better suited to encourage and service the expansion of post-compulsory secondary education. This can be seen in figures 5.1 and 5.2 which show that, compared with England and Wales in the last fifteen years or so, higher proportions of the age-group in Scotland have stayed on at school for a post-compulsory year (figure 5.1) and have achieved or surpassed threshold qualifications for entry to higher education (figure 5.2). However, although the fifth-year Higher at 17 years has continued to facilitate a greater take-up of what is now one year of post-compulsory secondary education, the fact that it is the terminal school examination means that Scottish schools have not retained as high a proportion of the age-group as in England for two post-compulsory years; for the Scottish system allows pupils to leave at 17 years with, if they are sufficiently able, qualifications that will be recognised by any Scottish tertiary-education institution, or professional body.

This distinctive Scottish pattern is a survival of arrangements that were explicitly intended to keep upper-secondary and tertiary education accessible to the children of families who could not afford to support them through what was considered to be an excessive further year of schooling (to 18 years); and, indeed, it is interesting that figure 5.1 shows that in the harsher economic climate of the 1970s Scotland has maintained its superiority over England with respect to the proportion taking one extra year (sufficient to achieve H-grade qualifications), but has deteriorated with respect to the proportion taking two extra years.[5]

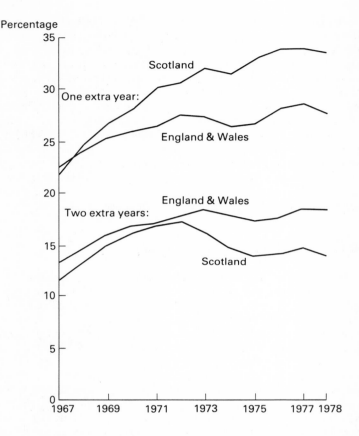

Figure 5.1 Percentages staying on at school for at least one extra year and for at least two extra years

The Scottish pattern has two implications for the management of the Highers curriculum. First, in attempting to maintain a broad spread of subjects in its final examination courses, Scotland has had to cater for a wider range of interests and abilities than has been the case with the GCE A-level in England. Second, Scotland must accommodate all of its arrangements for variety in curriculum in a shorter course (five years, or one post-O-grade year), for it cannot be assumed that all post-compulsory pupils will necessarily stay at school until 18 years to complete a sixth-year course. (The sixth year must not be confused with the English Sixth Form which, it may now be clear, has no equivalent in Scotland.) The related problems of difficulty, selection

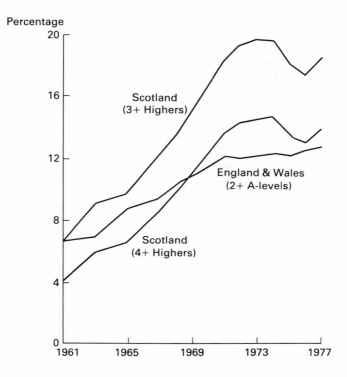

Percentage

Figure 5.2 School-leavers with minimum higher-education entrance qualifications

and motivation that we outlined in chapter 1 are therefore more pressing in the Scottish Highers system than they are in the current GCE A-level system, although recent English attempts to plan for a wider range of interests and abilities in post-compulsory second-ary education have had to anticipate these problems at a similar level.

We described in the previous section how the tactics that Scotland has used to cope with these problems have remained implicit. As a result there has been an uncomfortable lack of correspondence between the official descriptive (and prescriptive) account of Scottish provision, and what pupils have actually experienced.

Normatively, the Highers course has been, and still is, regarded as a five-subject, five-year course, the five subjects being the number required for the old group-leaving certificate. A report that was written in the 1960s, partly in the hope of persuading a mainly English audience

71

of the virtues of the Scottish system, had the following to say (Council for Scientific Policy, 1968, para. 92):

> [the] certificate examination structure . . . reflects different traditions and ideals. The aim in certificate courses has been to provide a general unspecialised education for five years (up to the age of about 17), i.e. the majority of pupils study at least four or five subjects, covering a wide range, for the whole of their secondary school course. This course lasts at most six years, and it is common for pupils to complete their secondary education in five years, moving straight from the fifth year to higher education. The pivot of this system is the Higher grade (taken after five years in the secondary school, at a standard considerably above the G.C.E. 'O' level, but below the G.C.E. 'A' level). The influence of universities in helping to maintain the key position of the Higher grade and, with it, the traditional broad pattern of education in Scottish schools is of great importance.

In 1965 the Scottish Education Department itself had commented (1965b, p. 43):

> an interesting feature is that, whereas in some schools the normal curriculum contains five major presentation subjects, in others it contains six. Although there may be exceptions in the case of highly selective schools, it must be said that the five-subject arrangement appears to be more in keeping with the capabilities of the majority of the pupils.

In the 1970s the second document quoted at the head of this chapter stated: 'Beyond the age of sixteen, the educational philosophy and *consequently* the educational systems and the examination diverge [the other system being that of England and Wales]. Scottish pupils undertake a broad general education and normally aim to sit for four–six SCE Higher grade subjects at seventeen' (our emphasis; see note 2).

Nevertheless, since the Second World War there has been only a poor correspondence between this view of the Highers course and what has actually been happening in the schools, in three respects. First, until recently, most Highers pupils have actually taken six years to complete their secondary schooling; second, until the mid-1970s only a minority presented five subjects, and then only by virtue of returning for a sixth year; and third, there have been substantial and persistent regional variations in rates of staying on from fifth to sixth year that have passed unacknowledged in the attempt to maintain a single, centralised national policy.

We may illustrate these points briefly and refer, first, to the length of the Highers course. Until 1951 the Scottish Leaving Certificate was taken as a group examination in fifth year (3 Highers and 2 Lowers or 2 Highers and 3 Lowers being recommended combinations). Once the fifth-year group requirement was abandoned, Highers pupils could, and did, spread their Highers presentations over fifth and sixth years. Some did this to ease the pressure of presenting five subjects for examination in one diet; and others did this because the changed conditions now allowed them to work meaningfully in the fifth and sixth year to the upper limit of their abilities, presenting one or two subjects each year for examination. This changing pattern had been anticipated at the time of the change in conditions in 1951[6] and it was later remarked as an actual empirical development.[7] When this happened, official policy set itself against the trend by trying to reassert the normatively prescribed five-year course as that which the schools should realise (Scottish Education Department, 1959b, para. 28):

> The Secretary of State . . . hopes that the proportion of pupils who succeed in obtaining in the fifth year all the Higher grade passes they require for university entrance or professional examinations will increase, and that the number who have to devote their sixth year mainly to preparing for Higher grade passes which they have failed to obtain in the fifth will diminish.

However, two developments in the 1960s worked against this hope. Both resulted from the planned use of certification policies to reduce wastage from academic courses (chapter 4) and both might, therefore, have been predicted when those policies were being formed. First, more pupils entered the sixth year to take one or two Highers; and second, as the demand for tertiary education expanded, more pupils in the sixth year needed more or better Higher passes to ensure their admission to tertiary institutions. The doors of the open Scottish university had begun to close. One feature of this institution was the Attestation of Fitness that at one time was awarded on the basis of a candidate's meeting minimum requirements in the Leaving Certificate or Universities' Preliminary Examinations. The Attestation allowed its holder to go to university though not necessarily to enter a chosen course. In 1968 its award was discontinued.

The Scottish Education Data Archive allows us to show in table 5.1 trends in the percentages of Highers pupils returning for a sixth year. The percentages are shown by year of leaving, by the number of Highers attempts in fifth year, and by whether or not the pupils were at schools in areas that were incorporated in 1975 into the Strathclyde Region. (This region includes Glasgow and the Clydeside conurbation and contains almost half the population of Scotland.) Several conclusions may be drawn. First, the table shows that a majority of Highers pupils did indeed return for a sixth year during the 1960s and early 1970s.

TABLE 5.1 Percentages of pupils returning for a sixth year (not leaving from fifth year) by number of fifth-year Highers attempts, region and year of leaving: among leavers from EA and GA schools passing at least one Higher

	1962-3			1969-70			1971-2			1975-6		
	Strath-clyde	Rest of Scotland	Differ-ence	Strath-clyde	Rest of Scotland	Differ-ence	Strath-clyde	Rest of Scotland	Differ-ence	Strath-clyde	Rest of Scotland	Differ-ence
1	76	72	– 4	63	63	0	55	61	+ 6	59	42	–17
2	62	62	0	64	68	+ 4	67	67	0	47	51	+ 4
3	59	63	+ 4	67	60	– 7	65	67	+ 2	54	55	+ 1
4	61	75	+14	59	73	+14	61	73	+12	56	60	+ 4
5	67	81	+14	60	77	+17	59	78	+19	56	72	+16
6+	60¹	79	+19¹	57	86	+29	64	81	+17	55	73	+18
All	65	69	+ 4	63	70	+ 7	63	71	+ 8	55	62	+ 7

Note: 1 These figures are based on 10 unweighted cases. All but five observations are based on over 100 unweighted cases.

74

Only in the mid-1970s did the proportion decline towards half (55 per cent in Strathclyde and 62 per cent in the rest of Scotland). Second, the table shows that the rate of fifth-year leaving among pupils with four or more Highers attempts in fifth year was consistently higher in the Strathclyde Region. We believe, although we have not the space to argue it fully here, that this persistent regional difference is a consequence of a long-standing preference, over a century old, particularly among the schools and tertiary institutions serving Glasgow and the Clydeside conurbation, for educational arrangements adapted to the needs of a less-than-prosperous population.

Five Highers after five years?

Table 5.2 shows the percentage of Highers pupils attempting different numbers of Highers at four points in time since the early 1960s. (During this period the proportion of the age-group attempting Highers increased from about 15 per cent to about 30 per cent.) The percentages are shown separately for fifth-year attempts at 17 years (table 5.2a) and for fifth- and sixth-year attempts combined (excluding repeated attempts in the same subject and counting both fifth- and sixth-year leavers in the 100 per cent base) (table 5.2b). The two parts of the table refer to the same pupils. The columns for all years but 1975–6 show substantial disparities between the traditional account and the actual situation. In the early 1960s for example, only a quarter of Highers pupils (27 per cent) attempted more than three Highers in their fifth year (table 5.2a), and this at a time when Highers courses were still, according to the SED, framed primarily for intending university entrants (chapter 4). By 1971–2 the comparable proportion was still under half (47 per cent) and by 1975–6 it was around two-thirds (64 per cent). But, even at that date, only a minority of Highers pupils were actually attempting five or more Highers in their fifth year (37 per cent).

A comparison between tables 5.2a and 5.2b shows how the received account of the Highers course as a broad, five-subject course depended heavily, if tacitly, on the sixth year. Table 5.2b shows the combined fifth- and sixth-year attempts. The percentages of all Highers leavers attempting at least four subjects by the time they left school were 55, 65, 68 and 82 per cent respectively at the four dates, and the percentages attempting at least five were 28, 41, 46 and 65 per cent. These percentages are all considerably higher than the corresponding percentages for fifth-year attempts. Thus, to the extent that one might wish to describe the Highers course as a five-subject course, one could not also describe it (as in the received account) as a five-year course. Moreover,

TABLE 5.2   Percentages of pupils attempting different numbers of
Highers by school stage and calendar year of leaving: among leavers from
EA and GA schools passing at least one Higher

(a) In fifth year

Number of attempted Highers	1962–3	1969–70	1971–2	1975–6	Change since 1962–3	Change since 1969–70
0	< 0.5	3	2	1	+ 1	− 2
1	23	13	11	4	−19	− 9
2	28	19	18	11	−17	− 8
3	23	22	21	20	− 3	− 2
4	17	21	21	27	+10	+ 6
5 or more	10	22	26	37	+27	+15
Total	101	100	99	100		

(b) In fifth and sixth years

Number of attempted Highers	1962–3	1969–70	1971–2	1975–6	Change since 1962–3	Change since 1969–70
1	7	6	7	2	− 5	− 4
2	16	11	10	7	− 9	− 4
3	22	19	16	11	−11	− 8
4	27	24	22	17	−10	− 7
5 or more	28	41	46	65	+37	+24
Total	100	101	101	102		

even when the sixth year is included, a large proportion of Highers
pupils did not take a full five-subject course, and substantial discrepancies
remain between the traditional account and the actual situation.

One might resolve this lack of correspondence in the following way.
Selection, it could be argued, was sometimes tacitly acknowledged in
the guarded terms in which the myth was expressed. It might talk, as
we have seen above, of 'presentation subjects' and of 'normal aims'. It
only implied, it did not insist, that presentation subjects were actually
presented, and that aims were actually fulfilled. In other words, the
myth attempted simultaneously to be both explanatory and evaluative;
in this instance it was as much an account of the goals that were
normatively prescribed for a course as it was a description of the
successful conclusion to which pupils actually brought their work.

Clearly much depends upon imprecision and on the ambiguity of terms like 'normal', which in everyday usage may be taken in both a prescriptive and a descriptive sense. Such ambiguities postpone critical dissent from the myth and they make it possible for it to function totemically, both as a focus for expressions of collective identity and also as an attempt at description. Logically, however, these functions can only be maintained at the cost of a lack of correspondence between the myth and the private experience of individuals to whom it ought to, but does not, apply. How are the pupils who are progressively selected out of a Highers course to make sense of their experience when this experience has no place in the received account? What coherence does a general or balanced course have when two, three or four of its elements (subjects) are removed? How are such pupils to construe such a course in the light of publicly received explanations and purposes? It is unlikely that they will disinterestedly interpret their situation in the light of the systemic, and ultimately political, problems of difficulty, selection and motivation. More probably they will understand their predicament in terms of their own individual moral and intellectual failure and perhaps take some comfort from the hope that an incomplete complement of Highers passes may, nevertheless, bring some extrinsic, occupational reward (McPherson, 1971, pp. 7-13; see also chapter 16, note 1).

The point of these questions and this example is not to argue that the prescriptive elements can and should be expunged from the terms that are used to describe the social world and the world of education. It is, rather, to pose two related questions to which there is, we think, a single answer. At what point does a lack of correspondence between myth and practice invalidate the myth? And at what point should one attempt to incorporate explicit reference to additional features (for example, selection, or the 'need' for a sixth year) that might improve the descriptive power of the myth, but only at the risk of sacrificing either its inner coherence or the values and identity that it asserts? The single answer towards which we work, by illustration in part 4 and by argument in our final chapter, lies in the attempt to admit all persons to the dialogue of research, and to help them to construe and publicly represent their own experience.

Various developments in the Highers course since 1963 are summarised in figure 5.3. All averages (lines) in the figure are based on the same pupils. Over the period 1963-76 there was a continuous upward trend both in the number of *subjects* attempted by Highers pupils (line b) and in the total number of Higher-grade examinations, including resits (line a). However, the increase in the overall number of attempts has mainly been in fifth year (line d). An 'average' Highers pupil made 2.6 fifth-year attempts in 1962-3 and 3.9 such attempts in 1975-6.

To this extent, the SED's wish to 'push' H-grade presentations back into fifth year (see the previous section of this chapter), and so restore the correspondence between actual practice and the official account, has been fulfilled. But it has only been partly fulfilled for there has been very little change over the period in the mean number of sixth-year Highers attempts (line e).

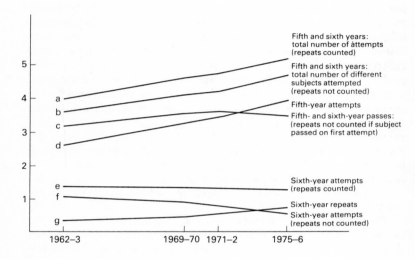

Figure 5.3 Mean number of Highers passes and attempts, by school stage and calendar year of leaving: among leavers from EA and GA schools passing at least one Higher

What has changed in the sixth year is not so much the number as the nature of these Highers attempts. This is shown in lines f and g of figure 5.3. The mean number of repeated (that is, second) attempts at H-grade subjects which had already been presented in the fifth year increased from 0.33 to 0.72 among all Highers pupils (line g). The mean number of H-grade subjects presented for the first time in the sixth year declined from 1.04 to 0.52 (line f). In practical terms, these are quite large changes.[8]

Finally, we might note that the experience of failure has become more common among Highers pupils in the 1970s. Although the increase in the mean number of passes flattened off in the 1970s and indeed had reversed slightly by 1975–6 (line c), the increase in the mean number of subjects attempted continued (line b). The widening gap between the mean number of attempts and the mean number of passes is one way of expressing the increasing incidence of failure in the Highers examination.

The O-grade examination

We described in the previous chapter how an O-grade examination that was originally intended for the most able 30–35 per cent of the age-group had expanded by the mid-1970s to a point where 70 per cent of pupils were presented for it. Another unexpected development has been that pupils have not generally chosen to follow the official recommendations to 'bypass' the O-grade in subjects which they planned to present at the H-grade in the following year or two. The O-grade examination now serves a very wide range of abilities. Many pupils attain A- and B-band awards in a full group of subjects, but many others have little chance of attaining anything other than D or E awards. The extent of such disparities is not revealed to the public in the Examination Board's annual report on the examination because the figures are presented in aggregated form (Scottish Certificate of Education Examination Board, annual).

If, however, we disaggregate the figures retrospectively, we can identify two groups of pupils: those who went on to attempt Highers (about 30 per cent of the age-group); and those who attempted only O-grades, most of whom left from fourth year at the age of 16 (roughly a further 40 per cent of the age-group). The chances of success or failure varied considerably between the two groups. In the 1977 survey 75 per cent of the first group (Highers leavers) took at least seven O-grade subjects, mostly in their fourth year, and 70 per cent (of all Highers leavers) achieved A, B or C grades (equivalent to the pre-1973 pass requirement) in at least six subjects. In other words, Highers leavers tended to take and 'pass' a large number of O-grade subjects.

Among the second group of leavers, however (those who attempted O-grades, but not Highers), the picture was rather different. Only 15 per cent of O-grade leavers attempted seven or more O-grade subjects and only 5 per cent of O-grade leavers 'passed' at least six subjects. Half the O-grade leavers attempted only four O-grades or fewer, and over half the O-grade leavers (54 per cent) 'passed' only one subject or none at all (Ballantyne and Taylor, 1979, table 2). In other words, a large proportion of Highers leavers 'passed' the majority of subjects they attempted at O-grade, but a large proportion of O-grade leavers 'failed' the majority of subjects they attempted. This widespread experience of failure among O-grade leavers, the 'middling' 40 per cent of all leavers, has provided arguments for the need for an alternative, and easier, examination.

Subject hierarchy in the Highers and O-grade examinations

In an investigation based both on the Scottish Education Data Archive and latterly on the records of the Examination Board, Kelly has shown how the folklore of 'softer' and 'harder' options corresponds to real differences between SCE subjects in the difficulty that pupils have in achieving good grades in them relative to their grades in all other subjects. She has also shown that this hierarchy of relative difficulty has been relatively stable at least for fifteen years (data for the period 1962–76 were analysed) and that the hierarchy of difficulty in the O-grade examination closely corresponds to that in the older H-grade examination (Kelly, 1975, 1976b, and 1976c). Interestingly, the Scottish hierarchy is very similar to that which has been shown to exist in the English GCE. Kelly (1976b, p. 22) writes:

> [a] strong hierarchy of subjects exists, in terms of both the standard of examinations and the average ability of the candidates attempting each examination. Languages are at the top of this hierarchy, followed by sciences, social subjects and vocational subjects. There is a marked tendency for the more difficult subjects to be attempted by the more able candidates.

She also found that the spread of difficulty was wide, especially in the O-grade examination, which catered for a wider range of pupil ability than the Highers examination. But, even in the Highers examination, the difference between the easiest and the most difficult subjects was such that the average pupil would have gained 21 per cent more marks in the easiest subject (metalwork) than he or she would in the most difficult (German) (ibid., p. 6).

The point is, of course, that pupils who presented German at the Higher grade tended not to present metalwork, and vice versa. Moreover, because clever pupils have tended to take the more difficult subjects, and less clever pupils have tended to take the easier ones, these variations in difficulty have not manifested themselves in large inter-subject variations in pass rates. Within certain restricted ranges of ability, clever and less clever alike have therefore been able to participate in the expanding award of credentials. But they have not, as we have just seen, been able to participate in the serious study of a range of subjects constituting a general or a common curriculum with the same assurance of success. The share that less able pupils have taken of the good examination grades that were awarded has therefore depended on their tendency to take different subjects to the more able pupils.

At any one time, in other words, the following factors have constrained each other and have placed limits on the extent to which each could be realised: the power of the examination to motivate pupils by offering a reasonable assurance of success; the credibility and extrinsic value of the grades that were awarded; considerations of fairness (equivalence between grades in different subjects); both the range of subjects in pupils' courses and also the amount of overlap between courses that was thought desirable in the light of curricular aims such as that of a general education; and the extent to which pupils were selected into different groups on the basis of measured ability, or attainment earlier in secondary school, or voluntary staying on at school.

Discussion

We may now draw together the implications of some of the positions and trends we have illustrated in this chapter. In recent years Highers pupils have on average attempted more Highers examinations in fifth year and they have repeated more of their attempts in sixth year. The increase in the pressure on fifth year has coincided with increased competition in the 1960s for places in tertiary education; aspiring entrants needed more or better passes than previously to distinguish their qualifications from those of their competitors.

At least on paper, the fifth year has become harder; pupils following a 'normal' academic course have taken subjects at Highers only, rather than at both Higher and Lower grades (as they could before 1962). And, in practice, fifth-year pupils in the mid-1970s took on average more Higher grades than they did in the early 1960s. Nevertheless, the proportion of Highers pupils who have presented five or more subjects at the H-grade in the fifth year has remained low. In 1976 the percentage doing this was 37 per cent. The majority of recent Highers pupils have not successfully completed a five-subject course at the Higher level either by the end of the fifth year or by the end of the sixth year. In 1976, only a third (33 per cent) of all Highers pupils had passed five or more Highers by the time they left school.

The difficulty of the Highers course helps us to understand why nearly all Highers pupils have disregarded official injunctions to 'bypass' presentation at the O-grade in subjects in which H-grade presentation was planned. Pupils wanted to be certain that they would achieve at least some recognised qualification in their subjects and even the offer of a compensatory O-grade pass for a creditable failure in the H-grade, first made in 1962, has not counteracted this. The schools, moreover, have found it convenient to use the O-grade examination in order to select pupils for H-grade presentation courses in their fifth year (and could justify this otherwise proscribed practice in terms both of the 1959-60 recommendations for the marginal H-grade pupil and the more general recommendation that they should not, as theretofore, regard all their certificate pupils as Highers pupils).

The presentation of most Highers pupils for examination at the O-grade in most of their subjects has had several important consequences. It has increased yet further the total number of examinations taken by Highers pupils and it has led to public examination in three consecutive years for those who leave school at 18. Between 1962–3 and 1971–2 the average number of public examinations taken by Highers pupils by the time they left school increased from 7.6 to 11.0.[9] Most people regard this as a trend towards over-examination, and its consequences can be seen both in attitudes to learning and in methods of study (next chapter). A further consequence is that, for many pupils, the Highers course consists of little more than two terms' teaching after the fourth-year O-grade examination.

The reluctance of Highers pupils to bypass presentation at the O-grade has also placed limits on the extent to which the O-grade examination itself might be adapted, as official policy in the later 1960s and 1970s wished to adapt it, to a much larger (and therefore, on average, less able) proportion of the age-group. The O-grade examination has grown incrementally out of the H-grade and has thereby incorporated, albeit in attenuated form, much of its content and its pattern of relative, between-subject, difficulty (Kelly, 1976b, p. 6). Thus the scope that was available to the O-grade examination to adopt an educational philosophy or standards other than those entailed in the Highers course was restricted.

In the context of comprehensive reorganisation, moreover, many Scots, mindful of the importance of a national system that allowed all pupils to progress up a single, accessible ladder, did not wish to explore alternative educational philosophies for less able pupils or indeed, for any pupils (chapter 13). The substitution in 1973 of banded awards for the pass/fail distinction was an attempt to make the O-grade a credible qualification at which the less able pupil might aim; the CSE was actively promoted only by one regional authority; and alternative philosophies for the curriculum for the less able child were rejected in favour of a diluted academicism. In 1977 the Munn Committee re-argued the case for a common curriculum based mainly on academic subjects for all pupils, whereas the Dunning Committee offered a solution to the problem of difficulty: first by abandoning any requirement for the comparability of standards between subjects and, second, by identifying three levels of difficulty, within one of which a pupil might present for examination when aged 16, in each subject. The Dunning Committee hoped that the early selection of pupils to courses at one of these levels might be avoided through the construction of curricula that overlapped between these levels. However, since the highest of these, the Credit level, was recommended for pupils who, a year after they had presented, would then present for the SCE H-grade, and since no changes of standard or content were mooted for the H-grade examination, it was unlikely that schools would have handled the problem of selection very differently from the way they handled it in the 1970s (described below). Government proposals in the early 1980s, moreover, were to restrict severely the amount of any internal assessment in courses at the top two levels, but to encourage more internal curriculum development and assessment in courses at the third and lowest level (Scottish Education Department, no date, 1980). These proposals were also likely, therefore, to inhibit overlap between the different course levels.

So far in this chapter our discussion of selection has, so to speak, put the cart before the horse. We have spoken of 'Highers' and 'O-grade' pupils but, in the way we have used these terms, they can only finally be applied to individuals after they have left school. In selecting pupils for courses, schools do not have the benefit of hindsight. Nevertheless, even by the end of pupils' second year, schools (and pupils themselves) often have a fixed view of the ability of their pupils and of the course and subject choices appropriate to this ability (Ryrie, Furst and Lauder, 1979). But schools vary as to how and when they formally differentiate their pupils. Some, it is claimed, start their potential Highers pupils on Highers courses at the beginning of their third year, following the first two years of a more or less common course (Scottish Certificate of Education Examination Board, 1979, pp. 30-1). But in general, it would appear that the long-hallowed Scottish practice in the schools of assuming a pupil to be a candidate for external presentation in academic subjects until experience proved otherwise has spread from the Higher to the O-grade. The 'democratic' strand in Scottish educational culture has been reluctant to withdraw pupils too early from the contest for credentials; the academic and meritocratic strand has been reluctant to provide a system of national certification that incorporated variety in its methods of assessment or in the recognised curricula.

Much of this selection in the past has been done by early leaving, especially until the late 1950s when the start of certification work was brought forward from the fourth to the third year in anticipation of the new fourth-year examination. Following the raising of the school-leaving age in 1973, schools have had to live with the consequences of the differentiation of pupils that is introduced at the beginning of third year for a further two years. Most schools at the end of second year make up classes of 'non-certificate' pupils who never embark on work for the O-grade. Many third- and fourth-year pupils, however, have started on courses that could lead to O-grade presentation, but have thereafter discontinued serious work to this end and have not presented for the examination. Estimates from the Scottish Education Data Archive of the frequency of this matter cannot be very precise, for pupils and teachers may sometimes be unclear about the purposes of the courses that pupils are taking in their third year. However, nearly one-third of the 1975–6 leavers who did not attempt O-grades reported having started an O-grade course in at least one subject (see chapter 8, figure 8.1). Also, it is likely that in particular subjects the drop-out from O-grade courses was even greater than the aggregate figure would suggest.[10]

Our picture, then, is of a process of selection which entirely rejects a minority of pupils from O-grade course work in third year and thereafter operates a continuous process of attrition upon the remainder through school examinations, 'prelims', 'mock SCEs' and the O-grade examination itself. The courses of the majority of pupils are sooner or later affected by this attrition, in the third or fourth year, or in the fifth year, if they are among the most successful third of pupils. But, even among those pupils who survive into the fifth year, only a minority end up by presenting for examination in a range of subjects that could possibly realise the notion of curricular breadth contained in (and sustained by) the Scottish myth. Formal discontinuation of O-grade courses (that is, stopping classes in the subject) is more common, especially among pupils who do not go on to take Highers; and, indeed, their prospects of 'failure' are so high that it is easy to credit that 'informal' discontinuation is common. This much indeed was recognised by the Munn Committee when it said: 'we felt from the outset some unease about the emphasis on balance in the remit, which seemed to make this the key concept for curriculum planning, whereas we saw pupil motivation as of comparable importance' (Scottish Education Department, 1977b, para. 1.4).

The abolition of selective transfer to secondary school, then, has arguably increased secondary-school pupils' initial expectations of success. But the incremental and downward expansion of certification over the years has distributed to 14 to 16-year-olds an examination based on an attenuated form of the Highers curriculum; the level of difficulty of this examination assures a majority of pupils either outright failure, when they are allocated to non-certificate classes in third year, or an experience in which they progressively drop their O-grade courses, or discontinue serious work in them, as the prospect of failure becomes more concrete. Expectation of failure also structures the courses taken by pupils aiming at Highers; attrition continues in the fifth year, and Highers subjects are repeated in the sixth year by pupils who are uncertain whether they have met the standards that will eventually be required by selectors. Conditions such as these are likely to militate against public purposes for the curriculum. They have upset plans for the bypassing of the O-grade and, as we shall show in the next chapter, they have upset other plans to change the curriculum of pupils between the ages of 14 and 18.

Chapter 6

General Education and Myth: Some Examples

Introduction

The previous chapter has described the way in which selection for certificate courses provided a framework for the curriculum, setting limits to the level, number and sequence for courses that were taken. This chapter explores examples of some of the ways in which this framework helped to shape both the content of the curriculum that pupils actually experienced, and also the methods of teaching and learning that were used.

The curriculum is an inexhaustible area of inquiry and our discussion is inevitably limited. We tend, moreover, to focus on the Highers curriculum; we describe curriculum mainly in terms of subjects (though we also make some reference to methods); and we employ only a few of the very many ways in which the subjects of a curriculum might be classified and grouped.

These emphases are partly dictated by the need for brevity. Within the bounds of the raw questionnaire data on pupils' subjects and courses, there is virtually no limit to the alternative conceptualisations of curriculum content that any user of the Scottish Education Data Archive may bring to the data. But our selection also reflects limitations in the data-base itself. We are, for example, less confident about the archive's present capacity to describe the curriculum of non-certificate pupils because, as we show in chapter 10, the question of whether or not these pupils were taught is just as important as what they were offered. Moreover, it is easier to survey courses that are known by a standardised or publicly recognised name (in practice, courses for external certification) than it is to survey purely local courses. Although the 1977 survey tried to overcome this difficulty, it is still likely that the archive's description of the curriculum of certificate pupils is more reliable than its description of the curriculum of non-certificate pupils and of the non-examined courses taken by all pupils.

What this chapter offers, then, is not an exhaustive description of the Scottish curriculum, but an illustrated discussion of the way in which some aspects of the Scottish curriculum have fared since the early 1960s. Our examples include: 'breadth' in the Highers curriculum; trends in Highers subject presentations since the early 1960s; the status of older and newer subjects; the place of science; methods of teaching and learning in fifth and sixth year; and the breadth of the curriculum experienced by certificate pupils, about 70 per cent of all pupils, in third and fourth year. We illustrate the influence of the Scottish myth on the way in which people have perceived and understood the curriculum and have consequently prescribed for it; and we show how prescriptions for change that have been based upon an inadequate understanding of the system have themselves gone astray. This leads us, in conclusion, to a somewhat pessimistic view of the capacity of the Scottish system to manage the problems of difficulty, motivation and selection, whilst developing and implementing the programme for curriculum and examination reform arising from the Munn and Dunning Reports of 1977.

'Breadth': an example of practice in search of a concept

We have argued in chapters 3 and 5 that an enduring feature of the Scottish myth has been the belief that education should be broad, and the belief that in Scotland it was indeed so. However, the persistence of these beliefs may be related to the fact that there has been little explicit discussion of what is meant by breadth in this context. In practice, breadth was once commonly taken to consist in the completion of the leaving-certificate group of subjects that would admit to university. By the 1940s breadth had thereby come to mean something approximating to the completion of a Highers course in English, mathematics, at least one language, and at least one science. In other words, a minimum of four subjects was required. Table 5.2a has already shown us, however, that in 1962–3 barely a quarter of Highers-qualified leavers had attempted four or more Highers in their fifth year. By the early 1970s the proportion was just under a half and by the mid-1970s it was just under two-thirds. Expressed as proportions of the age-group these proportions were respectively about 4 per cent, 12 per cent and 15 per cent. In terms of this implicit definition, therefore, large proportions of pupils have been excluded, at some stage, from study in a broad curriculum, simply because of the difficulty of carrying four subjects to Highers. But what of those who could meet these requirements? The first two rows of table 6.1 show trends in the percentages of pupils presenting, minimally, English, mathematics, a language and

TABLE 6.1   Percentages of pupils attempting various groupings of Highers subjects in fifth year by different total numbers of fifth-year attempts and calendar year of leaving: among leavers from EA and GA schools passing at least one Higher

Groupings of Highers subjects	Number of fifth-year attempts	Percentage of pupils attempting grouping			
		1962–3	1969–70	1971–2	1975–6
'Traditional breadth' (English, mathematics, at least one science and at least one language)	4	38	10	4	4
	5+	74	50	38	38
'Modified breadth' (English, mathematics, at least one science and at least one of languages, social subjects and creative subjects)	4	47	20	9	13
	5+	75	66	57	65
'Science' (English, mathematics and at least two natural sciences)	4	na	8	15	13
	5+	na	52	57	58
'Languages' (English and at least two other languages)	3	15	11	7	4
	4	33	28	22	15
	5+	79	36	27	22
'Social' (English and at least one of history, geography or modern studies)	2	8	21	24	31
	3	15	38	43	49
	4	20	53	49	55
	5+	27	57	58	60
'Vocational' (English and at least one vocational subject)	2	11	20	21	21
	3	9	28	31	30
	4	8	22	22	27
	5+	2	14	18	19

Note: The different subject groupings are not mutually exclusive. The table shows, for example, that among 1962–3 leavers who had attempted four Highers subjects in their fifth year, 38 per cent had attempted a combination of Highers subjects that met the requirements of 'traditional breadth', 47 per cent met the requirements of 'modified breadth', and so on.

na = not applicable.

a science in their fifth year ('traditional breadth') broken down by the number of fifth-year attempts. In the early 1960s well over half of those making five or more attempts met the minimal conditions of breadth, but well under half of those presenting just four subjects did so. The proportions fell sharply in the following decade, but then stabilised between 1971-2 and 1975-6.

New subjects arrived in the curriculum in the 1960s and others were revised and sometimes radically restructured. The remaining parts of table 6.1 describe the Highers curriculum in ways that take some account of these other areas. There has been an increasing incidence of courses with a social element and a vocational element; but courses with two languages have fallen off. If one redefines 'traditional breadth' (English, mathematics, 1 language, 1 science), substituting for the language element a subject from one of the newer areas (English, mathematics (1 language or newer subject), 1 science), then 'modified breadth' has not fallen as sharply as 'traditional breadth'. But what is a satisfactory definition of breadth? The question has never been publicly discussed in relation to the Highers course.

Breadth and congestion: an example of implicit value

The Scottish Advisory Council wrote in 1947 '[a] curriculum becomes congested precisely as a book case does with [the] passing of the years. New interests emerge, fresh claims are admitted, but old titles are seldom revised and still more rarely withdrawn' (Scottish Education Department, 1947, para. 72). Kelly's work on trends in the relative difficulty of subjects, already mentioned in chapter 5, illuminates the way in which new subject areas have been slotted in and older ones re-newed. Analysing trend data drawn from the 1962-3 survey and from later Examination Board records (Kelly, 1975, p. 7), she found that:

> by and large the most difficult subjects [at O and H-grade] were modern languages, followed by sciences and social subjects, with vocational and practical subjects much easier. Until recently classical languages have been even more difficult than modern languages. There was a similar ordering of ability. The most able group of candidates were those who took classical languages, followed by modern languages, sciences, social subjects and vocational subjects. Thus subjects taken by more able candidates were, on average, more difficult than subjects taken by less able candidates.

The ordering of classical languages, modern languages and sciences, and social subjects corresponds to the chronological ordering of these subjects' emergence in the Scottish university curriculum and in the schools. New subjects have had to compete for able pupils and for prestige against established subjects that opened the gates to the university.[1] Kelly also concluded that '[t]here appears to be a definite channelling of pupils by ability into different subjects, although whether this channelling is achieved by self-selection or by external direction cannot be determined from these figures' (Kelly, 1976b, p. 11).

An analysis by Hutchison and Littlejohn of the 1971 survey of school-leavers with Highers throws further light on the introduction of new subjects and on the selection of pupils in relation to them. They wrote (1975, p. 7):

> We have established the existence of two major curricular paths leading from school to university. The two-language course led mainly into arts while the two-science course led mainly into science. Few entrants gained effective qualifications for both paths. . . . By contrast to students in the established university curricula of arts and science, entrants to university social science courses showed no single defining characteristic other than a uniformly low measured ability.

Of Highers pupils who took up social subjects for presentation in their sixth year at school, they concluded: 'It seems that some pupils tend towards the social sciences in anticipation of relative academic failure within the established arts and science curricula' (p. 16).

Classical and modern languages are now less crucial qualifications for university entry and are no longer defining characteristics of an 'academic' secondary-school course.[2] This partly explains the declining proportion of pupils taking languages, as indicated in table 6.1.[3] Moreover Kelly's analysis shows that between 1962 and 1975 the difficulty of French and German, relative to other Highers subjects, was broadly maintained, whereas the social-studies subjects of geography, history and (from 1969) modern studies, and the science subjects of chemistry and physics, became relatively easier (Kelly, 1975, table 2). Table 6.1 shows that the subjects that, in Kelly's analysis, were becoming less difficult were the growth areas in the Highers curriculum during this period.

We commented in chapter 5 that the hierarchy of subject difficulty that emerged in the course of the historical growth of the curriculum has limited the extent to which pupils could study a range of subjects in common, with broadly similar prospects of success. Two other general points may also be made. A folklore of 'hard' and 'soft' options has been widespread, but subject 'managers' or pressure-groups have tended only to recognise the phenomenon and to seek to alter it either when they became insecure, for example, when their pupil numbers declined sharply, or when they wished to establish the 'qualifying' status of their subject, as in the case of the O-grade and H-grade subject of anatomy, physiology and health (Kelly, 1975, p. 14). Second, the formal management of the curriculum is such that people have only been able to react effectively to curricular problems within a subject framework. The Scottish Consultative Committee on the Curriculum (CCC) was founded in 1965 to advise the Secretary of State on curricular matters, but it quickly abandoned any initial hope of prescribing for the whole curriculum, preferring instead to approach it subject by subject (Scottish Education Department, 1972a, p. 6). The Munn Report of 1977, produced by a sub-committee of the CCC, marked a return to an attempt at general oversight, but it is significant that this was still confined to the pre-Highers years. In general, the CCC has avoided prescription for fifth and sixth years and it has tended to concentrate on less able pupils. What is studied and taught in fifth and sixth years is heavily determined by what is examined by the Scottish Certificate of Education Examination Board, and the Board works mainly through its subject panels.

Breadth: an example of incomplete conceptualisation

From time to time, educational reformers in England and Wales have looked to Scotland for arguments and examples that might support a case for changes south of the Border. Attempts to modify the GCE A-level, for instance, have invoked the apparent success of the Scottish Highers course in maintaining subject options throughout secondary education. It has been argued that Scottish Highers pupils can, and do, postpone subject specialisation and that those who enter tertiary education disperse into different subject areas in a manner that does not signify the existence of rigid tracks leading from specialisation at school to continuing specialisation in the same subject area thereafter. Arguments like these proved especially attractive in the 1960s to the Council for Scientific Policy (CSP), a UK body that was at the time highly concerned over what it called, rather dubiously, the 'swing from science'. The apparent rejection of science-based study by pupils and students was less likely to arise, it argued, and could more quickly be corrected, in a system like that of the Scots.

Much of the CSP's assessment, however, was based upon an account of the Scottish experience in which the influence of the Scottish myth loomed large. The account was prepared by the SED and was incorporated in one of the CSP's major reports, published in 1968 (Council for Scientific Policy, 1968). We have already reproduced and commented on aspects of this account in chapter 5. Here we mention a further feature to do with the way in which the myth influenced the construction that was put upon the Scottish curriculum, the concepts that were used to organise the data, and the conclusions that were reached.

In a section headed 'The secondary course still broadly based', the chapter on Scotland in the CSP report said: 'the general impression seems to be that there has been no fundamental change — for instance towards greater specialisation — in the course structure of Scottish schools. This impression was tested — and confirmed — by means of a 10 per cent sample survey carried out early in 1967' (1968, para. 97). The 'test' used in this survey was, however, incomplete. Pupils' curricula were classified according to whether or not they were studying certain *minimum* numbers of science and non-science subjects (the latter were also termed 'arts' subjects). No account was taken of the *total* number of subjects studied in these two subject areas. Using a 'minimalist' classification, the report found that 'the great majority of boys. . . were following science-cum-arts courses, and a very substantial group — indeed the largest single group. . . — were following genuinely balanced courses' (para. 100). In its own terms, this conclusion was empirically correct. However, when critics of the CSP report, using the 1971 survey, compared this minimalist classification with other ways of classifying the curriculum that took account of *all* of the subjects that pupils were studying, it became clear that there was much more specialisation in the Scottish Highers curriculum than the official account had identified. Most pupils took courses containing either a majority of science or a majority of non-science subjects. This 'specialisation' was reflected in the pupils' subject interests, as assessed by their favourite subjects (Hutchison *et al.*, 1974, table 4), and also in the content of the courses, if any, taken at university (ibid., and Jones, Littlejohn and McPherson, 1974). In a further analysis, of university entrants in the 1973 survey, McPherson and Neave (1976, p. 63) reported that:

> those who had followed biased courses at school tended to stay
> with that bias at university. Eight out of ten of the science-qualified
> (83 per cent) went on to take a science-based course at university
> in either a pure, applied or professional field. Only a tenth (9 per
> cent) of entrants from non-science (biased) courses followed them
> into science at university. Ten years earlier this proportion had been
> one third (31 per cent).

The authors also gave a fuller account than we can give here of the influence of the increasing competition for university places during the 1960s on specialisation in the Highers curriculum (1976, chapters 2 and 4).

Some lessons from this example are, first, that a minimal classification of curriculum is unlikely to be sensitive to subject specialisation, or trends therein; it is too incomplete. Second, if one is to monitor positions and trends and to learn from experience, it is important to organise the data using appropriate concepts. There must be opportunities to criticise existing concepts and to test alternative concepts on the data. Third, if inadequate concepts stop one learning from experience, inadequate actions may follow from one's misapprehensions. In this instance, 'breadth' was operationalised in terms of the classification of subjects into a science/non-science dichotomy. The decline in the study of modern languages therefore passed unheeded. Finally, the example is an illustration of how the Scottish myth may materially influence the perceptions and judgments of statisticians and of natural scientists, no less than of other persons.

Concepts, actions and learning: an example from the sixth year

The fate of attempts to reform the curriculum and pedagogy of the sixth year provides further illustrations of several of these lessons. At one time the Scottish sixth year was intended for pupils taking the Universities' Bursary Examinations or adding new subjects to their fifth-year Highers presentations. We have seen, however, how the sixth year has increasingly been used to repeat subjects already attempted in fifth year (figure 5.3). By 1976, for example, 38 per cent of sixth-year pupils were repeating at least two Highers subjects already attempted in fifth year and 61 per cent were repeating at least one.

In 1968 the Certificate of Sixth Year Studies (CSYS) was introduced in an attempt to 'liberalise' the content and methods of sixth-year courses for all Highers pupils, whether or not they planned to enter higher education. The CSYS examination in each subject was restricted to pupils who had passed the subject at the Higher grade in fifth year but, that apart, it was intended for all sixth-year pupils irrespective of the total number of their fifth-year Highers passes. Provision was made for a large internal element in many courses. The contents of this element were to be decided by pupils and teachers in partnership. Less emphasis was to be placed on didactic methods of teaching and more emphasis on independent approaches to learning and inquiry. Characteristic of the new courses were such things as dissertations, creative writing, field trips, the project notebook and the portfolio. The pupil was to be helped to value, and to become competent in, sustained independent study in depth, for its own sake. Thus, though there was to be an external examination, it was not to count as a qualification for entry to higher education or the professions. This 'proper sixth year' as it was called was, therefore, to offer a quite different experience from what was acknowledged to be an over-didactic Highers course.

In other words, it was to offer to Highers pupils for one post-Highers year an experience that closely approximated the education that the Advisory Council in 1947 had wanted to offer to all pupils for four years between the ages of 12 and 16.[4]

In the event, the courses that were subsequently developed have proved highly attractive to the sixth-year pupils who have taken them (Gray and McPherson, 1978, pp. 71–2). The problem has been, however, that very few pupils have taken CSYS courses, and even fewer have taken CSYS courses without combining them with continuing work for Highers in their sixth year. Hence the impact of the reform has been, at best, marginal and confined only to the very able. In recent years about 17 per cent of an age-group have entered the sixth year; about 7 per cent have taken at least one CSYS course; and about 2 per cent have taken only CSYS courses. Where Highers courses have been taken concurrently with CSYS courses the impact of the pedagogic reforms has been demonstrably reduced. Contrary to the original intention, few CSYS courses have been offered or taken in 'non-academic' subjects and only very able pupils have tended to present for the certificate.

Why was curricular reform undertaken in this way? First, the SED and the Examination Board were anxious to avoid any suggestion that they were trying to displace the fifth-year Higher by a sixth-year qualification. Specimen papers for a sixth-year course that the SED had issued in the early 1960s seemed to imply such a move. Teachers opposed them and they were hastily withdrawn. One of the core institutions of the myth had been threatened. Second, the normative belief that Highers was a five-year, five-subject course was allowed to pass as an adequate description of the situation that actually obtained in the schools. The Certificate of Sixth Year Studies was intended for pupils who had already achieved in fifth year the SCE H-grade qualifications that they would require for entry to their chosen job or course of higher education. In practice few pupils had achieved sufficiently good qualifications by the end of their fifth year to give them an unequivocal assurance of entry. A majority of pupils either knew that they must acquire better Highers in their sixth year or else they were uncertain whether or not their fifth-year qualifications were adequate (Gray and McPherson, 1978, table 3).

This situation was evident in the early 1960s and was, indeed, becoming more acute when the certificate was introduced in 1968. Yet it was disregarded. As a result, the system was put in the illogical position of trying, at a time of examination inflation, to reduce pupils' dependence on the extrinsic rewards of examinations, not by reducing the number of external examinations, but by adding to them. Moreover, because of the failure or reluctance to note that the myth's description of the structure and functions of the fifth year did not correspond to the reality that pupils experienced, the CSYS reform was never likely to have more than a marginal impact. Again, therefore, inadequate action was predicted upon inadequate understanding.

When things do not work out as expected, one may try to fit a new understanding to the situation in order to pursue one's original aim more effectively; that is, one may try to learn from experience. Alternatively, one may persuade oneself that any action that has been achieved is all that was originally intended and that further learning about the context of action is unnecessary. If anything, Scottish thinking about the sixth year has preferred the latter alternative. In the late 1950s, terms like 'a proper sixth year' or 'genuinely post-certificate pupils' were terms in good currency (Cmnd 603, para. 15; Scottish Education Department, 1959a, paras. 116–22; 1960). Even though the concepts were not fully explicated it was clear that reformers intended sixth-year pupils to kick the chalk dust of Highers off their heels. Nowadays the CSYS innovation is regarded as successful simply because it gives *some*, mostly very able, sixth-year pupils *some* experience of an alternative pedagogy to that of Highers. Statements of intention have been retrospectively, if informally, revised in such a way that expectations are not contradicted by the unexpected. Unserviceable though it proved to be in this instance, the myth's description of the fifth year has survived. Moreover, as early as 1972, an official description of the CSYS restated its function in terms that corresponded less to initial intentions for the reform and more to the way it was working out in practice.[5] To have acknowledged that the reform was not working out as planned would have required explicit, public recognition of the heavy academic selection that characterised fifth and sixth year; and, as we have said in chapter 5 (section entitled 'Managing expansion') there was at the time no place for selection in the publicly received account.

Relation between certification and pedagogy: an example from fifth and sixth years

The introduction of the Certificate of Sixth Year Studies was an attempt to change, if only at the margins, what a later Advisory Council in 1960 had called 'that unhappy rigidity and conservatism which in Scotland have hitherto tended to identify education too frequently with classroom teaching' (Scottish Education Department, 1960, para. 24). In the 1977 survey some questions addressed to fifth- and sixth-year leavers who had attempted Highers (including the minority who went on to attempt the CSYS) illuminated the relationship between the external examination system and methods of teaching and learning.

TABLE 6.2 Ratings of frequencies of various study methods and various attitudes to them: percentage of Highers leavers in 1975–6

Study methods	Studied in this way 'very often' or 'often'[1]	'Which helped most with your exams'[2]	'Which did you most enjoy'[2]	'Which helped you to learn most about things that interested you'[2]
Having notes dictated to you in class	60 (2)	24 (2)	11	8
Making your own notes from lessons	24	13	9	9
Using duplicated notes	49 (3)	14 (3)	5	6
Exercises, worked examples, proses, translations	73 (1)	30 (1)	12 (3)	9
Preparing essays or dissertations	42	5	4	5
Reading	47	8	10	29 (1)
Class/group discussion	14	2	17 (1)	12 (2=)
Laboratory/field work and writing up	20	2	14 (2)	12 (2=)
Creative activity: painting, music, creative writing, etc.	12	1	8	5
Practical activity: typing, making things, etc.	17	1	10	7
Total		100	100	101
Unweighted n		(4,209)	(4,341)	(4,289)

Notes: Each percentage in the first column is based on approximately 4,300 cases.
The numbers in parentheses indicate rank orders. Only the first three ranks are shown.
1 'Please indicate roughly how often you studied in each of the following ways in school hours during your last year.
The ways you studied may have differed for different subjects and different times of the year, so please try to make an "on balance" judgment of how often you studied in each of these ways.' A five-point scale was offered for each study method (see text).
2 Only one study method could be chosen.

Respondents were given a list of ten different 'study methods', or types of teaching/learning activity. They were asked to rate the frequency with which they had experienced each study method on a five-point scale ('very often/often/sometimes/rarely/never'). They were also asked to indicate which single study method they had most enjoyed, which they felt had helped them most with their examinations and which they felt had helped them to learn most about things that had interested them. The first column of table 6.2 (reproduced from Gray and McPherson 1978), shows the percentages who rated the frequency of each of the ten study methods as 'very often' or 'often'. Thus 60 per cent of respondents indicated 'having notes dictated' was a method they had used often or very often (the remaining 40 per cent, who are not shown, ticking 'sometimes', 'rarely' or 'never'). The figures in parentheses indicate the rank order of the three methods that were most often mentioned in each context. Overall, the most common single method of study was 'exercises, worked examples, proses, translations' (73 per cent), followed by 'having notes dictated to you in class' (60 per cent) and 'using duplicated notes' (49 per cent). ('Reading' was a close fourth at 47 per cent.)

The three most common methods were also those that leavers felt had been most helpful for their examinations (with reading, picked by 8 per cent, coming fifth after 'making your own notes from lessons', which was chosen by 13 per cent).

However, when asked which single method they had most enjoyed, two activity-based methods emerged as most popular: 'class/group discussion' (chosen by 17 per cent) and 'laboratory/field work and writing up' (picked by 14 per cent). The first column of table 6.2 shows that these two methods were among the least common. But this disparity between experience and preference is perhaps even more striking when preference is expressed in terms of the criterion of the fourth column: 'which helped you to learn most about things that interested you'. Over a quarter picked reading (29 per cent) and a further quarter chose either class/group discussion (12 per cent) or laboratory/field work and writing up (12 per cent). By contrast, only a quarter (23 per cent) picked *any* of the three most frequently used methods, dictated notes (8 per cent), duplicated notes (6 per cent), or exercises, etc. (9 per cent), as the method which they felt had helped them to learn most about things that interested them. One may infer that many felt there had been a conflict between studying for interest's sake and studying for examination success.

Aggregate comparisons like this should not be taken too far and, in particular, they should not be taken to imply either that any of the ten methods might not have its place in good practice, or that good practice might not vary between subjects and between different types

97

of pupils. Nevertheless, the pattern of responses in table 6.2 reflects a situation in which many pupils probably felt that their education was unduly shaped by the exigencies of the certification system. It was this very situation that the innovation of the Certificate of Sixth Year Studies was intended to redress; and by 1971–2 it had already achieved some success (McPherson and Neave, 1976, chapter 3). Nevertheless, comparative evidence from the early 1970s indicates that the motivation of Scottish pupils and students was more dependent on the sanctions and incentives of external examinations than was the motivation of their English counterparts (McPherson, 1976).

Definitions and distribution of a balanced curriculum

Although there has been little formal public discussion of the content and methods of the Highers curriculum, official attention has twice been given to the curriculum for 14 to 16-year-olds. The Brunton Report argued that 'the case is unanswerable for the use in schools of the vocational impulse as the core round which the curriculum should be organised' (Scottish Education Department, 1963, para. 55). This principle was proposed, however, mainly for those pupils who had been formally selected out of O-grade courses (ibid., para. 13). The Munn Report of 1977, by contrast, made recommendations for all pupils in third and fourth year, including those who would go on to take Highers, and it proposed a curriculum consisting of seven core areas plus electives. The core areas were: English, mathematics, science, social studies, religious and moral education, aesthetic education and physical education. Languages were excluded from the core. Vocational subjects such as technical subjects, home economics, or secretarial studies were consigned to the elective area (Scottish Education Department, 1977b). The core was to express 'balance', a term that in the 1950s and 1960s was loosely synonymous with 'breadth' in official usage. The problems of selection and difficulty were more acute for the Munn Committee, which was concerned with the entire age-group, than they were for the Brunton Committee, which had been mainly concerned with non-certificate pupils. The Dunning Committee, which had worked closely with the Munn Committee, proposed to handle these problems by offering courses at different levels with an overlapping content, the implication being that pupils might move up or down according to their achievement on the course. The need for any initial or irrevocable selection might thereby be reduced.

To what extent did the Munn proposals entail a change in the existing curriculum? One can only give an empirical answer to this question, if one is prepared to make certain assumptions about the correspondence between existing subjects and the areas proposed by Munn. Although the Munn Committee accepted the subject as the fundamental unit of the curriculum, it did not envisage an exact correspondence between existing subjects and the core areas; and it did envisage considerable curriculum development. Nevertheless, in framing a response to the Munn Report, a Working Party in 1978 felt able to model the new proposals using archive data on existing practice. Its analysis was conducted only on O-grade leavers in the 1977 survey (Collaborative Research Working Party, 1978). The Working Party systematically varied the assumptions concerning which existing subjects were to be included in each of the proposed core areas. For each set of assumptions it asked how far the Munn proposals corresponded to existing practice. Under 'narrow' assumptions that effectively required considerable syllabus change if Munn were to be realised, the curriculum of 83 per cent of O-grade leavers lacked at least one of the seven core elements, 45 per cent lacked at least two, and 13 per cent lacked at least three. Using more generous assumptions, the percentages were, respectively, 70, 27 and 4 per cent. Not surprisingly, leavers who had presented larger numbers of O-grade subjects were more likely than those who had presented fewer subjects to have studied a fully balanced curriculum which included all the areas recommended by Munn (Collaborative Research Working Party, 1978, table 4). A separate analysis showed that such balance was most common among pupils who were to go on to attempt Highers.[6] 'Balance', in other words, had been for the more able.

Summary and prognosis

This chapter has not attempted to give an exhaustive account of the Scottish curriculum. Instead it has illustrated some of the problems that are posed for the content and methods of education by the largely unacknowledged 'solution' that the Scottish system has adopted to the interrelated problems of difficulty, motivation and selection. Features of this solution have been the more or less exclusive recourse to a single, centralised system of external assessment for certification, based upon standards at 16 that are too easy for some, too difficult for many others, and virtually impossible, at present, for a significant minority. This is also true, but to a lesser extent, of the Highers examination at 17 years. To some extent the Scottish solution has become a victim of its own success, for it has helped, over the years, to persuade increasing proportions of the age-group to stay in post-compulsory secondary education and to compete for entry to scarce and favoured positions after school. Where the examination has been too easy for this purpose, examination inflation has occurred, pupils needing more and better grades to distinguish their attainments from their fellows. Most pupils taking the Highers examination have already achieved some psychological insurance by disregarding the official intention that they should bypass the O-grade examination at 16 in most of their Highers subjects; but, of those who start a sixth year, only a small minority feel certain that their Highers achievement at 17 years will qualify them for their chosen future. The Scottish solution has produced expansion but also competition, inflation and uncertainty. We doubt that this has done anything to ease a situation in which didactic and rote methods of teaching and learning have dominated academic courses and have been perceived as most useful for passing examinations; if anything, we suspect this situation will have been reinforced. Non-examinable elements and non-didactic methods in the curriculum have been displaced or excluded; interest and curiosity have been dominated by uncertainty and conformity as organising principles of the Highers curriculum.

The development of the O-grade out of the Higher in the 1960s, and the abolition in the 1970s of the fail category of the O-grade, have extended these principles to perhaps 80 per cent of pupils, in so far as they may start third year with some prospect of gaining some award, even if it is only one E award at O-grade. But the standard of the O-grade is, nevertheless, too difficult for the majority of 'middling' pupils, (say the middle 40 per cent who attempt some O-grades but no Highers). For them the improbability of success must harden during their third or fourth years into the certainty of failure in many of their subjects. For pupils who do not start O-grade course work in their third year, academic failure is an early and concrete certainty.[7]

Until recently, the debilitating effect of such processes on pupils' motivation and on their chances of mastering a broad curriculum had passed largely unacknowledged in public. Official perceptions and constructions of the curriculum have sometimes blurred the distinction between the descriptive and the prescriptive; sometimes they have implicitly discounted the many pupils to whom the descriptions cannot apply; and sometimes they have described the curriculum using concepts that incompletely represent pupils' courses. The effect has been to leave unchallenged, and seemingly unproblematic, the way in which the Scottish myth has described the curriculum and explained its purposes. Predictably, innovations predicated upon such descriptions have not worked out as expected, but resultant challenges to the myth, and resultant opportunities for learning from contra-indications, have sometimes been reduced through the retrospective revision of descriptions of the initial intentions for such innovations. At one time, for example, people wanted much more from a 'proper sixth year' than one CSYS course taken along with several Highers. However, the concept of the 'proper sixth year' was never fully explicated, even at the time that it was being most vigorously proposed in the late 1950s and 1960s. Nor, more importantly, was the fundamental concept of a general, or broad, or balanced education, and this vagueness and implicitness has also helped to immunise the myth from the infection of doubt.

As long as situations are stable, or can be represented as stable, it does not matter so much that the concepts underlying action are only implicit and only take their meaning from a superficial and unquestioned parallel between practice and the mythical construction. Their hollowness does matter, however, at the point of adaptation or resistance to change; at the point where, for example, new methods are proposed, new subjects are admitted to the curriculum, or new pupils. At that point, concepts that lack a meaning beyond that to be taken from their active application in the world have no use; and this was very much what the Munn Committee found when it had to interpret, in relation to the 'new' constituency of O-grade pupils and non-certificate pupils, a concept of balance that previously had had reference only in the rhetoric of the myth and the practices of the Highers curriculum.

In making its recommendations the Munn Committee addressed itself directly to the problems of difficulty and motivation, and it worked closely with the Dunning Committee in trying to harmonise curriculum with assessment. Events since the committees reported in 1977, however, give us little confidence in the likelihood of successful implementation. The government has rejected proposals for a large internal element in curriculum and assessment at the two higher (Credit and General) levels of the three levels of certification at 16 years proposed by Dunning; but there will be internal elements at the lowest (Foundation) level. The Credit level is meant to assess third- and fourth-year courses taken mainly by pupils who will go on to take Highers in fifth or sixth year. We find it inconceivable, therefore, that it will not be influenced by existing Highers courses. It is also highly likely that schools will be reluctant to deny third-year pupils the opportunity to start such courses, if they have some prospect of success. It is therefore to be expected that many of the pupils for whom the General level has been proposed will attempt courses in some or all of their subjects, at the highest, Credit, level of the new examination. In the same way, among pupils for whom the Foundation course was intended, there is likely to be strong competition to enter General-level courses. The exclusion of internal elements from the Credit and General levels will be taken generally as an adverse comment on their inclusion at Foundation level, and will encourage the pressure for General rather than Foundation courses. Moreover, future developments in provision for school-leavers' transition to the labour market may also undermine the viability of Foundation-level courses (chapter 9, section entitled 'Youth Opportunities Programme and education').

How will the schools arbitrate the competition for entry to the higher-level courses? 'Overlapping syllabuses' was the Munn and Dunning answer, allowing pupils to find their own level. But this is unlikely to be practicable where the Credit-level syllabus anticipates Highers, and where the Foundation syllabus contains internal elements. There are only two possible answers. One is to admit generously to the Credit and General levels, allowing pupils to transfer downwards thereafter. This tactic will secure the influence of Highers over the third- and fourth-year curriculum and will weaken the provision of coherent two-year courses for less able pupils based on other values. The alternative is to restrict the allocation of pupils to courses at the beginning of third year (or thereabouts) to the numbers for whom each level of course was notionally designed. If this allocation were to be done with an attempt at fairness, it would require a formal 14+ selection procedure. At present, however, few people are likely to agree that a fair procedure is possible. It may reasonably be objected that a precondition for such a procedure would be that society state the dimensions of ability that the curriculum should develop and in terms of which any selection should therefore be conducted.

Part 3

Education and Employment

Introduction

We have described in part 2 how policy and practice developed after the Second World War with respect to selection for, and during, secondary education. In part 3 we discuss the role played by certification in selection for employment and explore some of the consequences of this process for the school system itself.

A continuing feature of post-war policy has been that the value of certificates has been deliberately derived, in large part, from their use in selection for higher education and for preferred employment after school. Planning for the motivation of pupils has therefore been based primarily upon extrinsic, post-school goals. The way in which the interrelated problems of difficulty, motivation and selection have been faced by the schools has thereby been shaped by the developing links between certificates and post-school destinations; and also by pupils' and others' perceptions of these links.

Part 3 describes aspects of these developments and perceptions. The links between certificates and higher education are well established and we do not explore them further here.[1] Nor do we discuss the links between school certification and the different kinds of non-advanced further education available to school-leavers. (We would point out, however, that, in contrast to England and Wales, very few people of school age study for secondary-school certificates in Scottish colleges of further education.) Instead, we confine our attention to the link between the certification and the employment or unemployment of the five-sixths or so of school-leavers who entered the labour market on leaving school.

The 'Great Debate' of the late 1970s about education was occasioned, not by inherently educational problems, but by economic failure and by a desire to find its explanation in aspects of British society that could not be controlled by received techniques of economic management. The debate was, in other words, a further symptom of crisis in the expansionist perspective which had accorded education such an important role in the creation of economic and social well-being.

However, when the then Prime Minister, James Callaghan, made his speech at Ruskin College in October 1976, the Great Debate he started was not the first of its kind. Similar debates about the relation between education and industry had been conducted almost continuously for well over a century. Increasingly since the war, however, and especially since 1976, education has been on the defensive. Many of the earlier debates had been initiated by educationists who were critical of the philistinism of industry and of its failure to allow for the education and training of its workforce. Now, however, education and secondary schools in particular were attacked for allegedly low standards, for the neglect of basic skills and for inculcating inappropriate attitudes to work and to manufacturing industry.

Especially since the last war, the debate about the relation between education and employment has been essentially an argument about educational values. As Reeder (1979, p. 128) has written:

> The most important aspect of the continuing debate about
> education and industry in the years after 1944 was the way that
> new groups, within and outside of education, became critical once
> again of the dominant values and occupational interests of the
> school system at all levels, and beyond that, of what were considered
> to be unfavourable attitudes towards industry and the values of
> industrial culture more generally.

It would be wrong, however, to see this debate solely as one between education and industry. Educationists have often differed among themselves over the importance of employment and industry to the objectives of education. As we mentioned in chapter 6, one of the strongest arguments for building explicit vocational elements into schooling was made in Scotland by the Brunton Report, *From School to Further Education*. Brunton argued that such vocational elements provided 'meaningful incentives for learning', especially for children below the highest levels of ability: 'the case is unanswerable for the use in schools of the vocational impulse as the core round which the curriculum should be organised' (Scottish Education Department, 1963, para. 55). However, the purpose of the courses advocated by Brunton was claimed to be that of providing a general education, not a specific occupational training: the 'vocational impulse' was sought as a means to ends which were still to be determined by educationists.

Brunton's proposals were attacked on two main grounds. Rightly or wrongly they were represented as advocating the introduction of vocational training into the period of compulsory education. They were also criticised for presupposing, and therefore sustaining, a bipartite system of secondary education in which the initial selection, at 12 years, entailed the rejection of the large majority of pupils, some 65 per cent, from academic courses when they transferred to secondary school. In the years after 1963 'Brunton courses' were swept aside by the expansion of O-grade presentations and by those who thought that comprehensive reorganisation ought mainly to aim at expanding pupils' opportunities to compete for academic certification.

Appeals to the 'vocational impulse' might conceivably enable employers to influence the content of secondary education. But the position of employers is to be contrasted with that of the universities. Universities have exercised considerable influence over the curriculum, pedagogy and examination structure of secondary education through their power to specify entrance requirements. This influence is doubtless enhanced by their representation on examination boards and by their role in the socialisation of teachers: most secondary teachers attended university and are likely to have been influenced by this in their definitions of educational value. Moreover, 'downward incrementalism' (see chapter 1, 'Expansion and its dilemmas', and chapter 4) started from a situation in which the main function of secondary schools was to prepare pupils for university; and among these pupils were the majority of today's secondary teachers, those who trained them in colleges of education, and those who administer and inspect them.

The Great Debate, the respect among some educationists for the 'vocational impulse', and the influence of the universities over secondary education are all common, *mutatis mutandis*, to England and Wales as well as to Scotland. However, since the early 1960s, two important trends have overtaken many of the proposals of the Scottish Brunton Report and of similar policies elsewhere in Britain. The first of these trends has been the expansion of certification among secondary-school pupils, which we described in chapter 4. By 1976, two-thirds of school-leavers in Scotland and nearly five-sixths of school-leavers in England and Wales held an external qualification (table 2.1). Brunton had sought to work with the 'vocational impulse' through the intrinsic relevance of courses, believing that 'pupils can be stimulated by courses with a real vocational motive without the complication of external examinations' (Scottish Education Department, 1963, para. 235). By the late 1970s, however, education was seeking to harness a different vocational impulse among a majority of pupils by offering the extrinsic incentive of qualifications with a recognised value in the labour market. Yet the value of some qualifications has been in doubt. One consequence of the expansion of secondary-school certification has been that a large number of pupils have left school with 'marginal' qualifications, of uncertain value in the labour market. In England such pupils have held CSE awards, especially below grade 1; in Scotland they have held D or E awards at O-grade, or possibly just one or two awards in the A, B and C bands (which were formerly 'pass' grades and are still almost universally referred to as such).

The second trend has been the dramatic growth in unemployment among young people, and especially among school-leavers. Youth unemployment rose sharply from 1974 in Scotland as in the rest of Britain. It levelled off between 1977 and 1979, largely as a result of the Youth Opportunities Programme (YOP), but in 1980 it resumed an upward trend. The main governmental response to this problem, YOP, has offered schemes of work experience and training to unemployed young people. The mere scale of YOP has been such that its significance for secondary education cannot easily be overestimated; in 1981–2 it was expected to provide places for some 70,000 entrants in Scotland. This compared with an estimated number of school-leavers entering the labour market of less than 75,000. All previous proposals for the 16–18 age-group look like mere tinkering compared with the scale of YOP, a programme which has massive potential for the education and training of young people yet which is controlled by a government agency that is largely independent of traditional educational interests.

The following three chapters explore some implications of these two trends for the relation of education to employment. In chapter 7 we investigate the extrinsic connection between education and occupation: has Marshall's (1963, pp. 111–15) description of a 'tightening bond' between qualifications and employment applied to the qualifications gained in secondary school? In particular, has it applied to the new levels of qualifications, to the middle group of pupils affected by the expansion of certification? Have lower-level qualifications been worth anything in the job market? Has the association between certification and employment reflected the direct influence of qualifications, or do the better-qualified school-leavers have more success in jobseeking for other reasons? And what do employers value in qualified applicants?

In chapter 8 we ask whether, in the light of the relation between certification and employment, employers have been in a position to influence the content of secondary education, as universities do, by specifying entry requirements. Such an influence would presuppose that any entry requirements for employment were made explicit and that the importance of qualifications was appreciated by pupils; that requirements specified subjects or other details of the curriculum or pedagogy; and that pupils were motivated to meet such requirements. How far, if at all, do these conditions obtain?

In chapter 9 we extend our discussion of education and employment to take more account of unemployment. We analyse the patterns and levels of unemployment among the 1977 sample, and we consider the early development of the Youth Opportunities Programme. We argue that YOP may have helped to attenuate the link between certification and employment; and we suggest that YOP has revived several of the issues raised in earlier debates on the Brunton proposals.

Chapter 7

The Extension of Certification and the Tightening Bond

Introduction

The notion of the 'tightening bond' was coined by Marshall (1963, pp. 111-15) to designate the theory that individual occupational success has been increasingly determined in the course of this century by educational attainment and especially by certificates. Marshall was concerned with the educational implications of the tightening bond; it limited the possibility of 'mould[ing] the educational plan to the shape demanded by individual needs, regardless of other considerations. . . . Unless great changes take place, it seems likely that the educational plan will be adjusted to occupational demand' (p. 112).

In this chapter we do not offer direct evidence on whether or not the bond has been getting tighter, such as would be provided by data on certification and occupation for comparable samples drawn at different points in time. We lack such data. Rather, we investigate the effects of the substantially new situation which was created by the extension of certification to a large proportion of the secondary-school population in the 1960s and 1970s, and we ask whether the new, lower levels of certification were correlated with initial occupational success among school-leavers. In the past, the achievement of high-level school certificates by a small minority of pupils had been associated with entry to relatively high-level jobs; were the middle- and lower-level certificates of more recent years similarly associated with success in finding middle- and lower-level jobs?

Many operationalisations of the tightening bond have interpreted it as a statement about association rather than as one about causation; they have described and quantified the link between certificates and jobs, rather than asked whether employers' use of certificates directly influenced an individual's job chances. However, the educational significance of the tightening bond arises from the possibility that there may be a causal influence of certificates on individual occupational success. It is this influence which provides an externally defined and maintained value for the certificates for which school pupils are encouraged to work; the occupationally derived value of certificates helps to frame the context in which the schools confront the problems of difficulty, selection and motivation; and perceptions of this value influence the schools' responses to these problems. As the school system has extended the prospect of certification to larger proportions of the age-group, its success in resolving the problem of motivation has depended increasingly upon pupils' recognition of the occupational value of certification.

We first ask whether there was an association between the middle and lower levels of certification and the occupational success of the 1977 sample members. We then ask whether or not this association reflected a causal influence of certification on individual occupational success. Social science commonly finds that it is more difficult to establish a causal link than it is to describe and quantify an association; in the same way, in our discussion of the causal influence of certification on individual occupational success, our evidence is less complete, and our conclusions more qualified, than in our discussion of the empirical association. We end the chapter with a consideration of the nature of the bond between certification and occupation; we examine the importance of particular subjects compared with the general level of certification, and we consider whether employers use certificates as measures of the cognitive or of the normative qualities of the individual.

Certification and employment among the 1977 sample

The tightening-bond thesis is a statement about trends. It alleges not that the bond is tight, but that it has become tighter. Tests of such trends have usually been based on measures of the association between certification and occupation rather than on attempts to estimate the causal link between the two. Most of these tests have cast doubt on the notion of the tightening bond. Jencks *et al.* (1973, p. 186) reported that in America the correlation between educational attainment and occupation had been stable since the turn of the century. From a review of British and American data, Tyler (1977, p. 53) concluded that 'there is no evidence that the bond, weak and variable as it has been, is becoming tighter'. More recent British evidence on the tightening bond was provided by a comparison of different age-groups among the sample of adult males in England and Wales in 1972, surveyed by the Oxford Mobility Study (Halsey, 1975). The conclusions from this study were equivocal; whether or not the bond had tightened depended on the choice of statistic chosen to measure it.[1]

The parallel Scottish Mobility Study, based on a sample of adult males surveyed in 1974-5, did not attempt to test for trends in the tightness of the bond. However, it did reveal that the bond, as measured among this sample, was less tight than had sometimes been supposed. Even among men in upper-middle-class jobs, defined so as to include about one in eight of the sample, nearly half had low-level qualifications or no qualifications at all. One reason for this was that relatively few members of the whole sample had educational qualifications; most sample members had been educated when the expansion of educational qualifications had not caught up with the growing number of high-level jobs (Payne, Ford and Ulas, 1979).

However, all of these studies of the bond between certification and occupation were based on samples, most of whose members had received their secondary education before the 1960s. In investigating the bond, these studies therefore focused on the relatively small minority who had educational certificates, and on the narrow range of top jobs which this minority might fill. These studies were not able to take much account of the effects of the expansion of secondary-school certification since 1960.

In 1960 about one in six school-leavers had SCE awards; by 1976 the proportion was nearly two-thirds (table 2.1). New certificates and new awards were introduced, and existing certificates such as Highers were gained by a larger proportion of the age-group. If we define the bond between certification and occupation in terms of the extent to which certification was used as a criterion for selecting people for jobs at different levels, it is clear that the potential for the bond had increased, in that by 1976 there were more young people with certificates and there were more differentiations of academic level among those with certificates (figure 4.2).[2] Whether the bond had actually become tighter depended upon the use made by employers of the new levels of certification. In particular, it depended on whether there was, by 1976, an association between occupational success and the different levels of certification among those young people with middle- or lower-level certificates, whose counterparts twenty years earlier would all have left school uncertificated and therefore undifferentiated in this sense. It cannot yet be said whether these certificate levels correlate with occupational success later in life, say after the age of 35, since the young people concerned have not yet reached that age. However, other studies have suggested that the level of a young man's early occupation has been strongly correlated with that of his later occupation (for example, Halsey 1977); so in this chapter we investigate the extent to which the levels of school-leavers' occupations soon after entering the labour market were associated with their levels of certification.

TABLE 7.1   Destinations by SCE attainment: percentage of labour-market entrants from EA schools in the four regions

	No SCE awards	D or E awards only	O-grades			Any Highers
			1–2 A–C	3–4 A–C	5 or more A–C	
Boys						
White-collar employment	2	4	6	13	30	60
Skilled manual	16	27	35	44	41	13
Less skilled	56	54	44	31	20	15
Other employment	3	4	6	6	5	5
Unemployed	23	10	9	6	4	8
Total	100	99	100	100	100	99
Unweighted *n*	(2,038)	(510)	(1,243)	(740)	(516)	(1,081)
Girls						
White-collar employment	12	29	47	63	79	83
Services	20	28	25	18	9	7
Manual	42	30	20	13	7	2
Other employment	2	1	2	2	2	2
Unemployed	24	12	7	4	3	5
Total	100	100	101	100	100	99
Unweighted *n*	(1,741)	(680)	(1,071)	(737)	(400)	(1,139)

Table 7.1 shows the destinations of the sample of 1976 leavers from maintained schools in the four Scottish regions who had entered the labour market by early 1977. The table excludes those who continued with full-time education after school.[3] We have used different occupational classifications for boys and girls in order to reflect their substantially different labour-market experiences. For each sex we have identified three main categories of occupations, which form a rough hierarchy. For boys, these categories are white collar, skilled manual and less skilled manual; for girls, they are white collar, service and manual respectively. A fourth category of other employment includes the armed forces and those who did not describe their jobs in sufficient detail to be classified. The fifth and final category contains the unemployed.[4] As an indication of the level or desirability of jobs our scale is inevitably crude, partly because it aggregates disparate occupations and partly because the same specific occupation can vary greatly in its attractiveness to a school-leaver, depending on the

employer. More than 4 per cent of labour-market entrants were on programmes such as the Work Experience or Job Creation Programmes, and almost all of these are counted as being in employment. In chapter 9 we consider such provision in more detail and also explain our treatment of unemployment as a category of 'occupational level'.

TABLE 7.2   Selected measures of the association between SCE attainment and job level: labour-market entrants from EA schools in the four regions.

	Boys	Girls
Product-moment correlation	0.45	0.46
Gamma	0.57	0.64
Tau	0.43	0.48
Lambda (asymmetric)	0.16	0.22
Contingency coefficient (c)	0.55	0.52

Notes: All measures are based on the data and categories shown in Table 7.1 with the 'other employed' row excluded. All measures are positive. The more detailed SCE scale described in chapter 2 produces product-moment correlations of 0.51 and 0.52; this scale is used in table 7.4.

In table 7.2 we present alternative measures that summarise the strength of the association between certification and occupational level shown in table 7.1. These have been selected to correspond to varying assumptions about the way in which certification and occupation are best measured. The measures all show the association between school certification and the 'level' of a school-leaver's early occupational experience (including unemployment); all leavers who went on to further full-time education are excluded. The estimates in table 7.2 are therefore not directly comparable with the estimates of the association between education and occupation reported by other researchers, most of which refer to adult jobs and to the whole range of educational attainment.[5] The associations in table 7.2 are slightly lower than those usually reported for adults, mainly, no doubt, because they do not take account of the substantial amount of variation in educational attainment contributed by further and higher education. School-leavers entering full-time further or higher education are not covered in this chapter at all, yet they are the group whose experience has contributed most to previous statistical estimates of the strength of the link.

All the statistics in table 7.2 have a maximum value of 1.0, representing perfect association; the absence of an association would be represented by a value of zero. The values in table 7.2 show that there was a moderately strong association between certification and jobs. One may also see this association in table 7.1 by comparing the proportions from different SCE-attainment groups who entered the top and bottom destination categories, white-collar jobs and unemployment, respectively. The proportion of boys entering white-collar jobs varied from 2 per cent among unqualified leavers to 30 per cent among the most qualified O-grade leavers and 60 per cent among those with Highers. At all SCE levels, more girls than boys entered white-collar jobs, but their proportions also rose steeply with SCE attainment, from 12 per cent of the unqualified to 79 per cent of those with five or more O-grades and 83 per cent of those with Highers. Conversely, nearly a quarter of unqualified leavers were unemployed compared with only 4 and 3 per cent respectively of boys and girls with five or more O-grades. This trend did not extend to leavers with Highers, among whom 8 and 5 per cent of boys and girls respectively were unemployed; this could be either because Highers leavers were more selective in the jobs they sought or because they were too old to enter most apprenticeships.

Perhaps most remarkably, young people at the marginal qualification levels, that is, with D or E awards or just one or two A–C awards at O-grade, had substantially better job chances than young people with no qualifications. Leavers with only D or E awards were less likely than unqualified leavers to be unemployed, and those with one or two A–C awards had still lower unemployment rates. The marginal qualification levels were also associated with the kinds of occupations held by employed leavers, especially among girls. A majority of the unqualified girls who had jobs were in the lowest (manual) category. Girls with D or E awards who had jobs were split about equally between the white-collar, services and manual categories. Among girls with one or two A–C awards, about one-half of those in employment were in the highest (white-collar) category.

In other words, school qualifications at all levels, and including the lowest marginal levels, were significantly associated with initial success in the job market among the 1977 sample members. The extension of certification to cover a large proportion of secondary-school pupils may therefore have tightened the bond between certification and occupation.

Did qualifications directly influence occupational success?

Understood as an association, then, the bond appears to have tightened as a result of the extension of certification. However, earlier in this chapter we suggested a definition of the bond in terms of the extent to which certification was used as a criterion for job selection; this definition implies not merely an association, but a causal connection, such that an individual's occupational prospects were directly influenced by the level of his or her qualifications.

It is possible that certificates were correlated with job success merely because they were correlated with other factors (such as aspirations, home background or ability), which themselves directly influenced occupational success. We therefore pose the question: did school qualifications themselves affect a young person's chances in the job market? In answering it, we examine three plausible alternative ways of explaining the association between certification and occupation. These suggest, respectively, that:

1 better-qualified leavers aspired to, and applied for, the better jobs; qualifications may have affected the kinds of applications made, but not the success of these applications;
2 school qualifications were correlated with success in the tests set by employers, but employers used their own tests for selection and did not use school qualifications;
3 school qualifications were correlated with social background, attitudes and behaviour, but employers selected on the basis of these attributes and not on the basis of school qualifications.

Below we consider each of these three interpretations in turn.

Aspirations and applications: the 'socialisation' theory

Several British studies of school-leavers have shown an association between the school performance of secondary pupils and the level of jobs to which they aspired (Carter, 1962; Douglas, Ross and Simpson, 1968; Maizels, 1970; Thomas and Wetherall, 1974). The job aspirations of British school-leavers tended to be 'realistic' with respect to their likely level of educational attainment. A more recent Scottish study has shown how far secondary-school pupils were channelled into educational and occupational tracks even by the end of their second year (Ryrie, Furst and Lauder, 1979). By this stage pupils had already tended to develop clear perceptions both of their ability as judged by the school and of the educational and occupational choices appropriate to this ability level. It could therefore be argued that, as a result of this socialisation, pupils developed expectations appropriate to their future occupational levels even before they took their SCE examinations, and that their job applications simply reflected this socialisation; that the better-qualified leavers got the better jobs merely because they applied for them, whereas pupils with lesser or no qualifications did not apply for them. Thus qualifications did not *directly* affect the success of applications. We will call this the 'socialisation' theory.

We agree with that part of the socialisation theory which alleges a strong tendency for pupils' occupational aspirations to be pitched at a level corresponding to their educational performance. However, this channelling of aspirations does not explain all of the association between certification and employment, nor does it refute the claim that employers tended to prefer more highly qualified people when selecting recruits. Rather, young people tended to set their occupational aspirations at a level that anticipated these preferences; their aspirations were realistic precisely because they did not aspire to jobs which they would not have been able to enter with the qualifications they expected to obtain. Not all this anticipation was conscious on the part of the individual pupil or school-leaver; indeed, in chapter 8 we suggest that young people may frequently have underestimated the strength of the bond between certification and employment. Nevertheless, the various processes of occupational socialisation, including the advice given by careers officers and guidance teachers, were likely to have pushed pupils and school-leavers towards aspirations which were realistic in terms of their likely qualification level.

Employers also sometimes anticipated qualifications. Many leavers, about a third of the pupils who entered the job market by 1977, had arranged jobs before leaving school and before they could know their examination results. However, this does not necessarily mean that the examinations were not important. In such situations employers based their selection decisions on the level and content of the examinations being attempted by job applicants and on schools' estimates of their chances of success (see, for example, Lee and Wrench, 1981). Even when employers chose school-leavers for jobs before knowing their examination results, the examinations, or at any rate the processes which led up to them, were still important.

Although job aspirations, and therefore job applications, may often have been pitched at a level that anticipated employers' preferences for qualifications, it was still the case that, when young people of different qualification levels applied for the same job, those with higher qualifications tended to be more successful. O-grade leavers in the 1977 survey were asked 'Have you ever applied for an apprenticeship of any kind?'. Table 7.3 shows the answers of boys who had not entered full-time education or white-collar jobs (these were excluded to allow for the possibility that many boys would have entered full-time education or white-collar jobs in preference to apprenticeships). At all levels of O-grade attainment most of the boys in the table had applied for apprenticeships; the proportion applying for apprenticeships tended to be slightly higher among the best-qualified boys, but the difference was not great. This appears to contradict the socialisation theory, which would suggest a higher rate of applications among the better-qualified

117

TABLE 7.3 'Have you ever applied for an apprenticeship of any kind?': O-grade boys from EA schools in the four regions not in full-time education or white-collar jobs

O-grade attainment	(a) Percentage who answered 'yes'	(b) Percentage of applicants who were apprentices in early 1977
5 or more A–C awards	87% of 64	83% of 52
3–4 A–C awards	91% of 151	77% of 134
1–2 A–C awards	83% of 283	59% of 217
D or E awards only	80% of 117	48% of 84

Notes: Percentages in column (b) are based on the 'yes' respondents of column (a). Non-certificate leavers are not included as the question asked in their versions of the questionnaire was not directly comparable.

boys. However, the category of apprentice covers a wide range of occupations. Almost certainly the better-qualified O-grade leavers tended to apply for the more desirable trades such as electrician or engineer, whereas the less-qualified leavers tended more towards apprenticeships in building and other less sought-after trades. However, the socialisation theory as we have described it would also predict the success rate of applications to be independent of qualification level. Yet the second column of table 7.3 (column b) suggests that better-qualified applicants for apprenticeships were significantly more likely to be successful; and the difference in success rates is even more significant, if it is accepted that the better-qualified leavers tended to try for the more 'difficult' apprenticeships and the less-qualified leavers tended to try for the 'easier' ones. Certificates therefore directly influenced occupational success; socialisation cannot explain away this influence, although it may in part have anticipated it.

A further argument against the socialisation theory is that it fails to explain the concentration of unemployment among the least-qualified school-leavers. The theory would imply that many unqualified leavers aspired to unemployment; that is, that they actually wanted to be unemployed or did not try to find work. Yet other evidence suggests that even the most alienated of unemployed young people wanted to have some job and tried to find one (Manpower Services Commission, 1978; Roberts, Armstrong and Noble, 1980).

Employers' tests

Among the employed members of the sample, 30 per cent of the boys and 13 per cent of the girls had been given written tests by their employers when they applied for the jobs they held at the time of the survey. Those given written tests tended to be in the jobs that recruited the better-qualified leavers, especially skilled manual jobs (among boys) and white-collar jobs (among girls). The proportion of employees given written tests therefore rose sharply with SCE attainment (no table given), from 16 per cent of unqualified boys to 49 per cent of boys with five or more O-grades (falling again to 35 per cent of employed boys with Highers, who were less likely to be in skilled manual jobs). Among girls the proportion rose uniformly from 9 per cent of un- qualified employees to 24 per cent of leavers with Highers. If, as seems likely, success in these tests was correlated with success in SCE examin- ations, might not job level have been a consequence of performance in employers' tests and not directly a consequence of SCE attainment at all?

However, employers' tests cannot account for the association be- tween qualifications and jobs, for at least two reasons. First, a large majority of the employed young people in the sample, especially girls, were not given tests; only one-fifth even of girls in white-collar jobs were given written tests by their employers. Job level was strongly associated with SCE attainment among school-leavers who were not tested as well as among those who were. Second, employees who were given written tests by their employers were nearly twice as likely as other employees to consider that their O-grade results had been 'essen- tial' or 'quite important' for getting the job. Although we shall have more to say in the next chapter about young people's perceptions of employers' selection practices, their views support a conclusion that employers' tests provided a complement, but not an alternative, to the use of school qualifications as a criterion for selection.[6]

Background, attitudes and behaviour

Table 7.1 has shown that the influence of certification on employment, although substantial, was not absolute; other factors were also influen- tial. Several empirical studies have shown that employers attached considerable importance to the personal qualities, attitudes and behav- iour of new recruits as well as to their qualifications and cognitive skills. The Manpower Services Commission's employers' survey (1978, pp. 38– 40) suggested that employers placed less emphasis on the 'specific educational qualifications' of applicants than on their basic skills and

119

(especially) their 'willingness/attitude to work'; employers were most likely to refer to attitudes and personality as reasons for refusing job applications from young people. Other surveys of employers (for example, Maizels, 1970, pp. 190–4; National Youth Employment Council, 1974, pp. 72–7; Ashton and Maguire, 1980) have also shown how employers attached importance to non-academic criteria in the selection of young recruits.

Most of these studies suggested that employers took account of applicants' backgrounds, attitudes and behaviour in addition to their school examination record. However, since all of these criteria for selection tended to be correlated with school examination results, it could be argued that the association between qualifications and job success came about, not because employers cared for qualifications themselves, but solely because employers chose young people with favourable backgrounds, attitudes and behaviour, and these young people also tended to have good SCE qualifications.[7]

We can test for this possibility on the data for the 1977 sample. We have no direct measure of respondents' attitudes to work, but we do have measures of their truancy during their fourth year at school, of the frequency with which they were belted (received corporal punishment), of their reported satisfaction with their last year at school, and of their social class. If employers selected recruits solely on the basis of background, attitudes and behaviour, we would expect one or more of these four variables to have been strongly associated with job level and that together they would have accounted for much of the association between job level and SCE attainment. Table 7.4 tests this possibility; job level is measured by a four-point scale covering the three main job categories for each sex and with unemployment comprising the fourth category. Table 7.4a shows that these four variables together accounted for 12 per cent of the variation in job level among boys and 13 per cent among girls. However, SCE attainment explained an additional 15 per cent, over and above the effects of these four variables, and most of the variation that was explained by the four variables was 'shared' with attainment: the four variables added only 1 per cent to the variation explained by attainment (Table 7.4b). In other words, more than half the explained variation in job level was accounted for by SCE attainment alone; most of the remaining variation could be attributed either to SCE attainment or to the combined influences of background, attitudes and behaviour. Even if we had more and better measures of attitudes and personality, it seems unlikely that we could explain all of the association between SCE attainment and job level. Moreover, if background, attitudes and behaviour were the only direct determinants of success in the job market, it is remarkable that they accounted for so little of the variation in job

TABLE 7.4   Percentage of variation in job level explained respectively by SCE attainment and by background, attitude and behaviour variables (stepwise multiple regressions)

			Percentage of variation explained	
			Boys	Girls
(a)	Step 1	social class truancy belting attitude to school	12	13
	Step 2	SCE attainment	15	15
	Total variation explained		27	28
(b)	Step 1	SCE attainment	26	26
	Step 2	social class truancy belting attitude to school	1	1
	Total variation explained		27	28

Notes: Percentages have been rounded.

Population:	as in table 7.2 ('other employed' leavers excluded).
Job level:	as in Table 7.2.
SCE attainment:	see chapter 2.
Social class:	see chapter 2.
Truancy:	a five-point scale (see chapter 11).
Belting:	a four-point scale of frequency of corporal punishment at secondary school (see chapter 10).
Attitude to school:	whether respondent thought his/her last year at school was worthwhile (see chapter 10).

level that was not already accounted for by SCE attainment.

There is no doubt that many employers attached great importance to the attitudes, motivation and behavioural records of their recruits. However, for the 1977 sample members these criteria do not explain the relative success of better-qualified school-leavers in the job market. Our evidence suggests that SCE attainment influenced young people's chances in the job market, and that this was a direct influence which cannot wholly be explained in terms of other factors. Either employers used non-academic criteria alongside educational qualifications and not instead of them; or, as we suggest in the section entitled 'Mind or soul?', they may in part have used qualifications as proxy measures of the non-academic criteria in which they were interested.

Levels or kinds of attainment?

So far we have discussed SCE qualifications as though they formed a single hierarchy, as though more or fewer O-grades simply served to place school-leavers nearer or further from the front in a single queue of applicants for 'good' jobs. However, the certificates recorded not only the level of a young person's attainment, but also the particular subjects in which awards were made. Did employers regard qualifications principally as indicators of the specific skills and knowledge relevant to particular tasks or jobs? Or did they regard them principally as a measure of a more general factor, such as the general academic level of an applicant? If the former were the case, then the association between certification and occupation would have been multidimensional; a young person's qualifications would have tied him or her, not just to a particular level of job, but to a specific kind of job within that level. If, however, employers' main interests were in the general academic level of job applicants, the labour market would be more likely to have resembled the job-queue described by Thurow and Lucas (1972), where prospective employees formed a single job-queue, ranked in order of their attractiveness to employers, with those at the front of the queue being selected for the highest job levels without regard to their particular skills or knowledge. In the latter case the association between certification and occupation would be more appropriately measured along a single dimension, the level of certification being related to the level of occupation.

Clearly, at higher levels of education some specialist qualifications have always been important. In normal circumstances a medical graduate and an engineering graduate would be unlikely to apply for the same jobs, although they may possess qualifications at a similar level. However, our interest in this chapter is in qualifications gained in secondary school and in the O-grade examination in particular. Our attention focuses, therefore, on the O-grade, and on two questions: did employers seek school-leavers with qualifications in particular subjects of specific relevance to the jobs concerned? And, inasmuch as O-grades were used as an indication of general academic level, did employers count all subjects as being of equal value in this reckoning?

O-grade leavers were asked 'Did your employer require any particular subject(s) at O-grade?' The answers did not say whether a pass was required, or whether merely studying a subject was sufficient. Moreover, the question relied entirely on school-leavers' perceptions; the answers were likely to understate employers' requirements, and they did not reflect the unspecified, informal preferences of employers. Only specific subjects (and not more general answers, such as 'at least one science') were coded. Subject to these reservations, table 7.5

TABLE 7.5   'Did your employer require any particular subject(s) at O-grade?. . . If yes, which subjects?' By job category: percentage of employed O-grade leavers from EA schools in the four regions

(a)

Boys	White collar	Skilled manual	Less skilled	All employed boys
Any named subject[1]	49	17	7	15
English	35	8	2	7
Arithmetic	19	6	3	5
Mathematics	15	9	1	6
Arithmetic *or* mathematics	31	12	4	10
Physics	7	6	1	4
A technical subject	11	9	4	6
Unweighted *n*	(119)	(538)	(583)	(1,320)

(b)

Girls	White collar	Services	Manual	All employed girls
Any named subject[2]	35	3	3	18
English	26	2	1	13
Arithmetic	14	2	1	7
Mathematics	2	0	0	1
Arithmetic *or* mathematics	15	2	1	8
Accounts	2	0	0	1
A secretarial subject	12	0	1	6
Unweighted *n*	(617)	(291)	(304)	(1,231)

Notes: Of 119 boys (unweighted) in white-collar jobs, 49 per cent named any subject, 35 per cent named English, 19 per cent named arithmetic, and so on. The 'other employed' category is not shown, but is included in the figures for all boys and girls.
1   No other subject was named by more than 2 per cent of the boys in any category.
2   No other subject was named by more than 1 per cent of the girls in any category.

suggests that relatively little emphasis was placed on specific subjects. Fewer than one in six boys and fewer than one in five girls said their employer required any particular subject, although these proportions were much higher for those in white-collar jobs than for the other categories. Some 7 per cent of boys and 13 per cent of girls said they were required to have English, the most frequently cited subject; 10 per cent of boys and 8 per cent of girls named either mathematics or arithmetic; 6 per cent of boys named a technical subject, such as

TABLE 7.6 Percentages with at least one A–C award at O-grade in different groups of subjects, by labour-market destination: O-grade leavers who entered the labour market from EA schools in the four regions

	Boys				Girls			
	White collar	Skilled manual	Less skilled	Unemployed	White collar	Services	Manual	Unemployed
Any O-grade subject	85	78	60	57	78	56	46	40
Basics	76	57	34	34	65	38	33	28
Science	36	21	8	9	6	4	3	3
Modern languages	8	2	1	1	9	3	2	3
Other academic subjects	43	27	15	16	24	10	7	10
Arts	9	8	10	7	9	9	9	8
Home economics	1	*	1	*	20	18	14	8
Technical	29	44	34	24	0	*	*	0
Commercial	7	1	1	*	36	13	10	7
Other vocational subjects	1	*	*	*	2	2	1	2
Average number of A–C awards	3.1	2.3	1.3	1.2	2.2	1.1	1.0	0.8
Unweighted *n*	(219)	(1,076)	(1,207)	(230)	(1,241)	(616)	(605)	(221)

Notes: Of O-grade boys who were in white-collar jobs, 85 per cent had at least one A–C award in any subject, 76 per cent had an
A–C in at least one 'basic' subject, and so on.
Basics: English, arithmetic or mathematics.
Science: chemistry, physics or biology.
Other academic: history, geography, modern studies, economics, economic history, statistics, Latin or Greek.
Arts: art or music.
Commercial: accounting or secretarial studies (audio or shorthand).
Other vocational: anatomy, physiology and health, agricultural science, horticultural science, navigation, seamanship,
'another subject' or 'another science'.
* less than 0.5 per cent

engineering drawing or woodwork, and 4 per cent named physics; 6 per cent of girls named secretarial studies. Apart from these, neither the sciences nor 'vocational' subjects (such as home economics, accounting, or anatomy, physiology and health) seem to have been demanded of O-grade leavers by many employers. A more detailed analysis of jobs revealed that most of the girls who named secretarial studies were in clerical jobs, and that the two groups of boys most likely to name physics and technical subjects were technicians and electrical workers. Apart from these and a few other exceptions (such as the armed forces and employers of woodworkers), employers, if they specified any subjects at all, were likely to name English, mathematics or arithmetic.

Table 7.5 does not cover the occasions when an employer's preference for a particular subject was unknown to the job applicant. An alternative approach is to look at the subjects actually studied (or passed) by school-leavers entering different jobs, to see whether there were marked associations between particular subjects and particular jobs. Table 7.6 shows the subjects in which O-grade leavers in the different job categories held A–C awards. For reasons of simplicity and space, both jobs and subjects are described at a highly aggregated level.

In interpreting table 7.6 we need to bear in mind the differences in the average numbers of A–C awards among entrants to different jobs (shown at the bottom of the table). White-collar workers were, on average, better qualified than other O-grade leavers so, other things being equal, we would expect them to have had more passes in any given group of subjects. Allowing for this, we do notice some associations between subjects and jobs.[8] Relative to their mean number of A–C awards, quite a large proportion of girls in service or manual jobs had arts subjects or home economics. Boys with technical subjects tended to be in manual jobs. Boys and girls in white-collar jobs were relatively likely to have O-grades in commercial subjects, even allowing for their higher mean attainment. However, the associations between subjects and job types were mostly small and (except perhaps for commercial subjects) they may reflect not a demand for special skills in particular jobs, but rather the relatively low importance attached to the arts and vocational subjects by employers who wished mainly to gauge the general academic level of applicants.

This interpretation receives some support from table 7.7. This shows the correlations between job level and the total number of O-grade awards at A–C in different groups of subjects. The correlation of job level with the overall total of O-grades was 0.31 for boys and 0.35 for girls. However, the correlation with the total number of O-grades in the 'basic' subjects of English, mathematics and arithmetic was very nearly as high. In other words, the basic subjects provided nearly as

TABLE 7.7 Product-moment correlations of job level with number of A–C awards in different groups of subjects: O-grade leavers who entered the labour market from EA schools in the four regions

	Boys	Girls
All subjects	0.31	0.35
Basics	0.31	0.32
Other academic subjects	0.24	0.19
All academic subjects	0.31	0.30
All non-academic subjects	0.11	0.26
Non-academic subjects excluding commercial subjects	0.09	0.11

Notes: Basics: English, arithmetic, mathematics,
Other academic subjects: all foreign languages, chemistry, physics, biology, statistics, history, geography, modern studies, economics, economic history.
Non-academic subjects: all subjects *apart from* basics and other academic subjects.
Commercial subjects: accounting, secretarial (audio), secretarial (shorthand).
Job level as in table 7.2.

good a predictor of job level as did the overall total number of O-grades. The table shows that other academic subjects (equivalent to sciences, languages and 'other academic subjects' in table 7.6) were also correlated with job level, although the correlations were lower than for the basics. Finally, the table shows that non-academic subjects (equivalent to the general and vocational subjects in table 7.6) were very weakly associated with job level. (The correlation for non-academic subjects was considerably higher for girls than for boys, although, when commercial subjects were excluded, the correlation for girls was much the same as for boys.)

Table 7.7 suggests that employers selected in terms of a hierarchy of O-grade subjects, headed by the basics, followed by other academic subjects, and with general and vocational subjects at the bottom. (The principal exceptions to this were the commercial subjects, which appear to have been valued by employers of white-collar workers.) This hierarchy resembles that described in chapters 5 and 6, the principal difference being the greater value attached by employers to the basic subjects. Employers made reference to this hierarchy of subjects when using examination results to measure the general academic level of potential recruits. Employers of white-collar and skilled workers were therefore especially likely to select workers who not only had more O-grades, but who had O-grades in the basics and in academic subjects.

Employers' interest in the 'general academic level' of applicants, rather than employers' job-specific preferences for particular subjects, could explain most of the (relatively small) association between subjects and jobs in table 7.6.[9]

Mind or soul?

Why have employers valued the general academic level of their recruits? Perhaps the most accepted explanation is that employers have seen in academic attainment evidence of general ability and of a potential for acquiring the cognitive and technical skills required for effective performance of the job. It matters little whether ability and potential have been acquired in school or whether schools have merely ranked and labelled pupils in terms of them; the important point is that ability and potential have been defined in terms of cognitive and technical competence.

A rival explanation has been put forward by writers such as Collins (1971) and especially Bowles and Gintis (1976). They argue that employers have been more interested in the normative than in the cognitive qualities of their employees; that is, employers have mainly wanted their employees to have the right backgrounds, values, attitudes and personalities, and to show conformity or commitment to the social and organisational demands of the workplace; technical and cognitive abilities have been less important criteria, since the level of skill demanded in most industrial jobs has been within the range of most people. It is argued that, when employers have sought to recruit candidates at a high general academic level, they have done so in the belief that this, in turn, was a measure of their attitudes and personal qualities. Employers have not therefore chosen between qualifications and these 'normative' personal qualities as alternative criteria for selecting employees, as suggested by some of the studies mentioned above; rather, employers have valued qualifications as the best available indicators of normative qualities.

In three respects this argument receives some support from British evidence, although the support must be qualified. In the first place the surveys of employees which we cited in 'Did qualifications directly influence occupational success?' show that employers have attached considerable importance to the attitudes and personal qualities of their recruits, although most of these surveys suggest that employers have also valued the basic cognitive skills. Second, employers have tended to lack reliable information on young job-applicants, especially information which they could trust on these normative qualities which they valued. Third, educational attainment has been correlated with these normative qualities; in part 4 of this book we show how behaviour and attitudes to school have varied between pupils at different levels of the academic hierarchy, and in part 5 we measure the association between social background and attainment. However, school qualifications have probably been perceived by employers as imperfect measures of pupils' attitudes, behaviour and personal qualities. In this context it may be significant that Bowles and Gintis (and indeed Collins) were writing about the United States of America. There is a widely held view that British employers have been more hostile towards education than employers in other countries such as Germany and America (Cotgrove, 1958; Reeder, 1979). According to this view, British employers have been particularly critical of the values and aims of educational institutions; they have therefore been unlikely to regard the academic attainment certified by these institutions as a perfect indicator of a school-leaver's commitment to the values and aims which employers have considered appropriate for employment. However, we have already argued that employers have taken account of qualifications as a measure of general academic level. So what have employers believed this 'academic level' to represent: purely cognitive and technical skills and abilities, or some blend of these with attitudes and other personal qualities?

Of course, this distinction — between the cognitive and the normative — may not be one which employers have recognised or used in their selection decisions. They have wanted future employees who would get the job done, and perform the required tasks competently; the job has had to be done within a given organisation and system of authority; so conformity to such a system has been an integral part of job performance. Educational qualifications have been evidence of competence to perform set tasks competently within a system of authority not unlike that of the workplace. In accepting qualifications as (partial) evidence of competence, employers have not been required to make explicit their relative preference for the cognitive and normative aspects of performance, and it is probable that they have used qualifications as evidence of a competence which embraced both these aspects.

What is significant is that qualifications have not perfectly measured either the cognitive or the normative qualities which employers have sought in their recruits. Whereas academic level, as expressed in terms of qualifications, has been correlated with the kinds of qualities which employers have valued, the correlation has not been perfect; qualifications have also measured characteristics valued by educationists but not by employers. That qualifications have nevertheless been used by employers as selection criteria is largely a consequence of the scarcity of alternative convenient and reliable sources of information on both the cognitive and the normative qualities which employers have sought.

Moreover, employers have tended to invoke only a single dimension of educational attainment, the dimension we have called general academic level, and they have tended not to discriminate between the different abilities and qualities which have contributed towards this single dimension. Indeed, it is likely that many employers' knowledge of the educational process has not been sufficient for them to extract much more information from an individual's examination record than what it has said about his or her academic level. As a result, the criteria used in employers' selection decisions have inevitably incorporated educationists' definitions of the relative value of different examinations, subjects, syllabuses and standards; in other words, educationists' definitions of academic level.

We have argued that employers have tended to take account of only one dimension, academic level, of the various attainments and qualities of school-leavers that are measured by qualifications. As a result of this one-dimensional use of qualifications in selection, employers have had limited ability to influence, through their selection decisions, priorities within secondary education; we develop this argument in chapter 8. Then, in chapter 9 we examine some implications of the lack of fit between educational certification and employers' preferences. If alternatives were made available, would employers prefer to select recruits on other criteria than examination performance?

Conclusions

In this chapter we have investigated the claim that the extension of certification to a large proportion of secondary-school pupils contributed to a further tightening of the bond between certification and occupation. We have concluded that the evidence supports this claim; the lower-level qualifications were indeed associated with initial occupational achievement among members of the 1977 sample and, since these qualifications were held by sections of the age-group whose counterparts less than two decades earlier had held no qualifications at all, this is likely to have produced a tightening of the bond among the age-group as a whole. Even marginal qualification levels were associated with job chances substantially better than those of unqualified leavers. Qualifications, moreover, seem to have influenced job prospects directly; the association between certification and occupation cannot be entirely explained away in terms of job aspirations and applications, the use of employers' own tests, or the social background and behaviour of young people. Indeed, the association of aspirations and job applications with certification level may simply have reflected a realistic anticipation of the constraints imposed by certification level. We suggested that employers used school qualifications as evidence more of the general academic level of leavers than of specific skills or knowledge. Finally, we suggested that employers have perceived academic level as a reflection of both cognitive and normative qualities required for job performance. However, employers have had to take on trust educationists' criteria for defining a young person's academic level.

Chapter 8

The Limited Influence of Employers on Secondary Schools

Introduction

Many commentators of different theoretical persuasions agree that there have been strong links between education and the world of work, and that to a large extent the education system has been determined, or at least constrained, by the economic order. The bond between qualifications and jobs, described in the previous chapter, has been one aspect of this close relationship. We agree with this view. At the same time, however, it would be wrong to see secondary education as having been wholly determined by economic forces. The aims and objectives of secondary education have not always coincided with those of employers, and the outcomes of education have not always been those which employers would have wanted. In this chapter we suggest that there are structural explanations for this relative autonomy, which have to do with the nature of selection, respectively, for employment and for university.

In part 2 we referred to the historical influence of universities over the content, pedagogy and organisation of secondary schooling in Scotland. The academic values professed by universities have dominated much of the rest of the education system. Over the last three or four decades, secondary education has undergone a sequence of incremental changes, while evolving from a system whose dominant goal was to prepare the ablest children for university. Nevertheless, in Scotland as in England, the universities have continued to exercise considerable influence over secondary education through channels both formal and informal. University staff have advised governments and local education authorities and have sat on examination boards. Most secondary teachers have themselves attended university.

There have also been more informal mechanisms. Universities have also exerted an influence through their use of school certificates for selecting students and through their consequent ability to prescribe standards of attainment as well as to determine the relative value of different qualifications, subjects and (sometimes) pedagogies in school.

As we have seen in chapter 7, employers have also used certificates when selecting school-leavers. Has this given employers an influence over secondary education comparable to that of the universities? However, employers have had fewer formal channels of influence than the universities and their definitions of educational value have had to struggle for legitimacy. Moreover, in this chapter we argue that there have also been other, more structural factors which have limited the influence of employers over secondary education.

Three questions

To do this we must first spell out the mechanism through which such an influence might be exerted. One possible model is that employers offer rewards (jobs) as incentives in order to influence pupils' decisions over the qualifications they seek, the subjects they choose and the standards they aim at, and in order to motivate them to try to get good results. In this model, teachers would wish to maximise the job chances of their pupils, and they would also be subject to pressure from pupils and parents; they would therefore be influenced indirectly to offer courses in the subjects, at the standards, and for the qualifications desired by employers, and influenced also to advise pupils to make the choices which optimised their occupational prospects. Teachers might also be encouraged to provide the syllabuses and pedagogies which might be desired by employers.

This is, in effect, a free-market model of consumer power, with employers as the consumers of the output of schools.[1] However, for their consumer power to be effective, at least three conditions must be satisfied.

1 *The rewards*: the jobs offered, and the pecking order among these jobs, must be valued by pupils, otherwise they will have no incentive to make the desired educational choices and to get good educational qualifications.

2 *The perceived pay-off*: not only must there be a reasonably strong association between the outcomes of pupils' decisions (qualifications) and jobs, but this must be perceived to be strong by the pupils themselves (this is the assumption of 'perfect information', to continue the market analogy); moreover, pupils must perceive a *causal* relationship between qualifications and job chances.

3 *Employers' discrimination*: if employers are to influence
   secondary education through the effective use of their 'consumer
   power', they must discriminate between the different subjects
   and qualifications on offer to them, in a way that expresses their
   own values and preferences rather than values determined by,
   and borrowed from, the education system itself.

In the rest of this chapter we examine each of these three conditions,
to see how far they have been satisfied in the relation between certification and jobs as this is covered by the 1977 survey.

Condition 1: the rewards

Any attempt to influence behaviour through a system of incentives will
only be effective if the rewards that are offered in return for the desired
behaviours are sufficiently valued by the individuals concerned. In the
present model the incentives that may influence educational choices are
provided by the prospect of a job: a job rather than unemployment, or
a skilled and white-collar job rather than an unskilled job.

The desirability of such incentives may seem too obvious to need
spelling out. However, for some pupils, jobs, or good jobs, have not
been the most desirable of the immediate outcomes of secondary
schooling. Of the 1975–6 school-leavers who possessed the relevant
entry qualifications, a large majority went straight on to university.
Many others entered other forms of higher or further education, and
yet others expected to enter higher education after an interval. Of
leavers with five or more Highers, barely one in ten entered the labour
market directly from school, and many of those who did so entertained
plans to enter higher education eventually. Well under half of leavers
with three or four Highers entered the labour market. Only below the
three-Highers level did a clear majority of leavers seek employment
straight away (three Highers has been the notional qualification level
for higher education used in forecasting student numbers). So, of
school-leavers who had the choice, a large majority opted not for
immediate entry to employment but for higher education and especially
university.

However, only about 6 per cent of leavers from educational authority (EA) schools in the four regions in 1975–6 went on directly to
university.[2] How can the preference for university among this small
minority have affected the pattern of incentives for the majority,
whose only realistic aspirations were in the field of employment? The
answer lies in the hierarchical and sequential process of selection in
Scottish secondary schools, which has given the universities, a minority
destination though they may have been, a disproportionate influence

134

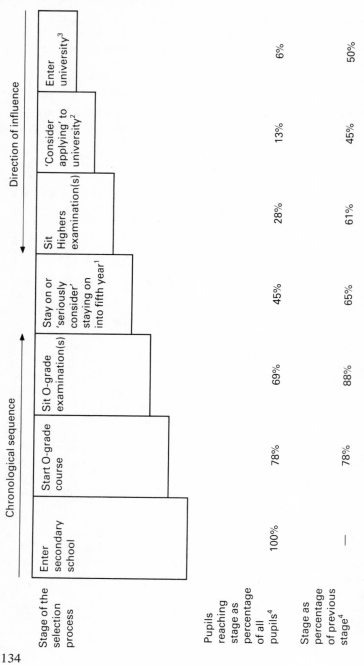

Figure 8.1   Stages of selection in Scottish EA secondary schools

which has stretched backwards and downwards over the education offered to a majority, if not all, of secondary pupils. Figure 8.1 shows the sequence of stages through which eventual university students were creamed off from the milk of Scottish secondary pupils. Although our description here concerns Scottish schools, we believe that a similar argument could be established in relation to comprehensive schools in England and Wales. The chronological sequence of these stages runs from left to right in the diagram, from transfer to secondary school through to the final selection for university. However, the conjectured chain of influence runs from right to left.

As we have said, only 6 per cent of pupils leaving EA schools in 1975–6 entered university directly on leaving. However, twice as many leavers had considered applying to university while at school, and these, in turn, accounted for nearly half of all Highers candidates and for considerably more than half of those (not shown in figure 8.1) attempting a full Highers course of at least five subjects. Universities could therefore exert considerable influence over the content, pedagogy and organisation of Highers courses and thus of the fifth and sixth years of secondary education.

This influence extended further back into the O-grade curriculum. Nearly two-thirds of O-grade candidates either stayed on for a fifth year or 'seriously considered' doing so (the proportion is much larger, if based on pupils who took several subjects at O-grade). For many pupils, O-grades were at least potentially a preparation for Highers, and the O-grade curriculum and pedagogy were accordingly influenced by Highers (see also chapter 5, 'The O-grade examination' and 'Subject hierarchy in the Highers and O-grade examinations').[3] Finally, a large majority of Scottish pupils at least began an O-grade course; the O-grade in its turn influenced the earlier years.

Thus, directly or indirectly, the universities have been able to exercise a substantial degree of influence over curriculum and pedagogy at several different levels of secondary education. This influence has been made possible, first, by the recognised hierarchy in education which is reflected in pupils' aspirations, such that pupils at any one level of education made the choices that preserved their options of attaining the next and higher level (with teachers, in turn, preserving these options when deciding the content and pedagogy of each stage). Second, the sequential nature of the selection process was such that, at each stage, a majority or near majority of pupils aspired to the next one. This effect was extended by the comprehensive reorganisation of education; previously a large majority of pupils had been selected out of the university-oriented side of education at the age of 12. It is perhaps ironic that comprehensive reorganisation has extended the influence of the universities over secondary education.

Condition 2: the perceived pay-off

If employers are to influence education through a system of incentives, not only must the rewards (jobs) be valued by pupils, but they must be perceived by pupils and others to be strongly and directly linked to the choices which employers wish to influence. In other words, pupils must also be aware of the bond between certification and occupation.

We argued in chapter 7 that there was an association between certification and labour-market success among school-leavers in the 1977 survey; even leavers with lower levels of certification were considerably more successful than leavers with no qualifications at all. Moreover, the association between certification and employment could not all be explained in terms of other factors; qualifications were important in their own right. Nevertheless, the association between school certification and employment was not absolute; it was much weaker than, for example, the associations between school certification and entrance to higher education. Employers, in other words, based their selection decisions not only on qualifications but also on a variety of non-academic criteria; qualifications were not the only means by which a young person could improve his or her chances in the labour market. To the extent that the bond between school certification and employment has not been strong, the ability of employers to use this bond to influence education has been reduced.

Moreover, it seems likely that many young people underestimated the vocational importance of qualifications. There are two main reasons why this may have been so.

The first reason is that when young people viewed the bond from a particular vantage-point in the educational or occupational hierarchy, their vantage-point was likely to structure their perceptions so as to lead them to underestimate the strength of the bond between certification and jobs. Although table 7.1 reflected a strong overall tendency for school qualifications to determine job level, the determination was far from absolute. Boys in skilled manual jobs, and even girls in white-collar jobs, had been recruited from all qualification levels. A young person leaving school was therefore likely to notice that former fellow pupils with similar attainments entered jobs ranging over several job levels. The same young person was perhaps less likely to appreciate the point made by table 7.1, namely that the ranges of jobs entered by pupils with different attainment levels were, on balance, very different. Once in a job, the young person was likely to notice that fellow workers, both young and old, possessed a range of school qualifications. Again, the young person would not have realised how the ranges of school qualifications in other jobs, although still wide, were nevertheless significantly higher or lower, on average, than in his or her own job.

In other words, any youngster who based impressions of the labour market on his or her own peers was more likely to notice the diversity among the peers than to notice the average, structural relationship between job level and qualifications that we have called the 'bond'. To perceive this structure accurately in the labour market would require a distanced, and global, perspective; close up, the impression was of haphazardness and randomness. From their own experiences and those of their friends, therefore, young people were likely to underestimate the significance of qualifications for jobs. Earlier studies of the job-seeking process have noted such subjective impressions of haphazardness and randomness (Carter, 1962; Maizels, 1970). Being in the right place, and knocking on the right door, at the right time, have seemed to be all-important.

The second reason was that employers themselves have understated the importance they attach to qualifications. Unlike universities, where academic achievement or potential has been (at least in principle) the sole legitimate criterion for admission, employers have selected on the basis of several different criteria and have had to find a balance between them. As a result, employers have been reluctant to specify precise entrance requirements in terms of any one criterion, such as educational qualifications. To do so would have restricted their freedom to choose applicants who had poor qualifications but who satisfied the other criteria, such as having the 'right' attitudes or background.

Employers have therefore tended not to formalise or make explicit their preferences for qualified applicants. Moreover, many employers (especially smaller employers) may never have consciously spelt out or rationalised their preferences, even to themselves. Indeed, one study of employers of young people mainly confined itself to larger employers, for 'it was found in practice that smaller firms, when seen, did not normally have an identifiable personnel and recruitment policy which could be discussed' (National Youth Employment Council, 1974, p. 73). Consequently, young people have been likely to underestimate the importance which employers have in fact attached to qualifications, because the employers have never told them of it. Indeed applicants for jobs may have been quite unaware that prospective employers even knew of their examination results or potential, since employers could have been informed of this, in advance of any interviews, by careers officers or schools.

Three additional factors may have further discouraged employers from making clear their preference for qualified applicants. The first is the fragmented nature of the labour market. There are eight universities based in Scotland; there are tens of thousands of employers, many of whom have taken on only one or two new employees each year. With an unpredictable flow of new applicants, many employers have found it hard to specify educational requirements with any precision, since they could not be sure of the demand for jobs at whatever educational price they set. Second, except for apprenticeships, most of the jobs for which young people applied were also open to older applicants (Manpower Services Commission, 1978, p. 38). Setting precise qualification levels for entry would have been unfair to older applicants who left school at a time when qualifications were only obtained by a small minority of pupils. Since many employers have tended to prefer the greater experience and allegedly better discipline of older recruits (ibid., p. 39), they have had an additional reason for playing down their emphasis on qualifications. Third, compared with universities, most employers have faced little pressure to justify their selection in terms of educational criteria. This is partly because qualifications have had less obvious relevance to job selection than to university selection, and partly because employers have generally been under less pressure than universities to legitimate choices in terms of universal criteria of any kind. Indeed, in many industries, ascriptive factors (such as having a relative in the firm or industry) have been useful or even necessary conditions for employment. Few employers have been called upon to explain their selection decisions, even to the applicants themselves.

In brief, whatever importance employers have in fact attached to qualifications, they have been under little pressure to legitimate their selection publicly and formally in terms of qualifications. The bond between qualifications and employment has therefore been perceived by many school-leavers to be considerably weaker than it really was, at least as far as qualifications below Highers level were concerned; and we conjecture that leavers' impressions of the bond were communicated to, and shared by, friends, brothers and sisters still at school.

More than half of the O-grade leavers in the sample who entered the labour market felt that their O-grades had not helped them at all when looking for a job (table not shown). Even among leavers with five or more A–C awards, 18 per cent felt that their O-grades had not helped them at all, and only a half considered that they had helped them 'a lot'. Less successful O-grade leavers were much less satisfied: the proportion of leavers who said that their O-grades had not helped them at all was more than a quarter among leavers with three or four A–C awards; more than half among leavers with one or two A–C awards; and more than three-quarters among leavers with only D or E awards. In spite of the empirical association between job success and examination achievements at the marginal qualification levels (table 7.1), few young people thought that these marginal qualifications had helped them in the job market. Of course, it is possible that by virtue of taking O-grades these leavers had raised their sights and that they were comparing themselves with more successful O-grade leavers, rather than with leavers with no O-grade awards. However, when O-grade leavers were asked 'Would better results have helped you when looking for a job?' only 28 per cent replied 'yes'; 42 per cent replied 'maybe'; and 30 per cent replied 'no' (table not shown). This pattern of answers was the same for leavers at all levels of O-grade achievement, including those with marginal qualifications. It therefore seems more likely that employers offering the kinds of jobs to which the less-qualified O-grade leavers applied simply did not communicate to the young people the importance that they attached to O-grades.

TABLE 8.1 'How important were O-grade results for getting the job?' By O-grade attainment: percentage of employed O-grade leavers from EA schools in the four regions

	D or E awards only	1 or 2 A–C	3–4 A–C	5 or more A–C
Boys				
Essential	< 0.5	5	21	41
Quite important	5	16	26	32
Not very important	23	27	22	11
Not important at all	65	44	27	15
Don't know	7	9	5	2
Total	100	101	101	101
Unweighted *n*	(294)	(474)	(263)	(117)
Girls				
Essential	1	4	9	30
Quite important	5	21	39	33
Not very important	31	29	21	15
Not important at all	50	37	23	21
Don't know	12	10	8	2
Total	99	101	100	101
Unweighted *n*	(230)	(536)	(297)	(158)

A similar story is told by table 8.1, which shows how employed O-grade leavers viewed the importance of their O-grades for getting the jobs they held at the time of the survey. Only among those with five or more awards in bands A–C did a majority consider that O-grades had been 'essential' or even 'quite important' for getting their jobs. At all other levels a majority either thought that their O-grades were 'not very important' or 'not important at all', or they simply did not know. Leavers with lower-level O-grade qualifications, especially those with only D or E awards, rarely considered that their qualifications had been important. A separate question asked: 'Overall, how useful is a D or E result at O-grade?' Fewer than 2 per cent of O-grade leavers replied 'very useful', 28 per cent thought it was 'quite useful', and more than 70 per cent thought it was 'no use at all'; and this despite the evidence of chapter 7 that leavers with D or E awards had a much better chance than unqualified leavers of escaping unemployment and of obtaining a job at a relatively high level.

Our conclusions are matched by those of a study by the Scottish Council for Research in Education, summarised in the Dunning Report (Scottish Education Department, 1977a, p. 114):

> This study was commissioned by us from SCRE and was based on completion of questionnaires by school-leavers (522 school-leavers responded out of a sample of 796 actual or potential leavers). 71 per cent indicated that their O grades had been of no importance in getting their job; and a number of the respondents apparently did not distinguish between an A, B or C 'pass' and a D or E grading. Some caution should be exercised in drawing conclusions, however, for many prospective employers are made aware, probably through a Careers Officer, of a candidate's examination record before deciding to interview him. Nevertheless, the survey showed further that only 26 per cent of those who had made more than one application for a job thought that more O grades would have been useful, and only 9 per cent of the employed school-leavers indicated that they had required a particular number of passes or set of subjects at O grade in order to gain employment. Of leavers applying for more than one job 52 per cent received some indication from the employer as to why their applications were unsuccessful. The most common reason young people said they were given was that there were no vacancies and in only 10 per cent of cases was the lack of sufficient O grade passes cited; again caution is required in interpreting this data since the reasons proffered by employers may not necessarily have been the accurate reasons.

Furthermore, a preliminary report on an English study of employers' selection strategies has suggested that, although many employers made use of educational qualifications in selection, their selection strategies differed from those used in 'educational circles'. Employers often used qualifications in the preliminary stages of selection, either directing their recruitment drive at young people with given qualification levels, or using minimum qualification levels to select short lists from which choices would be made on non-academic criteria. The result is that pupils may not have been aware of the actual importance of qualifications (Ashton and Maguire, 1980, p. 157):

In short, the rules governing selection in educational circles and those adopted in the labour market are different, and so too are the significance and meaning attached to educational qualifications. We suspect, judging from what little evidence there is available. . . that young people at school are all too aware of the rules governing educational selection, but are largely ignorant of the rules governing selection in the labour market. Here again, careers guidance could play an important part in ensuring that young people are fully aware of the rules that play such a large part in determining their success in the competition for jobs.

If pupils have been largely unaware of the nature or the strength of the link that has existed between school qualifications and jobs, they cannot, within the model we have described, have been motivated to do well at school or been induced to choose the courses, subjects or syllabuses that employers have preferred. Without such inducements, employers have not been able to use their position as selectors to influence the content of secondary education.

Condition 3: employers' discrimination

Consumers who invariably buy the cheapest product on the market have little influence over the design, quality or suitability of the products they buy; by choosing products on the single criterion of price, they fail to exercise their potential influence, as consumers, over other characteristics, besides price, of products on the market. We suggest that there is an analogy with the behaviour of employers in the labour market. The 'products' in this case are school-leavers; and the *educational* criterion which employers mainly use is not price, but the single dimension of 'academic level', which we discussed in chapter 7. We suggested that, although there was a modest association among 1977 sample members between types of jobs and particular subjects, this was not strong, and could largely be explained in terms of the varying degrees to which qualifications in different subjects were believed to reflect a high academic level.

However, consumers often buy the products of a complex technology that they do not fully understand; in such cases they may find it difficult to influence such things as the design, quality or suitability of products, because they are in no position to judge, in advance, what kinds of products are best suited to their needs. Similarly, we suggested in chapter 7 that most employers have been largely ignorant of the processes that have contributed to the attainment of educational qualifications; they have had little choice but to accept educationists' definitions of the criteria that composed 'academic level' and their judgments of the relative value of different qualifications, subjects and syllabuses. These definitions and judgments have been incorporated in the 'academic level' which employers have sought when using qualifications in selection. Employers have consequently been in no position themselves to influence the design and specifications of the educational products they have purchased.

Of course, employers can attempt to learn more about the value of different kinds of educational experience, in much the same way as consumers learn from the experience of using the product. However, such learning is inevitably a lengthy and difficult process. An individual's performance on the job can be very hard to measure and systematic attempts to learn in this way have mainly been confined to very large employers or industry training boards. They have, moreover, mainly concerned themselves with the higher levels of educational attainment. As employers gain more experience of recruiting young people with qualifications to lower-level jobs, they may gradually learn more about the relevance of different kinds of educational attainment to the performance of these jobs. However, to do so they would first have to learn to discriminate between the different kinds of educational attainment, and this implies a deeper knowledge of the educational system.

In the absence of such discrimination, employers have surrendered to educational interests the definition of the criterion of (academic) value which they have used in selecting recruits. If they do not invoke their own standards and criteria to discriminate between different educational qualifications, subjects or syllabuses, they cannot use their position as selectors to establish these standards and criteria within the education system. Indeed, their behaviour has merely reinforced the standards and criteria of the education system. The paradoxical consequence of employers' selection behaviour has been noted in a recent report by the Central Policy Review Staff. The report describes 'a conflict between the explicit statements made by employers and the implicit signals in the way that they select and recruit employees' (Central Policy Review Staff, 1980, p. 4). Employers who claim to prefer the more vocationally orientated courses on offer nevertheless tend to select students from the more academic courses (ibid., p. 5):

> This paradox seems to arise because for most employers general
> intelligence and ability are more important than particular
> knowledge or skills. Educational certificates are indicators both
> of specific knowledge and skills and of general ability levels.
> Employers will give preference to the qualification which attracts
> the ablest candidates even if they would have preferred them to
> study something else. This then is fed back, perversely, to students

as a message that the most popular course is the one best rewarded. The best students continue to choose that course and an enormous bias is created towards preserving the status quo.

Conclusion

Education does not exist in a social vacuum. The links which tie education to other institutions of society are strong and pervasive, and those which link education and the economic order are as strong as any others. Nevertheless, the education system has not been completely determined by economic forces. In this chapter we have tried to show how the structural links between secondary education and selection for employment have been such as to sustain some areas of relative autonomy.

In selecting among a large majority of school-leavers, employers are potentially in a position to exert a considerable informal influence over secondary education, through their ability to stipulate entrance requirements for jobs, or at least to state clear preferences for different kinds of educational qualifications. Yet in this chapter we have seen that the actual influence of employers has been limited: by the influence of the universities, enhanced by the structure of the selection process; by the tendency for young people to underestimate the existing connection between qualifications and jobs (a result in turn of employers' simultaneous use of other selection criteria and of their failure to make explicit their preferences for qualifications); and by employers' use of educationists' criteria (rather than of their own standards and preferences) when assessing the value of qualifications.

It is important to stress the limits to our argument in this chapter. We have demonstrated the relative freedom of secondary education from direct employer influence when this is exerted through just one mechanism, the 'free-market' model. There are many other mechanisms through which the economic order can and does influence education; our discussion has said little about these. Nevertheless, employers' use of qualifications in selection is, if not the only potential channel of influence over education, at least an important one. For structural reasons this channel has not been fully utilised as a means of control; the results can be seen in employers' criticisms of the education system.

The 'Great Debate' of 1976 was noteworthy for at least two things: political discussion invaded the 'secret garden of the curriculum' to an unprecedented extent, and the strongest criticisms were expressed by employers and others who had economic considerations in mind. Although the debate largely focused on secondary education, the universities, which, like employers, had an interest in the calibre of secondary-school leavers, remained largely silent. Perhaps the reason for this, and for the vociferousness of the employment spokesmen, was precisely that the universities did not need to be vociferous. Their influence over secondary education was already well established through the received assumptions and traditions of secondary education; through the incremental policy which gradually extended a university-oriented secondary education to steadily growing minorities of pupils and eventually to the majority; through their formal positions of power and influence; and finally, through those structural aspects of selection in education and employment which we have outlined earlier in this chapter. The employment interests, by contrast, were the most active in the Great Debate. That they needed to be so vociferous is an indication that the education system has been at least partially independent of the economic order.

Chapter 9

Education and Unemployment

Introduction

In chapters 7 and 8 we have spoken mainly of the bond between certification and employment, although it may be apparent from our argument that unemployment, too, has been an important aspect of this bond. In this chapter we turn our attention more directly to the problem of unemployment among young people. We briefly describe the recent increase in youth unemployment, and we chart the incidence of unemployment among the members of the 1977 sample and its relation to school certification. We argue that the respective problems of youth employment and of youth unemployment must be understood in relation to each other. We describe the early experience of the Youth Opportunities Programme (YOP) in Scotland, and its apparent impact on the bond between certification and employment. We suggest that the YOP may have important implications for the link between education and employment.

We have argued in chapters 7 and 8 that when employers have used school qualifications as a criterion for selection they have used them mainly as a source of information about the general academic level of job applicants. This level has been defined by academics and educationists, not by employers; it appears to have correlated only imperfectly with the qualities and abilities which employers have desired in their recruits. To some extent, therefore, qualifications have been used as a selection criterion because of their convenience and their legitimacy, and often for lack of a better alternative. YOP, however, may enable some employers to use additional information, and therefore alternative criteria, when selecting young recruits. The experience of YOP indicates what might happen, if both education and the labour market ceased to be dominated by the single criterion that is represented by 'general academic level'; among other things some of those who currently lose interest in school might have new bases for motivation.

We stress that we are not arguing that YOP, as currently organised, has all (or even most) of the answers to the problems either of education or of the labour market. But we do believe that one may learn from the experience of YOP, both about the nature of these problems, and about ways they might eventually be addressed.

Youth unemployment and the Youth Opportunities Programme

The level of unemployment among young people in general and among school-leavers in particular has been on a rising trend since the mid-1960s. Long-term trends are difficult to determine with precision, because youth unemployment is subject to large seasonal fluctuations. Moreover, the underlying trend was disturbed when the school-leaving age was raised in 1973 and a large number of would-be school-leavers were not released on to the labour market. However, the deterioration was especially sharp in the years after 1973; between July 1974 and July 1977 the number of unemployed 16 to 18-year-olds in Scotland rose from 17,046 to 46,389 (Cochran, 1980, p. 44).[1] After 1977 the numbers dipped slightly, to 41,186 in July 1979, largely as a result of government policies such as YOP. However, the underlying upward trend in youth unemployment continued, and accelerated sharply in 1980. Youth unemployment has continued to be much more sensitive than adult unemployment to the general level of economic activity (Makeham, 1980) and has risen sharply in the current recession. School-leaver unemployment, defined to cover under-18s who have not been employed since school, has been even more sensitive than youth unemployment as a whole to fluctuations in the level of economic activity. Groups most affected by the recent rise in youth unemployment have been the handicapped, girls, residents in areas of high unemployment, members of ethnic minority groups and the educationally unqualified. The sharpest increase has been in long-term unemployment; between July 1974 and July 1977 the number of 16 to 18-year-olds in Scotland who had been out of work for six months or more rose from 625 to 6,835 (Cochran, 1980, p. 44).

In 1977 the Manpower Services Commission (MSC) published the Holland Report, *Young People and Work*. The report surveyed the motley variety of special schemes for unemployed young people that were already in operation and made proposals to rationalise, co-ordinate and expand them. Its proposals were incorporated in YOP which came into operation in April 1978.

At the time of writing, in 1981, YOP provided a variety of schemes of work experience and training for unemployed young people. Schemes were sponsored by firms, local authorities or other (for example, voluntary) organisations. The MSC paid a weekly allowance (£23.50 in 1981) and some travel costs of such participants. The median length of schemes was six months. Most schemes consisted of work experience, most often in employers' premises such as shops, offices or factories, but sometimes on community projects or in specially established training workshops. Other schemes consisted of more explicit forms of training or 'work preparation'.

The programme had a variety of objectives; some of these were left largely unstated, such as reducing the unemployment figures and reducing the political and social disruption arising out of youth unemployment. The main objectives stated by the Holland Report were to help unemployed young people find jobs (and thus to give them a 'competitive edge . . . in the labour market' (Manpower Services Commission, 1977, p.43) compared with older people) and, in the longer term, to lessen the effects of unemployment on the future employability of young people. Most of the means by which these various objectives were to be pursued were to be educational in the broadest sense: the programme should equip its trainees with vocational skills — both specific skills, associated with particular jobs, and the more general skills of coping with the disciplines and demands of any job; and it should aid them in their search for jobs and make them more attractive to potential employers. The Holland Report proposed that the new programme should cater more adequately for those groups of young people who had tended to be overlooked by the earlier schemes; these included the unqualified and the unmotivated. 'Unemployment can easily lead to permanent disadvantage: if those without skill, knowledge or motivation have no opportunity to acquire them, they may well find themselves over the years suitable only for a diminishing range of unskilled jobs' (ibid., p.34).

In its first three years the scale of the programme was largely determined by the government's 'Easter undertaking', that no young person leaving school in 1978 and remaining unemployed at Easter 1979 should be without the offer of a suitable place on the programme. Similar undertakings were made with respect to school-leavers in 1979 and 1980, and a second group, the long-term unemployed, received a similar guarantee. In the first and second years of the programme there were respectively 23,600 and 36,300 entrants in Scotland (Manpower Services Commission, 1979, 1980a); a target of 37,000 was set for the third year (1980-1), but the actual total was more than 49,000. In November 1980 the Secretary of State for Employment announced new policies for the fourth year (1981-2) in which the Easter undertaking was replaced by a new Christmas undertaking, so that school-leavers would have less time to wait before being guaranteed a place on the programme; in 1981-2 entrants in Scotland were (in July 1981) expected to total 70,000. This figure double-counted those young people who would join more than one scheme; around one-fifth of trainees then did so, so the number of individuals entering YOP for the first time in 1981-2 was perhaps going to be around 55,000. These young people nevertheless comprised a large majority of the 73,700 young people expected to enter the labour market directly from school in 1980-1 (Scottish Education Department, 1980a, p.6), and most of them would enter YOP before finding their first job.[2]

Especially for the unqualified, who were the worst affected by unemployment and consequently most likely to enter the programme, YOP was becoming a 'normal' stage in the transition from school to work, catering for a substantially larger proportion of the age-group than is ever likely to attend either full- or part-time further education as currently conceived. As a result of its scale, the potential of YOP is immense, dwarfing all the other schemes proposed for the better training or further education of the 16-19 age-group and especially for the unqualified.[3] Of course, whether this potential can be realised depends not only on the content and design of YOP schemes and especially their educational components, but also on the expectations and motivations of the young people who enter them.

Unemployment and the tightening bond

One should take account of the rise in unemployment in analyses of the tightening bond between education and certification which we discussed in chapter 7. The bond is normally defined in terms of the type of employment of people with different levels of educational qualifications; in analyses of the tightening bond, those who are unemployed tend to be treated as 'missing information' and excluded from the analysis.[4] Their exclusion, we argue, is unjustified and serves only to obscure the relationship between qualifications and labour-market success, for unemployment has been an important aspect of this relationship.

In the first place, unemployment has been very unequally distributed, and those with no educational qualifications have been by far the worst affected. This was especially true of young people, as we saw in chapter 7; unqualified members of the 1977 sample had at least twice the rate of unemployment of any other group. This suggests that educational qualifications were used as a criterion for allocating people to *any* job, not just to skilled and higher-level jobs. Of course, unemployment was a transitional status and nearly all the young people who were unemployed at the time of the survey found jobs sooner or later. However, this does not mean that unemployment can be ignored in an analysis of education and labour-market success; most occupations have also been transitional, in the sense that there has been fairly frequent movement in and out of jobs, especially among young people; and these moves have often entailed substantial changes in occupational level. There is therefore no stronger case for excluding unemployed sample members from analysis than there is for excluding many employed sample members. Moreover, when sample members are excluded from analyses because of 'missing information', it is usually assumed that the excluded cases are randomly distributed, or at least that the remaining cases will still be representative of the population. However, the unemployed are far from typical of employed people, both educationally and also with respect to the kinds of jobs they will eventually find; if we excluded those currently unemployed, we would bias our study against many of those who will gain most of their employment in unskilled or minimally skilled areas of employment.

Second, unemployment has been an important feature of the way that the labour market has worked, especially for young people and especially for the unqualified. Occupational achievement should be seen in dynamic terms, as sequences of jobs and periods of unemployment. The tightening bond between education and occupation has therefore been reflected in the association of educational qualifications with different sequences of employment and unemployment, as well as with different levels of employment. The problems of youth employment and unemployment cannot be viewed in isolation from each other.

The median length of unemployment among young people has usually been shorter than among older people. In the late 1970s, most young people who were unemployed at any one time found work within a few weeks or months, and although the time it took them to find work was rising sharply, it was still shorter than for older people. This does not mean that unemployment was less of a 'problem' among young people than among older people; after all, aggregate unemployment rates were considerably higher among young people, and the corollary of the relatively short duration of unemployment among young people was that a very large proportion of the age-group was affected at some time or other.[5] Youth unemployment has historically been one aspect of a pattern of frequent job-changing; many young people, and especially those with no educational qualifications and those who were not seeking to acquire skills through apprenticeships or training, have spent the first few years of employment in a variety of occupations, rarely staying in one job for very long and with usually brief intervals of unemployment between jobs (Baxter, 1975; Phillips, 1973). However, as jobs became harder to find, these intervals of

149

unemployment became considerably longer and those who were un-employed between jobs were joined by growing numbers of school-leavers still waiting to find their first job.

TABLE 9.1 'How many months, if any, have you spent looking for work, since you left school?' By SCE attainment: summer-term leavers from EA schools in the four regions (mean number of months)

	All labour-market entrants	Unemployed (at time of survey)	Employed (at time of survey)
Boys			
Any Highers passes	1.8	5.5	1.4
5 or more O-grades (A–C)	1.2	5.7	1.0
3–4 O-grades (A–C)	1.4	5.6	1.2
1–2 O-grades (A–C)	1.6	5.2	1.3
D or E awards only	1.9	5.5	1.5
No SCE awards	3.0	6.1	2.0
All boys	2.1	5.8	1.5
Girls			
Any Highers passes	1.3	5.0	1.1
5 or more O-grades (A–C)	1.4	5.1	1.2
3–4 O-grades (A–C)	1.6	5.4	1.4
1–2 O-grades (A–C)	1.6	5.3	1.4
D or E awards only	1.9	5.4	1.4
No SCE awards	2.9	5.8	1.9
All girls	2.0	5.6	1.5

Note: Some respondents reported the total duration of two or more spells of unemployment, so the table does not show the mean length of single spells of unemployment.

The snapshot view of unemployment contained in table 7.1, where we compared the unemployment rate at a given point in time of young people with different SCE attainments, can therefore be complemented by a comparison of the average length of time for which young people had been unemployed. This is given in table 9.1. The table covers only those young people who left school in the summer term of 1976, and who had therefore been out of school for some eight or nine months by the time of the survey. The survey was conducted in 1977, exactly a year before the Youth Opportunities Programme came into operation. The first column describes all entrants to the labour market, whether or not they were employed at the time of the survey. The average leaver had spent about two months looking for work since leaving school. With the exception of Highers-qualified boys, the average length of unemployment varied inversely with the level of certification; it was particularly high among the unqualified. Among those who were currently unemployed, the average duration of unemployment was only very weakly related to qualification level. This may seem surprising but, as we shall see later, a relatively large proportion of the unqualified unemployed had had at least one job (and left it) since school, and this helped to reduce the average duration of unemployment for the unqualified. Among those currently in employment, on the other hand, the unqualified had on average experienced much more unemployment since leaving school (with Highers-qualified boys providing the only exception to the general trend). In other words, unqualified school-leavers were much more likely to have labour-market experiences which combined periods of employment with periods of unemployment.

This is shown in table 9.2, which offers an alternative summary of the first eight or nine months in the labour market of the young people who left school and entered the labour market in summer 1976. The first column shows the school-leavers who were still in their first job when they were surveyed early in 1977. As a proportion of all labour-market entrants, this group ranges from just over half, among the unqualified, to more than three-quarters among the best-qualified O-grade leavers. The second column shows the proportions who were already in their second (or later) job when surveyed; these proportions were much less dependent on SCE attainment, although they were relatively low for boys with O-grade 'passes', probably because many O-grade-qualified boys were on apprenticeships where continuity of employment was more common. The category most strongly related to SCE attainment comprises those who were unemployed at the time of the survey but who had held at least one job since leaving school. They are shown in the fourth column of table 9.2. The fifth category, those who had been continuously unemployed since school (and who alone would count as 'school-leavers' in the official statistics), was also related to SCE attainment, but less strongly. Fewer than one-half of all those who were unemployed at the time of the survey had not had any job since school.

A majority of the unemployed school-leavers in the sample had already had at least one job since leaving school. If we add together columns two and four in table 9.2 we find that one in four of all the summer-term school-leavers in the labour market had had, and left, at least one job; this proportion ranges from less than 20 per cent of the boys with good O-grades to more than 30 per cent of unqualified leavers. We do not know why these 1976 school-leavers left their jobs. However, in a similar survey two years later, 1978 leavers with low qualifications who had left their first jobs by the time of the survey

TABLE 9.2 Experience of employment and unemployment since school, by SCE attainment: percentage of summer-term leavers who entered the labour market from EA schools in the four regions

	Employed at time of survey			Unemployed at time of survey			Total	Unweighted n
	In first job	In second or subsequent job	Number of jobs not known	At least one job since school	No jobs since school	Number of jobs not known		
Boys								
Any Highers passes	71	18	3	4	4	0	100	(999)
5 or more O-grades (A–C)	77	15	4	2	2	0	100	(446)
3–4 O-grades (A–C)	78	13	3	3	3	0	100	(641)
1–2 O-grades (A–C)	70	16	4	6	4	0	100	(1,018)
D or E awards only	67	19	4	6	4	0	100	(402)
No SCE awards	54	18	4	15	9	1	101	(1,225)
All boys	66	17	4	8	5	<0.5	100	(4,731)
Girls								
Any Highers passes	72	20	3	2	3	0	100	(1,067)
5 or more O-grades (A–C)	76	20	1	2	2	0	101	(336)
3–4 O-grades (A–C)	72	21	2	3	2	0	100	(609)
1–2 O-grades (A–C)	73	20	1	3	3	0	100	(886)
D or E awards only	68	18	3	6	6	0	101	(549)
No SCE awards	56	16	2	15	10	1	100	(1,065)
All girls	66	18	2	7	5	<0.5	98	(4,512)

(in 1979) were asked why they had done so. Most young people offered reasons. A majority of those who gave their reasons had left voluntarily, either because they dislike the job (39 per cent) or in order to take up another job (18 per cent). About a quarter left involuntarily, either because their job was terminated (19 per cent) or because they were sacked (7 per cent). The remaining 17 per cent offered various other reasons.[6]

It can be seen from these analyses that youth unemployment and youth employment must be understood in relation to each other, especially as far as the unqualified school-leavers are concerned. About one-half of the young people who were employed at the time of the survey had experienced unemployment. More than half of the young people who were unemployed at the time of the survey had experienced employment. The overlap between employment and unemployment experience was greatest for the unqualified. To understand the problem of youth unemployment we therefore need to understand the factors which influence the movement of young people into *and out of* employment.

This dynamic interrelationship of employment and unemployment was also associated with the quality of employment when it was found. In conditions of high unemployment people seeking work have often had to settle for any jobs they could find, even if the jobs were not in the kind of work they would have preferred. Young people who were employed at the time of the survey were asked: 'Would you have taken this job, if other jobs had been easier to get?' Those who answered 'no' may be said to have settled for 'second best' in their search for jobs. Of course, their answers were probably influenced by a tendency to rationalise retrospectively, especially with respect to matters, such as occupations, which were important to a young person's identity and self-esteem. There was also a tendency for young people to regard their first job favourably, whatever it was, for the first year or so before the novelty wore off. More important, the answers were also subject to the trend (noted in chapter 7) for school-leavers' job aspirations to be realistic in relation to their level of educational attainment. In other words, our measure of second-best jobs is *relative* to aspirations, and many qualified school-leavers may have identified, as second best, jobs which unqualified leavers would have been only too happy to enter.

Young people were much more likely to say they were in second-best jobs the longer they had spent looking for work since leaving school. One-third or less of those who had spent less than a month looking for work were in second-best jobs (29 per cent of boys and 34 per cent of girls), compared with more than half of those who had spent two or more months looking for work (56 per cent of boys and 52 per cent of girls) (the relevant table is not shown). The link between unemployment experience and entering a second-best job was especially strong for better-qualified leavers, perhaps because they were seeking the kinds of jobs which were most likely to discriminate against young people who were unemployed or changing jobs. Overall, however, the better-qualified leavers were less likely to be in second-best jobs; fewer than a third of leavers with five or more O-grades were in such jobs compared with one-half of unqualified leavers. Even allowing for their 'realistically' low aspirations, unqualified leavers were least successful in finding the kinds of jobs for which they were looking.

Youth Opportunities Programme and the tightening bond

How did the Youth Opportunities Programme in its early years affect the bond between certification and employment?

In the first place, YOP clearly influenced the pattern and sequence of labour-market experiences which young people could expect to encounter when they left school. In principle (though not always in practice) each YOP trainee had experienced at least six weeks of unemployment before joining the programme. More than a third of YOP entrants had already had, and left, a job. Some two-thirds of trainees who entered YOP in the first year of the programme found permanent jobs within a few weeks or months of leaving their schemes (Manpower Services Commission, 1980a, p. 7), although this proportion has declined sharply since then.

Second, if YOP was at all successful, it would inevitably have affected the relativities between groups with different educational attainments in terms of their success in the labour market. YOP had little direct effect on the number of permanent jobs available; indeed, a proportion of YOP places, estimated as high as 30 per cent of work-experience places, substituted for permanent jobs. Its main effect may therefore have been to redistribute jobs, either between adults and young people, or between young people with different qualification levels. An evaluation of the programme needs to ask whether any redistribution favoured young people who left school with no qualifications, since a specific objective of the programme was to cater more adequately for the needs of the 'unqualified and least able among unemployed young people' (Manpower Services Commission, 1977, p. 29).

If successful, therefore, YOP would marginally have eroded the differences between the different educational attainment groups, and thus counteracted the tightening bond at least with respect to initial employment. However, its success in this respect was limited by the fact that unemployed young people with SCE qualifications were rather more likely to participate on YOP schemes than unemployed young people with no qualifications (Raffe, 1981a); more than a half of out-of-work young people with O-grades (of bands A–C) were on YOP schemes when surveyed in 1979, compared with just over one-third of those who had not sat O-grades.[7]

Nevertheless, YOP may have been successful in catering for the unqualified, in the special sense that it was more strongly associated with success in finding subsequent employment among non-certificate leavers than among some O-grade leavers. This is suggested by an analysis of the 1979 survey data (Raffe, 1981a). The analysis was restricted to sample members who had either not sat O-grades or who had sat O-grades but not gained any A–C awards. Sample members who had been on YOP schemes were compared with those who had been unemployed but had not been on schemes, to see which group had the higher rate of employment six months later. Among leavers who had sat O-grades (none of whom, as we have said, had A–C awards), those who had been on YOP schemes had only slightly better chances of regular employment than those who had not been on YOP. Among leavers who had not sat O-grades, however, the former YOP trainees were much more likely than the others to have found jobs. Moreover, whereas school-leavers without YOP had a much better chance of employment if they had sat O-grades, among school-leavers who had been on YOP, employment rates were similar for those who had and had not sat O-grades.

Whether, and in what ways, YOP schemes contributed to the future employment of their trainees is an issue which one of us has discussed at greater length elsewhere (Raffe, 1981a, 1981c). To the extent that YOP did contribute to their employment, its effect was to reduce the significance of attempting O-grades, since among the former YOP trainees, those who had sat O-grades were only slightly more likely to find jobs than those who had not sat O-grades. Since, in the study referred to, most of those who had sat O-grades had D or E awards (the first rung up on the qualification ladder), it seems likely that YOP in effect provided employers with a criterion for selecting recruits that was an alternative to low-level educational qualifications. Since (as we argued earlier) any tightening of the bond has probably been in relation to such low-level qualifications, the effect of YOP may have been to resist the tightening of the bond by providing an alternative dimension in terms of which young people could be differentiated and selected.

Youth Opportunities Programme and education

In chapter 8 we suggested that the tightening bond between secondary-education qualifications and jobs had provided employers with a potential channel of influence over schools but that, in practice, this potential influence had not been effectively exerted. The position of employers in relation to YOP has been somewhat different. First, its goals have been explicitly vocational; academic values, and educational interests, have had less influence over YOP than over secondary education. Second, young people were likely to have been aware of these vocational goals; we do not know to what extent young people have perceived a causal connection between YOP and jobs, but it seems likely that, by virtue of making its vocational goals explicit (and by making them the main goals of the programme), YOP has been better able to persuade its trainees of the vocational relevance of its endeavours. Third, many employers have had greater knowledge of YOP schemes than of secondary schools, not least because they have provided some of the schemes themselves. There has been no mystique of educational theory or professionalism to inhibit employers from making their own assessments of the value of schemes in the programme. Employers are consequently likely to have learnt to discriminate between trainees from different schemes. Fourth, by virtue both of the sponsorship system through which it has been organised, and also of its administrative and political separation from conventional educational interests, YOP has been provided and managed by agencies which are less resistant to the declared interests of employment than schools are alleged to be.

As a result, YOP has been more amenable than the secondary-education system to the influence of employers and similar non-educational interests. Those who have castigated the alleged deficiencies of schools have sometimes seen YOP as a remedy. In chapters 7 and 8 we described how employers who used educational qualifications in selecting recruits had had to accept the educational values and criteria which were incorporated in qualifications. We suggested that these values and criteria did not necessarily reflect the employers' own interests. In part 4 of the book we argue that the one-dimensional nature of these values has had serious implications for the motivation of pupils who were less successful in terms of this dimension. YOP, by contrast, has introduced an alternative dimension of evaluation after school. If YOP is perceived as a form of educational provision, then it has brought an element of pluralism into the education system, offering provision with alternative objectives and based on alternative values to those implied by the one-dimensional system of secondary-school certification. This alternative dimension may have been real to some young people too, since it has offered an alternative means by which they might pursue their occupational goals, albeit minimal goals. Young people who have been unsuccessful in school have measured themselves repeatedly against the school's dimension of attainment and have known, long before they left school, that they were going to fail. There have been few reasons for them to continue playing a game which they have seemed unable to win (chapter 10). YOP has provided such young people with an alternative game, success in which has apparently owed little to their former educational experience; YOP, in other words, may have provided an alternative basis for the motivation of young people who have had least reason to be motivated at school.

It is tempting to conclude from this discussion that YOP should be made the main vehicle for all future attempts to extend education among the 16–18 age-group and especially among those who would not expect to receive formal training or education through their work. This prospect seems especially inviting in view of the scale of YOP described at the beginning of this chapter. However, it is a worrying prospect for those who question the educational value of most YOP schemes. At the latest count only 38 per cent of trainees in work-experience schemes received any off-the-job training or further education (Manpower Services Commission, 1980a, p. 12). Moreover, the influence of employers and related interests over the design of YOP is seen by many as a threat to the educational potential of schemes. One of us has elsewhere discussed, not only how YOP may function as an instrument of social control, but also how, in some respects, it was deliberately set up to do so (Raffe 1981c). On the other hand, if the dominant educational interests took over the scheme, would they do any better? We argue at several stages in this book that the current balance of educational interests is not well suited to the education of less academic pupils.

However limited the educational content of YOP may have been, the experience of YOP nevertheless poses a series of questions for the secondary-school system. Can a principle of pluralism with respect to objectives and evaluation be applied to schools themselves? Can the current strategy of schools, which offer prizes for (nearly) everyone, but only in a single competition, be modified to provide new competitions? Those who are destined to fail (relatively) in the present system lack motivation because their realistic chances of bettering their position are limited and the prizes (certificates) which they will receive lack credibility. Might they not be more motivated by an alternative form of competition where their chances were less rigidly predetermined? In other words, should schools devise courses with curricula and assessment based on radically different principles, which pupils who lacked motivation for conventional courses could elect to take instead?

We do not know whether a strategy such as this could be made to work. We do, however, foresee several problems which would first have to be resolved. In the first place, any attempt to differentiate educational provision carries implications for the concept of equality in education, especially if the differentiation tends to correlate with differences in pupils' backgrounds. Is it possible, in principle, to have equality at the same time as differentiation; and, if so, how is equality to be defined and measured? Is it possible to establish parity of esteem among differentiated forms of provision, or would they merely re-introduce older forms of selection in a covert way? Second, the motiv-ating power of YOP is clearly enhanced by two factors which could not be incorporated into secondary education as presently organised: it is not compulsory; and it follows a period of 'unemployment experience' which is bound to affect the motivation and expectations of its trainees. Third, to motivate its 'pupils', it is not sufficient that YOP reflects a different dimension of objectives and evaluation to secondary education; it must also be seen to help them get jobs. An alternative dimension of provision in secondary education must also be seen to have practical occupational value. For this to happen, is it necessary that it should primarily reflect the interests of employers? If so, can it still be educational?

The early history of YOP thus revives some of the issues that were raised in the discussion of the Brunton proposals nearly two decades ago (see Introduction to part 3). It highlights the theme of the balance of influence between economic and 'educational' interests over public educational provision. This theme should not be seen simply as one of choice between competing values in education, for such a choice is constrained by structural factors to do with the nature of assessment and its consequences for post-school selection, the motivation of pupils, and their ability to choose the criteria in terms of which they will be assessed. The experience of YOP appears to confirm our view that employers' use of educational qualifications (especially at the lower levels) has to some extent been arbitrary with respect to their professed interests and preferences, which are imperfectly related to the factors that qualifications actually measure. Does this indicate an area of freedom which secondary schools have in determining their objectives, and which a reformed school system could exploit? Or will programmes like YOP themselves provide the competitive pressure through which this area of freedom is to be restricted, and schools brought more closely into line with economic demands? Finally, if pupils who were experiencing failure at school could all realistically expect a 'second chance' through YOP, would they be motivated to compete for the sorts of certificates that are currently planned for them, for example, at the Foundation (lowest) level in Scotland (chapter 6, Summary and prognosis)? Will YOP, or some sort of guaranteed national traineeship for all school-leavers arising out of YOP, in fact deprive the secondary-school system of the main, extrinsic, source of control that it might otherwise try to exercise over its academically least able pupils?

Part 4

Selection and Rejection

Introduction

The first of the two chapters that follow has been written largely by school-leavers themselves, in that it draws heavily upon their own accounts of their schooling and of, in particular, the consequences for them of selection during their secondary education. The accounts of non-certificate leavers predominate. Chapter 11 then explores mainly quantitative evidence about leavers who had, so to speak, selected themselves out of school by playing truant. Was this a reaction to their schooling and, if so, was it an unreasonable reaction? Or were other factors responsible?

How do these chapters fit into the general argument of the book? We said in part 2 that one of the consequences of the way in which the education system has managed the related structural problems of difficulty, motivation and selection was the extension in the late 1960s and early 1970s to the 'middling' 40 per cent of pupils of an attenuated academic curriculum through the medium of public examinations and certificates. These examinations were, in fact, too difficult for pupils at this level. Part 3 has shown how employers have, nevertheless, made use of certificates to select school-leavers for employment. The extrinsic value placed upon certificates has helped the school system towards a solution to the structural problems mentioned above, but there have been costs none the less. Among these were, first, the exclusion of a substantial minority of pupils in third and fourth year from the dominant reward system of the school and, second, the restriction of the schools' capacity to develop alternative curricula and methods.

The consequent experience of such pupils should therefore be regarded as one source of possibly disconfirming evidence about the expectations and assumptions underlying expanded provision. But these very assumptions have also sustained the selective production of

161

public information about the education system in a way that has filtered the experience of failing pupils out of the public account. Official statistics on school-leavers focused for many years mainly on 'qualified' school-leavers, whose abilities and skills would, it was antici-pated, expand the national supply of trained manpower and create new wealth for further expansion. In Scotland at least, the modifications of the official school-leavers' survey in the later 1970s, which resulted from our programme of collaborative research, began to redress this imbalance. It became possible regularly to evaluate the experience of all leavers within a common survey research approach, although, even then, the methods that were used to some extent still failed adequately to represent the experiences of unsuccessful school pupils and leavers (McPherson and Raffe, 1978).

Truancy also presents a challenge to the expansionist perspective, indicating as it does that not all pupils are convinced of the value of schooling for themselves. Chapter 11 describes the incidence of truancy in Scotland, showing that it was a more extensive phenomenon than was commonly supposed, and arguing against attempts to discount the relevance of extensive school absence to evaluations of the strategy by which the problems of difficulty, motivation and selection were managed.

Chapter 10

Pupils' Experiences of Selection

Introduction

We have argued that planned and unplanned changes in the last two decades have produced a situation in which schools themselves have had to adjudicate and reconcile unresolved issues of value, often by using informal methods of selection and differentiation with little external guidance, scrutiny or standardisation. Who should be educated, in what sort of curriculum, by which methods, for how long, and with what promise of success? We return now to an exploration of some of the ways in which the schools have addressed these questions, but we use a rather different method from that adopted in part 2. In this chapter we tell the story mainly using a selection of the accounts written by the leavers themselves about their time at school.[1] Then, towards the end, we briefly set these against a more systematic and quantified perspective on how schools have differentiated pupils and on how pupils themselves have reacted. Both types of evidence, we argue, must be admitted to any overall judgment of the school system.

Selection after second year

We said in part 2 that the incremental extension of academic certification since the 1950s, allied to a historically rooted reluctance among Scottish teachers to withhold from pupils the opportunity to compete for certification, has resulted in a situation in which pupils and courses are now judged overwhelmingly in terms of criteria and standards derived primarily from the university curriculum. Also, we have talked in chapter 5 of a process of selection which entirely rejected a minority of pupils from O-grade course work in third year and which thereafter operated continuously upon the courses of the remainder through school examinations, 'prelims', 'mock SCEs' and the O-grade examination itself. We said that the curricula of the majority of pupils were sooner or later affected by this attrition, in third or fourth year if they were less able, or in fifth year if they were among the most able third of pupils.

How were the dominant values of school perceived by some of the pupils involved? This girl left school to study social sciences at university:

> Although I realise what the teacher has to cope with, each teacher could be more concerned with the pupil rather than the pupils attainments, without detracting from what she teaches or from what is being learned. Most of our teachers concentrated on bright pupils, encouraging them which is wrong because bright people get on fine without help, while the less able pupils get moved into a lower non-certificate class and the attitude was, 'we only have to put up with them until they reach SLA, we'll just keep them occupied until then,' with no care about preparing them for life outside school in any way.

But it was not only the budding student of social science who saw matters in this way. This boy worked for the O-grade examination in four of his subjects, leaving school after fourth year to go into the mines:

> In my school, and many others I believe, there are two different 'classes' of pupils . . . the '2nd class' of pupils is people like myself, who like to get on well at school but cant be bothered with work at home, and [there is] the intellectual pupil, who shows off his outstanding 'IQ' to all other 'not so bright' pupils. . . . SOME teachers are the main reason why pupils are embarrased to answer questions in class in case they are quietly laughed at by the 'Intellectuals', and also to work for future exams, (I will write later on, on this page about my plight on this subject). Most teachers love attending to, and helping the 'brainy' pupil and can't be really bothered with the ones that need more help, although the teachers will testify to the exact opposite. . . . the more school went on, the more the teachers made it unbearable for you, as this is shown in the classes I was in. This 'slump' from 1st year in my case, was due to being sick and tired of the treatment, and attitude of teachers towards you, and this resulted in my own 'slump' in attitude towards my own work, and confidence in doing so. . . I never bothered to attend 2 exams because I lost all confidence in myself leading up to the exams because of teachers continually saying things like, 'You'll never do', 'useless', 'thick', and other words, never uttered to an intellectual.

Another boy, who took O-grades and then started an engineering apprenticeship, put it more succinctly: 'School is still geared to the academically minded child and some teachers think the rest are all nit-wits! The chosen few are still catered for.' Indeed, because the 1977 survey had adjusted the level and content of the questionnaires in advance to the certification level of the leaver (see chapter 2), it was seen by some respondents as having itself accepted uncritically the judgments of pupils that school had made:

> Firstly I would like to say that some of the questions asked require only a yes or no answer but I feel that some of them need more explanation. . . . Also I think that some of the questions are put in such a way that a ten year old could understand rather than a seventeen year old, because this reminds me of the way I was treated at school. At Secondary school, I would like to see more pupils treated as individuals rather than being just recognised by their grades or ability.

The girl who wrote this was working on an assembly line. She had been in a non-certificate class at school.

Leavers at all levels, therefore, and leavers with different types of experience both at school and afterwards, volunteered similar observations on the dominant values their schools had used in judging and selecting their pupils. What was the initial impact of selection on the pupils themselves? This girl eventually took Highers and went into nursing:

> When I look back to when I was at school I feel we were influenced by how clever or bright we were. In the first year we were divided into any class not depending on our IQ or intelligence from our primary schools. Though our marks in Exam's in 1st year, we(re) put together and from there we were put in classes for 2nd year. The best marks being class 2A. I for one was in class 2A, and we were all called the 'brainy lot'.

And this non-certificate boy, who later became an apprentice turner, said: 'In my last year at school I was in a class which wasn't sitting O levels. The reason for me being in that class was because I didn't get a good mark for my 1st year French Exam so I was put into that non O grade class.'

In other words, differentiations were sometimes formalised during the first two years of secondary schooling, the years that had been ear-marked for a largely undifferentiated common course under the policy for comprehensive reorganisation (see chapter 13). There was also some informal differentiation (Ryrie, Furst and Lauder, 1979). For most pupils, however, the first formal selection that affected a majority of school subjects was made with the selection of pupils for certificate and non-certificate courses at the end of second year, and it often had major consequences:

> After my second year at school my class was just thrown aside.
> As we did not qualifie for O levels. So it was just a case of to hell
> with yous. In my opinion this was to push the O level pupils on.
> And from 3rd year on it was part-time education. We could sit in
> a arithmetic class and end up writing a stupid essay because the
> arithmetic teacher had to take an O level class while we had a PE
> teacher. As for guidance we sometimes got the odd film, but usually
> ended up playing football or some other game, because teacher
> was to busy. Our last year and a half school was made up mostly
> of metal work, woodwork, PE & Art. We would go into school in
> the morning and get sent home 2 hours later. Out of all the last
> year & half you could have put what we where taught into three
> months.

For this pupil at least, a non-certificate boy who worked afterwards as a venetian-blind fitter, the raising of the school-leaving age had not effectively increased the amount of education he was offered. It had only extended the period during which he was subject to what he saw as pointless compulsion. And so it was with pupil after pupil.

Several short accounts must suffice to illustrate the bitter sense of rejection that so many non-certificate pupils expressed over the lack of regard in which they felt they were held by their schools after second year. This, for example, was how the apprentice turner (above) saw the consequences of his poor mark in French in first year:

> I think the teachers could have learnt the class I was in a lot more
> than they did when I was in my 3rd year some teachers couldn't
> be bothered teaching the class anything so they told us to play
> cards in the classroom or go outside to play football. Some teachers
> didn't like our class behaviour I dont blame them but if they hadn't
> put us in a non O Grade class they wouldn't behave like this in class.

A girl who became an apprentice book-binder told us: 'At our school we were put into groups one's who can sit there O grades and one's who can't which is unfair. The one's who did not sit there O Grades the teachers never Botherd to learn them anything.' A girl who became a sewing machinist said: 'I didn't like the way a lot of the teacher's ignored us, well our two classes that were not O grade classes.'

About 20 per cent of pupils were excluded entirely from certificate work at the beginning of their third year and a further 10 per cent or so acquired the non-certificate label over the following two years as they withdrew from work for O-grade presentation, or were excluded from it (figure 8.1). It seems unlikely that many pupils recommenced work for the O-grade once they had been left behind. Few Scottish schools by the mid-1970s provided the 'bridge' that CSE courses might have offered in some subjects; and some schools were thought by pupils to be too ready to consign non-certificate classes to what pupils saw as the irredeemable status of 'remedial'. A non-certificate boy who became an engineering tracer and entered a college of further education to study for O-grades and Highers said:

I feel that the whole system of education in Scotland is a complete failure due to the lack of interest in pupils from members of staff. In my eyes they were only interested in the already bright pupils and were not prepared to really try and help the unfortunate less bright ones, instead they made massive classes of outcasts or as they would call them remedials. I spend my last term in a class without a teacher along with another twenty or so doing nothing at all. . . . It was clear that the school wasn't interested in us.

Once established, the labels were often confirmed in use by teacher and pupil alike: 'I wouldn't go to school as the class I was in well it was filth and nothing else, but I went and decided to work my way up (headmaster said, work hard and get your own standard). I did for about 2 or 3 months, nothing. Science teacher told me "you won't be going back up", "once your down you stay down". which was true.' This non-certificate girl added that 'teachers tend to under estimate pupils. I'm quite intelligent really but you just don't get a chance to show what you can do.' Nevertheless she regarded her non-certificate class as 'filth'. This is how a non-certificate boy found that a label stuck:

Teachers could make it more usefull by treating us with more respect than just the common thicky. They could have also got rid of the remedial classes for these people are intelligent but just never got the chance to prove themselves. I was one but I got an understanding teacher and he gave me a chance so I was moved into an O level english class but I was ignored because I was remedial. Pretty soon I was back in my old class not because I could not do the work but because of the atmosphere that was set of(f) by the other pupils. So you see, if there was no such thing as a remedial class, then there would have been no such thing as the common thicky.

These, then, were pupils who tried to resist the implications of the initial judgments their school had passed on them. Others, however, accepted the label, but put their own evaluation on it. This non-certificate pupil eventually worked as a van boy:

> When I was at school I was known as one of the class rowdies after
> your second year teachers didn't want to know you because they
> couldn't handle you. My last year at school I was put into a class
> entitled May leavers. It consisted of pupils who were not sitting
> exams so instead of trying to help us they put us all together and
> formed what they called ML and what we called the Rowdies.
> Once in this class there was nothing you could do you couldn't
> start behaving because you were branded and that was you teachers
> just didn't want to know you.

A future clerk also thought that escape was impossible, in this case as a
result of coercion by fellow pupils:

> the school I was at is one of the toughest in . . . and the teachers
> are too soft. You found it hard to study when there was a load
> of evil lads around. Depending on the the the class, some you could
> work in (although I always had a laugh anywhere) some you
> couldn't (I never had laugh in them). The teacher was so soft in
> my arithmetic class every week was games. But you couldn't ask
> for a move because if the rest of the class found out you were for it.

This particular boy had taken O-grades in several subjects, although he
did not achieve any awards at A–C. Others on the margins of the
chosen group in a school encountered other difficulties in combining
certificate-course work in some subjects with non-certificate classes
in others:

> School was alright in my last year but I very seldom went as I
> found not very much interest was put into it and it was a bit of a
> waist of time in most classes I sat and done nothing and after sitting
> doing nothing it takes away your concentration for your next class
> where work had to be done.

The last compulsory year

The size and membership of the non-certificate group in a school
appears to have been established, therefore, partly by formal processes
of selection, and partly by informal processes, including self-selection
and coercion, that continued to operate after second year as they
confirmed and extended the logic of the initial selection. That logic
stated that value lay in academic certificates and that, measured against
this criterion, certain pupils were not worth much. The subsequent
teaching of such pupils could therefore quite logically become a matter
of empty ritual. This was how one girl described the situation that had
arisen by fourth year:

I did not like my last year at school at all. Those who were doing a non-certificate course were asked to sit in a class with a book opened at any page at all and pretend to be reading in case the head-master or someone like that would come into the room. If you were not interested in O-levels then the teachers couldn't be bothered with you.

A panel-beater from another school said:

Well about my last year at school it was virtually a waste of time going because there was not all that many members in the class 8 people to be precise. Very often a few members would not turn up and the teachers did not think it worth while teaching the class. I think it would have been much better if we had not been branded as being thick and not worth bothering about.

Elements both of ritualistic teaching and of truanting, by pupils and teachers alike, appear in this next account:

Well to tell you the truth about the last year at school I hated the whole lot of it because every class we went into the majority of the teachers would be their about 5-10 minutes then go off and leave us until about 5 minutes before our two periods were up. And it was very boring and thats why in the last year I and my friend played truant. The teachers could have made it more useful if they were in the class teaching us instead of leaving us an exercise to do which never got done because they never asked for it when they came back.

Sometimes pupils and teachers struck an implicit bargain over how to cope with the logic of their situation. A nursery assistant had found that:

we more or less spent our time sitting our-selves, in classrooms or in the Cloakroom. I did not like that at all. The teachers done their best but that wasn't much help we all wanted to leave and look for work, some teachers even told us *although not in so many words* that we were all just wasting our time and their time. (Our emphasis.)

In this boy's school, however, the bargain was explicit: 'We just went to our subjects and were told by teachers, "Do something to ocupie yourself," consisting of talking, laughing around and often playing cards.' The bargain could go further and apply outside the classroom and even outside the school. This non-certificate girl truanted 'a lesson here and there': 'I felt that in the last year at school the teachers did not bother about you if you were not taking O levels eg. (they know we played truant and never sayed anything to us about it).' And a girl at another school wrote:

It was right boring. There was hardly anybody there as the year went on more and more people would stay of they didnt bother getting us back again you could walk pass a teacher in the street and say "hello" they would just return the remark and just walk past.

Many fourth-year pupils still had expectations that made them resent what they saw as the connivance and indifference of some of their teachers:

The last year at school was terrible. We would go into a class and the teachers might not even come in so we were left there by ourselves. Nothing to do. Sometimes the teachers would come in and say I have some correcting to do, Well that wasn't teaching us anything.

But others had abandoned any assumption that their school owed them anything in return for the compulsion to which they were subject. One leaver, for example, absolved teachers who corrected other classes' work, rather than provide teaching for her own class, with the comment that teachers 'had their own work to do'.

The school's judgment, nevertheless, often bit deep:

My teachers made me feel thick really stupid so I did not bother to study, they made me feel as if it was not worth my while thinking of what I wanted to be . . . so I shall never forget my teachers and how they made me feel. . . . I dont think my teachers meant to be like this.

And here is another girl of no account, acknowledging the school's judgment of her, and yet struggling at the same time to assert her worth ('just like other people'):

I was a girl that was not very good at my work. We were all put into a group and forgoten. there was no hope for us. but there is we can all work. My two little sisters are the same. (forgoten children) Help them please. they need help I hope they can do something for them. . . . I have been interviewed by millions of people and not yet got a job. We school leavers all have to started somewhere just like other people. (School. Forgoten children). (Her parentheses.)

Pupils such as this were demoralised in two senses: first, they had lost confidence and their enthusiasm for school work had slumped. But they were also demoralised, in that they felt that value had been taken from them; they were no longer members of the moral community of the school. Many such pupils felt that their views were no longer regarded, that they could no longer legitimately give an account of themselves to their teachers by bringing their own story into the discourse of the school. They did not figure in its morality tale. This pupil, for example, saw the curriculum as coercive, for it meant that only certain sorts of talk were admissible:

> the teachers gave you a book which you were to answer the
> questions, and that was it, never any class discussions about what
> we would like to do or what we did do outside school. I think
> when you go into a class and there's a different teacher he should
> talk to us more like an adult they always said we should act. He
> or she should tell us about themselves what they do when at school
> and when not at school and he should ask us individualy what
> we do.

Another wrote, 'the only thing in my point of view to help pupils now is the teachers listen to the children's views, and realise how STRONG the pupils feel'.

As we have seen, when the May leavers had found themselves demoralised in this second sense ('the teachers just didn't want to know you') and when they had seen this situation as irretrievable ('you were branded and that was you'), they had started to tell their own story about themselves: 'what they called ML *and what we called the Rowdies*' (our emphasis). The Pack Committee (Scottish Education Department, 1977c) thought it important to go beyond a strict interpretation of its remit and to discuss the relevance of curriculum to the questions of truancy and indiscipline. Many non-certificate pupils themselves made such a connection; and they also saw the prevalent Scottish practice of belting or strapping as directly related to coercion in the curriculum and to the demoralised status of non-certificate pupils after second year. Some pupils, again, made their own morality out of this situation: 'I remember in my class boys would have compitions who could get belted the most within a week'; but many more remembered it with bitterness and hostility: 'To them you were shit, and they pushed you around a lot. When I got the belt it did not cure me.' Another non-certificate boy wrote:

> I did not like the teacher so we picked on him then I got expelled
> for fighting with him and refusing the belt. My own fult. Thasts
> why me and my mates went to school to cause trouble cos we
> did not like teachers. They teachers could of treated us like peapole
> instead of animals. I have called all sorts of names by the teachers
> included a Bastard.

Expulsion was not, however, the only way in which schools dealt with a polarising situation:

I was discouraged from staying on at school by some of the teachers. They said I was anti-social and I should leave at Christmas. I was not sixteen till January. therefore I could not get any unemployment payment for over a month. I had no money at all. When I went for interviews they would not concider me because I was only fifteen at that time. I think it is wrong for teachers to be able to tell you to leave school when you are fifteen. I now wish I had been able to stay on at school and finish off the O grade courses I had begun to study. I was taking five O grades and I was going to stay on but opted out of school before the O grades were given out.

This girl eventually found employment in a bakery.

Selection within the certificate population

We have focused so far mainly on the processes by which pupils were selected, or selected themselves, into non-certificate courses and classes and then ended their effective education at, or often well before, the summer of their fourth year. We have done so for several reasons. First, the creation of 'massive classes of outcasts' in third year itself stimulated or reinforced other behaviours (truancy, indiscipline, demoralisation) that informally continued the processes of selection and that then provided the occasion for further formal exclusions (from school itself, or perhaps from whatever O-grade classes had been commenced). Second, much of this experience was grimly predictable. If the O-grade were indeed set at a standard at which 30 per cent of the age-group might have 'a reasonable prospect' of attaining three A–C awards, then many more would attain one such award and more again could reasonably expect to be prepared for the examination.[2] In 1976 the percentage attaining at least one A–C award was 56; 69 per cent presented at least one O-grade subject and 78 per cent had started on O-grade work in their third year (chapter 8). The position of the remaining pupils, the non-certificate minority, has become more invidious as the proportion of pupils involved in certificate-course work has increased over time. Also, as 'outsiders' whom the school must nevertheless formally attempt to retain in third and fourth year, non-certificate pupils were perhaps well placed to pronounce on the main dimension of value by which schools differentiated and judged their pupils.

Nevertheless, the line that divided the certificate from the non-certificate pupil was not the only line to be drawn. Non-certificate pupils tended to see selection in dichotomous terms: 'ones who can sit there O grades, and ones who can't'. This, however, was how matters were seen by a girl who took O-grades, though who failed to achieve any A-C awards. She talked about pupils who were 'thrown to the back of the class and forgotten about' and said: 'One thing I'll always remmember is the more O grades a pupil was sitting the more interested the teachers were in helping you' (but see Williams, 1978). An apprentice plasterer who did achieve certification with awards in the A-C bands wrote: 'Non-academic people like myself feel like second class citizens at school.' Similar sorts of feelings were expressed by some Highers pupils. A computer operator said: 'Too much emphasis was put on going to university at my school, when the careers teacher discovered I did not want to go to university, or college, he never gave me a second thought'; and a student of commerce in further education wrote: 'I think that in my school teachers had no interest in "middle of the road" pupils and where only interested in pupils that were going to universities.'

For such pupils (Highers pupils who had ruled out university entrance), the related curricular differentiation was not so much to do with whether there was a taught curriculum, as with its composition. A student nurse remembered:

> When deciding our subjects for 3rd year it was all accepted that
> 2A should take latin, physics, chemistry etc. . . . It was expected
> that a large majority of our class should go to University. I
> personally had no wish to go to University. . . . I always remember
> some teachers shocked that I was the only one in my class not
> taking physics and chemistry, but taking secretarial studies and
> biology. . . . I found we were never advised about our future at all.
> If you were above average in our school you took Latin, Physics
> and Chemistry if you were below average, like most girls took
> Food and Nutrition.

At another school, a girl who became a student teacher had a similar experience:

> One thing I regret about my secondary education is the fact that
> I was in a class with others who were labelled as 'academic pupils',
> with the result that in my second year, whilst others were given
> secretarial studies or food and nutrition, I was given German. I
> then felt that because I had started the subject, I may as well carry
> it on. . . . All in all I feel any help I did receive were very fragmented
> and I think more help should be given to pupils further down the
> secondary school, because it is then that they have to choose
> subjects — which is tantamount to choosing their career.

We have already seen how academic selection operated partly through the choice of examination subjects (chapter 5) and how a hierarchy among subjects was tacitly recognised by employers (chapter 7). To

TABLE 10.1 Selected opinions and experiences by SCE presentation level: percentage of leavers from EA schools in the four regions

	Boys			Girls		
	Highers	O-grade	non-SCE	Highers	O-grade	non-SCE
How much did your teacher help you:						
to do as well as you could in your exams or studies[1] (Percentage answering 'a lot' or 'quite a lot')	87	74	51	87	76	50
to learn things that would be useful to you in a job (Percentage answering 'a lot' or 'quite a lot')	25	38	30	32	43	33
to learn about different sorts of jobs and careers so you could decide what to do (Percentage answering 'a lot' or 'quite a lot')	32	44	34	36	48	35
Did you ever get the belt, strap, or other form of corporal punishment at secondary school (Percentage answering 'often' or 'quite often')	22	50	61	2	14	25
On the whole, do you feel your last year at school was worthwhile (Percentage answering yes)	73	52	23	76	52	22
On the whole, would you say you enjoyed your last year at school (Percentage answering yes)	80	62	44	78	70	48

Notes: 1 In the non-certificate version the question referred to 'lessons' and not to 'exams or studies'.
All percentages are based on at least 500 unweighted cases.

finish with a Highers pupil who entered the civil service as a clerical officer: 'The feeling of suffocation I felt in sitting my prelims was almost unbearable. One minute I was happy as a lark the next I was told I was about to take the first big step of my life.'

Some correlates of selection

Table 10.1 shows the answers given to six questions by three groups of leavers, namely non-certificate leavers, those who attempted at least one O-grade examination (but not Highers), and those who attempted Highers examinations. Two of the questions relate to the leavers' last year of education and four to experiences that were not year-specific. Under a quarter of non-certificate leavers thought their last year had been 'worthwhile', compared with roughly half of the O-grade leavers and three-quarters of the Highers leavers.[3] Smaller proportions of non-certificate leavers than other leavers had 'enjoyed' their last year, and the differentiation between the three levels of pupils was again quite marked. Fewer non-certificate leavers than other leavers thought they had been helped to do as well as they could in their examinations or studies; and fewer non-certificate than O-grade leavers thought they had been helped in relation to learning about employment. A higher proportion of non-certificate boys than of other boys had been belted 'quite often' or 'often' during their secondary schooling and the proportion of non-certificate girls was also higher than for other girls. Indeed, all but 3 per cent of the non-certificate boys and all but 18 per cent of the non-certificate girls reported that they had been belted at least once while at secondary school (not shown in table).

These figures do not tell us about the processes of selection in secondary school, but they do give us a perspective on the consequences of selection for the way pupils were treated, and for the way they then evaluated themselves and their schooling. In part, this differential treatment was itself a consequence of the system of values within which schools worked. Of course, it was easier for teachers to help pupils who were candidates for public examinations with their 'lessons or studies'; and in a system that converted the currency of public examinations into jobs, it was easier for schools to help the pupils who were candidates for public examinations to find out about jobs for which they might be suited by virtue of their certificate work. As one candidate who eventually achieved only D and E grades remembered: 'They always reminded us about not taking O grades, and how hard it would be for the ones who didn't take O grades to get jobs.' But it would, we think, be difficult to justify the inferior treatment that non-certificate pupils felt they had received simply by reference to the fact that some of it

175

was institutionalised in the certification system and in the relation of certification to employment.

Conclusion

We argued in part 2 that the public account of Scottish education could be maintained logically in its two forms, as an explanation of the system and as a statement or celebration of its moral values, only for as long as it was tested against an incomplete body of evidence. In effect, it could continue to command assent only by disregarding the experience of large numbers of children, the children of no account. This chapter has described some of the processes by which some such children have become 'demoralised', have been excluded from the moral community of the school and have been diminished in confidence and self-respect. This process of demoralisation has helped to maintain the public account, for it has removed from public attention the very children whose example and experience might have stretched the account's correspondence with events to a point where its credibility would be lost. In the past such demoralised children removed themselves from school at the earliest opportunity, but, since the raising of the school-leaving age and comprehensive reorganisation, their continuing presence and example have proved a continuing challenge in a moral, theoretical and practical sense. The point of this chapter is not simply to document the confusion, disbelief and despair that so many non-certificate pupils have felt about the last two years of their secondary schooling. It is partly also to show that, to differing degrees and in differing ways, such pupils have reflected on and interpreted their experience, and have also sometimes acted on it. An adequate account of secondary schooling cannot afford to discount as evidence this body of experience, reflection and action; and, indeed, in its interpretative aspect alone, there is clearly much to be learned from it. We develop and generalise this argument in our discussion of the politics and methods of social research in chapter 17.

Ultimately, however, the moral, theoretical and practical arguments for paying attention to the views and experience of all children converge on one another. In practical terms the teacher who is accountable to his or her class and is prepared to discuss pupils' perspectives on how and why they should or should not approach the learning that is offered to them, is engaging in a process of negotiation that may itself be educational. It is also to offer pupils the respect of adult treatment and regard that so many complain was lacking. Negotiation implies, of course, that the authority of the teacher and of the curriculum is put at risk; that moves to help pupils towards a wider understanding of their position in the education system and of the system's position in wider society, would loosen controls that rely on the twofold process of demoralisation that we have described. It is surely, however, both practical and moral to regard pupils as educable and to regard the ability to understand one's social situation as part of being educated. Clearly, also, it is a contradiction of morality to exclude certain pupils from the moral community of the school on the grounds that they do not measure up to the dominant value of certified academic success. It is clearly a contradiction of the idea of science to discount as evidence the experience of pupils that might cast doubt on a received account; and it is also a contradiction of science to exclude from public consideration and testing the theories and explanations that participants in a situation themselves have to offer, whether or not they fully appreciate the potential explanatory force of their beliefs. This is not to argue that the pupil's view is necessarily correct; nor to argue that rival explanations can easily be stated in such a way that data on pupils' experiences then allow one to choose decisively between them. But it is to argue for a greater catholicity of inclusion with respect both to the arguments that are canvassed and with respect to the persons that are admitted to the argument. And it is to warn against the perspective that would discount certain sorts of pupils or behaviours, on the grounds that, being beyond the pale of the moral community, they are irrelevant to an assessment of the public account. We develop this point in the discussion of truancy that follows, and we formalise it in our final two chapters.

Chapter 11

Truancy: Rejection is Mutual

Introduction

Most British research has seen the school system as playing an essentially passive role in the development of truancy: after all, schooling is something that all pupils share, but not all pupils play truant. The research has tended to focus instead on the supposed pathology of the families and family backgrounds of persistent truants, and especially of those who have been identified and treated as such by the various legal, social, medical and educational agencies that process pupils regarded as problem children. Using the 1977 survey data, we argue in this chapter that the phenomenon of truancy cannot be explained solely in terms of the pathology of individuals and families, quite simply because it has been so widespread. We then show that the patterning of this phenomenon has, nevertheless, corresponded to that which is predicted by explanations couched in terms of individual and family pathology. Next we show that this patterning could, in its turn, largely be explained statistically in terms of the different effects of the school system on different pupils. In particular the data reveal that the pupils who truanted most frequently tended to be those pupils who were excluded from work for certification; the pupils who were rejected tended, in turn, to reject school. We argue that it is dangerous and misleading to discount the role of the school system itself in the promotion of truancy. Selection in third and fourth year has been one of the ways in which the school system has attempted to manage unresolved issues of difficulty and motivation (part 2) and it has given different pupils different experiences of schooling. It is therefore possible to see the scale and patterning of truancy as evidence that forces us to acknowledge limits to the application of the theory concerning the potency of education that has underpinned educational expansion in general (chapter 1) and the incrementalist strategy for certification in particular (chapter 4). Where that theory cannot be applied, it may be rational for pupils to truant and for teachers to connive. The pathology may be systemic, however much it may also be individual.

The Pack Report

Most people, argued the Pack Report on *Truancy and Indiscipline in Schools in Scotland*, have a 'working definition' of truancy; but 'such definitions [are] not formulated on a common basis'. The committee therefore framed the following definition: 'Truancy is unauthorised absence from school, for any period, as a result of premeditated or spontaneous action on the part of pupil, parent or both' (Scottish Education Department, 1977c, para. 2.17). It also conducted a survey of attendance in 55 Scottish secondary schools involving some 40,000 pupils over a six-week period in January–February 1976. Class teachers were given the committee's definition of truancy and were asked to record how many of each child's recorded absences were 'satisfactorily explained'. About 9 per cent of first-year boys and 7 per cent of first-year girls were absent without 'satisfactory' explanations at some period during the survey. Among third-year pupils the figures were 18 and 17 per cent respectively; and among fourth-year pupils they were about 25 per cent for each sex.

The committee identified three main types of causes: those arising from the general social attitudes of the public; those arising from characteristics of the child's family background; and those arising from characteristics of the school attended (para. 2.36). On family circumstances it suggested that '[w]hat emerges from the Evidence about those children whose truancy is high is the dominance of the effect of family circumstances on their behaviour' (para. 2.38); and on factors associated with the school, it remarked that '[p]ractically all our discussions of truancy and indiscipline, and almost all of the Evidence, eventually came to examine what goes on in our schools' (para. 4.30). The committee also decided to 'discover how children viewed the main causes of truancy'. It found that pupils emphasised the part played by the school (para. 2.33):

> On the whole . . . the information gathered (mainly from known truants and secondary schools with high truancy rates) indicated that the children saw the causes of truancy as fairly well rooted in the school. . . . Questionnaires put to classes of secondary school children (not all of whom were truants) showed that they attributed truancy to boredom with school work, difficulty with school work, dislike of a particular subject, and conflict with some teachers.

179

The committee continued, however (para. 2.35):

> [s]ome children seem bored with everything, but boredom often
> turns out to be symptomatic of home factors that are unsatisfactory
> or of a general feeling of inadequacy. . . . All the Evidence taken
> from children, including conversations with classes during the
> Committee's visits to schools, confirmed what we know very well
> to be true — that children's dislikes in school, such as those listed
> above and named as causes of truancy, are not experienced only
> by those who play truant . . . serious truancy is usually induced
> by a 'clustering' of factors . . . several. . . [of which] originate
> outside the school, but add to the pressures felt at school by
> the child.

The incidence of truancy

What is one attempting to explain in research on truancy? If it is the
behaviour of a small minority of pupils (say 1 or 2 per cent), then it
is perhaps easier to see how a conventional wisdom regarding exceptional
family circumstances might emerge; and also how remedies might be
sought through agencies charged with a responsibility for handling
problem pupils and their families. On the other hand, if it is the
behaviour of at least a quarter of pupils in their fourth and final compulsory year of secondary schooling (and possibly, as we show later,
more than half), such solutions begin to break down, on purely practical
grounds if nothing else. If the solutions themselves seem impossible are
the explanations any more adequate?

How widespread is truancy? The answer to this question depends
partly on the definition of terms, but it is also affected by the methods
that are used. One of three starting-points is typically adopted: the
attendance register; teachers' estimates; or pupils' self-reports. Occasion-
ally two of these approaches are combined. Each, none the less, has its
problems. However, if one asks about primary-school children or
children who are in the first or second year of secondary schooling,
then estimates from attendance registers and from teachers indicate
no more than 1 or 2 per cent of pupils. With older children, on the
other hand, a divergent picture emerges. Estimates from attendance
registers suggest figures around 4 or 5 per cent of pupils (Carroll,
1977). However, several researchers (May, 1975; Tibbenham, 1977;
and Rutter *et al.*, 1979) report considerable discrepancies between
the estimates of persistent absentees on the basis of recorded school
attendance and estimates based on teachers' reports or on pupils'
reports about fellow pupils. Generally, the attendance register gives

lower estimates. This suggests either that secondary-school teachers and pupils do not have a very accurate picture of who is persistently absent or that attendance registers pick up only a part of truancy (missing out, for example, pupils who register and then leave), or both.

Asking pupils themselves how frequently they truant is the least common of the three approaches. If circumstances can be created in which pupils will be honest, self-reports can offer an important perspective. However, no 'official' survey to date has used self-reports and only a handful of researchers have done so (for example, Belson, 1975; Fogelman, 1976; Rutter *et al.*, 1979). In the 1977 survey we asked: 'Did you ever play truant in your fourth year at school?' There were five response categories: 'never', 'a lesson here and there', 'a day here and there', 'several days at a time', and 'weeks at a time'. A separate investigation of this question indicated that respondents tended to share a common view of what constituted truancy and to apply that view with honesty when replying (Cope and Gray, 1978).

Section (a) of table 11.1 shows the leavers' responses to the question on truancy. Some 63 per cent of leavers reported that they had truanted at some point during their fourth year at school. But the extent of truancy varied: 6 per cent of the sample said they had truanted 'weeks at a time'; 7 per cent reported 'several days at a time'; 24 per cent reported 'a day here and there'; and 26 per cent reported 'a lesson here and there'.

If we return to our earlier question about the incidence of truancy, it is clear that several answers are possible. If we adopt Pack's initial definition ('truancy is unauthorised absence from school, for any period'), then for fourth-year pupils the answers might range from 25 per cent (the 'unexplained absences' over the six-week period of the Pack survey) to 37 per cent (those admitting to a 'day here and there', 'several days at a time' or 'weeks at a time' over their fourth year in the 1977 survey). Indeed, if we also include absences that would not have been revealed by the attendance register ('a lesson here and there'), then the self-reported level was as high as 63 per cent. On the other hand, if we focus on the idea of 'persistent truants' we find that some 5 per cent of fourth-year pupils were absent for more than half the six-week period of Pack's survey 'without adequate explanation' and some 6 per cent of the 1977 survey sample reported that they truanted 'weeks at a time' during their fourth year.[1]

Any argument over the incidence of truancy thus hinges either on the definitions that are explicitly employed or on those that are implied in operational form by the data source or methods that are used. Researchers have sometimes, apparently, been unaware of the implications of the methods they have adopted for the definition of the problem of truancy. They have sometimes used ways of identifying

TABLE 11.1 'Did you ever play truant during your fourth year at school?'[1] By social class, sex and SCE attainment respectively: percentage of leavers from EA schools in the four regions

	Never	A lesson here and there	A day here and there	Several days at a time	Weeks at a time	Total	Unweighted *n*
(a) All leavers	37	26	24	7	6	100	(15,682)
(b) I Professional	49	32	15	3	2	101	(812)
II Intermediate	42	32	20	4	2	100	(2,406)
IIIN Skilled non-manual	44	29	19	5	3	100	(1,258)
IIIM Skilled manual	35	25	26	8	6	100	(6,449)
IV Partly skilled	36	24	24	9	7	100	(2,497)
V Unskilled	33	22	24	11	10	100	(557)
Unclassified	32	22	26	10	10	100	(1,703)
(c) Boys	32	25	27	8	7	99	(7,678)
Girls	42	26	21	6	5	100	(8,004)
(d) Any Highers passes	50	36	13	1	< 0.5	100	(5,039)
4 or more O-grades (A–C)	41	32	24	3	1	101	(1,779)
1–3 O-grades (A–C)	37	27	27	6	3	100	(3,590)
D or E awards only	35	24	30	8	3	100	(1,302)
No awards	28	17	28	13	14	100	(3,972)

Note: 1 For non-certificate leavers the question referred to the 'last year' at school.

truants (referrals to child-guidance clinics or samples drawn from juvenile-court records) that restricted their studies to small and to deviant minorities. On occasion, a dichotomous definition has been used that explicitly confined the problem to a small minority of pupils. There are, however, several ways in which the 1977 survey distributions might be summarised, each of which implies a view of the 'problem'. One approach is based on the view that the distribution of truancy was dichotomous: some pupils were truants; others, the vast majority, were not. The other approach, in contrast, implies that the distribution of truancy was more continuous. A majority of pupils truanted to a greater or lesser extent in their fourth year.

Leavers' backgrounds and truancy

The conventional wisdom on truancy holds that truants tend to come from disadvantaged backgrounds. Although researchers may often acknowledge that both family circumstances and school factors contribute to the incidence of truancy, in practice nearly all the research has concluded by cataloguing the background and individual characteristics of so-called persistent or hard-core truants, showing that they have many of the characteristics that are more generally attributed to disadvantaged groups: truants tend to perform less well academically, to come from lower social-class backgrounds and larger families, and to live in overcrowded homes. Surprisingly, perhaps, this is frequently the extent to which background factors and other attributes and attitudes of truants are explored. Individual pathologies are inferred, but most of the studies, as Carroll (1977) remarks, seldom permit causal relationships to be established with any confidence. Since Carroll (1977) has recently reviewed most of the relevant research evidence, we comment on it only briefly here. Carroll has cited some twenty books and articles as containing significant research on truancy and school absence. The studies vary in their methods, quality and authority. Only two major studies, however, have deliberately included a focus on the part that the school may play in the generation of truancy; one is by Reynolds (1976) and the other by Rutter *et al.* (1979). Both emphasise the effects of schools as social institutions on the behaviour and attendance of their pupils. They suggest that to understand more about truancy we need to know more about the quality of the experiences pupils are offered by their schools and more about pupils' reactions to them.

To what extent is the 1977 survey's evidence on the correlates of truancy compatible with earlier studies? In general, these have shown that truancy has been associated with a number of background

183

TABLE 11.2 'Did you ever play truant in your last year at school?' By social class: percentage of non-certificate leavers only from EA schools in the four regions

Socio-economic grouping	Never	A lesson here and there	A day here and there	Several days at a time	Weeks at a time	Total	Unweighted *n*
I Professional	(35)	(4)	(17)	(26)	(17)	99	(23)
II Intermediate	28	16	29	15	12	100	(156)
IIIN Skilled non-manual	33	10	30	15	12	100	(137)
IIIM Skilled manual	26	16	29	14	14	99	(1,571)
IV Partly skilled	28	17	27	13	15	100	(713)
V Unskilled	28	17	21	15	19	100	(228)
Unclassified	26	16	27	14	17	100	(716)

Note: The percentages for class I (professional) are based on small sample numbers.

characteristics. Truants have tended to come from lower social-class backgrounds, from larger families and from families with no male head; they have tended to be boys and to have had poor educational attainments. Section (b) of table 11.1 confirms that leavers in the sample from unskilled home backgrounds and from those not classified were indeed more likely to have truanted than those, say, from professional or other non-manual backgrounds. For example, 49 per cent of children of professional parents said they had never truanted compared with only 33 per cent of children of parents in unskilled employment and 32 per cent of unclassified children. (Many of the unclassified children were from families with no male head.) Children truanting 'weeks at a time' comprised 2, 10 and 10 per cent respectively of these three groups. Moreover, among leavers as a whole, the number of siblings was positively associated with the incidence of truancy. One way of summarising this relationship, for which we do not show a table, is to say that the percentage of leavers who had truanted for 'several days at a time' or 'weeks at a time' was 9 per cent for those with one brother or sister and 12 per cent for those with two; thereafter it continued to rise towards a plateau (15, 17, 18 and 19 per cent); the percentage for only children (14 per cent) was an interesting exception to the overall trend and perhaps merits closer investigation.

Part (c) of table 11.1 shows that boys were more likely to have truanted than were girls; finally, part (d) of the table indicates that the 1977 survey data were also broadly compatible with earlier studies' conclusions about the lower educational attainments of truants. For instance, among those who achieved no SCE awards, 28 per cent had never truanted and 14 per cent had truanted for weeks at a time. Among those who achieved Highers passes, half had never truanted and a negligible percentage had truanted for weeks at a time.

None of these measures describes family or individual pathology as such, but their associations with truancy indicate how they might be used (and, indeed, have been used in some hands) to derive an explanation in terms of family and individual deficiencies. Nevertheless, there is a competing explanation that is also largely consistent with the data. If one confines one's attention to pupils at any one of the three broad SCE-presentation levels, the associations of truancy with the other family measures largely disappear. By way of example, table 11.2 shows the association between social class and truancy for non-certificate leavers only, and may be compared with part (b) of table 11.1 which covers all leavers. The association in table 11.2 is considerably weaker; much of the apparent link between family background and truancy therefore disappears when the effects of presentation level are controlled. A similar analysis (not shown) reveals that the association between family size and truancy was also considerably weaker among non-certificate leavers than among leavers at all levels. The association between sex and truancy, however, is largely not explained by presentation level (also not shown).[2]

It is clear that truancy has been most widespread among non-certificate pupils. It might be fruitful to explore some of the factors related to the school system that differentiated between the experiences of non-certificate leavers who truanted to a greater as opposed to a lesser extent. It is to these aspects that we now turn. There are several types of evidence that may be adduced; what pupils said; their other school experiences; the prevalence and distributional nature of truancy across individuals and across schools; and the employment record of truants after leaving school.

What leavers said

The previous chapter has already illustrated that, in the view of some leavers, truancy was a reasonable response to the perceived indifference of some schools to their non-certificate pupils and to the ritualism and coercion that became features of what many teachers and pupils, tacitly or explicitly, regarded as a pointless curriculum. We do not think it necessary to give many more illustrations here. The limiting case was, perhaps, that in which, during a period of teacher strikes and of teacher shortages in some subjects and in some areas, scarce teaching resources were given preferentially to the certificate classes:

> I did not do my last year at school because when we went in to school in the morning we got our mark and were sent home. So we did not have to play truant in our last year we just got sent home and that was that. Some times my mother did not believe me and told me to get back to school she thought, I was playing truant but I wasint: she told us to go and get a letter.[3]

At another extreme, perhaps, were examples of what is commonly thought of as personal inadequacy. But in what sense is the inadequacy in the following example entirely personal?

> The reason I played truant so much was because I hated the teachers, for the simple reason that I wasn't to bright at school, and if I didn't catch something the teacher said, or couldn't do something right, I was scared to ask the teacher because eight out of ten (he) would just tell me I should have been listening or to just get a copy off a freind so when it came to exams I just didn't have a clue what to do.

And what about this?

All I can say about my self is I am shy and nervous and do my fare share of work and I never go out at night. I was hardly ever at school the last year cause I never liked it as I never had anybody to go about with and when I had to answer a question my face went all red because the people in my class started to look at me and I would get all mixed up and the teacher would make it worse for me as they made me sit at the front of the class and I was scared to answer in case I was wrong and they would all laugh at me. I don't really know if he could have made the time more useful. I'm sure it was up to myself to make the time more useful.

Between these two extremes of, on the one hand, what amounted to a virtual lock-out by the school and, on the other, an inability by the school to understand or to respond to the difficulties of a very isolated pupil, were the large majority of leavers' accounts, reiterating again and again the demoralisation of non-certificate status. Reference was rarely made to factors from outside the school, coming from the home or from the wish for employment, though many leavers voiced the view that their time could have been better spent working, preparing for work, or finding work. From a systematic content-analysis of 750 accounts written by non-certificate pupils, Cope and Gray (1978, p. 25) concluded:

we can legitimately infer that for non-certificate pupils, the perceived irrelevance of much of their school work, the perceived inadequacy of the provision and their sense of being treated as relatively unimportant, all of which comes through so vividly in their volunteered statements, must at the very least have legitimised their truancy in their own eyes, may indeed have triggered it off, and certainly could not have countered other factors operating to induce them to absent themselves from school.

Aspects of non-certificate pupils' school experience

We may set leavers' open-ended accounts of their schooling against a more systematic, quantitative picture of their views and experiences. Table 11.3 is confined to non-certificate leavers and it shows responses to a variety of fixed-alternative items asked of different random sub-sets of pupils. The percentages are given for each of the different levels of self-reported truancy.

The items presented in table 11.3 provide evidence of a consistent pattern. Those who truanted for the longest periods reported more negative attitudes and experiences than those who truanted briefly or not at all. The differences were, not surprisingly perhaps, large with

187

TABLE 11.3   Perceived help from teachers, various experiences and attitudes, by extent of self-reported truancy: percentage of non-certificate leavers only from EA schools in the four regions

		Never	A lesson here and there	A day here and there	Several days at a time	Weeks at a time
	Percentage reporting a lot of help from teachers with:					
1	lessons	66	62	48	35	31
2	learning things useful for jobs	44	36	33	19	13
3	learning about jobs	44	37	34	33	17
4	learning useful things	51	46	34	39	26
5	becoming independent	45	34	32	27	23
6	spare-time activities	29	22	22	22	13
7	getting on with others	36	35	27	23	23
8	personal problems	23	18	19	18	15
9	Percentage treated too much as a child	12	19	17	21	29
10	Percentage belted often or quite often	21	39	50	60	64
11	Percentage enjoying last year	66	63	42	26	21
12	Percentage saying last year worthwhile	30	29	21	16	8
13	Percentage saying last year very or quite useful	53	42	31	22	12
14	Percentage finding reading easy or quite easy	56	55	63	68	70
15	Percentage finding writing easy or quite easy	61	60	56	63	62
16	Percentage finding sums easy or quite easy	29	29	30	29	36
17	Percentage with part-time job while at school	33	33	39	40	39

Note: Since many items were asked in different versions of the questionnaire, the numbers on which many percentages are based vary. All percentages are based on more than fifty unweighted cases and most on more than a hundred cases. All items are based on leavers' own reports. Full details are given in Raffe *et al*. (1978).

respect to perceptions of teachers' help with lessons, but there were differences on all of the other seven items concerning help from teachers. Similarly, those who truanted for the longest periods were also more likely to report that they had been treated too much as children, and that their last year at school was, in the main, neither enjoyable nor worthwhile. By way of reinforcing these views, they were also considerably more likely to report that they had been belted often or quite often. In brief, they tended to feel that their last compulsory year at school had been an unpleasant experience. Although the truants tended to have even more negative attitudes than other non-certificate leavers to their school experiences, there is no evidence of lower self-esteem among truants than among non-truants. A majority of all non-certificate leavers said that they had found reading and writing easy or quite easy, although this confidence did not so often extend to 'doing sums'. Roughly two-thirds of all non-certificate leavers reported some difficulty in doing sums. Those who truanted more extensively were as likely as their non-certificate peers to regard the 3 Rs as easy; indeed, they were more likely than the others to regard reading as being easy.

The distribution of truancy and its correlates

There is another argument to be made from table 11.3 and, indeed, from the earlier tables in this chapter. If the persistent truant had been a different animal from other pupils, we should expect to find this reflected in the correlates of truancy; those truanting a lesson here and there or (perhaps) a day here and there ought to have been relatively homogeneous and to have resembled those who never truanted more closely than they resembled those who truanted weeks at a time or several days at a time. In general, however, the associations were linear and tended towards monotonicity; that is, the intervals between adjacent percentages tended to be similar within each scale. There is very little indication that 'serious' or 'hard-core' truants could be identified by a cluster of opinions, experiences or attributes that distinguished them from occasional truants any more than occasional truants could be distinguished from non-truanting pupils in such respects. Perhaps the best example of this monotonicity was in the case of the association of truancy with the item 'How useful was your last year at school?' The percentages saying 'very' or 'quite' useful fell, from 53 per cent (among those who never truanted) to 12 per cent among those who truanted weeks at a time, by almost equal intervals of about 10 percentage points. One would be hard put to find a consistent point in the truancy scale at which a significant split occurred across many items. Indeed there were only two items that might have indicated an appreciable hard core. Both were to do with perceptions of teachers' help in the vocational domain (items 2 and 3), but even these two items differed in the positioning of the split. We may conclude that, statistically, the extent of truancy was associated with the extent to which leavers reported negative experiences at school and that this was true among the majority of the non-certificate population.

Truancy and subsequent experience in the labour market

Our evidence so far suggests that truancy was generated at least in part by factors pertaining to the school. At the same time, however much the level of truancy may have been a consequence of school factors, Pack's contention remains true, namely that, among pupils with apparently similar experiences at school, there were wide variations in the extent of truancy. Different individuals responded in different ways to the same situation; at least part of the explanation of truancy, it would seem, must be couched in terms of personal characteristics.

Like other studies to which we have referred, our data on the individual characteristics of truants (let alone on individual pathology) are limited. However, indirect light is thrown on this point by the subsequent experiences of truants and others in the labour market. For, as we argued in chapter 7, employers have been interested in the personal characteristics of their recruits. If they perceived former truants as being less disciplined, more work-shy or more antisocial than other applicants, they would have been reluctant to employ former truants, who would thus have had higher rates of unemployment.

However, comparing the unemployment rates of leavers with different levels of truancy is not a test of the individual pathology explanation of truancy. Whereas it may be true that former truants had personal characteristics which made them less attractive to employers, it does not follow that these characteristics were pathological in any commonly accepted sense of the word. Indeed, it might be argued that truants showed signs of independence, self-assurance and even rationality which made them less attractive to employers. To say that the most persistent truants tended to differ, in certain respects, from other pupils is not to say that they were pathological or even that they were any less well-adjusted, on other criteria, than other pupils.

As we argued in chapters 7 and 8, employers have had very limited stock of information on the school-leavers who have applied to them for jobs. Their selection decisions regarding truants and non-truants may have reflected, not so much their preferences for the personal characteristics of recruits, as their basic ignorance of the characteristics of individual applicants. The more useful source of evidence on truants and others may well be not the ease with which they first found employment, but their persistence in employment once they had found it. Table 11.4 attempts to take account of this point. It is restricted

TABLE 11.4   Experience of employment and unemployment since school, by extent of self-reported truancy: percentage of non-certificate leavers who entered the labour market from EA schools in the four regions

	Employed at time of survey			Unemployed at time of survey			Total	Unweighted n
	In first job	In second or subsequent job	Number of jobs not known	At least one job since school	No jobs since school	Number of jobs not known		
Boys								
Never	60	23	3	8	5	1	100	(416)
Lesson	49	22	4	15	9	1	100	(275)
Day	52	22	2	17	7	<0.5	100	(539)
Several days	49	21	3	17	9	1	100	(279)
Weeks	38	26	2	24	8	1	99	(314)
All boys	50	23	3	16	7	1	100	(1,823)
Girls								
Never	57	18	3	12	8	2	100	(486)
Lesson	59	20	2	15	5	<0.5	101	(266)
Day	55	19	2	17	7	<0.5	100	(391)
Several days	47	24	1	17	10	1	100	(196)
Weeks	43	20	2	25	8	2	100	(189)
All girls	54	19	2	16	8	1	100	(1,528)

to non-certificate leavers, and therefore controls for the influence of SCE attainment on employment. It shows the labour-market experiences of boys and girls with different levels of truancy, using the same destination categories as table 9.2.

The total level of unemployment among non-certificate sample members at the time of the survey may be calculated by adding the three columns under the heading 'unemployed at time of survey' in table 11.4. This level varied considerably between the different categories of truancy. Among those who had never truanted, 14 per cent of boys and 22 per cent of girls were unemployed; at the other extreme, among those who had truanted for weeks at a time, 33 per cent of boys and 35 per cent of girls were unemployed. However, the proportion who had never had a job since school (column 5) was only very weakly, and erratically, related to the level of truancy. Where the different levels of truancy differed most was in the proportion who had held at least one job since school but who were unemployed at the time of the survey (column 4). In other words, the higher rate of unemployment among truants owed more to their greater propensity to leave jobs than to their smaller success in finding them.

We do not know the details of the jobs which the unemployed sample members had formerly had, so we cannot tell the extent to which the former truants' propensity to leave jobs was a function of the jobs they left rather than of the characteristics of the young people themselves. However, in the 1979 survey, respondents who had left their first jobs were asked why they had done so. Among non-certificate school-leavers who had left their first jobs, those who had truanted more extensively were less likely to say they had done this because they had another job to go to, or because they had been made redundant. They were equally likely to have been sacked. The most common single reason (given by 37 per cent of boys and by 42 per cent of girls) was their dislike of their first job, and this was a reason that those who had truanted more often mentioned more often. For example, 45 per cent of non-certificate boys who had truanted days or weeks at a time gave this reason compared with 34 per cent among those who had never truanted. The comparable gap among girls was a little larger (no table shown).

Truants were therefore rather more likely than non-truants to have left their jobs for negative, reactive reasons, and rather less likely to have left them for positive reasons, such as the offer of a better job elsewhere. Although they may well have had worse jobs, and therefore more to be negative about, the evidence does suggest that former truants were relatively likely to walk out on unpleasant experiences at work, just as they had formerly been relatively likely to walk out on unpleasant experiences at school. This is not to deny that those experiences at school may have occasioned their truancy, nor does it indicate pathology; but the evidence on employment does suggest that personal characteristics played some part in deciding which young people played truant and which ones responded in other ways.

Conclusion

In this chapter we have questioned explanations that locate the root cause of truancy in problems associated with particular types of disadvantaged family circumstances. Because only the activities of a very small minority are commonly characterised as truancy, the search for causes is largely confined to establishing ways in which the minority differ from the majority. Pupils' experiences of the school system are held to be common to all pupils and are therefore discounted as a possible explanation for the difference between truants and nontruants; family circumstances, in contrast, are seen to differ widely among pupils. The explanations offered by pupils themselves (regardless of whether they truant or not) are also largely discounted. By defining 'truancy' so that it refers to a very small minority, by assuming that school experiences are common to all pupils, and by discounting the reports of one group of participants (the pupils), such explanations easily lead to the conclusion that disadvantage associated with 'family circumstances' is the single major cause of truancy.

We have subjected this conclusion to a number of criticisms. First, we have shown that, by the final year of compulsory schooling, truancy has been far more widespread than these explanations would suggest. Among members of the 1977 sample, we found not a deviant minority, but a substantial majority (63 per cent) admitting to some truancy in their fourth year. Our estimate, we note in passing, is similar to that reported in the National Children's Bureau's study of England and Wales where 52 per cent of 16-year-olds claimed to have 'stayed off' school at some point in their last year when they 'should have been there' (Fogelman, 1976).

Second, we have argued that the school-leavers' accounts of why they had truanted cannot be lightly dismissed. In the leavers' accounts the part played by the school system was paramount; those who truanted did so because they did not like school. Pupils did not share a common experience of schooling. To have been a non-certificate pupil in a Scottish secondary school was almost certainly a different and, in many ways, more negative experience than to have been a certificate pupil. Furthermore, among the non-certificate respondents, those who truanted more extensively reported more negative attitudes and experiences than those who truanted less or not at all. We have emphasised that such accounts cannot be considered adequate by themselves, any more than can official or other explanations; the accounts of other participants (teachers, for example) would be necessary for a more complete picture to be established, but the collection of such data was beyond the scope of our project. We would be surprised, however, if such additional research did not allow considerable validity to leavers' reports of their experiences.

In arguing for the role of the school in the generation of truancy, and in opposing explanations based solely on family circumstances or individual pathology, we are not denying that personal characteristics have no influence at all. When studying the labour-market experiences of former pupils who had truanted to different extents, we found a tendency for the former truants to leave their jobs within a relatively short space of time, and a tendency for them to do so for negative reasons. Truants apparently tended to be individuals with a relatively low tolerance of unpleasant experiences, who were more likely to walk out on such experiences whether at school or at work.

The relatively low tolerance of truants is not necessarily a sign of pathology or irrationality on their part. To many of them it seems to have made sense to truant, because this was one way of improving their immediate short-term position. We have argued in this chapter that an account which locates the causes of truancy mainly or exclusively in 'family circumstances' is likely to be deficient; the part played by the school and the fact that different pupils have different experiences of the institution of schooling needs to be recognised. But until efforts are devoted to establishing the interaction between young people's experiences of family and school, such accounts will continue to be inadequate. This discussion has established that there is an overwhelming case for 'bringing the school back in', if only to do justice to the consumers' viewpoint. But at present it represents no more than a preliminary to the more sustained research that is required.

Part 5

Education and Class

Introduction

For many people what we have termed the expansionist perspective on education involved a belief in equality of educational opportunity between the classes. The perspective combined the belief that equality was possible, given enlightened government reforms, with the belief that it was desirable, both for its own sake and also for the efficient functioning of a modern society. The goal of equal opportunity has influenced much of post-war policy for secondary education in Britain. It inspired the establishment of a bipartite system in the 1940s and also the switch to a comprehensive system from 1965. The 1950s and the 1960s saw a series of official reports (in England, although not in Scotland) which condemned the waste of talent resulting from working-class failure in education and which proposed a series of modest reforms: the concept of 'positive discrimination' was invented and applied on a small scale. Above all, it was widely believed that educational expansion itself was the best way to promote equality. This belief arose partly out of an individualistic perspective which attributed inequalities to a lack of opportunity in education, and to tangible barriers placed in the way of working-class children. Expansion, or the policy of increasing opportunity, was implicitly identified with a policy of increasing equality of opportunity.

In Scotland these ideas blended with two of the essential components of the 'Scottish myth' which we described in part 2. The first of these was the 'lad o' pairts', the young person of talent, often from humble origins, whose rise up the educational ladder and thence to the professions was believed to be facilitated by the special features of the Scottish education system. The second component was the omnibus school, wherein all the children of the parish, rich and poor alike, were educated under the same roof, and which was believed to encourage

197

both equality of opportunity and a strong sense of communal solidarity.

However, both the expansionist account and the Scottish myth have been found wanting as guides to policy and practice with respect to educational inequality. Sometimes they have simply turned out to be false or self-contradictory; and sometimes they have been too vague and general to provide clear guidelines.

In the first place, the concept of equality has shifted. Before the war, and in the early post-war period, equality (or equality of opportunity) was identified with the absence of barriers to opportunity which unfairly discriminated against children of particular social backgrounds. Over the years the notion of 'unfair' discrimination subsequently broadened, to include all forms of pre-secondary selection, and the absence of barriers came to be identified with comprehensive secondary education. During the post-war period, however, attention has focused increasingly on the outcomes of education rather than on formal opportunity; equality has been defined in terms of the equality of educational attainments between classes. This is the sense in which we define and measure inequality in chapter 12. Yet the distinction between the two concepts has often been confused, not least because the old individualistic terminology, and in particular the concept of 'opportunity', has often been used in connection with the equality of educational outcomes (for example, by Coleman, 1968). Another reason for the confusion is that 'attainment' in one context may be 'opportunity' in another; for example, a particular level of attainment in Highers examinations leads to the opportunity for higher education.

Second, the presumed connection between educational expansion and educational equality was never spelt out. Equality and inequality are relative and not absolute terms. Give everyone twice as much education and class inequality will be unchanged, even if it is made rather more tolerable. Only if the distribution of the additional education favours the working class will expansion reduce inequality. This is a conceptual dilemma as well as an empirical one. Suppose that the additional education is distributed disproportionately in favour of the middle class, but to a lesser extent than the initial amount of education. The total proportion of education that goes to the middle class will have fallen; but can we talk of expansion producing greater equality if the middle class have nevertheless taken more than their share of the increase? Any attempt to identify and measure greater and smaller degrees of inequality is especially problematic in the context of expansion (or, for that matter, of contraction too). When the content of education and the ways in which society defines and measures educational attainment also change, the search for a trend in the level of inequality in education becomes even more problematic, because there is no longer a common yardstick by which to measure it. We discuss these problems in chapter 12 and, on the basis of our favoured solution, we then analyse trends in class inequality in education in Scotland since the war, answering three main questions: what has been the level of class inequality; has inequality been associated to different extents with different stages and sectors of education; and, has inequality been decreasing since the war?

In chapter 13 we turn to the movement for comprehensive reorganisation in the 1960s, a movement that was intended to expand educational opportunity and to diminish class inequalities. There we show how, in addition to the types of conceptual problems discussed in chapter 12, there were further problems to be solved in stating the purposes of the reform: problems arising partly from the uncertain knowledge of what the social and psychological sciences could offer as to the potential of a reformed education system; and partly from a related tendency for people to claim that a variety of goals could all be served by the same means. We characterise the movement for reform as polyvalent and in some respects confused, offering a clearer account of what it wished to remove than of what it wished to achieve. It was clear enough that selective transfer to secondary courses at the age of 12 was to be abolished. But which of the many possible purposes for secondary education were to be served by this move? And how, in particular, were the dilemmas of difficulty and motivation to be handled, once the control that could be achieved through early selection was gone?

We argue, however, that no programme for planned social or educational change can expect to be able to specify all its goals and means in advance. This can only be done in the context of social learning about the potential and possibilities for change, learning that arises, in part, from observation of the early progress of reform. Much of chapter 13 illustrates the way in which these issues and problems were interpreted in a Scottish context and how these interpretations were sometimes materially influenced by the Scottish myth. Did Scotland really need comprehensive reorganisation (the argument ran), if educational provision was already more generous in Scotland than in England and Wales, and if Scottish society was already less class-based? Did Scotland not already have a comprehensive-school system in the form of the traditional omnibus school? Moreover, even among those Scots who argued the need for change, the myth influenced the kinds of changes that were envisaged. Was comprehensive reorganisation to diversify the criteria by which the school system evaluated pupils, or was it merely to extend to many, or all, pupils the possibility of being evaluated in a single, academic dimension?

Chapter 14 offers an empirical assessment of the impact of the early stages of comprehensive reorganisation in Scotland. By dividing the school system of the early–mid-1970s into two exclusive and exhaustive sectors — a comprehensive sector and a selective sector — and by making several empirically grounded assumptions about the similarity of the pupil intakes to the schools in these two sectors, we are able to judge reorganisation in terms of four measures covering both cognitive and non-cognitive outcomes of schooling. We also find evidence that the early impact of comprehensive education was closely bound up with the much older omnibus tradition. The myth's account of a class-less education was, to a degree, valid for some pupils in some areas.

Together with those arising from the earlier parts of this book, the issues arising from part 5 are then dealt with in our final three chapters. What is the relation between a mythical account and that offered by social science? What is the relation between social science and politics? What are the possibilities for learning more about the potential of education to change the world?

Chapter 12

Social-Class Inequality in Educational Attainment since the War

Introduction

A recent study of Englishmen born between 1907 and 1952 has shown that, despite the educational reforms that followed the Second World War, the educational inequality in post-war England and Wales that was associated with social-class background was as great as it had been before the war. Moreover, actual class differences in educational attainment were substantially larger than class differences in intelligence as measured at the age of 11 (Halsey, Heath and Ridge 1980). Yet the expansionist perspective had implied that educational reform, and a consequent trend in society towards greater wealth and openness, would increase educational equality. Are these findings a consequence of an irredeemably class-based society and education system in England, as (we suspect) many Scots and not a few English might suppose? What have been the consequences of expansion and reform for educational equality in Scotland with its different history and forms of provision? The Scottish Mobility Study (1976) has in fact reached similar conclusions to those of the English study as far as historical trends are concerned. However, education and society have continued to change during the post-war period. By virtue of their timing, neither of these studies could reveal any effects of more recent changes.

In this chapter we examine social-class inequality in education in Scotland, and ask three questions: what has been the level of class inequality in educational attainment? Has inequality been associated to different extents with different stages and sectors of education? Has inequality been decreasing since the war?

Data

To help us answer these questions, we have assembled data on samples representing three age-cohorts of pupils who passed through Scottish secondary schools at different times since the war. These are:

> *the 1948 transfer cohort*, who entered secondary school in 1948, and who left between 1951 and 1954;
>
> *the 1957–8 transfer cohort*, who entered secondary school in 1957 or 1958, and who left between 1960 and 1963;
>
> *the 1970–2 transfer cohort*, who entered secondary school between 1970 and 1972 and who left during or at the end of the 1975–6 session. These are the leavers covered by the 1977 survey, whose progress and attitudes we have been examining throughout this book. Our data on this cohort are confined to the four regions, which comprise about three-quarters of the Scottish population.[1]

We use data on the social class and educational attainment of members of all these samples. We define social class in terms of father's occupation.[2] Our measurement of educational attainment is more complex. For each cohort we have recorded a number of different measures of what we term *criteria of educational attainment*. These are listed in table 12.1. They include measures of course placement (for example, 'stayed on beyond age $15\frac{1}{4}$'), of course completion ('completed any five-year course') and of achievement ('passed at least one Higher'), as well as of continuing education ('entered any post-school education'). Many of our criteria of attainment differ between the three cohorts; this is partly because of the available data and partly because the criteria themselves have changed, for instance when new examinations were introduced.

Each of these criteria is expressed in a way that identifies a certain proportion of the cohort as having reached or surpassed it. Thus we express attainment in terms of reaching or surpassing a particular rung on the ladder of attainment; for instance, passing one or more Highers as distinct from passing exactly one Higher. (Put technically, all our criteria of attainment are dichotomous.)[3]

We are therefore able to report the percentage of a cohort which reached (or surpassed) each criterion level of attainment; this is shown in column (i) of table 12.1. This percentage is important because, across the three cohorts, it indicates the progress of educational expansion, and expansion has been widely believed to facilitate greater equality. Columns (ii) and (iii) of table 12.1 show the percentages of middle- and working-class children respectively who reached (or surpassed) the criterion. Column (iv) shows the ratio of these two percentages; this so-called *disparity ratio* is easily understood as showing the relative class chances of reaching the criterion. For instance, the first line of table 12.1 reveals that middle-class children in the 1948 cohort were exactly three times as likely as working-class children to be on a five-year course at the age of 15.

Many studies have used the disparity ratio, or statistics based on it, to measure the level of educational inequality, and thus to make comparisons and assess trends in inequality over time. However, we believe that the disparity ratio is an inappropriate way of measuring trends across time when expansion (or contraction) has occurred. We therefore prefer an alternative measure of inequality, using a statistic known as Yule's Q, and we report estimates of inequality based on this measure in column (vi) of table 12.1. We justify our preference for this measure in the next section of this chapter. Inevitably this discussion must be somewhat technical, so readers who are prepared to accept our own judgments on this may prefer to pass on to the section entitled 'The level of inequality', where the main story of the chapter resumes. However, if they do so, they must also take on trust a further assertion which some readers may find intuitively puzzling or even unacceptable: that there is no incontestable definition of the 'level' of educational inequality, and that any statement that this level has risen or fallen will therefore partly depend on the way in which inequality is defined and the measure that is used to put this definition into practice.

Measuring inequality

For each criterion of attainment listed in table 12.1, we have constructed a table of the form represented below, where the numbers in the four cells of the table are represented by the letters a, b, c and d.

	Number reaching or surpassing criterion level of attainment	Number not reaching criterion level of attainment
Middle class	a	b
Working class	c	d

The statistics in the first three columns of table 12.1 can be formally represented in terms of these symbols as follows:

column (i) Percentage of cohort reaching criterion level $= 100 \times \dfrac{a + c}{a + b + c + d}$

TABLE 12.1 Measures of class inequality for selected criteria of educational attainment among three cohorts

Criterion of attainment	(i)	(ii)	(iii)	(iv)	(v)	(vi)	(vii)
(a) 1948 transfer cohort							
On a five-year course at age 15	24	49	16	3.0	1.7	0.67	0.59 to 0.75
On a five-year general course (with a language) at age 15	20	44	13	3.4	1.6	0.68	0.59 to 0.76
Stayed on beyond December 1951 (boys only)	25	54	17	3.1	1.8	0.70	0.59 to 0.81
Stayed on beyond July 1952	16	43	9	5.0	1.6	0.78	0.68 to 0.87
Completed any five-year course	13	33	7	4.6	1.4	0.73	0.64 to 0.81
Completed a five-year general course (with a language)	11	30	6	5.0	1.3	0.74	0.65 to 0.83
Entered any post-school education	29	41	25	1.6	1.3	0.35	0.22 to 0.47
Entered a university course	4	12	2	8.0	1.1	0.80	0.68 to 0.92
(b) 1957–8 transfer cohort							
On a five-year selective course at age 15 (NS)	24	45	18	2.5	1.5	0.58	0.46 to 0.71
Stayed on beyond age $15\frac{1}{4}$ (NS)	30	65	20	3.4	2.3	0.77	0.69 to 0.85
Stayed on beyond age $16\frac{1}{4}$ (NS)	22	53	12	4.3	1.9	0.78	0.69 to 0.87
Stayed on beyond age $17\frac{1}{4}$ (NS)	12	35	5	7.3	1.5	0.83	0.72 to 0.94
Passed at least one O-grade or Higher (NS)	26	61	16	3.9	2.1	0.78	0.71 to 0.86
Passed at least one Higher (NS)	15	43	6	7.0	1.7	0.84	0.75 to 0.94
Passed at least two Highers (NS)	12	34	5	7.3	1.4	0.83	0.70 to 0.95
Passed at least one Higher (SEDA)	15	36	8	4.4	1.4	0.73	–
Passed at least two Highers (SEDA)	13	32	7	4.6	1.4	0.72	–
Passed at least three Highers (SEDA)	10	25	5	4.9	1.3	0.72	–
Passed at least four Highers (SEDA)	7	17	3	5.3	1.2	0.72	–
Passed at least five Highers (SEDA)	3	9	1	6.1	1.1	0.74	–
Entered a degree-level course (SEDA)	6	16	3	5.7	1.2	0.74	–
(c) 1970–2 transfer cohort							
On an academic 'B' course at 15 (see note 17)	55	76	45	1.7	2.3	0.59	0.56 to 0.63
On an academic 'A' course at 15 (see note 17)	24	43	15	2.9	1.5	0.63	0.60 to 0.66
Attempted at least one O or H-grade	73	90	66	1.4	3.3	0.64	0.61 to 0.68

	(i)	(ii)	(iii)	(iv)	(v)	(vi)	(vii)
Attempted at least one Higher	32	60	20	3.0	2.0	0.72	0.70 to 0.74
Stayed on beyond first term of S5	37	64	25	2.6	2.1	0.69	0.67 to 0.71
Stayed on to sixth year	17	34	10	3.5	1.4	0.65	0.62 to 0.68
Any SCE award (including D or E)	67	87	59	1.5	3.2	0.65	0.62 to 0.68
1+ O-grade at A–C or 1+ Higher pass	58	82	48	1.7	2.8	0.66	0.63 to 0.68
2+ O-grades at A–C or 1+ Higher pass	49	75	38	2.0	2.5	0.67	0.64 to 0.69
3+ O-grades at A–C or 1+ Higher pass	42	70	31	2.3	2.3	0.68	0.66 to 0.70
4+ O-grades at A–C or 1+ Higher pass	37	65	25	2.6	2.1	0.69	0.67 to 0.71
5+ O-grades at A–C or 1+ Higher pass	33	61	22	2.8	2.0	0.70	0.68 to 0.72
6+ O-grades at A–C or 1+ Higher pass	30	57	19	3.1	1.9	0.71	0.68 to 0.73
Passed at least one Higher	27	53	16	3.4	1.8	0.72	0.70 to 0.74
Passed at least two Highers	22	46	12	3.8	1.6	0.72	0.70 to 0.74
Passed at least three Highers	17	38	9	4.4	1.5	0.73	0.71 to 0.75
Passed at least four Highers	13	30	6	5.0	1.3	0.74	0.72 to 0.77
Passed at least five Highers	8	20	3	6.0	1.2	0.76	0.73 to 0.79
Passed at least six Highers	3	9	1	8.4	1.1	0.80	0.76 to 0.85
Any (full-time or part-time) post-school education	47	65	39	1.7	1.8	0.49	0.46 to 0.52
Any full-time post-school education	23	41	16	2.6	1.4	0.58	0.55 to 0.61
Advanced or degree-level education	14	31	7	4.4	1.4	0.71	0.69 to 0.74
Degree-level course	10	23	4	5.6	1.3	0.75	0.72 to 0.78
University course	8	20	3	6.1	1.2	0.76	0.73 to 0.79

Key

(i)   percentage of age-group reaching or surpassing criterion level
(ii) percentage of middle class reaching or surpassing criterion level
(iii) percentage of working class reaching or surpassing criterion level
(iv) disparity ratio (ii)/(iii)
(v)   residual disparity ratio (100−iii)/(100−ii)
(vi) inequality (Yule's Q)
(vii) 95 per cent confidence limits for Q

Notes: For sources see note 1 to this chapter (NS = National Survey; SEDA = Scottish Education Data Archive). All values are
subject to rounding.

column (ii) Percentage of middle class reaching criterion level $= 100 \times \dfrac{a}{a+b}$

column (iii) Percentage of working class reaching criterion level $= 100 \times \dfrac{c}{c+d}$

The fourth column contains the disparity ratio, which is the ratio of columns (ii) and (iii):

column (iv) Disparity ratio $= \dfrac{100 \times \dfrac{a}{a+b}}{100 \times \dfrac{c}{c+d}} = \dfrac{a}{c} \times \dfrac{c+d}{a+b}$

The disparity ratio can be easily interpreted: the first line of table 12.1, for instance, shows that among the 1948 cohort a middle-class child was exactly three times as likely as a working-class child to be included on a five-year (selective) course at the age of 15. Perfect equality would be represented by a disparity ratio of 1.0, and levels above this represent increasing levels of inequality. However, it is also evident from table 12.1 that the disparity ratio varies substantially between the different criteria of attainment studied for each cohort. It tends to be higher, the smaller the percentage of the whole population (column (i)) reaching the criterion level of attainment. Among the 1948 cohort, for example, the most exclusive criterion of attainment was university entrance, achieved by only 4 per cent of the cohort; university entrance also had the highest disparity ratio (8.0) of any criterion measured for the 1948 cohort (this may seem inconsistent with the estimates of 12 per cent and 2 per cent respectively, in columns (ii) and (iii), but these are both rounded). Between the 1948 cohort and the 1970–2 cohort, however, university entrance became less exclusive, and the proportion entering university doubled; the disparity ratio declined to 6.1. This tendency for disparity ratios to fall with expansion is also apparent in Little and Westergaard's (1964) survey of trends in class inequality in England and Wales.

Commentators who accept that the disparity ratio is an appropriate measure of inequality would argue from such examples that inequality tends to be considerably greater at the higher levels of attainment and that it tends to fall with educational expansion. However, there are other available measures of inequality. One of these is the *residual disparity ratio*:

$$\text{column (v)} \quad \text{Residual disparity ratio} = \frac{100 \times \dfrac{d}{c+d}}{100 \times \dfrac{b}{a+b}} = \frac{d}{b} \times \frac{a+b}{c+d}$$

Like the disparity ratio, it is easily interpreted; it shows the relative class chances of failure, that is of *not* reaching the criterion level of attainment. A value of 1.0 indicates perfect equality and levels greater than 1.0 represent increasing levels of inequality. However, it is evident from table 12.1 that the residual disparity ratio, shown in column (v), tends to move in the reverse direction to the disparity ratio, shown in column (iv); that is, as educational expansion increases the percentage reaching or surpassing the criterion level of attainment, the residual disparity ratios tend to show an *increasing* level of class inequality. For example, we have already shown how the proportion of the age-group entering university rose from 4 per cent (of the 1948 cohort) to 8 per cent (of the 1970–2 cohort), and the disparity ratio for university entrance fell from 8.0 to 6.1. However, in the same period, the residual disparity ratio rose from 1.1 to 1.2: this rise may seem small, but it indicates a proportionately large departure from perfect equality, which is represented by a ratio of 1.0. Once again, a similar conclusion was noted by Little and Westergaard (1964), who found that although post-war expansion had led to a slight narrowing of the relative chances of going to selective schools, the relative chances of *not* attending such schools had widened.

So we have two different ways of measuring inequality, which may yield opposite conclusions about the direction of trends in inequality when expansion has occurred. Which is the more appropriate? At heart this is not a technical question, but a conceptual one: what do we mean by inequality? The disparity ratio measures inequality of access: the relative chances of reaching or surpassing a given level of attainment. The residual disparity ratio measures inequality of exclusion: the relative class chances of not reaching it.

The importance of equality of access is easy to accept. Stages of education, such as university or upper secondary education, are made available through the spending of scarce educational resources, and it is natural that one should want these resources to be distributed fairly. Moreover, educational attainment is a criterion for distributing positions of influence and the more widely these can be distributed the better it may be. A measure of inequality should therefore take account of inequality of access. On the other hand, from all that we have said in the earlier chapters of this book (especially chapters 9 and 10), it follows that, as education expands, the plight of those who are still excluded from this expansion becomes increasingly serious. The extension of certification to a majority of school pupils makes the relative deprivation of the uncertified minority increasingly dire. We therefore consider that exclusion is both sociologically and normatively important, and we favour a measure of inequality that also takes account of inequality of exclusion.

Our view is therefore that both the disparity ratio and the residual disparity ratio represent important but partial aspects of inequality, and that a more adequate summary measure of inequality is their product:

$$\frac{a}{c} \times \frac{c+d}{a+b} \times \frac{d}{b} \times \frac{a+b}{c+d} = \frac{ad}{bc} = \frac{a/b}{c/d}$$

This is termed the *cross ratio*. It is the ratio of two ratios (or odds); that is, it is the ratio of the odds of a middle-class child reaching the criterion rather than not reaching it, to the odds of a working-class child reaching the criterion rather than not reaching it. Although the cross ratio has rarely been used in the study of educational inequality, it has been used in the analogous context of social mobility and it is the basis for log-linear analysis.[4] However, in one respect the cross ratio is an unwieldy measure: it ranges from zero (representing the limits of inequality favouring the working class) through one (representing equality) to infinity (representing the limits of inequality favouring the middle class). We have therefore chosen as our measure of inequality a statistic which is directly based on the cross ratio, but which ranges from -1.0 to $+1.0$, with equality represented by zero. This is Yule's Q, our sixth statistic in table 12.1, which is represented by the equation:

$$\text{column (vi)} \quad \text{Inequality (Yule's Q)} = \frac{(ad/bc)-1}{(ad/bc)+1}$$

Q is a way of adjusting the cross ratio to make it symmetrical with known and attainable limits of -1.0 and $+1.0$.[5] Also, it is normally distributed for large samples, with a known and calculable variance; this enables us to calculate 95 per cent confidence limits for Q in table 12.1. The confidence limits indicate the range within which the true value of Q for the population is estimated to lie. The 95 per cent confidence limit is such that, if we were to draw a new sample twenty times over, we would expect only one of these samples to produce confidence limits which did not include the true (population) value of Q.

The confidence limits take account of predictable error arising out of the use of a sample to represent the population; however, they do not take account of possible *biases* in the samples, which result from the sample being unrepresentative rather than merely small. It should also be noted that the several estimates of Q for each cohort are based on a single sample;[6] consequently any error, whether due to sample size or to bias in the sample, is likely to have a similar effect on all the estimates of Q for that cohort.

The level of inequality

In the rest of this chapter we measure inequality in terms of Yule's Q statistic, and for simplicity of expression we shall simply refer to it as 'inequality'. The maximum possible level of inequality in favour of the middle class is represented by a value of 1.0, and perfect equality by a value of zero. In figures 12.1, 12.2 and 12.3 we report the levels of inequality in relation to the criteria of attainment listed in table 12.1 for the three cohorts respectively. Inequality (from column (vi) of table 12.1) is shown on the vertical axis; the higher a point in the diagram, the greater the inequality associated with the corresponding criterion of attainment. The horizontal axis shows the percentage of the cohort reaching or surpassing the criterion level, from column (i) of table 12.1. By representing this percentage on the diagrams we can see that, within each cohort, the level of educational inequality tends to be slightly lower for those criteria of attainment which are reached by larger proportions of the cohort.

The data on the 1957–8 cohort (figure 12.2) comes from two sources, neither of which is as reliable for our present purpose as the data on the other two cohorts. Our first source, indicated by a ⊗ in figure 12.2, is the National Survey sample born in 1946, which contained only 405 Scots whose social class could be determined. Only 86 of these had any Highers passes, of whom only 18 were working class. Because of these small sample numbers the estimates of inequality obtained from the National Survey are subject to wide confidence intervals (or margins of error), especially at the higher levels of attainment where there were very few working-class children in the sample. Moreover, the National Survey sample excluded illegitimate children, which may well have affected its estimates of class inequality. Our second source, indicated by × in figure 12.2, is the 1962 population survey of Highers-qualified pupils in the Scottish Education Data Archive. In itself this source is highly reliable. However, since the 1962 survey only covered Highers-qualified leavers, we have adjusted the data to produce measures of inequality based on the whole cohort by adding estimates (from the National Survey) of the class composition of those who did *not* have Highers qualifications (see note 1). Because

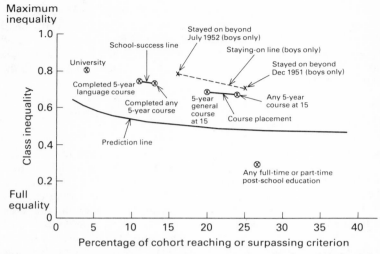

Figure 12.1 Class inequality for selected criteria of educational attainment: 1948 transfer cohort

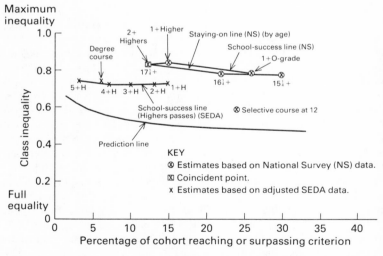

Figure 12.2 Class inequality for selected criteria of educational attainment: 1957–8 transfer cohort

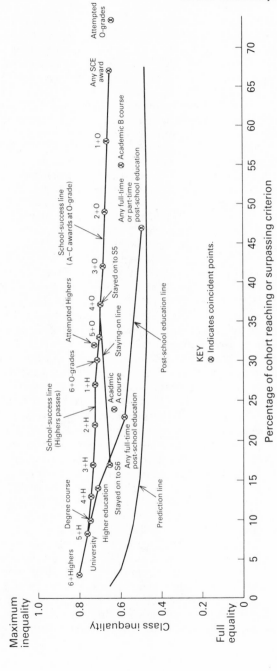

Figure 12.3 Class inequality for selected criteria of educational attainment: 1970–2 transfer cohort

211

the National Survey data are subject to sampling fluctuations, due to the low sample numbers, the archive estimates for the 1957–8 cohort are sensitive to the assumptions used in this adjustment. Any comparisons between the estimates from the two different sources, or between these sources and either of the other two cohorts, should allow for wide margins of error.[7] However, because the different observations from each source are subject to the same biases, we may be more confident in making comparisons between the levels of inequality of different criteria of attainment covered by any *one* source.

In figures 12.1, 12.2 and 12.3 we have plotted the level of inequality corresponding to the 45 measures of attainment listed in table 12.1, spread across the three cohorts. The most important conclusion to be drawn from the three diagrams is that there was class inequality in relation to each of the 45 measures of attainment. This is seen from table 12.1, columns (ii) and (iii), and shows that a larger proportion of middle-class children than of working-class children attained or surpassed each criterion. All of our measures of inequality, therefore, are substantially greater than zero, despite the wide range of data at our disposal; for none of our three cohorts have we been able to find any criterion of educational attainment in terms of which working-class children performed as well as middle-class children.

To each of the three diagrams we have added a line which we call the 'prediction line'. This shows the level of class inequality which would be expected if each individual's attainment were wholly determined by a factor (or combination of factors) which was external to the education system and which was differentially distributed between classes. In order to estimate this line we have assumed the factor(s) in question to be approximated by the verbal reasoning (VRQ) scores of pupils at the age of 11. The prediction line, as we have drawn it, therefore reflects class differences in measured ability, although, as we use it below, it has relevance for explanations which do not rest upon any concept of ability. We have constructed the prediction line on the basis of data from the Scottish Mental Survey (Scottish Council for Research in Education, 1953, p. 47).[8] Those data are roughly summarised in figure 12.4, which is offered as a heuristic device to explicate the prediction line.

The line AA' in figure 12.4 represents a given level of measured ability (VRQ). From the figure we may measure the proportion of middle-class and working-class 11-year-olds respectively with ability scores at, or above, AA'. From these we can then calculate, first, the proportion of the whole age-group with ability scores at or above AA' and, second, the level of class inequality in relation to reaching or surpassing this level of measured ability. In other words, for each level of measured ability at 11 years we can estimate a level of class inequality,

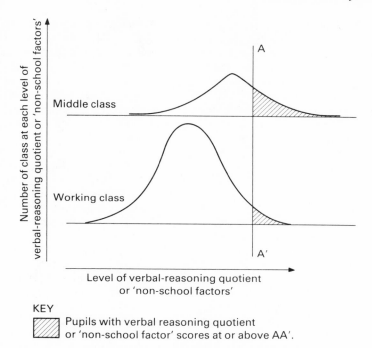

KEY

Pupils with verbal reasoning quotient
or 'non-school factor' scores at or above AA'.

Figure 12.4 Distribution of Verbal-Reasoning Quotient or 'non-school factors' by social class.

just as we did for each level of educational attainment, and these levels of class inequality in measured ability are represented by the prediction line. Our calculations allow for the changing class composition of the three cohorts, but they do not allow for any effect of these changes on the difference between the average ability scores of middle- and working-class children.[9] Nor do they allow for any widening or narrowing of the gap between the two classes' ability scores which may occur after the age of 11.[10]

The prediction lines show levels of inequality greater than zero, reflecting the finding (shown in figure 12.4) that, by the age of 11, the average middle-class child in Scotland in the 1940s had a higher measured ability than the average working-class child. We are aware of no comparable study that has failed to find such a difference. Even in a 'meritocracy'[11] where ability, as measured by VRQ tests, wholly determined subsequent educational attainment, there would have been differences in the average attainments of middle- and working-class children.[12] However, figures 12.1, 12.2 and 12.3 show that actual

213

levels of inequality in attainment were substantially greater than the levels of inequality predicted from ability scores. For 44 of the 45 criteria of attainment which we have measured across the three cohorts, class inequality was greater than for the equivalent level of measured ability at 11 years. In other words, all but one of the estimates of inequality which we have plotted in the three figures lie above the prediction line. Ability, at least as measured by the VRQ scores at the age of 11, cannot explain all of the class inequality in attainment between roughly 15 and 18 years.

The prediction lines therefore demonstrate that, on certain assumptions about the class distribution of ability (and assuming also that this distribution does not change too dramatically beyond the age of 11), Scottish secondary education since the war has not been 'meritocratic'. However, the role which ability plays in mediating class influences on attainment is hotly contested; see, for example, the discussions in Jencks *et al.* (1973, chapter 5), Tyler (1977, pp. 54–114) and Halsey, Heath and Ridge (1980, chapter 9). Alternative explanations of class differences in attainment point to a variety of additional factors, such as 'cultural capital' or the material circumstances of the home, and in the rest of this chapter we use the term 'non-school factors' to describe all the influences on attainment, including ability, which are located outside the education system, in the family or elsewhere. Non-school factors are distributed unequally between classes; moreover, it is possible that non-school factors may also be distributed in a way similar to figure 12.4 (that is, normally distributed within each class). If this were so, then the prediction line in our diagram would indicate the levels of inequality which would be expected, if non-school factors were the sole influence on attainment.

In this context we should emphasise that the prediction line is a heuristic device that is intended solely to clarify certain aspects of the social-class distribution of educational attainment. We are in no position to say whether the distribution of non-school factors is adequately represented by the distribution of VRQ test scores at the age of 11. Many people would argue that the gap between social classes in non-school factors is very much wider than the class-gap in ability scores alone; if this is true, the prediction line should be placed higher on the diagram, that is, it should predict higher levels of inequality than it does at present. The vertical gap between actual inequality and the prediction line therefore probably overestimates the school system's own contribution to class inequality over and above the contribution of non-school factors. We must also add that clear-cut distinctions between individual attributes such as ability, factors associated with the school system, and social factors located outside the school system, oversimplify situations in which these may interact.

The heuristic value of the prediction line arises more from its slope than from its level. Its slope shows how inequality would vary over a range of different levels of attainment, even if the institutions of education made no contribution to inequality over and above the effects of non-school factors. In each of figures 12.1, 12.2 and 12.3 the prediction line is not perfectly horizontal, but slopes downwards over much of its length; the slope flattens out and eventually starts to rise again as the line approaches the lower levels of attainment which were reached by large proportions of the population.[13] (This is visible in figure 12.3.) If our assumption about their distribution is correct, therefore, non-school factors alone would cause the level of educational inequality to rise, the smaller the proportion of the age-group reaching the criterion of attainment concerned. In relation to the factor of ability, the same effect was noted by Halsey, Heath and Ridge (1980, p. 140): 'a meritocratic selection procedure that creams off smaller and smaller numbers of pupils for higher levels of education will be yielding larger class differentials at succeeding levels'.

In each of figures 12.1, 12.2 and 12.3 we can see a tendency for *actual* class inequality to be greater, the smaller the proportion of the age-group reaching the level of educational attainment. This is most evident in figure 12.3, where inequality is recorded for the largest number of criteria of attainment. There were larger class differences in attainment at the upper levels of secondary education, and in entrance to university, than at the lower levels of attainment in secondary education.[14] However, the vertical distance between the actual level of inequality and the prediction line remains roughly constant over the range of levels of attainment. In other words, if some of the class inequality in attainment was caused by non-school factors with a class distribution such as we have postulated in figure 12.4, then the highest levels of education may have had the widest class differences because of the class distribution of the non-school factors and not because the highest levels of education were in some sense more class-biased than other levels of education.

Of course, not all the observations of inequality recorded in figures 12.1, 12.2 and 12.3 are at an equal distance above the prediction line. Some variations in inequality result from institutional factors associated with the separate stages and sectors of education. We describe these in greater detail below.

Stages and sectors: success in secondary-school courses

For the 1948 cohort we have data on two criteria of success in secondary-school courses: completion of any five-year course, and completion of a five-year general (or language) course. The data surviving for reanalysis do not record the number of Higher and Lower passes achieved. Among the 1957–8 and 1970–2 cohorts, success may be measured by attainment in SCE examinations, so for these cohorts we have used criteria defined in terms of various numbers of Highers passes or A–C awards at O-grade. We have drawn 'school-success lines' to connect the points representing these criteria on each of figures 12.1, 12.2 and 12.3. There is a logical connection between the points on each school-success line: to reach the level of attainment indicated by any point on this line, one must have surpassed the levels indicated by all the points further to the right along the line. (We have assumed that anyone with one Higher surpassed the level of attainment represented by six or more O-grade awards at A–C.)

The data on the 1957–8 cohort in figure 12.2 came from two separate sources which are not comparable and we have drawn two school-success lines, one for each source. Neither source gives a reliable estimate of the general level of inequality, for reasons outlined in the section above. However, since the different estimates of inequality based on any one source were subject to the same biases, they can more reliably be compared with each other. So, even though there must be some uncertainty about the overall level of inequality in the 1957–8 cohort, we can speak with more certainty about variations in equality between different stages and sectors of education for that cohort.

Figures 12.1, 12.2 and 12.3 indicate the educational expansion that has taken place since the war. The two criteria of school success for the 1948 cohort were reached by a mere 11 per cent and 13 per cent of the cohort respectively (figure 12.1). Among the 1970–2 cohort, however, as many as 67 per cent gained some kind of SCE award, the lowest criterion of school success used here. The school-success line for the 1970–2 cohort slopes downwards from left to right, indicating that there was less inequality at the lower levels of attainment, and more at the higher levels (figure 12.3). However, this does not necessarily mean that class bias was greater at the higher levels of secondary education, for the gap between the prediction line and the school-success line is roughly constant over the attainment range. As we argued above, if some of the class influences on attainment are mediated by non-school factors with a class distribution similar to that shown in figure 12.4, then the tendency for inequality to be greater at the higher levels of attainment may therefore have been a result, not of greater institutional bias at these levels, but of the class distribution of non-school factors which was also more unequal at higher levels.

For the 1957–8 cohort the school-success line connecting the levels of inequality for one Higher pass and one O-grade pass respectively is roughly parallel to the prediction line (figure 12.2: National Survey estimates, indicated by ⊗). However, at levels of attainment above one Higher pass (moving from right to left) the inequality line for Highers achievement (SEDA estimates, indicated by ×) and the prediction line converge. The National Survey data (⊗) also show convergence and indeed show inequality falling between one and two Highers, although these estimates are based on small sample numbers and are subject to wide margins of error. The SEDA data show inequality falling very slightly between one and two Highers; it then remains steady up to four Highers before increasing at five Highers. Overall, the trend is for inequality to remain virtually constant over the different criteria of Highers attainment. We have already argued that any biases in the 1957–8 data were unlikely to affect the *slope* of this school-success line, so we can dismiss the idea that this finding is a consequence of limitations in the data. Yet it is a remarkable finding, as we can readily see by comparing the (more or less) horizontal school-success line with the sloping prediction line. At higher levels of attainment (above one Higher) the level of inequality differed less and less from the level of inequality which one would have predicted from non-school factors distributed as in figure 12.4.

In the 1957–8 cohort, therefore, the distribution of achievement *among* Highers pupils was less class-biased than at the other levels of secondary education.

There are at least two possible explanations for this, both of which may be applicable here. On the one hand, because of class inequality earlier in secondary education, the working-class pupils who survived into the Highers population may have been more rigorously selected than the middle-class survivors in terms of ability, determination or whatever. As far as ability is concerned, however, it seems unlikely that differential selection is a major part of the explanation, for within the Highers population working-class pupils scored lower by roughly one-fifth of a standard deviation on a test of verbal aptitude administered two months before the SCE examinations (McPherson, 1973b, pp. 14 and 27, n. 4). The second explanation is that the working-class survivors who reached the Highers population were thereafter relatively insulated from the pressures which had created inequalities lower down the school. In this view Highers pupils in Scotland had been selected for what Turner (1960) has described as a 'sponsored' form of educational mobility, and once selected they were relatively protected against the influences on survival and success which characterise the alternative ('contest') mode of mobility.[15]

By the time of the 1970–2 cohort, much of this effect seems to have disappeared. Inequality continues to increase with higher levels of Highers achievement; it rises almost continuously in figure 12.3 from 0.72 (for at least one Higher pass) to 0.80 (for at least six Highers passes). The vertical gap between the school-success line and the prediction line does get narrower at the highest levels of attainment; the gap is 0.24 for one or more Highers, 0.21 for five or more Highers and 0.18 for six or more Highers. However, this convergence is much less pronounced than for the 1957-8 cohort, among whom the gap falls from 0.23 for one or more Highers to 0.13 for five or more Highers. The influences which prevented inequality from increasing at the upper levels of attainment among the 1957-8 cohort had significantly weakened by the 1970s.

We can only speculate on the reasons for this change. We suggested above two possible explanations for the 1957-8 patterns: one arising from the highly selected nature of the Highers population (which we are inclined to discount), and the other relating to the institutional arrangements of sponsorship, which insulated this group from the continuing influence of social class. The Highers pupils in the 1970-2 cohort were less highly selected than those in the 1957-8 cohort, in the sense that a much larger proportion of the age-group passed a Higher, 27 per cent compared with 15 per cent, but they were just as rigorously selected in terms of class (inequality for one Higher was almost the same in the two cohorts). The data do not reveal whether the nature of this inequality changed between the periods concerned, but this seems unlikely. We therefore seek an explanation in terms of institutional factors affecting class influences among Highers pupils. The expansion of Highers may well have made a difference: institutions which successfully insulated 15 per cent of the age-group from external social influences may have been less effective when the numbers nearly doubled. Alternatively, the comprehensive reorganisation of the 1960s and 1970s might have encouraged a move away from 'sponsorship' to 'contest' norms for organising educational mobility, with a consequent decline in the system's willingness or ability to protect the ablest working-class children against any adverse influences arising from their class background. However, the evidence we review in chapter 14 does not support this last speculation.[16]

Whatever the explanation, by the early 1960s Highers classes in Scottish secondary schools, like sixth forms in England, were relatively insulated from the factors which fostered class inequality; a decade later, much of this effect had slipped away in Scotland.

Stages and sectors: staying on and course placement

Research in England and Wales has suggested that class differences in the age of school-leaving explained much of the overall class difference in educational attainment (Halsey, Heath and Ridge, 1980, p. 188) and that, if education is seen as a sequence of stages, social class has strongly influenced staying on to each stage, but has had little influence on the subsequent success of those who have done so (ibid.; Little and Westergaard, 1964). However, this does not seem to have been the case in Scotland.

In each of figures 12.1, 12.2 and 12.3 we have drawn a 'staying-on line', similar in principle to the school-success line, to connect the levels of class inequality associated with staying on beyond different dates or ages. The staying-on line for the 1948 cohort appears to confirm the English experience: class inequality for staying on was greater than for school success. However, for the 1948 cohort our staying-on data cover boys only. Class inequality was higher for boys than for girls in respect of all criteria of attainment except university entrance (not shown), so the school-success line for boys only (not shown in figure 12.1) was also higher than the one for both sexes shown in figure 12.1. Among boys, attainment and staying on showed similar levels of class inequality and, in the absence of evidence to the contrary, we would expect the same to have been true for girls.

For both of the later cohorts staying on and school success respectively showed similar levels of class inequality. Indeed, in the 1970–2 cohort there was rather less inequality in staying on into a sixth year than in school success.

The Scottish data do not, therefore, show the pattern observed in England, where class inequality in rates of staying on has been higher than for levels of subsequent attainment among the stayers. In Scotland, school success and staying on were associated with similar levels of class inequality; so, too, were school success and course placement. For the 1948 cohort we have estimates of inequality in relation to being on any five-year course or on a general five-year course respectively at 15 years (but before attaining the minimum leaving age); although inequality for these criteria was lower than inequality for completion of the same courses, the difference can be explained in terms of the slope of the prediction line. For the 1970 cohort the measures of inequality for attempting Highers and attempting an O-grade respectively lie almost exactly on the school-success line or its extrapolation.

Stages and sectors: post-school education

Among the 1948 cohort the criterion of attainment associated with the greatest level of inequality was entrance to university (figure 12.1). However, only a small proportion of the age-group (4 per cent) entered university; and the prediction line also predicts higher levels of inequality at these more exclusive levels. The greater level of class inequality associated with university entrance compared with school success may therefore reflect the class distribution of non-school factors rather than any additional bias in university admission procedures.

This conclusion is reinforced by our data on the two later cohorts (figures 12.2 and 12.3). For each of these cohorts we have recorded criteria of school success reached by about the same percentage of the cohort as entered degree courses, and we can therefore compare the level of inequality associated with degree-course entrance with levels of inequality associated with criteria of school success attained by comparable proportions of the age-group. Inequality in relation to degree-course entrance is fractionally above the school-success line among the 1957–8 cohort (figure 12.2) and fractionally below the school-success line among the 1970–2 cohort (figure 12.3); among both cohorts the differences are negligible, and among the 1970–2 cohort the inequality associated with university (as distinct from degree-course) entrance is identical to that associated with passing at least five Highers, a level reached by the same proportion of the cohort. Degree-course and university entrance have been no more and no less class-biased than equivalent levels of attainment in school.

For the 1970–2 cohort we obtained measures of inequality relating to several different levels of post-school education. In figure 12.3 these are joined by a 'post-school education line', which connects the observations for entrance to university and degree courses with observations for higher education, any full-time course and any full- or part-time course respectively. (Higher education in this definition includes advanced non-degree courses, such as those leading to Higher National Certificates and Diplomas, and the teaching diplomas awarded in the Colleges of Education.) The effect of following the post-school education line down from left to right is progressively to include the non-university sectors of tertiary education and the various levels of courses below degree-level. Following the line from left to right therefore reveals the contribution of the 'alternative route' of further education towards class equality in entry to tertiary education (Raffe, 1977). The line slopes downwards, revealing that this contribution was a positive one. In other words, the alternative route reduced the level of inequality in post-school education. As one mcves progressively down the post-school education line the level of class inequality falls more rapidly than inequality in the equivalent levels of success in the secondary school. The 'alternative route' pattern of further education therefore persisted among the 1970–2 cohort; the non-university sectors of post-school education, and especially their less advanced and part-time courses, continued to attract working-class entrants in sufficient numbers to have a favourable effect on the class inequality associated with post-school education as a whole, bringing it well below the level of inequality associated with equivalent levels of attainment in school.

The lower level of class inequality in entrance to post-school education does not necessarily mean that the content of further education was in any sense more 'working class' in orientation than that of secondary education, nor that the formal criteria for selection to other forms of post-compulsory education were class-biased. The criteria for selection to further education were generally less academic than those relating to higher education. Most further-education courses had a fairly specific vocational purpose, and going to further education depended more on the kind of job one was doing or hoped to do than on any criterion of academic 'merit'. Since further education tended to be oriented towards the more technical and skilled manual jobs, the relatively high level of working-class participation could have resulted from a relative propensity of working-class youths to enter such jobs.

Post-war trends in the level of class inequality

In the previous four sections we have mainly compared actual levels of inequality for different criteria of attainment *within* each cohort. In the section 'The level of inequality' we compared levels of inequality with those predicted from assumptions about the social distribution of ability or of other factors influencing attainment, and in the three sections immediately preceding this one, we compared levels of inequality associated with different criteria of attainment for each cohort; for instance, we compared inequality in school attainment with inequality in university entrance. In each case we mainly compared levels of inequality for the same cohort; our comparisons were therefore relatively unaffected by any lack of comparability of the data *between* cohorts.

We now wish to compare class inequality over the different cohorts to find out whether inequality has tended to increase or decrease over the two or three decades covered by our data. For these comparisons it is more important that our data for the three cohorts should be comparable. For reasons which we summarised in 'The level of inequality' we place least confidence in the estimates of inequality obtained for the 1957–8 cohort; in particular we consider the estimates of the general level of inequality for this cohort to be less reliable and therefore less suitable for comparison with the other cohorts. We will therefore restrict most of our discussion of trends to a comparison of the 1948 and 1970–2 cohorts only. A further discussion of the technical factors affecting the comparability of these two cohorts is contained in the Addendum at the end of this chapter.

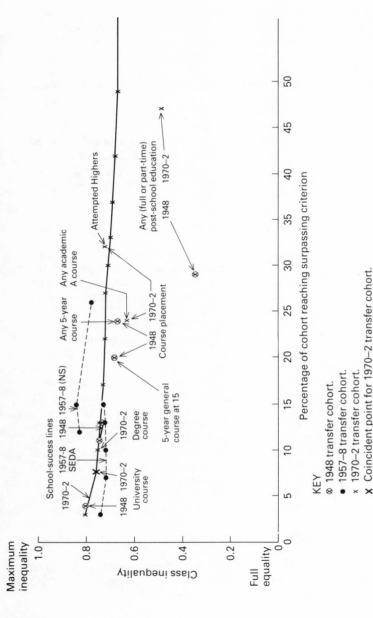

Figure 12.5 Class inequality for selected criteria of educational attainment: three transfer cohorts (selected from figures 12.1, 12.2 and 12.3)

In figure 12.5 we have plotted the level of inequality for selected criteria of attainment for the 1948 and 1970-2 cohorts, taken from figures 12.1 and 12.3 respectively. (We have also added the school-success lines from each source of data on the 1957-8 cohort, from figure 12.2.) We can infer trends in inequality by comparing the observations for the 1948 cohort (marked by ⊗ in figure 12.5) with those for the 1970-2 cohort (marked by ×).

When we compare these two cohorts we naturally wish to compare like with like, but this is not always easy or possible. For the 1948 cohort we measured school success in terms of course completion; there was no SCE O-grade at that time and the individual Highers results were not available to us. Yet the school-success line for the 1948 cohort (based on course completion) almost exactly coincides with the school-success line for 1970-2 (based on SCE achievement). The apparent conclusion is that inequality remained constant between the two cohorts; but this conclusion rests on the assumption that course completion in 1948 was equivalent to SCE attainment in 1970-2.

Comparing like with like in course placement is even more difficult. What we have termed an 'academic A course' for the 1970-2 cohort roughly corresponds in curricular terms to a five-year general (or language) course for the 1948 cohort. Yet the significance for educational attainment of such a course may have been very different in the institutional context of the 1970s. The requirements of our construct, the academic A course, are that the pupil should minimally have started in S3 or S4 courses with a view to SCE presentation in mathematics, English, a language and a science. This construct was an attempt to realise in a contemporary setting the contents of the older, academic certificate course.[17] It is interesting that the class inequality associated with this type of course fell between the earliest and most recent cohorts but only slightly (0.68 to 0.63 respectively), and that the estimated percentage of the age-group taking such a course increased only slightly from 20 to 24 per cent. With the rider that the academic A course had less formal status by the 1970s than it had in the 1940s and 1950s (the language requirement in particular being more questionable), we may say that some twenty years of educational change had had little effect on class chances of access to 'academic' education among pupils who were 15 but below the minimum leaving age. We may also note that the level of inequality associated with attempting Highers for the 1970-2 cohort is somewhat larger (at 0.72) than those for course placement in the 1948 cohort (0.67 and 0.68).[18]

Inequality in university entrance declined between the 1948 and 1970-2 cohorts. However, the proportion of the age-group entering university doubled, from 4 per cent to 8 per cent and, although the institution of the university remained formally unchanged, some might argue that expansion somehow devalued university education. How should we compare measures of inequality for the two cohorts with respect to university entrance or, indeed, to any criterion of attainment whose 'value' might have been affected by expansion in the proportion of the age-group achieving that criterion?

There are at least two ways of assessing trends in inequality where expansion has occurred. The first, which could be called a 'consumption' view, considers that the intrinsic value to an individual of a form of education is not diminished by its expansion (always provided that resources per capita do not fall and that 'more' provision does not mean 'worse' provision). On this view university expansion brought about a slight fall in class inequality. For most criteria of attainment in figure 12.5, inequality tends to fall as larger proportions of the age-group reach the level of attainment concerned. (In terms of our diagrams, the level of inequality, like the prediction line, usually slopes downwards from left to right.) Other things being equal, educational expansion tended to produce a very slight decline in class inequality as we have measured it.[19] However, this decline was probably due to the class distribution of the non-school factors which influenced attainment, rather than to qualitative change in the education system itself.

The second view could be termed 'a personal investment' view of education. It assumes that individuals value their education only in terms that are relative to the achievements of others. Thus the value of education to an individual depends on his or her ranking in the overall hierarchy of educational attainment. It implies that, in systems that select for employment on the basis of certification, what counts is not an absolute level of attainment that may have a fixed value in the 'consumption' view, but, rather, the level relative to others. Since educational expansion did not bring about an expansion in jobs at the equivalent levels, it might therefore be said to have devalued the kinds of education that were expanded. Only 4 per cent of the 1948 cohort entered university. Adopting a 'personal investment' view, we should therefore compare inequality in university entrance among this cohort, not with university entrance among the 1970–2 cohort, but with some criterion of attainment reached by 4 per cent of the later cohort. The outcome of such a comparison suggests that the level of inequality did not change; the level of inequality in university entrance for the 1948 cohort virtually overlapped the school-success line for the 1970–2 cohort (as indeed did inequality in university entrance for the later cohort). The decline in inequality in university entrance between these dates was precisely what we would expect as a result of expansion; the underlying pattern of inequality did not change.

Figure 12.5 has been constructed to facilitate comparisons from both the 'consumption' and the 'personal investment' points of view. For the latter, inequality can be compared for criteria of attainment which were reached by the same percentage of different cohorts. There was no change in inequality in relation to university entrance and school success. The trends in inequality in course placement were more erratic, and also more difficult to interpret (as we suggested above). There was one clear exception to our general rule that expansion induced a modest fall in the level of inequality: post-school education (considered as a whole) expanded considerably between the two cohorts, but the level of class inequality associated with it *increased* by a statistically significant margin. The influence of the 'alternative route' appears to have diminished. One possible explanation of this trend is the nature of the expansion of further education, which catered for young people entering a wider range of occupations than previously; it therefore became less strongly linked to the occupational routes on which working-class children were relatively well represented.

With this exception, however, figure 12.5 supports our view that expansion accompanied a very modest increase in equality, but only on the 'consumption' view of education outlined above. In terms of the 'personal investment' view, which compares levels of attainment reached by similar proportions of the age-group, inequality did not decline; indeed our data suggest that the level of inequality remained remarkably constant between the two cohorts.

From our review of the available data we conclude that none of our evidence suggests that overall class inequality in secondary-school attainment or university entrance was substantially different between the 1948 and 1970–2 transfer cohorts. Educational expansion may have led to a modest decrease in inequality in relation to particular criteria of attainment, but this can wholly be explained in terms of the continuing tendency for the greatest inequality to be associated with the most exclusive levels of attainment. If we compare levels of attainment of equivalent exclusiveness (that is, reached by similar proportions of the age-group), we find no evidence of any decline in inequality.

Conclusion

We are now in a position to answer the three questions which we posed at the beginning of this chapter. The first question asked what has been the level of class inequality in post-war Scottish education. Our answer is that inequalities in almost all areas of educational attainment have been consistently large, and in almost all cases larger than class differences in measured ability at the age of 11 years would predict.

The second question asked whether inequality varied between different criteria of attainment, in other words whether inequality was different for different stages and institutional sectors of education. We noted a tendency for inequality to increase slightly at levels of attainment reached by smaller proportions of the age-group; but this could well have been a result of the class distribution of the factors external to the education system which influenced attainment, and not a result of differential institutional bias. Allowing for this, entrance to university or degree courses has been no more or less class-biased than school attainment; and, contrary to English experience, we discovered no tendency in Scotland for class inequalities to be greater in relation to school-leaving and dropping-out than in relation to examination attainment. The main apparent institutional effect was among the Highers pupils in the 1957–8 cohort, whose examination success was relatively independent of class; but this effect had waned by the 1970s. We found that selection under the bipartite system produced class differences at 15 years (but before the minimum leaving age) comparatively near those predicted from differences in measured ability at 11 years, but this did not seem to reduce the overall level of class inequality in eventual attainment at school. We also confirmed that the 'alternative route' provided by non-university further education showed less inequality than comparable levels of secondary-school attainment; this effect also appeared to be waning in the 1970s.

Our third question asked whether the overall level of inequality has declined since the war. This question was inevitably harder to answer, partly because our sources did not yield precisely comparable data for the three cohorts, and partly because of the difficulty of making fair comparisons when basic categories have changed. However, not only has our evidence failed to show any trend in the level of inequality; we believe that, taken together, the data from various sources justify a stronger conclusion: that the general level of class inequality in Scottish education has remained remarkably constant since the war.

Our conclusions in this chapter call into question part of the received account of the Scottish education system on which much post-war educational policy has been based. In the first place, the folk image of the lad o' pairts, and the accompanying notion of equality receive a sharp knock. Scottish education since the war has been neither meritocratic nor equal; the levels of inequality reported in this chapter are similar to those observed in England and other Western societies. We argue in chapter 14 that the received account of Scottish equality had some validity in the rural and small-town areas whence it derived. However, it has not offered an accurate description of the experience of most of Scotland. Second, what we have termed the expansionist perspective, with its belief in progress, in the potency of educational institutions, and above all in the beneficence of expansion itself, is called into question. An increase in opportunity is not the same as an increase in equality of opportunity. Educational expansion has been accompanied by only very small gains in educational equality (except in instances such as staying on to 16 years, where total equality has been legislated into existence). Moreover, if one argues that, by definition, expansion lowers the relative value of a nominally unchanged level of attainment, then these gains were spurious, since there was no increase in equality of attainment at comparable levels of exclusiveness.

Educational expansion may be valued for the intrinsic benefits of the extra education for individual and society; but there is no evidence that it has changed social-class relativities in educational attainment in post-war Scotland.

Addendum

We list here the various ways in which the sources of data for the 1948 and 1970–2 transfer cohorts differed, and say why these differences probably do not invalidate our general conclusions from the comparison.

The target samples varied slightly; the 1948 subsample was drawn from all Scottish children attending school in 1947, whereas the 1970–2 sample covered only the four regions of Fife, Lothian, Strathclyde and Tayside, and excluded independent schools. However, these differences are unlikely to have affected our comparisons; only 1 per cent of the 1948 sample attended independent schools, and the four regions in 1970–2 accounted for three-quarters of the age-group in Scotland. The remaining quarter would have had to have been very different, if it were to affect the national average.

The 1948 sample was subject to the attrition and non-co-operation associated with longitudinal studies; the 1970–2 sample was subject to (possibly different) biases in non-response to a postal survey as well as to largely unknown biases in the construction of the sample. The 1948 sample was not subsequently weighted (or post-stratified), whereas the 1970–2 sample was weighted to produce population estimates based on sex, attainment and type of school; and the weights therefore compensate for sampling and non-response biases related to these variables. We described our procedures for weighting the 1970–2 data in chapter 2; we believe that our use of weighted data is justified, even in this chapter, because sampling and non-response biases affected the 1970–2 sample more than they affected the 1948 sample. Nevertheless, it is probable that we over-corrected for the 1970–2 biases in comparison with the 1948 sample. We therefore re-estimated our measures of inequality for the 1970–2 cohort using unweighted data, and found that the effect of having used weighted rather than unweighted data on the 1970-2 sample was to have increased our estimate of inequality by an average of 0.04 over the thirteen criteria of SCE achievement; over the criteria of achievement in the higher ranges, reached by less than 30 per cent of the age-group, the average increase was 0.06. If our use of weighted data for 1970-2 did indeed over-correct for the differential bias between the samples, we might expect that the appropriate comparable levels of inequality for 1970-2 lay somewhere between the weighted and the unweighted estimates, that is, marginally below the levels reported in figure 12.5.

The other main potential sources of non-comparability arise out of differences in the definition, collection and classification of information about social class (father's occupation). Discrepancies could have arisen out of differences in the actual occupation asked for, in the treatment of missing data, and in the methods of classifying the data.

Maxwell (1969) does not say at which date the occupations of the fathers of the 1948 transfer cohort were measured; the basic information was collected in 1947, when the sample children were aged 11, but Maxwell implies (p. 24) that the information was updated to account for later occupational changes, although he does not make clear how and when this was done. For the 1970-2 transfer cohort the measures refer to 1977, after the sample had left school. However, these differences are unlikely to have a significant effect on comparisons between cohorts. Possibly more serious is the different treatment of missing or unclassifiable data. Father's occupational class was recorded for all but 2 per cent of the 1948 cohort, whereas 12 per cent of the 1970-2 cohort could not be classified. These omissions cannot be treated as random, since they tend to affect categories (such as one-parent families) for whom the effects of background on educational attainment might be especially strong. Indeed, it is likely that the unclassified group resembles the working class much more than the middle class with respect to educational opportunity. We therefore recomputed our estimates of inequality for the thirteen SCE-achievement criteria among the 1970-2 cohort, counting unclassified children as working class. The estimates of inequality thus obtained were almost identical with those reported in table 12.1. Over the thirteen criteria reached by less than 30 per cent of the age-group (the part of the range that was of interest to our inter-cohort comparisons) the average difference was a mere 0.007. If we are correct in assuming that most children with no information on class should 'really' have been classified as working class, then the effect of their omission on our estimates of inequality seems to have been negligible.

Probably the most serious discrepancy between cohorts is their use of different definitions of social class. For the 1970-2 cohort we used the aggregated version of the Registrar-General's classification employed elsewhere in this book. In the 1948 data, however, this classification was only available for the boys in the sample, and we have created middle- and working-class categories by reaggregating the nine occupational classes described by Maxwell (1969). (See note 1 to this chapter.) However, since the occupations of the fathers of the boys in the 1948 sample were coded into both the Registrar-General and the Maxwell classifications, we were able to test the effects of the different classifications on the estimates of inequality among boys in the sample. (We are grateful to Dr Keith Hope of Nuffield College for his assistance with these and other analyses.) More boys were middle class in terms of the Maxwell classes (22 per cent) than in terms of the Registrar-General's classes (15 per cent). When the two class measures were applied to the same data to produce alternative estimates of inequality, the Maxwell measure tended to produce the higher estimate, with an average difference in inequality of just under 0.04. This estimate of the effect of the class categories is very tentative: the difference between the two estimates of inequality varied substantially over the eight criteria for which a comparison is possible, and if we exclude the university criterion, which was based on a small sample number, the average difference falls to 0.03. The estimates of inequality reported for both sexes of the 1948 cohort in figure 12.5 are therefore probably slightly greater than those that would have been estimated had we been able to use the Registrar-General's classes. (The weaker predictive power of the latter class measure seems to confirm widespread doubts about the validity of this measure. See, for example, Bland, 1979.)

The conclusions of this discussion of the comparability of the data on the 1948 and 1970-2 cohorts can be summarised as follows. To produce estimates of inequality that were comparable for the two cohorts, we would slightly reduce those for the 1970-2 cohort in figure 12.5, to offset some of the effects of weighting, and we would slightly reduce those for the 1948 cohort, to allow for the use of the Maxwell class categories. These two adjustments would largely cancel each other out. The other possible sources of non-comparability have probably not affected the estimates either way. As far as we can tell, therefore, the comparison between the two cohorts in figure 12.5 provides a relatively unbiased indication of trends in class inequality since the war, or to be more precise, of the absence of such trends.

Of course, our data on both cohorts were obtained from samples and are therefore subject to the possibility that, by chance, the samples were unrepresentative of the cohorts they were meant to represent. We can quantify this possibility by providing 95 per cent confidence limits, such that the chances of the true level of inequality *not* falling between these limits is only one in twenty; these are shown in table

12.1. The estimates of inequality would have to differ substantially between the two cohorts for there to be a statistically significant difference; except in the case of post-school education, the differences fall far short of statistical significance.

Chapter 13

The Reorganisation of Secondary Education[1]

Introduction

The Labour government of 1964, the first for thirteen years, outlined its intention to reorganise secondary education on comprehensive lines in two circulars, Circular 10/65 to the English local authorities (Department of Education and Science, 1965) and Circular 600 to those in Scotland (Scottish Education Department, 1965a). With only the half-hearted mention of a possibility of experiment with a middle-school system 'in a few areas', Circular 600 recommended the 'all-through' comprehensive school as the only acceptable form of secondary provision for Scotland. Such schools were to provide courses for all six of the secondary-school years, including courses that led to presentation at the SCE O-grade and H-grade. Where distance and accommodation allowed, all pupils from the local area were to attend, and only those pupils. In 1965, roughly a fifth of Scottish education-authority (EA) secondary schools were already comprehensive in this omnibus sense (although pupils were streamed on entry) and roughly a third of EA pupils attended them (Scottish Education Department, 1966a, pp. 33–4). Circular 10/65, by contrast, recommended no less than six models to the English local authorities where only 4 per cent of local education-authority secondary schools were already comprehensive and only 8 per cent of state-school pupils attended them (Department of Education and Science, 1974, table 3(3)). By 1971, 40 per cent of Scotland's EA schools were officially designated as all-through comprehensives in that they offered five- or six-year courses to an entry from a fixed catchment area, an entry that had not been formally selected in terms of attainment or intelligence. A further 21 per cent of EA schools had comprehensive intakes, but transferred some or all of their certificate pupils to other schools, usually after second year (Scottish Education Department, 1972b, table 4.4). In England

and Wales in 1971, only 29 per cent of local education-authority secondary schools were comprehensive (Department of Education and Science, 1974, table 3(3)). By the mid-1970s, nearly all of Scotland's EA schools were either all-through comprehensives or four-year comprehensive schools serving isolated communities, but with the possibility of transfer to a neighbouring all-through comprehensive. In 1974, 98 per cent of all pupils in Scottish EA secondary schools attended schools with a comprehensive intake (Scottish Education Department, 1975, p. 1) and the grant-aided (GA) sector accounted for only 3 per cent of all EA and GA secondary-school pupils (Scottish Education Department, 1977e, table 1(4)).

By 1965, therefore, Scotland had proportionately more comprehensive schools than England and Wales and thereafter moved more decisively towards a predominantly comprehensive secondary *system*. No doubt the pace and character of this change in Scotland owed something to the higher levels of comprehensive provision that already existed and to other distinctive features of Scottish political and educational life: to the greater influence of the central administration in education north of the Border; to the more widespread control of local authorities by the Labour Party; and to the resultant harmonisation of policy at national and local levels.

Nevertheless, other aspects of the Scottish experience of comprehensive reorganisation reflect at least three interrelated features that are relevant to a wider British context. First, as in England and Wales, the thrust of central government and administration in Scotland towards a single, uniform model has been mediated by the local interplay of a variety of factors: religion, community aspiration, the size and dispersion of the population, the architectural, organisational and intellectual inheritance from the earlier system, and the influence on occasion of the educational directorate. As we show in the next chapter, any attempt to learn from the national experience, whether in Scotland, England, or elsewhere, must take account of such variations in local circumstances.

Second, although omnibus schools were more common in Scotland by the mid-1960s and although the issue was less bitterly disputed between the Scottish Labour and Conservative Parties, reactions to Circular 600 and its consequences contributed in Scotland to the declining consensus on policy for secondary education in much the same way as was the case with Circular 10/65 in England. Thereafter in both countries, the educational professionals, and especially the teachers, inspectors and directors who had earlier been involved in the formulation of advice on educational policy, were to find their claims to professional expertise or to authoritative knowledge increasingly exposed to the determined and sometimes impulsive criticism of local and national politicians. What mainly impelled such politicians were the manifest inequalities of provision that they saw among young secondary-school pupils. And these inequalities seemed to have a diminishing justification even in their own terms, for by the early 1960s the critique of school transfer procedures that used tests of intelligence or attainment for 10 or 11-year-olds was firmly established in the public mind (though far from fully accepted by many professionals in Scotland).

Third, in Scotland, as in England, the purpose of reform was more easily stated in the negative terms of opposition to existing procedures for selection at 11 or 12 than in the more positive terms of the new forms of education that might be possible or desirable. In other words, Scotland, like England, has experienced dispute and uncertainty over the purposes and feasibility of comprehensive reorganisation, and over what part, if any, was to be played by the selection of pupils during compulsory secondary education. These were questions that Scotland's earlier experience with comprehensive schools could not easily illuminate, for omnibus though the schools had been, pupils entering them had always been streamed to one of a number of courses, usually on the basis of primary-school tests of intelligence and attainment. Though the term 'comprehensive' had been used to describe such schools at least since the 1940s, the provision of a common course for all pupils was not generally regarded as essential to its meaning (Scottish Education Department, 1947, chapter 7; 1951, para. 23).

In the next section of this chapter we briefly examine the Scottish inheritance of educational forms and values. We then show how these influenced both the forms of post-war school provision in Scotland, and also Scottish reactions to the emergent issue of reorganisation. After that we analyse the various aims that were entertained for comprehensive reorganisation and show how, at the heart of the movement for change, there were doubts, uncertainties and conflicts of value and purpose. Finally, we briefly discuss what perspective sociology might bring to bear both on the political movement for change in the schools and on the question of how one evaluates, and tries to learn from, the aims, methods and consequences of this movement. Chapters 14 and 15 are examples of such evaluations.

The inheritance of forms and values

In the course of the protracted nineteenth-century dispute over the maintenance of a distinctively Scottish form of university education, Scottish protagonists articulated a prescriptive and descriptive view of their educational institutions whose influence on educational thought and policy in this century has been substantial. As we have indicated in chapters 1 and 3, this view (though not unanimous) emphasised the social, economic, intellectual and moral importance of the generous public provision of educational opportunity at all levels. Balancing this 'collective' emphasis or value, as one of us has termed it, was an emphasis on individualism (McPherson, 1973a): the elect individual of merit, talent or parts was believed to be a minority (though he might be found in any social class); the purpose of generous public educational provision was, *inter alia*, to make initial opportunities available to all such individuals; what they thereafter made of these opportunities depended on their merit; the struggle to realise talent in the face of economic adversity was morally and intellectually enhancing; the public economy that was necessary to distribute educational opportunity to all those of talent led therefore not only to public economic and spiritual growth, but to individual virtue as well.

Twentieth-century Scottish policy for secondary education was formed initially in the light of these ideas: of the economy that spreads scarce resources more generously; of the ladder to an accessible university; and of talent and worth defined in terms of the single academic capacity to mount that ladder. The right to free secondary education was not recognised in England until 1944. But in Scotland, it was recognised in the 1918 Act (Knox, 1953, p. 242) and higher proportions of the Scottish age-group thereafter received secondary schooling. Nevertheless, after 1918, the intellectual inheritance from the nineteenth century could be invoked in support of two different types of post-primary-school system. In towns, burghs and rural areas with certain characteristics of population size and distribution, economy required that provision for all post-primary pupils should be made in a single school (often by enlarging the existing school). But where population size and density were higher, and especially in the four cities, more differentiated and larger units were practicable. There economy indicated that provision for pupils who might eventually aspire to the accessible university (chapter 3) might be made separately from that for the new, non-academic types of post-primary-school pupils. Circular 44, whose rehearsal of the 'immemorial Scottish tradition' of university education we have already cited in chapter 3, recommended for such pupils 'an entirely separate organisation even in subjects which are common to the Secondary and to the non-Secondary group. Combination may be convenient, but it is educationally unsound' (Scottish Education Department, 1921, para. 7).

Out of this advice there eventually developed, especially in the Scottish cities, the bipartite pattern of senior and junior secondary schools paralleled in England after the war by the grammar school and secondary modern school respectively. New provision for non-academic pupils was, to some extent, made in those parts of the more densely populated areas of the country where there had not previously been sufficient demand for, or sufficient concern to provide, academic secondary education – in the less favoured areas of the inner cities or on new council estates, and perhaps more in the industrial conurbation of the west, rather than in the towns and rural areas of the east, north and south.

Arguably, therefore, the bipartite secondary provision in the cities was from the outset partly correlated with their social class and residential segregation. Nevertheless, this provision had been made in the name of the same values that were used to justify the development of omnibus secondary schools, especially in those areas where much of Scotland's educational history had previously been made, in the east and the north. Developed and maintained as one institution for all on the grounds of economy, the outer form of such schools could easily accommodate inherited ideas about the classlessness of Scottish communities and the universal recognition they gave to merit rather than to inherited position. Indeed, in the minds of the members of the 1947 Advisory Council, the omnibus school, as an expression of inherited values, could also be a vehicle for new thinking about a comprehensive ideal that could be realised in an urban, industrial, twentieth-century Scotland where social-class differentiation bit deep.

Some Scottish reactions to comprehensive reorganisation

It is somewhat ironic, therefore, that the Advisory Council's supreme attempt to reinterpret the inheritance of Scottish character and of forms of educational organisation should itself contribute to the continuing and uncritical acceptance of the Scottish myth. The fact that the Advisory Council in 1947 had prescribed the omnibus school as 'the natural way for a democracy to order the post-primary schooling of a given area' was often thereafter taken as an adequate description of the system that subsequently developed; and the correspondence of that description to the organisation of what, by the mid-1960s, was still only a minority of Scottish secondary schools, nevertheless was taken as a sufficient basis for the claim that Scotland did not need comprehensive reorganisation because it had comprehensive schools already. Moreover, the Advisory Council Report of 1947 also supplied sufficient arguments to support the view that bipartite provision 'in cities and other areas of dense population' (para. 180) was nevertheless consistent with a Scottish ideal of general omnibus education.[2] In the early 1960s therefore, many in the professional world of Scottish education argued that comprehensive reorganisation was more than a political incursion into a world where professional judgments should

235

reign; it was an *English* political incursion that would never have arisen solely from the endogenous processes of Scottish society, education and government; it was a product of the political union, and it was a product of a new phase in Labour Party thinking and of new relationships between national and local policies.[3]

Issues of national and local identity were therefore involved in the debate over comprehensive reorganisation. One reason for this was the earlier success of the Scottish local authorities in expanding the percentage of the age-group for whom they were able to provide selective secondary education (chapter 4, 'The university inheritance'). It has been estimated that one result of the more generous Scottish provision was to give Scottish working-class pupils a better opportunity of entering a selective secondary course than that enjoyed by middle-class pupils of the same level of ability in England and Wales (Douglas *et al.*, 1966). Many found it difficult to resist the corollary that, *if* the purpose of comprehensive reform south of the Border was to improve working-class opportunities of access to academic education, the greater public provision that Scotland made had already achieved for the Scottish working-class pupil the level of opportunity that, in practice, was desired for his or her English counterpart. Moreover the transferring Scottish pupil was typically allocated to one of a more differentiated range of courses than was the case in England and Wales and, following from this, for courses that were not so exclusively associated with one of two types of secondary institution and therefore with a clear-cut distinction between success and failure.

Arguments about the character of the national system also had a local purchase which had often proved persuasive to a post-war generation of Labour councillors. The selective secondary school offered a ladder of opportunity to some working-class pupils. As in some parts of England and Wales as well, pride in the wider social engineering which socialists and others felt they were achieving through public secondary provision was mixed with civic pride in the achievements of the local school. Support for selective schools was not, therefore, confined to the middle-class parents of able children; it could also be found in more homogeneous working-class communities, for example, in Fife and Lanarkshire. And where in such communities Catholics (who tended to be Labour supporters) experienced prejudice at work and elsewhere against their faith, the selective secondary school was perhaps even more important as the major legitimate means of advancement that was likely to open to their children (Payne and Ford, 1977). And did not the historical continuity of characteristically Scottish educational provision over the years give to such local communities a more solidary, less differentiated character? To quote at greater length than in chapter 3 the argument with which the Director of Education for Lanarkshire questioned the movement towards all-through schools when writing for his committee members in 1965 (McEwan, 1965, p. 1,680):

> The arguments about comprehensive schools in England frequently refer to considerations of 'the middle class' and 'the working class' which are hardly mentioned in Scottish debates on the subject, partly because there is in fact less social distinction in Scottish and Lanarkshire communities, but largely because our senior secondary schools, even when selective, carry pupils who constitute a complete cross section of the community. In Scotland there is little point in making changes to ensure that middle class children meet working class children at school; they do already.

The Lanarkshire example is worth pursuing for a moment, for it well illustrates how the issue of selection at 12 and thereafter was not easily separable from considerations of the historical relation between school and society in Scotland. Lanarkshire was Scotland's most heavily populated county, but its largest town at the time numbered only 75,000 inhabitants and only two others exceeded 40,000. Moreover, the authority was obliged to make separate provision for the 35 per cent of Catholics in the county's school population; and since, in Scotland generally, a higher proportion of the Catholic working population was manually employed and its children tended to be under-represented relative to the non-Catholic population in post-compulsory school courses, it was especially difficult for a thriftily-minded county authority to provide denominational schools of an economic size without recruiting pupils from more than one catchment area to schools providing upper-secondary certificate courses. Hence after the war the older academies, high and grammar schools, there and elsewhere, were supplemented by schools offering only shorter courses. Until the late 1960s in Lanarkshire there was a complex pattern of three-year junior secondary (secondary modern) schools, four-year schools offering O-grade courses, and only ten six-year senior secondary schools, three of which were Catholic. Only in one town in the rural south was there an all-through comprehensive school serving a single community, although there were several other grammar schools and academies that admitted local pupils on a non-selective basis at 12 years and others from junior secondary or junior high schools (the latter offering SCE O-grade course work) on a selective basis thereafter. The senior secondary schools each drew selected pupils from extensive catchment areas, which even encompassed the entire county in the case of one school (Scottish Education Department, 1977d).

Was such a system selective or comprehensive or something of both? The same question could be asked of the system in Fife. Perhaps more than any other Scottish authority, Fife had determinedly expanded access to academic, selective secondary education in order to broaden and lengthen the ladder of opportunity available to working-class pupils. In the early 1960s, in the words of the 1972 Inspectorate Report (Scottish Education Department, 1973a, p. 16):

> the Authority embarked on a policy of reorganisation which involved the closure of a large number of small secondary departments and the centralisation of pupils in larger units. The aim was to achieve a two-tier system of junior and senior high schools; the former were to take all the pupils in their areas for the first two years, after which those able to profit from courses leading to Higher Grade examinations would transfer to the senior schools which would cater for SIII–VI pupils only; the others would remain in the junior high schools and follow courses for Ordinary Grade examinations or courses for early school leavers.

By the time the authority's education committee changed to a policy for all-through six-year comprehensives in 1967 the two-tier system had been established, sometimes with new buildings, in several areas, and more than half the schools were housed in modern, post-war buildings often of a location, size or design that was inappropriate to the new policy. The authority decided 'to continue the two-tier system, where it existed, as an interim compromise arrangement; and indeed it was felt desirable to create some new junior high schools in order to spread the benefits of non-selective entry to as many parts of the county as possible' (ibid., p. 16). A similar junior/senior high-school system continued in parts of Renfrewshire until 1974, but that was the only county authority to delay the adoption of a predominantly all-through six-year school system (Young, 1971; Scottish Education Department, 1973b; McKechin, 1976).

By the eve of Circular 600 Scotland had therefore evolved through practice and argument various notions of the comprehensive school and of a comprehensive-school system. The annual report of the SED for 1964, the last year of the Conservative administration, distinguished between 'comprehensive schools of the older traditional kind' (a six-year omnibus school, and probably one that had served an entire community for a considerable period), and 'new comprehensive schools', (also six-year and omnibus, but founded out of a more recent and explicit concern with the comprehensive ideal). The latter might still, nevertheless, serve a community as only one among several types of secondary school and find itself 'creamed' of more able pupils in consequence. The report (Scottish Education Department, 1965b, pp. 33–4) also distinguished three types of four-year school, at least two of which could be designated as comprehensive, either in themselves or else as part of a comprehensive system:

There are in the City of Glasgow four-year comprehensive schools which may pass on very promising pupils to associated six-year schools at the end of SII, but which tend to hold the majority of their Certificate pupils until they have completed the Ordinary grade course. Secondly, there are in the other cities and in many towns former junior secondary schools which have added Certificate courses leading to the Ordinary grade in SIV. Thirdly, in many areas, mainly rural, three-year schools which were formerly comprehensive throughout now pass on to a central school at the end of second year those pupils thought likely to secure passes on the Higher grade in the fifth year and retain the other Certificate pupils for presentation on the Ordinary grade in SIV. This type of school, which has emerged mainly for local historical and geographical reasons, is a close parallel to the junior high school that forms part of the two-tier system introduced in parts of England and now also in some counties in Scotland.

None of these organisational forms precluded the allocation of pupils to different levels of course on their entry to secondary school (streaming) nor their subsequent reallocation. In the words of one Director of Education, the only criterion for a comprehensive school was that 'children of all degrees of academic ability should have their secondary education under one roof' (Young, 1967, p. 58).

By the early 1960s, therefore, the four-year schools might be regarded in one of several ways. Some saw them as an evolutionary development in a system that could be called 'comprehensive' and that was pragmatically tailored to considerations of population, topography, religion, resources and traditional forms of local provision. Others regarded them as an attempt to maintain the identity, status and selective functions of the older, six-year academies and senior secondary schools by underpinning them with feeder schools that might transfer, on an academically selective basis after second year, some additional pupils who intended presentation for the Certificate (the possibility of a further transfer after a fourth, O-grade year being regarded as little more than token deference to an ideal of opportunity for slower developers). And some saw them as an inevitable expedient in the necessarily lengthy move to a national system of all-through, six-year schools.

Circular 600

The Labour government presented the case for reorganisation as a natural and modest development in an evolving Scottish tradition of common education and of common opportunities to acquire certification, saying (Scottish Education Department, 1965a, para. 4):

> the majority of all secondary pupils in education authority schools are now in schools which provide both non-certificate and certificate courses or, at least, their earlier stages. About 20 per cent are in schools which provide certificate courses only and a further 20 per cent are in schools which provide no certificate courses at all.

All that the circular absolutely required of the local authorities, without qualification, was that they should 'no longer . . . allocate pupils to "certificate" and "non-certificate" courses when they start the secondary stage' (ibid., para. 6). And even this condition was represented, in the annual SED report for 1965 (the first under the new Labour administration), as no more than the realisation of an inherited ideal: 'The effect of the firm allocation of pupils, before they enter the secondary school, to either certificate or non-certificate courses has all along precluded the schools from being *as truly comprehensive as their form suggests they should be*' (Scottish Education Department, 1966a, p. 35, our emphasis).

But what was the 'truly comprehensive' ideal that was indicated by the various extant comprehensive forms? Here the guidance was more problematic, for the circular's insistence on the six-year, all-through school (where circumstances permitted) did not so much answer this question as restate it: how was the six-year, all-through school itself to be organised? Pupils were to transfer to the same secondary school 'as a first step', but as a first step towards what? Here the answer seemed to be that the content and levels of later secondary education should remain unchanged. The circular affirmed government support both for the existing SCE system of examinations and for the continuing implementation of the 1963 Brunton Report, *From School to Further Education*. The Brunton Committee had been asked to consider in particular the 'educational needs, both vocational and general, of those young people *who either do not follow or do not complete courses leading to the Scottish Certificate of Education*' (Scottish Education Department, 1963, para. 1, our emphasis), and it had recommended separate courses in this respect in third and fourth year, aimed at about 65 per cent of the age-group, and centred increasingly on what the committee had called the pupil's 'vocational impulse'. The provision of such courses was clearly predicated on the selection and differentiation of pupils before work began for the SCE O-grade, in other words, towards the end of the second year or at the beginning of the third year. Logically, therefore, Circular 600 seemed to require not so much the abolition of selection, but the postponement of initial selection from 12 to 14 years; and it implied, more by its silence on the matter than by anything it said, that such selection should no longer be conducted according to publicly administered procedures, but should be entrusted to teachers within each school, though with some regard to the wishes of parents and pupils.[4] All it required (with certain negotiable exceptions) was that allocation to differentiated courses at 14 years (or 16 years) should not entail allocation to new schools for pupils intending certificate work. And this seemed to many people not to be so very different from the situation that already obtained in the traditional omnibus school.

One may conjecture a number of different purposes that supporters of 'the first step', the abolition of selective transfer at 12 years of age, may have had for that and any second or subsequent step. First, there was the view expressed in the circular itself, that 'young people will greatly benefit in their personal and social development by spending the formative years of early adolescence in schools where the pupils represent a fuller cross section of the community' (Scottish Education Department, 1965a, para. 5).

Second, for those who viewed education as a consumer or citizen right, a common course for 12 or 13-year-olds could be regarded as an end in itself: as, so to speak, a commodity that pupils were entitled to consume rather than as a possible product of transactions between pupils and teachers that might be affected by individual differences in ability or motivation.

Then there were several views that rested on the (sometimes implicit) belief that the common course, however achieved, would have new consequences. It might lead, third, to an increase in the proportion of 16 or 17-year-old pupils attaining certification at different levels (see, for example, Scottish Education Department, 1966b, paras. 3, 4 and 12); and, fourth, it might lead to a redistribution of certified attainments between the social classes (in effect, so that the average level of certification of working-class pupils would come to resemble that of middle-class pupils). These two goals might be held separately or jointly. For example, it might be hoped that the expansion of certification would occur particularly among working-class pupils and lead consequently towards an equalisation of educational outcomes between the classes. Both goals could also be differently stated, according to particular beliefs about the distribution of ability between the social classes, and about whether or not this distribution itself could be changed.

Indeed, the realisation of the belief that individual ability might not be fixed, but might yield to educational interventions that identified it more accurately and developed it more effectively, could be regarded as a fifth purpose that some had for comprehensive reorganisation (though often it may have overlapped with the fourth and third).

Taking this view further, there were, finally, those who felt that the talk should be of 'abilities' rather than of 'ability', and that the former should be rounded out to include aspects of the individual's moral, social and aesthetic sensibility that were not easily described in cognitive terms. Amongst other things this view implied a reduced emphasis on the academic and certifiable elements in the school curriculum, and a reduced emphasis on making public, certified judgments about the differences between pupils' attainments; what pupils could do or be relative to *absolute* moral and cognitive standards was judged to be more important than whether they were simply better or worse than other pupils.

Discussion

Comprehensive reorganisation, then, meant different things to different people and the question 'Has it worked?' requires us to distinguish these various goals and expectations, for they have differing implications for how one might work towards an answer or answers. Some of the resultant questions, then, appear to be more of the form 'Has comprehensive reorganisation happened?' (For example, has there been mixed-ability teaching; has a greater social mix been achieved within schools? and so on.) Other questions, however, are more of the form 'Have the things that (may) have happened had the expected consequences?'

But there are problems. The first concerns the role of theory in specifying political goals. Apparently factual questions about events, when pressed, often then take on the character of questions about expectations: persons who thought they wanted an increased social mix in the schools may later turn out actually to have wanted increased social mixing between children. They may have regarded a changed social mix as a precondition for greater social mixing; or, more likely, they may have thought that a changed social mix was sufficient to achieve greater social mixing. In the latter case further assumptions or expectations would be involved: an implicit theory of how pupil groups were organised and of how such organisation might influence the choices individuals made about mixing. In such instances the political goal can only be adequately stated when politicians know the correct explanation of human behaviour (or, more modestly, the generalisation about people that will apply best for the foreseeable future). Failing that, politicians may, nevertheless, attempt to improve their statement of goals, when they see evidence that the change that they thought would achieve their goal has not in fact achieved it.

Goals come to be stated, in other words, in dialogue with facts and as a part of a social process of doubting and learning. At each stage in this process, statements about both the facts and the goals are predicated partly upon implicitly theoretical or proto-scientific ideas about 'how society works' and about how one thing leads, predictably, to another. Bad theories or explanations may therefore lead to inadequate political programmes, and lack of theory may have the same effect. Comprehensive reorganisation itself was partly a result of collapsing faith in the theory of intelligence and learning that was taken to support the bipartite secondary-school system in England and Wales. But the lack of an accepted theory did not make it any easier to specify what the goals of reorganisation should be. Here, for example, is a Labour Member of Parliament in the annual Scottish Estimates Debate stating his purposes in terms of an understanding of ability, its definition, distribution and fixedness, that shifts several times as he speaks, with implications for the type of educational programme that is implied (House of Commons Debates, 1966):

> They [the Scottish Conservative Party] believed that 65 per cent
> of our school children would be the hewers of wood and drawers
> of water. . . . My argument in favour of comprehensive education
> is not because of party doctrine but because of the age of technology
> and science in which we live, and in which we cannot afford to
> waste the talents of our children. Of course, there is a pool of
> ability, but we have never accepted that it was for only 35 per
> cent of our children and that the other 65 would not have the
> opportunity of higher education . . . we must give to all children
> of aptitude and ability more opportunities in this day and age. . . .
> If we neglect to provide for the progress of our educational system,
> and to widen the pool of ability and so give our children an
> opportunity according to their aptitude and ability, this nation
> will suffer.

From this the purpose of comprehensive reorganisation could be variously construed: (i) as identifying all children 'of aptitude and ability' in a fixed pool of ability that would exclude some children; (ii) widening the pool of ability, possibly to include all children (and possibly not); and (iii) recognising different levels of ability among (implicitly) all children ('our children . . . according to their aptitude and ability'). Ability is defined implicitly as that which leads to 'higher education' and away from manual work; and higher education is valued as that which, through science and technology, keeps the nation from suffering; a moral view is also implied.

But if intelligible and plausible political goals are predicated upon 'good' understandings, the converse is also sometimes the case. Inadequate political programmes may sometimes lead to bad social explanations. To mobilise concerted action towards some goal, a politician must 'talk the same language' as those whom he or she wishes to influence: he or she must try to ensure that people share common purposes, a common understanding of how those purposes might be achieved, and a common, and explicit, will to achieve them. Under such conditions, something can, perhaps, be learned from the resultant course of events; a knowledge of society can emerge. But when one or more of these conditions does not apply, it becomes very difficult to learn about the world (and our potential to change it) from the often confused and disputed events of an unfolding political programme. One cannot, for example, easily say whether comprehensive education might work under certain conditions, when those involved in implementing it have shared neither a common understanding of what was entailed, nor a common will to achieve it. Such a situation may well arise when those who attempt to change the moral order find that this requires them also to try to change the terms of common discourse. Here, for example, is a minister, speaking a year later, also in the Scottish Estimates Debate (House of Commons Debates, 1967, our emphasis):

> I should now like to turn from the comprehensive reorganisation of our schools and its implications on their internal organisation and say a word about what is taught in the schools. We have always been concerned, and rightly . . . about the education of the more academically inclined boys and girls. . . . But the schools must also prepare our young people for the work they will do and the life they will lead outside. . . . [We require] a fundamental change in the thinking of many Scottish teachers and educationists about the balance of the secondary school curriculum, and particularly about its relationship to the requirements of examinations. This is some-thing which has been virtually a shadow over Scottish secondary education. The memorandum 'Raising the School Leaving Age — Suggestions for Courses', which was published at the end of last year, emphasised that in planning the non-certificate work of their pupils — *and I do not talk, and indeed we must not talk about 'non-certificate pupils' because even certificate pupils should take non-certificate work* — schools should think less of the traditional individual subjects and more of how the work relates to the three basic elements of social and moral education, preparation for leisure and vocation based activities.

In his attempt to change the priority given by teachers and others to academic subjects, pupils and examinations, the minister had to try to change the terms in which teachers thought of education. But in doing this, he was constrained to use terms they could understand. The result in this instance was an apparent logical confusion: some pupils were still to be termed 'certificate' pupils, but there were no longer to be 'non-certificate' pupils, a term that many regarded as one of implicit moral opprobrium arising from the moral approval that was given to the 'lad o' pairts' or the academically certificated pupil.

Thus, when we explore the crucial question of policy for selection *within* the comprehensive school, we find we have entered an area of uncertain theory, of value conflict and of logical confusion. If the first step was to abolish selection at the age of 12, it was not at all clear in which direction any second step would lead.

We emphasise that the purpose of these examples is not to argue that the language of politics is so hopelessly confused, or so cynically detached from the 'real' purposes of action, as to render it useless. Nor is it our purpose to imply that academics are knowledgeable and clever, whereas politicians are not. On the contrary, our argument is that the problems of politics and of social knowledge are interrelated; that politicians naturally find it difficult to be clear about political goals, and about the relationship of such goals to political means, when social scientists (or others) cannot provide knowledge about the world in which politicians must act. Equally, social science has difficulties in learning about that world when actions are undertaken in the name of political programmes that are confused, unexplicated and willed only by some. Moreover, even political programmes that fit this description may sometimes be politically 'adequate', in the sense that they are sufficient to the politician's immediate purpose. Political programmes are often an amalgam of different goals, expectations and beliefs that must be negotiated and argued within the party and beyond, developing and changing in the course of this process as they seek to gather or retain support.

We can therefore acknowledge that, in at least two respects, the interests of politicians make it difficult for social scientists to observe and learn from organised human activity. First, the more issues a political programme can cobble together, and the greater the success of politicians in representing these as a common, or at least mutually consistent, set of issues, the more likely it is that a major political programme like comprehensive reorganisation will command support, at least in the first instance. To the extent that the actions which social scientists study are themselves guided by the actors' interpretations of the purposes of such a programme, social science therefore faces problems. It must deal with a multiplicity of goals or purposes and it must expect to find that some of these have not been stated fully, consistently or exhaustively. Vagueness can be a political asset in maintaining coalitions. Second, it is not in politicians' interests to confess to uncertainty over the theoretical basis of their actions, the beliefs about 'how the world works' that ultimately are used to justify the means that are chosen to achieve ends. Nor, in the shorter term,

245

are politicians or governments much concerned to search energetically for negating evidence, for evidence that 'things are not working out as planned'. The public practice of scepticism undermines the claims to knowledge that parties and governments must use in attempting to maintain their authority, and with it, their executive effectiveness in carrying programmes through. Yet doubt and criticism are nevertheless part of the very methods by which knowledge is tested or tried, and goals are clarified. To the extent that social science is dependent upon government for access, data or resources, its ability to learn from the experience of political programmes is thereby diminished.

Despite all these considerations, there is sense, we think, to be made of Circular 600 and a clear role for social science to play in relation to it or other public programmes. The language and arguments of the circular, and its emphasis on the continuity of its proposals with previous trends and practices, bear all the marks of a document that was framed to command as wide support as possible from those whose practices it was nevertheless trying to change. 'As a first step' it was trying to remove unacceptable hindrances to the programme it envisaged.

But the subsequent stages of the programme could not be exhaustively specified in advance, for two reasons. First, the viability of the programme, and the scale of the goals it could adopt, depended partly on the will that could be mobilised nationally and in the classroom. Second, as people tried to make the first step work, public learning had to occur about what was possible, and how. It was hoped that this learning would itself feed back to influence the will and understanding of those who initially lagged.

From this perspective, the circular can usefully be understood as outlining an agenda for the school system to work out in the context of certain broad parameters (such as 'no selection at 12' and 'six-year comprehensives where possible'). The hope was that the underlying values and the first guidelines were such that a critical review of the consequences of the first actions would provide a surer basis for filling in the goals and means of further action. It is in this light that one may read the treatment by the department (in Circular 614 and in its annual reports for 1966-9) of the system's growing experience of the common course: critical discussion of examples of good practice that had been evolved in response to Circular 600 are recommended for further extension and become the fine details of a developing policy.[5]

Ten years later, however, we find exactly the same method of argument used in the annual report of the department to support the view that the common course was *not* working.[6] Our point, then, is not that the proto-scientific element in the making and reformulation of policy necessarily produces immutably true statements. It is, rather, that there is a rational element in policy arguments that social science can engage and must engage, if one is to explicate, observe and learn from historical experience.

To say that policy-making and social science share a partly overlapping logical ground is not to reduce social science to the study of existing policies nor to say that policy-making may ever be wholly scientific. Nor is it to argue that logically persuasive arguments are necessarily persuasive in practice, nor to minimise the considerable difficulties of knowing how best to learn from historical experience about the parameters and possibilities of action. Not only is there a tension between the social scientist's interest in open, sceptical evaluation and government's concern to maintain public credibility on the basis of often unexamined claims to knowledge; there is also a variety of goals, understandings and expectations that are mobilised, with varying degrees of success, as policy develops. In order to learn from the outcomes of action, one must ideally be able to describe what people thought they were doing, and how wisely and energetically they did it. And one must do this in the context of differing local situations, whether in the classroom or the council chamber, that may themselves have affected the conception of national policy and constrained its execution.

It seems to us that one can only work towards meeting such requirements through a dialogue that is open, critical and inclusive of all the parties to the situation under review. It is not the exclusive prerogative of social research to initiate such dialogues; but it may, nevertheless, do so by trying to infer purposes, understandings and constraints on action from publicly available evidence, and by offering provisional judgments on at least the consequences of a programme as initially understood by the researchers. This is the main purpose of the empirical chapter that follows. What might emerge from such a dialogue we leave for discussion in our final chapter.

Chapter 14

The Early Impact of Comprehensive Reorganisation

Introduction

Having discussed the movement for comprehensive reform, we turn now to an examination of the impact of reorganisation on the schools and schooling of the members of the 1977 sample, the oldest of whom transferred to secondary school in 1970. Our strategy in this chapter is to compare leavers from two groups of schools: first, from schools which had become fully comprehensive (in a sense that we will explain) by 1970; and second, from all other schools in the sample. The comparison focuses mainly on pupils' SCE attainment, if any, but is also made in terms of various 'non-cognitive outcomes' of schooling, namely truancy, corporal punishment and whether pupils judged their last year at school to have been worthwhile. Important though these may be, they represent, of course, only some of the many criteria of evaluation that might be applied to a reform that we have characterised as essentially polyvalent.

The early stages of reorganisation

We first describe aspects of the pace and pattern of the early stages of reorganisation. By the time the sample members left school in 1975–6, most schools in Scotland were comprehensive (chapter 13, 'Introduction'). However, the sample members had entered school between 1970 and 1972. At this time many schools had yet to become comprehensive, so many sample members transferred to secondary schools under selective arrangements (even though most of their schools subsequently became comprehensive). Table 14.1 summarises the history and organisation of the schools entered by sample members from the four regions (Fife, Lothian, Strathclyde and Tayside). More

TABLE 14.1   Schools attended by 1975–6 leavers in the four regions (percentage of leavers)

Type of school		Percentage of school-leavers
EA schools with fully comprehensive intakes by 1970:		55
established (Highers offered by 1970)	(33)	
non-established (Highers first offered between 1971 and 1974)	(22)	
EA schools with comprehensive first-year intake by 1970, selective intakes after first year		10
EA comprehensives founded after 1970		<0.5
EA selective schools in 1970:		17
selection abandoned by 1972	(8)	
still selective in 1972	(9)	
EA schools with no provision for Highers courses by 1974		13
Grant-aided schools		3
Independent schools		1
All leavers		99
Unweighted n		(16,926)

than half of the sample (55 per cent) left schools which had fully comprehensive intakes by 1970. More than half of this group (33 per cent of the whole sample) left schools which were 'established' in the sense that SCE Highers courses were already being offered to pupils in 1970. The other fully comprehensive schools, which accounted for 22 per cent of the leavers' sample, first offered Highers courses between 1971 and 1974 (that is, before the oldest of the sample members, those who transferred in 1970, reached fifth year. Sample members in these schools can therefore be presumed to have had the opportunity to attempt SCE examinations at both O-grade and H-grade). A further 10 per cent of the sample left schools which had comprehensive first-year intakes, but which were still partly selective because they still offered the only local EA provision of SCE courses to pupils who transferred from other schools at some time after the first secondary year. A few pupils (just under 0.5 per cent of the sample) attended comprehensive schools which were founded after 1970. The sample of leavers from these few schools is unrepresentative in the sense that there were no sixth-year leavers (and sometimes no fifth-year leavers) from these schools by 1976. One in six sample members (17 per cent) left EA schools which still had selective intakes in 1970, in the sense that entry still depended upon doing well in tests at the age of 11. However, this category was shrinking rapidly; nearly half of these leavers (8 per cent of the whole sample) were from schools which had ceased to be selective by 1972, the year in which a majority of the sample members entered secondary school. The remaining leavers from EA schools, 13 per cent of the whole sample, were from junior second-ary schools and other schools which had no provision for SCE Highers courses by 1974. None of the leavers from these schools could have completed a six-year course which involved starting Highers subjects in 1974. All the schools in this last group had intakes from which pupils attending selective schools had been creamed, or they had arrangements for the transfer of able pupils to other schools at a later stage, or both. Finally, 3 per cent of the sample had attended grant-aided schools, and just over 1 per cent had attended schools which were fully independent.

It is clear, therefore, that the sample relates to a specific stage in the early development of comprehensive education in one country; one should be cautious about drawing general conclusions from this sample concerning the effectiveness of comprehensive education at other times or in other countries. In particular, if the full potential of comprehensive education can only be realised when teachers, resources and the infra-structure of education have had time to adapt, then not all of its potential can be revealed by the data on 1977 sample members.

In this context one should also be aware that the schools that had become 'established comprehensives' by 1970 (in the sense that a full range of SCE courses was already available by that date, and that the intake was entirely non-selective) did not do so at random. Many had already been omnibus schools before Circular 600; and others may have been reorganised quickly because they presented fewer problems (of size, staffing or siting) than schools which took longer to reorganise. Also, the pace of early reorganisation varied between local authorities. By 1970 the proportions of established comprehensives (as we have defined them) were as follows (in descending order): the Lothian counties (other than Edinburgh) (17 out of 25 EA and GA schools), Dunbartonshire (11/22), Glasgow (29/68), Tayside (other than Dundee) (8/21), Ayrshire (9/29), Fife (5/21), Dundee (2/14), Lanarkshire (5/36), Edinburgh (3/25), Renfrewshire (2/33), Argyll (0/8; four of these schools had comprehensive first-year intakes but accepted transfers after first year). It is possible that, where established comprehensives had not yet become the modal form of provision within an authority, the support they enjoyed (of resources, services, advice and so on) was less emphatic than in authorities with a more established commitment to an omnibus, and later a comprehensive, ideal.

Definition of 'the comprehensive sector'

Another problem for a comparison between comprehensive and other schools is that even most of the 'selective' schools in the sample had turned comprehensive by the time the sample members left them in 1975-6. Does it make sense therefore to compare them with the other (comprehensive) schools in the sample, which merely made the change a little earlier? However, most arguments for comprehensive education stress the social and intellectual heterogeneity of pupils as a distinctive, or even a defining, feature; and since the only requirement on which Circular 600 insisted without qualification was that transfer to secondary-school courses should be non-selective, we regard the arrangements for selecting a pupil's own year-group as the criterion for deciding whether that pupil attended a 'comprehensive' school. The first of the sample members entered secondary school in 1970; so in analysing the 1975-6 leavers' data we count as comprehensive only those schools with fully comprehensive intakes by 1970. A pupil who entered a school in 1970 under selective arrangements would not have experienced comprehensive education (by our definition and by that of the circular), even if the school was reorganised while he or she was still a pupil there.

Our next problem is that, even if we have properly identified 'comprehensive' schools, a comparison between these and the other schools in the sample would be misleading, if they recruited pupils who differed in terms of ability or background characteristics which were likely to influence attainment. A longitudinal study conducted by the National Children's Bureau (NCB) has shown how children entering comprehensive schools in England had lower average test-scores at 11 years and were more likely to be working class than children entering the selective sector of grammar and secondary modern schools (Steedman, 1980). We might expect a similar pattern in Scotland. It is likely that catchment areas served by comprehensive schools differed on average from catchment areas served by other schools, and in particular that the social and intellectual composition of the intakes to the two types of school differed, prejudicing any simple comparison between comprehensives and other schools. These differences are compounded by 'creaming', which occurs when children in a catchment area served by a comprehensive school attend another, selective school in any of the maintained, grant-aided or independent sectors; since such children are more likely than others to be able or middle class (or both), their absence means that the comprehensive school is left with a group of pupils from which many of the more promising pupils have been creamed.

We cannot estimate the number of potential pupils lost by each school as a result of creaming; and, even if we could, we could not easily estimate how this creaming affected the average ability of the pupils attending the school. We can, however, identify schools whose proximity to selective schools made it likely that their intakes were creamed. This category of potentially creamed comprehensive schools included all the comprehensive schools in the cities of Dundee, Edinburgh and Glasgow, since each city contained at least one selective school. A few other schools in counties such as Lanarkshire, Renfrewshire, Dunbartonshire and Fife were also sufficiently near to selective schools to be affected by creaming.

Overall, one-quarter of the sample, and nearly half of those attending schools which were fully comprehensive in 1970, attended schools which we have considered to be creamed; rather fewer than one-third of the sample attended 'uncreamed' comprehensive schools, that is schools which were comprehensive by 1970 and which were sufficiently far from the nearest selective school to be considered (relatively) unaffected by creaming (no table shown).

We do not have data on the ability of the sample members when they entered school, so we cannot judge the effect of creaming on the ability range within schools. Creaming was, however, associated with substantial differences in the class composition of schools: 27 per cent of leavers from the uncreamed comprehensives were middle class, compared with only 17 per cent of leavers from the creamed comprehensives. Not all of this difference was necessarily a consequence of creaming, of course, as the uncreamed schools may have served catchment areas with proportionally more working-class families.

Nevertheless, we have two reasons for excluding the creamed comprehensive schools from our category of comprehensive schools, when comparing this category with other schools. The first reason is a conceptual one: the creamed schools served pupils who were unrepresentative of the population as a whole, because these schools had relatively few middle-class pupils. In this sense they were not comprehensive. Our second reason is more practical. Since we lack a measure of pupils' ability on entering school, a blanket comparison between comprehensives and other schools would be unfair to the comprehensives, some of whose most promising pupils had been creamed off to selective schools. However, this objection does not apply to the uncreamed comprehensives in the sample. If we have identified them correctly, they catered by definition for the entire age-group in their catchment areas. Their pupils may still have differed from pupils in other schools, but at least these differences were linked to geography and not compounded by the more elusive processes of creaming by ability.

With what schools should we compare the uncreamed comprehensives in the sample? Not with the bipartite senior and junior secondary schools alone, for the comments about creaming would apply, in reverse, to them: they would be unfairly advantaged in a blanket comparison since they would, on balance, have gained able pupils through creaming. In the uncreamed comprehensives we have identified a self-contained sector of Scottish secondary education, based on residence; all pupils, and only those pupils, who lived within the boundaries of this sector attended its schools. It is clear from our discussion of creaming that there was only one other such sector in Scottish education; this included all schools except the uncreamed comprehensives. Our comparison is therefore between the uncreamed comprehensive sector and a heterogeneous sector containing senior (selective) and junior secondary schools, schools with partly selective entrance arrangements after first year (whether or not they had comprehensive first-year intakes – those accounting for 10 per cent of leavers in table 14.1), and creamed comprehensives. We also include grant-aided schools in this sector, since they were responsible for much of the creaming within this system, and to exclude them would exclude important sections of the ability range from one half of the comparison. On the other hand, as in chapter 12, we have not included independent schools, principally on the grounds that they did not draw their pupils from their local surroundings to the same extent as did the grant-aided schools (especially at the time covered by the survey). Also they are harder to locate in terms of residential sectors. The boarding schools at least are likely to have drawn their pupils from both sectors, so any further creaming by the independent schools will affect both sides of the comparison. (Only 1 per cent of the sample attended independent schools, and even this total includes some English pupils.)

Although our second sector is a mixture of different types of schools, many of them formally comprehensive, it is distinguished by the selection of pupils to schools within it. This selection may have been formal or informal; it may have been based on ability or on the social and economic criteria that determined attendance at grant-aided and senior secondary schools. It is in this sense that we identify this group of schools as a 'selective' sector and compare it with the (uncreamed) 'comprehensive' sector.

The comprehensive sector thus defined accounted for less than a third of school-leavers in the sample. This results in part from our earlier judgment that all comprehensives in the cities of Dundee, Edinburgh and Glasgow were creamed and therefore a part of the selective sector. However, the two sectors were virtually identical in terms of social class. In the comprehensive sector, 27 per cent of leavers were middle class; in the selective sector, the proportion was

26 per cent. Later in this chapter we investigate more subtle differences between the social compositions of the two sectors; for the moment we proceed to a simple comparison between the two in the knowledge that, in terms of the best available predictor of attainment (social class), they were very similar. This does not necessarily mean that the two sectors were identical with respect to the pupils' ability or other determinants of attainment; however, since both sectors represented an entire cross-section of residents in their respective localities, there are perhaps fewer *a priori* reasons for expecting one sector to have had more promising pupils on average than the other.

Non-cognitive aspects of schooling in the two sectors

Table 14.2 compares the pupils from the two sectors in terms of three aspects of schooling which were discussed in chapters 10 and 11: truancy, satisfaction with the last year of schooling, and corporal punishment. On none of these three items did the two sectors differ more than trivially. Fewer pupils from the comprehensive sector reported extended truancy during their fourth year at school, and fewer reported receiving frequent corporal punishment. In both cases the differences between the sectors were statistically significant, but this is hardly surprising in view of the large sample numbers involved; the differences were very small. Slightly more pupils from the selective sector than from the comprehensive sector considered that their last year at school was worthwhile, but this difference was not even statistically significant.

All comprehensive schools in the cities were creamed and therefore included in the selective sector. Since truancy was higher in cities than in smaller towns or rural areas (no table given), the apparently lower truancy rate of the comprehensive sector might simply have been a result of the absence of large cities from this sector. We therefore re-estimated the figures in table 14.2 for the selective sector *excluding* the large cities, to give a fairer comparison. This did indeed show that the rate of extended truancy in the selective sector excluding the cities was 12 per cent, identical to the comprehensive sector (table not shown). The rate of frequent corporal punishment for the non-city selective sector was 29 per cent, fractionally above the comprehensive sector. On the other hand, 52 per cent of pupils from the non-city selective sector said that their last year at school had been worthwhile, 1 per cent more than among the selective sector as a whole.

The NCB report (Steedman, 1980) which compared pupils from comprehensive schools with pupils from other kinds of schools in England found that the former were much more likely to be reported

TABLE 14.2   Percentage of 1975–6 leavers in the four regions from the uncreamed comprehensive and selective sectors who. . .

	Uncreamed comprehensive sector	Selective sector	Statistical significance
. . .truanted several days or weeks at a time	12% of 5,131	14% of 10,474	$p < 0.05$
. . .thought their last year at school was worthwhile	50% of 4,582	51% of 9,049	$p > 0.1$
. . .received corporal punishment often or quite often	28% of 2,475	30% of 5,040	$p < 0.05$

by their teachers as having truanted; the highest rates of teacher-reported truancy were among pupils of the earliest comprehensives. Our own comparison between uncreamed comprehensives and other schools in Scotland reveals no such differences; there were negligible differences in relation to self-reported truancy, as well as in relation to corporal punishment and pupils' satisfaction with their last year at school. We now turn to a fourth aspect of schooling: the SCE attainments of pupils.

The level of SCE attainments in the two sectors

Table 14.3 shows the SCE attainments of leavers from the two sectors. The first row of the table shows the mean score of leavers from each sector on a scale of attainment, described in chapter 2, with a range of 1 to 18. The comprehensive sector had a higher average score than the selective sector, but the difference is not large, less than 0.4 of a point. More revealing differences between the two sectors may be seen in the second part of the table. This shows the distribution of leavers across the various levels of attainment. Fewer leavers from the comprehensive sector were at the very top of the attainment range; only 15 per cent had three or more Highers (a notional qualification for higher education) compared with 17 per cent of leavers from the selective sector. However, more comprehensive leavers had one or two Highers, so the total proportion of Highers-qualified leavers was about the same in each sector. At the other end of the attainment range, however, the picture is different. More leavers from the selective sector than from the comprehensive sector were completely unqualified, without even a D or E award at O-grade; the proportions in each sector were 37 per cent and 31 per cent respectively. This was not a consequence of any greater willingness among comprehensive-sector schools to present doubtful pupils for O-grades. Such a policy would have resulted in a relatively large number of pupils leaving comprehensive schools with only D- or E-band awards; yet the proportion of comprehensive pupils with only D- or E-band awards was the same as in the selective sector.

TABLE 14.3   SCE attainment by school sector: among 1975–6 leavers from the four regions

	Uncreamed comprehensive sector	Selective sector
(a) Mean SCE attainment	7.53	7.15
(b) Distribution of SCE attainment		
(percentage)	100	99
5 or more Highers passes	7	8
3 or 4 Highers passes	8	9
1 or 2 Highers passes	10	8
5 or more O-grades (A–C)	7	6
3 or 4 O-grades (A–C)	10	8
1 or 2 O-grades (A–C)	18	14
D or E awards only	9	9
No SCE awards	31	37
Unweighted *n*	(5,236)	(11,615)

Note: The between-sector differences in both parts of table 14.3 are highly statistically significant (based on unweighted figures). See chapter 2 for the scaling of SCE attainment used in part (a) of the table.

If, as we think probable, the two sectors served comparable ranges of ability, the data would suggest that comprehensive education had a levelling effect on attainment, raising fewer pupils to the highest levels of attainment, but helping more of them to progress beyond the minimum. It appears to have raised *average* attainment, although the definition of this average clearly depends on the relative importance of different levels of attainment implied by our scale. In the same way, practical conclusions about the overall value of comprehensive education must depend upon the relative importance attached to different levels of attainment, as well as to the importance of examination attainment in relation to other objectives of education.

The slightly better performance of the selective sector at the highest levels of attainment (that is, the higher proportions of leavers with three or more Highers passes) can be attributed to the contribution of grant-aided schools. Of leavers from EA schools within the selective sector, only 14 per cent had three or more Highers passes, slightly fewer than in the comprehensive sector. Of course, grant-aided pupils were highly selected from within the selective sector (at any rate in social terms; fewer than 10 per cent of grant-aided school-leavers were working class), so it would be inappropriate just to compare EA schools within the two sectors. On the other hand, any attempt to extrapolate from table 14.3 to the situation in the 1980s cannot ignore the continued existence of the former grant-aided schools, most of which have now assumed independent status outside the reorganised state system. They are likely to continue to cream able pupils away from the state sector.

Class inequality in the two sectors

Pupils from each sector came from a similar range of home backgrounds, as measured by their fathers' occupational classes. The comprehensive sector had slightly more leavers from social class II (15 per cent compared with 13 per cent), but for none of the other social classes did the proportions in the two sectors differ by more than 1 per cent. Overall, 27 per cent of comprehensive-sector leavers were middle class compared with 26 per cent of selective-sector leavers.

Given this similarity between the two sectors, we would not expect 'controlling' for social class to have much effect on the overall differences in SCE attainments which we saw in table 14.3. However, table 14.4 reveals a less predictable outcome of such controls: the direction of difference in attainment between the two sectors varied between the social classes. Children from social classes I and II achieved rather better SCE results at schools in the selective sector than at schools in the comprehensive sector. Children from each of the three manual classes, and unclassified children, did better in the comprehensive sector than in the selective sector. As a result, the gap between the middle and working-class average scores was narrower in the comprehensive sector than in the selective sector. In the comprehensive sector the class-gap was 4.4 (10.9 − 6.5) points, as measured by our scaling of SCE attainment; in the selective sector the class-gap was 5.7 (11.6 − 5.9) points. The average difference between the classes in the comprehensive sector was therefore about three-quarters of the difference in the selective sector.

Can this be taken as an estimate of the early effects of comprehensive reorganisation: to reduce class differences by a quarter? To reach such a conclusion we would have to be more certain of several of the partly-grounded assumptions we made earlier, not least that the two systems probably served comparable ranges of ability.

TABLE 14.4   Mean SCE attainment by school sector and social class: among 1975-6 leavers from the four regions

| | | Mean SCE attainment | | |
		Uncreamed comprehensive sector	Selective sector	Difference
I	professional	12.2	14.2	−2.0 **
II	intermediate	11.0	11.5	−0.5 ns
IIIN	skilled non-manual	9.8	9.8	+0.0 ns
all middle class		10.9	11.6	−0.7 **
IIIM	skilled manual	6.6	6.1	+0.5 **
IV	partly skilled	6.4	5.5	+0.9 **
V	unskilled	5.0	4.3	+0.7 *
all working class		6.5	5.9	+0.6 **
Unclassified		5.2	4.5	+0.7 **
All leavers		7.5	7.2	+0.3 **

Notes: See chapter 2 for the scaling of SCE attainment.
  ** = $p<0.05$
  * = $0.05<p<0.1$
  ns = $p>0.1$

However, early reorganisation did not affect a random sample of schools; nor did it affect a random sample of pupils. Moreover, in confining our attention to uncreamed comprehensives, we have introduced further systematic differences into the comparison. Each of the large cities in the four regions (Dundee, Edinburgh and Glasgow) still retained at least one selective school in 1970, so the comprehensive schools in these cities were all considered to be creamed and they were therefore included in the selective sector. Consequently, the comprehensive sector in our analysis was disproportionately based on the omnibus schools, which were most easily adapted to meet the requirements of comprehensive reorganisation. So, although the pupils attending schools in the two sectors were broadly similar in terms of social class, they differed in other aspects of their environment. Is our comparison between the sectors therefore invalid?

One source of difference between sectors might be the range of occupations included *within* social classes. Each of the six classes covers a wide variety of occupations, and one would expect the pattern of occupations within (say) social class I to differ between the big cities (which were all in the selective sector) and the small towns (which made up much of the comprehensive sector). To test this, the six classes were further broken down into 38 more homogeneous occupational groups, such as professional engineers, policemen, schoolteachers and skilled woodworkers. We computed a second set of average-attainment scores for the selective sector, adjusted to match the distribution of the 38 occupational groups in the comprehensive sector. That is, we left the children of (say) schoolteachers in the selective sector with the same mean attainment score, but we weighted them to match the proportion of children of schoolteachers in the comprehensive sector. The adjustments were thus designed to show what the selective-sector scores would have been, other things being equal, if the occupational distribution had been the same as in the comprehensive sector. However, once we had adjusted the selective-sector scores in this way, we still found a class difference of 5.6 points, only slightly less than the unadjusted difference which was 5.7 points, and still much greater than the class-gap in the comprehensive sector which, as we have seen, was 4.4 points.

Differences associated with fathers' occupations cannot, therefore, explain the different levels of class inequality found in the two sectors. Of course, not all of the respects in which the catchment areas differed were necessarily reflected in their occupational structure. The comprehensive sector comprised smaller towns and rural areas, whereas half the leavers in the selective sector lived in the large cities of Dundee, Edinburgh and Glasgow. Even with comparable occupational distributions, the local class structures of cities and small towns respectively might have different effects on norms, culture, patterns of interaction and, possibly, on educational attainment. However, if the figures for the selective sector in table 14.4 are recalculated to exclude the large cities, the gap between middle- and working-class scores within the sector actually increases from 5.7 to 6.2 points. The greater inequality within the selective sector was therefore not a result of its greater urban concentration.

The lower level of class inequality in the comprehensive sector, therefore, must be attributed either to comprehensive reorganisation or to more subtle differences between the sectors than mere differences in the occupational distribution between cities and towns. However, if these more subtle differences were independent of comprehensive education, we would expect them to have existed before the process of reorganisation was set in train by Circular 600 in 1965. To test this we would need to know whether class inequality in the schools in the comprehensive sector was already lower than in the schools in the selective sector *before* 1965. Unfortunately, we do not have data on class and attainment for a full cross-section of pupils in each sector for the years before 1965. However, the Scottish Education Data Archive does hold information on pupils leaving school with at least one Higher pass in 1962-3 (and also in 1969-70 and 1971-2); and we can retrospectively divide their schools into comprehensive and selective sectors in terms of their admission arrangements in 1970. In the following analysis we continue to identify the two sectors in terms of the status of schools when the 1977 sample members entered them in 1970 or later, but we look back into the past of the schools in these sectors before reorganisation.

Table 14.5 shows class differences in the mean number of Highers passed among Highers-qualified leavers in each of four years, for the two sectors defined in terms of their 1970 admission arrangements. In 1975-6, the last year covered by the table, the average middle-class leaver in the comprehensive sector had 0.49 of a Higher more than the average working-class leaver. In the selective sector, however, this 'class-gap' was 0.83 of a Higher. The average class-gap was therefore greater in the selective sector than in the comprehensive sector by about one-third of a Higher. The pattern of class differences among Highers-qualified leavers therefore resembled the pattern among the whole age-group, namely that class differences were smaller in the comprehensive sector than in the selective sector.

However, table 14.5 also shows that this pattern extended back at least as far as 1962-3; among leavers in that year from the schools which later comprised the uncreamed comprehensive sector, the class-gap was negligible (one-hundredth of a Higher), whereas among leavers from schools which later comprised the selective sector, the class-gap in that year was already more than one-third of a Higher (0.35). Similar differences between the sectors are visible for the two intermediate years for which we have data. The apparently greater equality in the comprehensive sector had existed in those schools well before comprehensive reorganisation and cannot therefore be a consequence of reorganisation. It either stemmed from other, longer established attributes of the schools that comprise it, or it was produced by the social environment of the catchment areas they serve.

Of course, Highers-qualified leavers in 1962-3, as in later years, were a highly selected group, and class differences among them might merely reflect the process of selection to this group. An alternative explanation for the pattern in table 14.5 might be that comprehensive reorganisation did improve working-class attainment overall, but that, since many more working-class pupils now stayed on to pass just one or two Highers, the average number of Highers passes among *Highers-qualified* working-class pupils did not increase. However, table 14.5 shows that reorganisation did not in fact encourage a disproportionate growth in the number of working-class pupils passing Highers.

TABLE 14.5   Difference between mean number of Highers passes held by middle and working-class leavers respectively, by school sector and year of leaving school: only leavers with at least one Higher pass, in the four regions

	Uncreamed comprehensive sector	Selective sector
1962–3		
Difference between class means	0.01	0.35
Working class as a percentage of		
Highers-qualified leavers	*47%*	*42%*
1969–70		
Difference between class means	0.07	0.60
Working class as a percentage of		
Highers-qualified leavers	*49%*	*43%*
1971–2		
Difference between class means	0.24	0.56
Working class as a percentage of		
Highers-qualified leavers	*44%*	*42%*
1975–6		
Difference between class means	0.49	0.83
Working class as a percentage of		
Highers-qualified leavers	*44%*	*40%*

Note: The difference scores show the extent to which the middle-class mean exceeded the working-class mean: for example, in 1962–3 Highers-qualified middle-class leavers had, on average, 0.01 of a Higher more than Highers-qualified working-class leavers. These means are based only on pupils leaving with at least one Higher pass. The percentages indicate the proportion of working-class leavers among this group. The sectors are identified in terms of admission arrangements in 1970 (the first year in which the 1975–6 leavers could have entered school). Many of the schools in the uncreamed comprehensive sector did not, of course, have comprehensive intakes when the 1962–3 leavers entered them.

Working-class pupils were, at least in the 1970s, a declining proportion of the Highers-qualified leavers in the comprehensive sector as well as in the selective sector. So our comparison seems not to be affected by such selection effects (unless any net population shift between the two sectors were strongly linked to social class). Of course, the comparison is restricted to Highers-qualified pupils; it tells us nothing about trends in inequality at other levels of attainment.

Must we therefore reject any conclusion that comprehensive education can promote social equality? Not necessarily; but much depends upon how we define 'comprehensive' education. The schools in our comprehensive sector were the first in Scotland to go comprehensive. Many of them were able to reorganise quickly because they were already omnibus schools, where all the pupils from the area were often taught under the same roof, albeit in streamed courses. The transfer to comprehensive status was relatively easy, and therefore quick, for such schools. We explained above why we chose, as the defining feature of comprehensive education, the arrangements for selecting entrants; and, on this criterion, the omnibus schools were not very different from the comprehensives that replaced them. Moreover, the differentiation of pupils within omnibus schools may not have been much different from the streaming and setting that have been characteristic of many comprehensive schools, at least in their early years. Indeed the omnibus school was the chief bearer of an indigenous Scottish comprehensive tradition, and our data seem to confirm the effectiveness and endurance of this tradition. Of course, uncreamed omnibus schools served only a small proportion of Scottish children, and other schools had very different traditions. What we are describing was a tradition within Scottish education, not one that governed all of it.

We have examined the lower level of class inequality in the comprehensive sector and concluded that it was a result neither of different occupational structures nor of the city/smaller town distinction; nor, apparently, was it entirely a result of the reorganisation following Circular 600, if at all. Instead we have suggested that it may in large part have been a result of the much older tradition of the omnibus school in Scottish education. Of course, there may in fact have been other differences between the two sectors which may explain the class effect: other differences, perhaps, in the social and cultural characteristics of their catchment areas. However, we feel it might be inappropriate to seek too precise a distinction between, on the one hand, the effects of the schools themselves and, on the other hand, the effects of these characteristics of their catchments. The relatively low level of inequality seems to have been a feature of schools in our comprehensive sector for a long period of time. The long history of omnibus schools in these areas might be both a consequence and a cause of a more egalitarian class structure, which in turn influenced the educational attainment of children. The effects of education are not exhausted in one generation; the omnibus schools may have created in earlier generations a climate of greater social equality, which is now reflected in the educational attainments of the present generation of children. A static, ahistorical distinction between 'school effects' and 'home effects' would ignore the continuing effects of school and home on each other.

Reorganisation and the elite

If the lower level of class inequality in the comprehensive sector in the mid-1970s was largely or entirely a lasting effect of the omnibus-school tradition, did the reorganisation after 1965 have no important effect on these schools and on class differences within them? This is a broader question than we could hope to answer with the evidence presently at our disposal. However, we can try to estimate the effects of reorganisation on one aspect of the omnibus tradition which might well have been threatened: its academic emphasis, especially in relation to the able working-class child. The ideal of equality coexisted in the old tradition with a strong emphasis on traditional academic values and on the ablest sections of the age-group. Indeed these two aspects of the tradition were closely linked: it was the 'lad o' pairts', the boy of high ability and often of low social origin, whom the tradition most clearly identified as deserving special treatment. More recent versions of the comprehensive ideal, however, have reacted against the meritocratic principles of selection at 11 or 12 years and have placed more emphasis on the education of the intermediate and lower-ability groups. If the reorganisation since 1965 has diverted resources and attention towards these groups, has it at the same time diverted them away from the lad o' pairts, the able working-class child, and thus increased class inequality at the very highest levels of attainment?

In table 14.5 we saw that inequality among Highers leavers, though consistently lower in the schools that formed the uncreamed comprehensive sector for 1970 entrants, increased substantially in both sectors between 1962–3 and 1975–6. Moreover, working-class pupils declined slightly as a proportion of all Highers-qualified pupils, although this may have simply reflected population trends. The 1962–3 leavers overlap with the 1957–8 transfer cohort we described in chapter 12. In that chapter we commented on the low level of class inequality among Highers-qualified pupils in the cohort and speculated that it might be a consequence of a 'sponsorship' pattern of educational selection. By the time of the 1970–2 transfer cohort (the same as our 1975–6 leavers) much of this sponsorship effect had disappeared. Table 14.5 also gives figures for 1969–70 and 1971–2 leavers which confirm that this increase in inequality among Highers-qualified leavers was a continuing trend, and not just a freak consequence of the data for either 1962–3 or 1975–6 leavers.

However, table 14.5 shows that the class-gap amongst Highers-qualified leavers increased by exactly the same amount (nearly half a Higher) in each of the two sectors. The trend to greater inequality was not therefore a consequence of comprehensive education as we have defined it. However, it may have resulted from aspects of

263

reorganisation which also affected pupils whose schools turned comprehensive while they were there. (Such aspects might include, for example, a diversion of resources from Highers pupils to less able pupils.) Most schools in the selective sector were formally comprehensive by 1976, so any such developments might have affected 1975–6 leavers in both our comprehensive and selective sectors. We lack the information to say how reorganisation affected the education of sample members whose secondary schools were reorganised whilst they attended them. However, we do know that most of the schools in the uncreamed comprehensive sector had reorganised before most of the schools in the selective sector; yet table 14.5 shows that the increase in inequality occurred earlier in the selective sector, with a substantial rise already evident by 1969–70, before most of these schools were reorganised. It can hardly be a consequence of reorganisation.

We conclude, therefore, that there is little evidence in the data to link the increasing level of class inequality among Highers pupils specifically with comprehensive reorganisation. To what, then, do we attribute this trend? Our answer can only be speculative, but we would draw attention to two points.

First, in an important sense the anomalous pattern was that of the 1962–3 leavers and not of the 1975–6 leavers. The general pattern observed in chapter 12 was for inequality to exceed the level predicted from non-school factors by a more or less constant amount over the whole attainment range. However, for the 1957–8 cohort (the 1962–3 Highers leavers) the level of inequality among Highers leavers had grown closer to the prediction line at the higher levels of attainment (figure 12.2). In the 1970–2 cohort (the 1975–6 leavers), on the other hand, the deviation from the prediction line was more nearly constant across the attainment range (figure 12.3). In other words, 1962–3 was the odd year out; inequality at the highest levels of attainment among 1962–3 leavers was affected (and reduced) by some additional influence which did not affect the other levels of attainment and which had disappeared by 1975–6. *Post hoc* we may call this a sponsorship effect: it operated to reduce the levels of inequality which might otherwise have been expected among leavers with Highers passes.

Second, we note that between 1962–3 and 1975–6 the proportion of secondary pupils leaving with Highers qualifications increased from 15 per cent to 27 per cent, most of this expansion occurring by 1970. Arguably, the system could no longer provide the same level of attention for each Highers pupil; the system may have expanded past a threshold, beyond which a sponsorship effect could not be sustained at the previous level of resources. During the same period the school-leaving age was raised, the O-grade examination became established and other measures increased the amount of attention paid to pupils of average and below-average ability. These trends were largely independent of comprehensive reorganisation; they may have accompanied a further diversion of resources per capita away from Highers pupils towards pupils lower down the attainment range. This is not to say that the secondary-education system could not have provided such a sponsorship effect for an expanded Highers population, but to do so would probably have required a change in the level and type of available resources, of staff and materials, and of administrative and advisory infrastructures. It might also have required some institutional changes.

Conclusions

Before summarising our conclusions in this chapter we must stress the limits to their generalisability. First, the data reflect only the early years of comprehensive reorganisation, while the new system was still settling down, and before attitudes, expectations and more tangible resources had had time to adapt. Second, we have taken account of only a limited number of outcomes of secondary schooling; there are many other criteria which both friends and foes of comprehensive education might consider relevant to a proper comparison. Third, we have restricted ourselves to a particular definition of comprehensive education: one based on the selection arrangements in force at the time pupils entered school, and one which does not include schools with a creamed intake. As a result, the selective sector in our comparison includes both creamed comprehensives and schools which reorganised while the sample members were pupils.

We compared the two sectors in terms of three 'non-cognitive' aspects of schooling: truancy rates, the proportion of leavers expressing satisfaction with their last year of schooling, and the incidence of corporal punishment. On none of these criteria could we discern appreciable differences between the two sectors, even if we excluded the large cities from the comparison.

We found that the leavers in the sample from the comprehensive sector had levels of attainment which were, on average, slightly higher than those of leavers from the selective sector. Rather more leavers from the selective sector had three or more Highers passes, a level of attainment that is often regarded as a threshold qualification for higher education; this seems to have been attributable to the grant-aided schools in the selective sector. Conversely, fewer comprehensive-sector leavers left with no SCE awards at all, and this difference could not be explained in terms of a more generous presentation policy.

The level of class inequality was somewhat lower in the comprehensive sector than in the selective sector. This difference was not due to the different occupational or geographical (city/town) composition of the two sectors. However, class inequality in the schools in the comprehensive sector had already been comparatively low *before* comprehensive reorganisation took place (at least among Highers pupils), so we tentatively attributed the lower inequality mainly or entirely to the continuing tradition of the former omnibus schools in our comprehensive sector, rather than to reorganisation as such. Finally, we examined the increase in the level of inequality among the Highers-qualified elites of our samples, and concluded that there was little evidence to link this increase specifically to comprehensive reorganisation.

Our conclusions in this chapter have supported many of the optimistic claims made by advocates of comprehensive education. However, the form of comprehensive education that sustains these claims is not the one introduced by the post-1965 reorganisation, but one arising out of an older and traditional form in Scottish education, the omnibus school. The relative equality of opportunity in the comprehensive sector was not the result of reorganisation, but was a continuation of the equality already established by the omnibus-school tradition. Moreover, this tradition has involved much more than a particular mode of selection of pupils. It implies an interdependence between the school and community and the kinds of social relationship found in each, and in practice it implies a particular kind of community, typically a small town. All this means that comprehensive reorganisation will not necessarily bring about an equivalent transformation in the areas not previously affected by the omnibus tradition, and especially not overnight; and it means that the success of reorganisation in these areas will depend upon the factors that encourage or impede the growth of such traditions. The resources and infrastructure available to schools, the attitudes and expectations of teachers and parents, continued creaming by the grant-aided schools, most of which have now assumed fully independent status – all these influence the probability that the conditions of the omnibus school will be reproduced in a reorganised system of secondary education.

Part 6

Myth and Reconstruction

Introduction

The concluding part of our study has several purposes. Chapter 16 summarises our arguments and empirical findings. It also opens up the problems that are raised by the conflict between our own account of the world of post-war education in Scotland and the descriptive account of that world sustained by the Scottish myth. These problems are partly philosophical, concerning as they do the logical status of the two accounts. Our own account is social-scientific, but it is acknowledgedly incomplete and arbitrary in some respects, resting on definitions and assumptions that must be made if empirical inquiry is to continue. Nevertheless, we claim it is superior to the account offered by the myth. The problems are also partly political. If, as we have shown, myth not only describes the world, but also expresses human values *in* the world, what are the consequences for social science and for politics of the myth's shaky status as science? Are all human belief systems inadequate as science? Must they be? If so, what are the possibilities for politics and, in particular, for a politics of progress? And can social science never expect to become established in the world, offering as it apparently does only another (also arbitrary) perspective on, and challenge to, the received opinions of the day?

A further purpose of part 6 is to suggest a solution to these problems that has a general application and that is not restricted solely to education and to myth. We do this in chapter 17, where we argue that philosophical problems to do with the logical status of social-scientific accounts, and political problems concerning the possibilities for government and for political accountability, are two dimensions of the *same* problem. The single solution that is indicated by our analysis leads us to prescribe for new relations between social science and government, and therefore for a new form of social science and of government: a form in which the right of all citizens to be knowledgeable is a focus of both political and intellectual endeavour. Our discussion in chapter 17 casts doubt on the generalisability of our empirical findings, indeed of any empirical findings, about the potency of education; for, we argue, the way in which the right to be knowledgeable has been ignored, misunderstood, or denied has itself substantially influenced the capacity of persons to act effectively, whether in providing public systems of education or any other form of collective provision.

How then can one learn to improve? This is a question that underlies chapter 15. But the chapter itself is mainly substantive, concerned as it is to elucidate the question 'How much difference can and do individual schools make to an individual pupil's educational prospects?' The chapter exemplifies how the application of one, very restricted, social-scientific method can nevertheless help one to learn about the limits and possibilities of schooling; but it also illustrates how the possibilities for further learning about how to improve provision are very soon blocked by the difficulties in our political and intellectual culture with which our final chapter tries to deal.

Chapter 15

School Differences and School Effects: Knowledge and the Potency of Schooling

Introduction

Our analysis in the previous chapter of the early impact of comprehensive reorganisation took advantage of a historically unique opportunity; this was that the 1977 survey could be used to describe a school system that was in the process of reorganisation. We could identify a sector of (substantially) uncreamed comprehensive schools and another, more heterogeneous, selective sector. In our analysis we were able to compare leavers from schools in these two sectors. This opportunity was not available, for example, to the National Children's Bureau in their study of comprehensive schools in England (Steedman, 1980). They found evidence of substantial creaming of comprehensives, and virtually no local authorities in England had reorganised all their schools on fully comprehensive lines by the time their sample entered them.

The distribution of 1977 sample members across the two sectors was not the product of pure chance or of an experimenter's randomisation, but the result of a systematic if complex process of historical development, some of whose complexities we started to unravel in chapter 13. When interpreting our comparison between sectors, we found it necessary to refer to their historical origins. We found differences between sectors which appeared to be consequences of the history of the organisation of the schools within them, of the local contexts of these schools, and of the continuing interaction between schools and their local contexts. In this chapter we suggest, in the course of an exploratory analysis, that the same historical awareness must inform the study of differences between individual schools *within* any sector. The history of a school has effects on its pupils' attainments over and above the effects of its other characteristics. The influence of the school's history is communicated, we conjecture, partly through the quality of the understandings of that history held

271

by the teachers and others involved. Thus the potency of schooling may vary according to the collective understanding of the place of the school in its historical and social context.

Our discussion in the previous chapter was inevitably a very restricted evaluation of the possibilities for change in the school system. It did not take account of any lessons that might be learned from comparisons between schools within sectors; examples of outstanding success or failure were obscured in the anonymity of the average. Our comparison could not illuminate the school factors, inherited or planned, which may make some comprehensive schools more successful than other comprehensive schools. In this chapter, therefore, we turn to questions associated with the performance of individual schools, with particular emphasis on schools within the uncreamed comprehensive sector, as we defined it in chapter 14.

Everyone knows that schools can differ greatly one from another. As Jencks *et al.* (1973, p. 256) put it: 'Some schools are dull, depressing, even terrifying places, while others are lively, comfortable and reassuring.' Schools differ not only in terms of the quality of life that they offer to their pupils, but also in terms of the more tangible outcomes of the education that they offer. Universities are well aware of how even their state-educated students tend to be drawn from a restricted range of schools; at some schools a single university place is still an achievement to be celebrated. League tables of schools' examination results would, and do, show enormous differences between schools. Such differences are often assumed to reflect differences in the effectiveness of schools; and the schools with the best examination results may be oversubscribed by parents who believe that those good results promise equally good chances of achievement for their own children. However, an accumulating body of research indicates that variations between schools in their average examination results owe much more to variations in the social and intellectual compositions of the pupil intakes than to the differences in the contributions made by the schools themselves. We suspect that many parents would, in their bones, acknowledge the truth of this. The question therefore remains: is it possible to go beyond a knowledge of school outcomes and to study and measure the extent to which characteristics of individual schools can affect and enhance these outcomes?

In this chapter we focus on four outcomes of schooling: O-grade results, truancy rates, the incidence of belting, and pupils' reported satisfaction with their last year of school. We first map the extent to which schools differed in respect of these four outcomes. We then examine the relation of these outcomes to the characteristics of the pupil intakes to each school. Next, we introduce the concept of a school's 'difference score', which reflects the difference between two averages or two percentages measuring, on the one hand, the actual outcomes of a school's pupils and, on the other, outcomes which would be predicted on the basis of its social composition. We discuss the possibility that a difference score may be a rough measure of a school's own contribution to the outcome. Then, in a more exploratory spirit, we apply the concept of difference scores to three issues which affect schools: the extent to which schools which are effective with respect to one outcome of schooling are effective with respect to another; the factors associated with the history of a school's organisation and context which influence its effectiveness; and the implications of the publication of examination results on a school-by-school basis. First, however, we briefly review the history of research into school effects.

Previous studies of school effectiveness

The debate over school effects in the last two decades has passed through three stages. We shall describe these briefly in order that our own contribution may be placed in context.

The first stage culminated in the publication of the Plowden Report (Central Advisory Council for Education (England) 1967). The report brought together a variety of studies whose assumptions about the role of schooling in creating and sustaining life-chances were essentially optimistic. Schools, it implied, were important places, with important effects on the lives of the children they served. Unfortunately, it argued, they varied in the quality of education they offered, especially to disadvantaged children. Problems of 'poor' home backgrounds were compounded by problems of 'poor' schools in a 'seamless web of circumstance'. What was required was a programme of 'positive discrimination', whose 'first step must be to raise the schools with low standards to the national average; the second, quite deliberately to make them better' (ibid., p. 57). But aspirations were not matched by actions, and whether Plowden's initial findings were justified has subsequently been questioned (Acland, 1973).

Meanwhile, the second stage of the debate was already under way, fuelled by a number of influential American studies. Some knowledge of the work of Coleman and his colleagues (1966) is necessary at this point. Coleman conducted a cross-sectional study of educational opportunities in the United States. He had expected to document major inequalities in the educational opportunities offered to white and black children (Hodgson, 1973). To his surprise he found that his data did not sustain such a conclusion. Far from schools having powerful independent effects, he concluded that they 'brought little influence to bear on a child's achievement that [was] independent of his background and general social context' (Coleman *et al.*, 1966, p. 325). He argued that equality of educational opportunity should be pursued not, as previously, through resource inputs to the educational process but through those 'elements . . . that are effective for learning'. In the process he exposed the poverty of much educational theorising about the relationships between educational resources, on the one hand, and pupils' performances, on the other.

Coleman's rather pessimistic conclusions about the part played by schools were augmented by Jencks and his colleagues in their study of inequality (1973). Casting the contribution of schooling against the background of societal differences in life-chances, Jencks argued that differences in the 'quality' of primary schools had only small effects on levels of cognitive inequality and that effects attributable to differences between secondary schools were smaller still. He added, almost as an aside, that, as far as he could see, practitioners themselves did not know much about how to change matters to make schools more effective. The foundation was thus laid for the view that 'schools don't make a difference'.

The third stage of the debate has in many ways been a response to the conclusions of Coleman and Jencks, and has stressed the methodological and conceptual weaknesses of these and earlier studies. Criticisms have focused on four main issues. First, the studies were mostly cross-sectional. They lacked information on how schools have changed their pupils over time. For this one would require information on pupils when they entered school and a longitudinal research design. Second, the studies usually employed psychometric tests of basic skills to measure the outcomes of schooling. These tests had usually been designed in such a way as to discount any differences that there may have been between schools in their effectiveness. Outcome measures like public examinations, for which teachers had actually been preparing pupils, were largely ignored or unavailable. Third, narrow measures of cognitive skills were typically employed, thereby ignoring important non-cognitive outcomes of schooling. Finally, the studies were thought to have measured the wrong aspects of schools. They concentrated on things which were easily measured and susceptible to administrative manipulation, like class size and teacher qualifications; factors concerned with the process of schooling, such as pupil–teacher relationships and school 'ethos', were ignored. We ourselves would extend this criticism, arguing that the studies ignored history as well as process; they did not allow for the continuing influence exerted by the history of a school's organisation, of its local context and of the interactions between school and context (chapter 14, 'Organisation, context and the effectiveness of schools', below; and also Byrne, Williamson and Fletcher, 1975).

Four recent studies of British and Irish secondary schools have taken account of some of these criticisms. Each, in its separate way, claims to have cast doubt on the earlier conclusions. Of the four, that by Rutter and his colleagues (1979) is probably the best known. It was based on twelve inner-London secondary schools. The other studies are Reynolds's study of nine South Wales secondary modern schools (Reynolds, 1976); a study of some forty English secondary schools of various types, both state and independent (Brimer *et al.*, 1978); and a related study of some fifty Irish secondary schools (Madaus *et al.*, 1979). There are, however, problems in the interpretation of each of these studies (Gray, 1981), and our general view is that the question of school effectiveness in contemporary Britain is unresolved.

We mention these points partly to underline some of the limitations of what follows, as well as some of the strengths. Ours is a cross-sectional study; our information on intakes was collected retrospectively and did not cover all the factors which might influence attainment; and we did not gather detailed information about the practices of the schools attended by our sample of leavers. None of this is very surprising, since we did not set out to design a study of school effects. At the same time, we find ourselves in a position to contribute to present discussion by virtue of the very large number of secondary schools on whose pupils we have amassed information. Moreover, by the standards of many previous studies we are particularly fortunate in having data both on public examinations and on various non-cognitive outcomes. We can therefore help to establish a framework for the debate and, to some extent, to delineate the limits and possibilities of secondary schooling for a national system. Although we have some empirical conclusions to offer, the analyses that follow are mainly important as preliminaries to, and indications of, some of the kinds of investigations that would be entailed in better studies of school effectiveness. But we also hope that, as they stand, our analyses are sufficiently informative to persuade people that it would be worth their while to try to establish more securely the conditions in which such studies can be made.

Differences between schools with respect to four outcomes

Our analysis in this chapter is based upon four outcomes of schooling:

1 *O-grades*: the percentage of pupils in each school obtaining one or more O-grade awards at grade A, B or C (regarded as pass grades until 1973 — see chapter 4);
2 *truancy*: the percentage of pupils reporting that they truanted 'several days at a time' or 'weeks at a time' (see chapter 11);

3 *satisfaction*: the percentage of pupils saying that their last year at school was 'worthwhile' (see chapter 10);

4 *belting*: the percentage of pupils reporting that they were belted 'often' or 'quite often' during their secondary schooling (see chapter 10).

Our choice of these outcome measures is intended to combine brevity with variety. It goes without saying that there are other outcomes of schooling (some of them represented in the Scottish Education Data Archive) in terms of which one might wish to assess schools; and our map of the differences between schools in their outcomes or in their effectiveness may well depend strongly upon the particular outcomes under consideration. Later in this chapter we criticise the view that most of the variation in effectiveness between schools can be represented in terms of a single dimension; we suggest instead that a school which is 'good' in terms of one outcome may not be particularly 'good' with respect to another outcome. This may apply also to different outcome measures of the same general area of a school's endeavour, such as academic attainment. Our O-grade outcome measure reflects on the success of schools in helping their pupils to cross a relatively low hurdle in the academic race; more than one-half of the age-group in 1975–6 (55 per cent) obtained at least one A–C award at O-grade. A school whose pupils are relatively successful in jumping this hurdle may be much less successful, relative to other schools, with respect to more difficult hurdles, such as gaining Highers passes or entrance to higher education. The possible importance of these distinctions has tended to be glossed over in research which has looked for undifferentiated 'school effects'. We would stress the need for studies that systematically explore the consequences for conclusions about school effects of varying the outcome measures in terms of which effects are represented.

We also stress the need for evaluations which are responsive to the variety of different goals which schools may set themselves or which may be set for schools by the political process. We have therefore chosen, in addition to our examination outcome, three measures of non-cognitive aspects of schooling. The significance of pupils' reported satisfaction with their last year at school and also of truancy is, we hope, clear from our discussions in chapters 10 and 11. The fourth outcome, the reported frequency of belting, is more ambiguous than the others as a direct measure of school processes, since it reflects both the behaviour of pupils at a school and the school's policy on discipline. Nevertheless, we feel it may be of interest as some kind of evidence about the type of school regime in which pupils found themselves involved.

Table 15.1a summarises the range of variation among the 273 education-authority schools in the four regions with respect to the four outcomes of schooling. Six figures are shown for each outcome. These

TABLE 15.1 Distribution of school scores on (a) four measures of
school outcomes and (b) one measure of school intake: all EA schools
in the four regions ($n = 273$)

	Lowest score	Score at the lower quartile	Score at the median	Score at the upper quartile	Highest score	(Inter-quartile range)
(a) School outcome						
Percentage of leavers obtaining one or more A–C awards (O-grades)	4	32	46	64	100	(32)
Percentage of leavers reporting that they had truanted several days or weeks at a time (truancy)	0	7	14	21	50	(14)
Percentage of leavers saying their last year was worthwhile (satisfaction)	10	36	46	57	90	(21)
Percentage of leavers reporting that they were belted often or quite often (belting)	0	10	18	26	100	(16)
(b) School intake						
Percentage of leavers with middle-class fathers	0	13	25	32	84	(19)

figures describe the 273 schools as if they were ordered in four separate
rankings according to their scores on each outcome. The first and fifth
figures show the scores for the schools at each end of the ranking; we
therefore find that at one school only 4 per cent of leavers had any
A–C O-grade awards, at another school the figure was 100 per cent,
and all the other schools were between these two extremes. The schools
at the lower quartile, median and upper quartile are the schools which
are placed respectively one-quarter, one-half and three-quarters of the
way up the rank ordering of schools. The median score is therefore
the score of the middling school. One way to read the table may be
illustrated with respect to the O-grade outcome: in all schools at least
4 per cent of leavers had A–C awards at O-grade; in three-quarters of
schools 32 per cent or more had A–C awards; in half of the schools
46 per cent or more had A–C awards; and in one-quarter of schools 64
per cent or more had A–C awards; and in no school, not surprisingly,
did more than 100 per cent of leavers have A–C awards.

277

The sixth column in table 15.1a shows the inter-quartile range for each outcome. This is the difference between the scores of the schools at the upper quartile and the lower quartile respectively. It therefore shows the range of variation across the 'middle 50 per cent' of schools. We use the inter-quartile range as a summary measure of the range of variation among schools on each outcome. We believe that it is more useful than the overall range (that is, the difference between the highest and lowest scores) for two reasons. First, it is statistically more robust; it is unaffected by the odd one or two schools where sampling bias or sampling error may have produced a freak high or low score. Second, even when the estimation of the extreme points is reliable, knowledge of the overall range does not tell us about the distribution of schools over that range, for example, about any tendency for the schools to be grouped together or to be scattered. The first five figures shown for each outcome in table 15.1a give a relatively full description of the range of variation for each outcome, and the sixth, the inter-quartile range, gives a summary measure of that variation.

Table 15.1a shows considerable variation among schools with respect to each of the four outcomes. This variation, at least as measured by the inter-quartile range, was greatest with respect to the O-grade outcome.

Intakes and outcomes

Part (b) of table 15.1 describes school variability in terms, not of an outcome of schooling, but of one aspect of a school's intake of pupils: the percentage of leavers whose fathers were in middle-class occupations. Rather than describing the output of schools, this measure says something about the raw materials with which schools had to work. Strictly speaking it is not a measure of intake, since it is retrospective and refers to pupils after they had left school. However, although retrospectively collected data on, say, the ability of school-leavers would not be a valid measure of their ability on entry to school, we believe that no such objection applies to a social-class measure. A measure of the social-class composition of a school's leavers will almost always be very strongly related to a measure of the social-class composition of the same school's intake a few years earlier, with changes in class membership among the pupil body having largely cancelled each other out. In keeping with the logic of our argument in this chapter, we refer to measures of pupils' social backgrounds as describing the intake of pupils to schools.

Table 15.1b also reveals considerable variation between schools in their intakes, as measured by the percentage of leavers with middle-class fathers. The amount of variation is broadly comparable to that between schools with respect to the four outcomes of schooling. Similar between-school variability may also be observed with respect to other aspects of intake such as the education of leavers' mothers and fathers. However, these variables are measured in a different way that requires more space to reproduce, so they are not shown in table 15.1.

In chapter 12 we demonstrated a strong association between social class and the educational attainment of individual pupils. The question naturally arises whether a similarly strong association might be found between the social-class composition of a school's intake and the attainments or other outcomes of its pupils as a whole. This question has practical significance. If schools' outcomes merely reflect schools' intakes, then the argument that '[particular] schools don't make a difference' might be vindicated. At least, it would be the case that particular schools made less of a difference than a simple comparison of their outcomes might suggest. The use of outcome measures, such as examination results, as measures of a school's effectiveness (or contribution to the outcomes) would be called into question, because, if outcomes principally reflected intakes, they would be poor measures of effectiveness.

In order to study the relation of schools' intakes to their outcomes we have restricted our analysis to uncreamed comprehensive schools (see chapter 14, 'Definition of "the comprehensive sector"'). We do this partly in order to minimise the effects of selection and creaming on school intakes in subsequent analyses. It is possible that both formal and informal selection processes generated differences in schools' intakes which we may not be able to represent adequately with our available measures of intake. By eliminating creamed schools from this part of the analysis, we thereby err on the side of caution. Moreover, we believe that now that Scotland (though perhaps not England) has virtually completed its comprehensive reorganisation within the maintained (EA) sector, the practical contribution of an exploratory study such as this is greatest if directed towards variations in school effectiveness among comprehensive schools. We have excluded a further 15 schools from the uncreamed comprehensives, 84 in all, which we identified in chapter 14, mainly because observations for them were based on an unweighted sample size of less than forty leavers. Exclusion was not necessary where, as in chapter 14, we were pooling all leavers within the sector (because possible sampling errors associated with the size of the sample from particular schools would tend to even out over a large number of schools); but it is necessary where we wish, as in this chapter, to talk with some confidence about observations for particular schools.[1] The net effect of the exclusion of these 15 schools is therefore to bias our study slightly against discovering any different

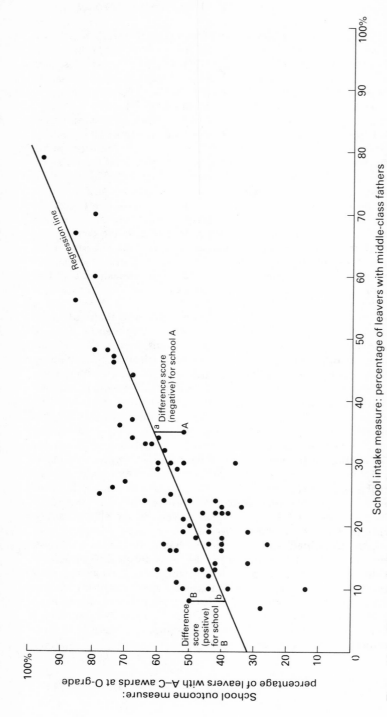

Figure 15.1 Percentage of leavers with A–C awards at O-grade, by percentage of leavers with middle-class fathers: uncreamed comprehensive schools in the four regions (*n* = 69)

relationships which might obtain in a sample including smaller schools.[2]
Our study in the rest of the chapter is mostly based on the remaining
69 uncreamed comprehensive schools that offered the leavers in our
sample a full range of SCE courses over the six secondary-school years.
(These schools had fully comprehensive intakes to first year. None of
them accepted pupil transfers from neighbouring four-year schools.)

Figure 15.1 plots these 69 schools in terms of one outcome measure
(the percentage of leavers with at least one A–C award at O-grade) and
one measure of intake (the percentage with fathers in middle-class
occupations). Each school is represented by a cross in the diagram.
Figure 15.1 shows that schools with higher percentages of middle-class
pupils in their intakes tended to have higher proportions of pupils
leaving with A–C O-grade awards. This tendency can be represented
by a correlation coefficient (r) of 0.79. The regression line drawn
across figure 15.1 shows the line of 'best fit' between intakes and
outcomes; it shows, on certain assumptions, the best prediction of a
school's outcome score, based only on knowledge of its intake. A
perfect correlation would be one of $r = 1.0$, describing a situation in
which all the crosses fell exactly on the regression line and in which,
therefore, statistical prediction was perfect.

The association in figure 15.1 is not, however, perfect. In other
words, the correlation coefficient is less than 1.0 and some schools do
not lie on the regression line. This is to be expected; unless particular
schools made no difference at all, we would expect to find some
variation in the outcomes even of schools with comparable intakes.
The dispersion of schools at varying distances above and below the
regression line therefore partly reflects the difference between schools
which are more and less effective at boosting the outcome. However,
the fact that the correlation between intake and outcome is less than
perfect also partly reflects the inadequacy of our intake measure. The
percentage of leavers from middle-class homes describes only one aspect
of a school's intake; there are many other characteristics of a school's
intake which might exert an influence on outcomes and which should
therefore be controlled when assessing the influence of the school itself.

Table 15.2 shows the (zero-order) correlations between the four
outcomes and each of five different measures of school intake. In the
case of the first outcome, O-grades, we find that the highest correlation
is with the percentage of leavers with middle-class fathers ($r = 0.79$).
Nevertheless there are high correlations between O-grades and other
intake measures, including measures of the average level of education
of pupils' parents. More surprisingly perhaps, the O-grade outcome is
correlated with the percentage of leavers who were male. At the bottom
of table 15.2 we report the multiple correlation which is obtained when
all five intake variables are simultaneously used to predict the outcome.

TABLE 15.2   Correlations between five school-intake measures and four measures of school outcomes: uncreamed comprehensives in the four regions ($n = 69$)

	O-grades	Truancy	Satisfaction	Belting
School-intake measure				
Percentage of leavers with middle-class fathers	0.79	−0.42	0.59	−0.30
Percentage of leavers with no classified father's occupation	−0.42	0.15	−0.26	0.22
Average father's education of leavers	0.73	−0.25	0.57	−0.38
Average mother's education of leavers	0.50	−0.31	0.39	−0.10
Percentage of leavers who are male	0.29	0.04	0.11	0.04
Multiple correlation based on all five intake measures	0.84	0.50	0.62	0.41
Percentage of between-school variation in each outcome measure explained by the five intake measures	70%	25%	39%	17%

Notes: Father's and mother's education were reported in terms of the following categories: left school at 15 years or less, 16 years, 17 years or more, don't know. The average is based on the first three categories.
The scoring system should be remembered in interpreting the direction of the correlations. For truancy and belting, high scores indicate that *more* leavers said they truanted or were belted.

For O-grades, the multiple correlation is 0.84. The square of this value, 0.70, indicates that 70 per cent of the variation between schools in their O-grade outcomes can be statistically 'explained' in terms of these five characteristics of their intakes. We must stress that even these five intake measures do not exhaust all the aspects of a school's intake which might influence outcomes.[3] In particular, we do not have any measure of the ability or attainment of pupils when they entered secondary school. Other evidence suggests that such a measure would further increase the proportion of school variation in examination outcomes which could be statistically explained by intake characteristics; a study of secondary-school results in inner-London showed that, depending on the number and type of other intake variables employed in conjunction with a measure of the average verbal-reasoning scores of each school's intake, between 80 and 85 per cent of variation between schools in examination results could be explained by intake variables (Inner London Education Authority, 1980 and unpublished analyses).

Table 15.2 also reports the correlations between the five intake measures and the three other outcomes: truancy, satisfaction and belting. These correlations are consistently lower than those for O-grades; the proportion of between-school variation in each outcome measure, which can be explained by the five intake measures in tandem, is 25 per cent for truancy, 39 per cent for satisfaction and only 17 per cent for belting. The fact that these estimates are lower than for O-grades may mean that school differences are simply more important in relation to these other outcomes than in relation to O-grades. It seems likely that, for example, the incidence of belting is strongly determined by disciplinary policies which vary substantially between schools, so it is not surprising that relatively little of the variation in belting can be explained by intake variables. On the other hand, we saw in chapter 11 that, although truancy can at least in part be attributed to factors within the school, many of these factors are structural in nature and cannot easily be varied across schools with similar intakes. In other words, some school *effects* may not emerge as school *differences* in the kind of study we are conducting here. The alternative explanation for the relatively low correlations of intake with truancy, satisfaction and belting suggests that these outcomes may be as much determined by intake as are O-grades, but that they are influenced by different aspects of intake from those which influence O-grade results.

Compared with the correlations between the intake measures and O-grades, therefore, the correlations between the intake measures, on the one hand, and, on the other, truancy, satisfaction and belting are relatively low. This may reflect greater variability in school effectiveness with respect to these outcomes, or it may reflect our use of inappropriate intake measures. We have no way of choosing between these two explanations, although we suspect that both may be partly valid.

Difference scores

We hope that the analogy between the multiple correlations, reported at the bottom of table 15.2, and the simple (zero-order) correlations, represented diagrammatically in figure 15.1, is now clear. Both statistics attempt to predict a school's outcome score from its intake, but the multiple correlation attempts to improve the prediction by basing it on more extensive information on the intake. In this section we will, for the sake of simplicity, base our exposition of the concept of difference scores on the (zero-order) correlation shown in figure 15.1. Our practical application of the concept of difference scores, however, will be in terms of the multiple correlations of table 15.2. The logic and limitations of our approach are the same in both cases.

The regression line in figure 15.1 expresses our 'best prediction' of any school's outcome score, given our knowledge of its intake. We must emphasise that it takes its standard from the relationships that actually prevailed among the 69 schools. It is not a prescriptive statement about the outcomes which any school *ought* to achieve. Moreover, the regression line is based on a technique (regression) which incorporates several assumptions about the relation of intake to outcome.[4] However, since our main purpose in this chapter is to explore and illustrate certain broader questions, we feel that, in this instance, the relative conceptual simplicity of regression analysis outweighs the technical limitations.

In figure 15.1 we have identified two schools, A and B. The O-grade outcome scores for the two schools are similar: that for school A is 2 percentage points higher than that for school B. However, more than one-third of school A's pupils are middle class; for school B the proportion is a mere 8 per cent. On the basis of this intake measure, therefore, we would predict a considerably higher outcome score for school A than for school B; these predictions are shown respectively by points a and b on the regression line in figure 15.1. The vertical distance Aa is equivalent to about 10 per cent of leavers on the outcome measure; the vertical distance Bb is about 11 per cent. In school A, therefore, about 10 per cent fewer leavers have O-grade A-C awards than we would predict from knowledge of its intake, and in school B about 11 per cent more leavers have O-grade A-C awards than we would predict from its intake. We will use the term *difference score* to describe the difference between a school's actual outcome and the outcome which would be predicted on the basis of its intake. Difference scores can be positive or negative; the difference score for O-grades for school A is −10 per cent and for school B it is +11 per cent.[5]

A school's difference score will depend on the outcome measure concerned; a school with a positive difference score for one outcome, say O-grades, may well have a negative difference score for another, say belting. Difference scores also depend upon the choice of intake measures; generally speaking, the better the prediction of the outcome measure from the intake measure, the smaller will be the average difference score (plus or minus) among schools. If the prediction were perfect, all schools would have a difference score of zero.

Difference scores can be computed for multiple regressions as well as for simple regressions. In the rest of this chapter we will use the term *difference score* to describe the difference between a school's actual outcome and the outcome that would be predicted from a knowledge of all five intake measures listed in table 15.2.

Table 15.3 shows the range of variation among the 69 schools in terms of the actual outcomes and the difference scores respectively for the four outcome measures. The first part of the table refers to actual outcomes; it is identical to table 15.1, except that it describes the 69 uncreamed comprehensives rather than all 273 schools in the sample. As we might expect (given the narrower range of variation in intakes to comprehensives), the variation in terms of all four outcomes is narrower for the uncreamed comprehensives (table 15.3a) than for all schools (table 15.1).

TABLE 15.3 Distribution (a) of actual school scores and (b) of school difference scores for four outcome measures: uncreamed comprehensives in the four regions ($n = 69$)

	Lowest score	Score at the lower quartile	Score at the median	Score at the upper quartile	Highest score	(Inter-quartile range)
(a) Actual school scores (percentage of leavers)						
O-grades	14	43	52	64	96	(21)
Truancy	0	7	12	18	37	(11)
Satisfaction	28	37	47	55	80	(18)
Belting	0	10	15	24	50	(14)
(b) School difference scores						
O-grades	−25	−5	0	+5	+22	(10)
Truancy	−13	−4	−1	+3	+22	(7)
Satisfaction	−18	−6	−1	+7	+23	(13)
Belting	−18	−6	−2	+6	+28	(12)

The second part of table 15.3 shows the range of variation among the 69 schools in terms of their difference scores for each outcome measure. The dispersion is summarised by the inter-quartile range. On each outcome the inter-quartile range is narrower for the different score than for the actual score. The reduction in ranges is greatest for the O-grade outcome, where the inter-quartile range of the difference scores is rather less than half that of the actual scores; the reduction in ranges is smallest for belting, where the inter-quartile range is only marginally smaller for the difference score than for the actual score. This reflects the fact that our five intake measures predicted the O-grade outcome most successfully and the belting outcome least successfully (table 15.2).

Where, as with the O-grade outcome, we have been able to predict a large proportion of school variation in outcome from knowledge of schools' intakes, we have found that the range of variation between schools in their difference scores is considerably smaller than the variation in their actual scores.

Nevertheless, even for O-grades, schools' difference scores *do* vary, and this leads us now to consider the question of what it is that difference scores, as we have defined them, measure.

Difference scores are residuals; they represent that part of a school's outcome which is still statistically unexplained, when allowance has been made for the five intake measures. It is therefore tempting to regard a difference score as a measure of a school's own contribution to the outcome, over and above the influence of the characteristics of its intake. However, this is, at best, an over-simplifying interpretation.

On the one hand, it can be objected that difference scores may overestimate a school's contribution to outcomes. The difference scores are not based on direct observations of the characteristics of schools which contribute to outcomes; they are merely the residuals obtained when we try to predict outcomes from the intake measures. As we have argued above, additional information about intakes would increase our ability to predict outcomes. If we were able to use other intake variables in our analysis, the range of variation among the difference scores would have been smaller. Difference scores, therefore, partly reflect characteristics of intakes which we have not been able to measure. They also reflect the consequences of error in our measures of the intake variables and the outcome variables. To the extent that either intake or outcome variables have been imperfectly measured, the correlation between the two will be attenuated, or weakened, and the range of variation in schools' difference scores will be overestimated.

On the other hand, it could also be argued that difference scores might underestimate a school's contribution to outcomes. Some of the variation in school's actual outcomes could probably be attributed *either* to intake differences *or* to differences between schools in terms of the school characteristics which influence the outcomes. Since we have no direct measures of these school characteristics we cannot gauge the extent of this covariation. However, in estimating difference scores we have, in effect, attributed all of this shared variation to intake rather than to school factors. (We have also discounted possible statistical interactions between intake and school factors.) Difference scores merely represent what the intake scores cannot statistically explain; the 'true' effects of schools might account for some of the variation in outcomes which we have attributed to intake differences. School effects might therefore be larger than the difference scores indicate. With the data at our disposal we cannot evaluate the validity or substantive significance of this claim. In any case it is fundamentally a question which data alone cannot resolve, but which has to be decided partly on theoretical grounds; for even if we did discover that some variation in outcomes was 'shared' between intake and school variables, we would need a theoretical basis for deciding on their relative importance.

Our own view is that, on balance, the difference scores probably overestimate the contributions made by schools to outcomes. This, we must stress, is a view based on judgments which inevitably exceed anything that any set of empirical data can tell us directly. The two problems described above, concerned with the adequate measurement of intake differences and with the interpretation of shared variation, are problems faced in one form or another by all researchers in this field. Both theoretical and empirical advances would be needed, if we were to produce difference scores which accurately measured a school's own contribution to outcomes. Moreover, advances in the social organisation of data-collection and research would also be needed. For a school might have a high or low difference score as a result of idiosyncratic features of its intake, history or organisation which would not be adequately represented in any standard set of measures. A research design for the study of schools must provide the means to assimilate and apply local knowledge of these idiosyncratic features.

Although we believe that difference scores are imperfect measures of particular schools' contributions to outcomes, the contributions that we also call school effectiveness, they are better than no measures at all. More importantly, we believe that difference scores are better measures of school effectiveness than are the actual outcome scores of schools. We have, we hope, established that, with theoretical and empirical advances, the concept of school difference scores as measures of school effectiveness could be improved and refined. In the rest of this chapter we continue to look at the school difference scores as we have operationalised them, and cautiously regard them as measures of school effectiveness. In a more tentative and exploratory spirit than we have so far adopted, we now use the difference scores to explore three questions in relation to comprehensive schools: are schools which are effective with respect to one outcome effective with respect to another? Is the effectiveness of a school related to aspects of the history of its organisation and context? What are some of the implications of requiring schools to publish data on examination results or other outcomes?

Correlations between school outcomes

A number of studies of school effects have concluded that a school which was effective with respect to one outcome was very likely to be effective with respect to another; that, say, a school that was effective at securing a good level of attendance from its pupils was also effective at boosting their examinations results. If this were generally true, it would simplify the task of both researcher and policy-maker. If there were a single dimension of school effectiveness, then the task of the researcher would be to explore that dimension and the task of the policy-maker would be to maximise schools' positions on it. If, however, there were several dimensions of school variability which contributed respectively to different types of school outcomes, then the definition of an effective school would be more problematic.

TABLE 15.4   Correlations between four measures of school outcomes

	O-grades	Truancy	Satisfaction	Belting
Truancy	−0.53 (−0.46) [−0.29]	−		
Satisfaction	+0.73 (+0.63) [+0.29]	−0.47 (−0.38) [−0.20]	−	
Belting	−0.37 (−0.28) [−0.07]	+0.24 (+0.08) [+0.01]	−0.28 (−0.31) [−0.16]	−

Notes: Unbracketed correlations are for the actual school scores among all EA schools in the four regions ($n = 273$).
Correlations in parentheses are for the actual school scores among uncreamed comprehensives in the four regions ($n = 69$).
Correlations in square brackets are for the difference scores among uncreamed comprehensives in the four regions ($n = 69$).

Table 15.4 shows three sets of correlations between the four outcome scores for schools. The first two correlations respectively refer to the actual outcome scores among all 273 schools (the unbracketed correlations, as in table 15.1) and among the 69 uncreamed comprehensives (the correlations in parentheses, as in table 15.3). With one exception (the correlation between belting and satisfaction) the correlations among the uncreamed comprehensives are lower than the equivalent correlations among all 273 schools. This may reflect the lesser variability, in terms of intake, among uncreamed comprehensives, which is reflected in their lesser variability in terms of outcomes (see table 15.3 in comparison with table 15.1). Whether these correlations are large or small is a matter of judgment; Rutter *et al.* (1979) and Reynolds (1976) felt able to conclude, on the basis of correlations that were, in general, somewhat larger than these (but based on different outcome measures and on much smaller samples of schools), that school outcomes could be collapsed into a single dimension, essentially defined by academic performance, and therefore capable of yielding a single order of merit for schools. Our own verdict is different. We feel that the correlations (especially among the uncreamed comprehensives) are sufficiently low to suggest that researchers should investigate school effectiveness in relation to different outcome criteria, and should remain open to the possibility that different outcomes may be influenced by different school variables.

One reason for our saying this is that studies of school *effects* should base their conclusions, not on correlations between the actual outcomes of schools, but on correlations between the best available measures of schools' own contributions to those outcomes. The third set of correlations in table 15.4, in square brackets, refers to the difference scores for the four outcomes among the 69 schools. In all cases the correlations between difference scores are considerably lower than the correlations (in parentheses) between actual outcomes. The highest correlation between difference scores for two outcomes is 0.29; subject to the qualifications discussed in the previous section, this suggests that less than 10 per cent of the variation in schools' effectiveness with respect to O-grades overlaps with the variation in schools' effectiveness with respect to truancy or satisfaction.[6] It is probably, but not necessarily, the case that, if we had additional measures of intake characteristics, the correlations between difference scores would be reduced still further.

In other words the apparent one-dimensional nature of school effectiveness may be an artefact of the tendency for the same aspects of a school's intake to predict, at least in part, the different aspects of a school's outcomes. The apparent single dimension is a dimension based on intakes; it is not based very strongly on schools' effects on outcomes. On the evidence of table 15.4, we would argue that future research into school effects should start from the premise that there may be several different aspects of schooling which respectively contribute to the effectiveness of schools in different areas of their endeavours.

Organisation, context and the effectiveness of schools

We have suggested that difference scores may be regarded as proxy measures of school effectiveness. In this section we explore the possibilities inherent in the difference-score approach by investigating some of the known characteristics of schools with positive and negative difference scores (that is, with 'high' and 'low' effectiveness). We restrict our investigation to a single outcome, O-grades; this is sufficient for our present analysis, which is largely exploratory and illustrative. Nevertheless, we believe that the general strategy we are illustrating could, given an appropriate social organisation of the research process, offer a chance to advance understanding of the effectiveness of schools. We will enlarge upon this claim at the end of this chapter and in chapter 17.

Our present discussion is limited by a restriction which is largely self-imposed. Under the code of practice for collaborative research (see chapter 2) the identity of individual schools covered in the Scottish Education Data Archive may not be revealed without the consent of the schools concerned and of individuals who might be identified through the data on a single school. Nor may aggregates of fewer than five schools be publicly identified, except in a collaborative context. The limitations which confidentiality principles impose are an important sociological fact, and we comment upon their significance later in this chapter. The practical consequence for the present analysis is that we do not identify individual schools. This raises difficulties for our general argument, that knowledge of a school's history, organisation and context is required in order to learn from comparative studies of school effectiveness. It is not easy to make this general point without the use of specific illustrations. We therefore examine O-grade difference scores in relation to some of the variables which can be expressed in more general terms. These variables concern the organisational history of schools and the education authorities to which they belong.

Among the 69 uncreamed comprehensives we can identify three groups of schools which first presented pupils for Highers between 1970 and 1975; in other words, they were in the process of acquiring 'academic tops' as the sample of 1976 leavers passed through them. It may take time for a school to consolidate its new-found academic status; the schools with new 'academic tops' may therefore have been handicapped relative to other schools during this process of consolidation. If so, we would expect these schools, other things being equal, to have been less effective than prediction during this period, and to have, on average, negative difference scores as revealed among our 1976 leavers. Of course, our analysis refers only to O-grade attainment; any handicap experienced by schools with new academic tops may have affected Highers but not O-grade results, or vice versa.

The first of these three groups consists of eleven schools which were founded as comprehensive schools in the late 1960s and which had had no previous existence as two-, three- or four-year schools. The average difference score for O-grades of these eleven schools was +0.7 per cent.[7] In other words, their O-grade performance was marginally better than would be predicted on the basis of intake alone and their newness apparently did not prove to be an overriding handicap.[8]

The second group consists of four schools which had previously been two-, three- or four-year schools, and which had served communities of insufficient size to support at least one six-year school. So, although these schools had not offered full academic courses before comprehensive reorganisation, this was not simply a result of any bipartite philosophy. The mean difference score for O-grades of these four schools was −0.1 per cent; these schools were achieving almost exactly at the level which would be predicted from their intakes.

The third group contains ten schools which had also been two-, three- or four-year schools before reorganisation; unlike the second group, however, this did not usually reflect the size of their communities, and was primarily a consequence of the bipartite system in which these schools had been the junior partners. The average difference score for these ten schools was −3.2 per cent. So, although schools which were developing new academic tops were not *per se* disadvantaged (and new schools may even have had an advantage over the rest), schools with the stigma (and perhaps also the more material handicaps) of former junior-secondary status appear still to have been disadvantaged, even relative to their intakes, in 1976.

It seems that the previous organisation of a school and, more important, the meaning of its organisational history in the context of the educational policy of the local authority, may continue to influence the performance of the school over and above factors associated with the characteristics of its intake.[9]

The three groups we have examined so far together accounted for 25 schools. The remaining 44 of our uncreamed comprehensives were all 'established' comprehensives, in the sense that they had first offered Highers courses by 1970. Most of them had had a long existence as academic secondary schools. (At an earlier time, however, they had varied among themselves in terms of whether or not they had also offered non-certificate courses, and whether or not they had admitted all pupils from the area; see chapters 13 and 14). The mean difference score of the 44 established comprehensives was relatively close to zero (+0.6 per cent).

Until 1975 the schools were administered by the old education authorities. Two authorities were represented in the group of 69 schools by one school and two schools respectively. The other schools were distributed across eight authorities, and table 15.5 shows the mean of the difference scores for schools in each of these eight education authorities, first for the established comprehensives and, second, for the established comprehensives together with the 25 comprehensives first presenting pupils for Highers between 1971 and 1974.

TABLE 15.5   Mean difference scores for O-grade attainment by pre-1975 education authority (a) among 'established' uncreamed comprehensives in the four regions and (b) among all[1] uncreamed comprehensives in the four regions

| Education authority | Mean difference score (for percentage of leavers with A–C awards at O-grade) | |
	'Established' uncreamed comprehensives	All[1] uncreamed comprehensives
A	+ 7.3	+ 6.9
B	+ 8.3	+ 1.7
C	+ 5.0	+ 1.8
D	− 8.3	− 7.2
E	+ 4.2	+ 4.2
F	− 1.1	− 1.1
G	− 0.1	+ 1.8
H	− 4.4	− 4.8
All authorities[2]	+ 0.6	±0.0
Standard deviation	(9.0)	(8.8)

Notes: 1   Excluding 15 schools (see chapter 15, 'Intakes and outcomes').
          2   Including the three schools omitted from the education authority figures (see chapter 15, 'Organisation, context and the effectiveness of schools').

The variation in mean difference scores between education authorities was large, especially with respect to the established comprehensives. The mean difference score of one authority was almost a standard deviation above zero, whereas that of another authority was almost a standard deviation below zero. Only two of the eight authorities were within 4 percentage points of prediction. The differences between authorities are somewhat reduced when the 25 newer comprehensives are pooled with the 44 established comprehensives, but there is still one authority (A) whose schools did substantially better than prediction (+6.9 per cent) and one (D) whose schools did substantially worse (−7.2 per cent). These are large differences. Given the assumptions of our model, they mean that the school system in authority A had itself caused 14 per cent more of the age-group to be raised to, or above, the criterion threshold of achievement (at least one A–C award at O-grade) than had the school system in authority D.

One may make such comparisons in greater detail. Four of the five 'least effective' schools in our sample, the five schools with the lowest (that is, most negative) difference scores, came from two authorities. In the one authority there were three neighbouring schools with difference scores of −20.3, −19.9 and −12.4 per cent respectively. In the other there was a school with a difference score of −25.1 that served a burgh in which the two other schools had difference scores of −2.0 and −6.8. These were, in terms of our O-grade outcome, noticeable educational blackspots. More significantly for our present argument, they had already been identified as blackspots in official reports and by observers with knowledge of the local circumstances and context.

There were also bright spots. For example, the seven schools in the three new towns had not enjoyed the advantages that had accrued, say, to the long-established academies in the most 'over-achieving' of the education authorities shown in table 15.5. Nevertheless, the new-town schools had a mean difference score of +3.2 per cent.

Our exploration of the types of schools with positive and negative O-grade difference scores leads us to reiterate and extend the conclusion already reached in the last chapter on the basis of a comparison between the comprehensive and selective sectors of the system: namely that it is essential that the contribution which schools can or do make to their pupils' performance be understood in the context of the schools' history, of their local context and of the continuing interaction between the two. Of the three stages in the school-effects debate which we outlined earlier in this chapter, the first two largely ignored this point. The third phase accommodated it partially in terms of concepts such as 'ethos', although the accommodation has not, in our view, gone far enough. The ways in which one understands schools and their effects must be grounded in their history and local context.

Education is not, however, the irrevocable prisoner of tradition and past practice. Where, for example, comprehensive schools have begun anew in a community, or where entire communities have begun anew, the schools concerned appear to have done at least as well as, or even better than, one would have predicted from the nature of their intakes alone. More generally, the importance of history and context does not mean that a school's effectiveness is wholly determined by factors beyond the control of its teachers and administrators. We believe that *some* of the difference between more and less effective schools does lie within their control; there are ways in which the effectiveness of schools could, with better understanding, be improved. The better understanding, however, requires (among other things) an awareness of history and context; and the better practice that may result should also be conducted in the light of these factors. The history and context of a school live, in part, through the ways in which teachers, parents and others interpret their inheritance (for example, the reputation of a school) and act in the light of it, whether in the classroom or elsewhere. Chapter 10, for example, has shown how the Scottish myth has penetrated many classrooms through the culturally conditioned interpretations and actions of teachers. If education is to become more effective, it is clearly important that practitioners achieve a better understanding both of their own situation and of the theories and interpretations that influence their relations with individual pupils.

It follows, therefore, that schools and teachers should themselves be involved in the study of schools (an argument developed in Burnhill, Raffe and Weston, 1981). An effective school system may require that all practitioners attempt to act in the light of a better understanding of the cultural and historical constraints on their actions as well as of the theories and interpretations that guide these actions.

The publication of schools' examination results

Our argument in this chapter can be applied to the debate about the publication of examination results by schools. Much of this debate has concerned the political wisdom of this move: would the publication of examination results give undue weight to academic performance? Would it detract from the desired level of school autonomy? Can one do justice to all of a school's objectives? And so on. We believe that more fundamental problems have sometimes been overlooked. The publication of results is desired in order to disseminate information, but what is the quality of the information that would be disseminated? In terms of whose interests is the idea of school effectiveness to be judged? And in what ways would better information lead to better choices, and thereby, to an improving system?

As a mere description of how pupils from a school perform in examinations, the publication of results cannot be faulted, always provided that the results are based on all pupils in the age-group and not just on those who are entered for the examinations. Moreover, examination results are a very good measure of at least two charac-teristics of a school: the social composition and the intellectual com-position of its intake. This is because of the high correlations between a school's intake and its examination performance; a school with 'good' examination results is likely to have a relatively large proportion of pupils who are bright and a relatively large proportion who are middle class. Some parents may prefer their children to attend schools where a large number of their fellow pupils are bright or middle class or both; if governments believe that this is a legitimate preference, it is appro-priate for them to insist on the publication of examination results, since these offer indirect measures of a school's intake and can there-fore assist parents to implement their preferences.

The more usual assumption, however, is that many parents wish their *own* children to do well in examinations and that published examination results will help them to identify the schools at which their children would have the best chance of examination success. However, although it is undoubtedly true that many parents place a high value on examination results, we feel that the argument that examination results are a good indicator of a school's effectiveness deserves careful scrutiny.

We have already shown that more than two-thirds of the variation between schools in the O-grade performance of their pupils can be explained by measured differences in their intakes. Almost certainly a larger proportion could be explained in this way, if we had evidence on other intake characteristics. Therefore less than a third of the variation in schools' O-grade performance, and probably considerably less than a third, is due to variations between schools in their effectiveness at preparing pupils for O-grades.

Some consequences of this can be expressed more concretely. The publication of examination results by schools could, if the results were presented in a standard form, easily facilitate the production of 'league tables' of schools. Not only would these league tables show which schools apparently do better than others, but they would also suggest that the range of variation among schools was very wide, with some schools doing extremely well and others very badly. If, however, schools were to publish, not their actual examination results but their difference scores (that is, their results 'controlling for' intake) a different picture would emerge. In the first place the ranking of schools in the resulting league table would be different. Some schools with apparently good examination results would have negative difference scores; other schools with apparently poor examination results would have positive difference scores. If we took, for example, all the possible pairs of schools out of the 69 uncreamed comprehensives discussed above, we would find that, for at least 30 per cent of these pairs, their ordering would be reversed if the comparison were based on difference scores rather than on actual examination results.[10] In other words, if parents chose schools on the basis of examination results, in the belief that these results reflected the schools' relative effectiveness, they would very often choose the wrong school.

Basing league tables on difference scores would not only change the rank ordering of some schools; it would also reveal a much narrower range of variation among schools. We have already seen (table 15.3) how, among uncreamed comprehensive schools, the inter-quartile range for O-grade difference scores was rather less than half the inter-quartile range for the actual outcome scores; and we believe that, if difference scores were estimated using additional intake data, the observed range would be further reduced. This range would not be negligible; it would still indicate significant differences between schools,

295

but the differences would be much smaller than actual outcome scores would suggest.

The evidence, both from our own study and from others, is sufficient to show clearly that, if the unadjusted examination results of a school were to be used as a measure of the school's effectiveness, this would be seriously misleading and unfair to schools, parents and pupils alike. And in this context one should entirely dismiss from consideration studies which claim to reach conclusions about the effectiveness of schools or types of schools, but which do not clearly state, and take account of, the nature of the intakes to these schools or of other factors, external to the schools themselves, which influence their outcomes.

But of which of these factors should one take account? The answer depends on the purposes and interests which the study of a school's effectiveness aims to serve.

The interest of teachers is that they should be judged fairly and should not be held accountable for things which, as teachers, they cannot influence. The local context and history of a school, its organisation and its physical fabric are not within their power, as teachers, to change. The interest of teachers is therefore to discount (and statistically to control for) the effects of these factors, as well as the effects of intake characteristics, when estimating school effectiveness.

The interest of parents, however, is different; it is to identify the school which would be most effective for their own child. For this purpose the only factors whose effects should be controlled in the study of school effectiveness are those which are fixed for any child, that is, factors directly related to children's individual or family characteristics. All other influences on outcomes, including the history and local context of a school, would affect the outcomes of schooling for their child. The parents' interest is therefore that the effects of such influences should not be controlled in the estimation of the effectiveness of particular schools.

A third interest is that of administrators, policy-makers and all whose interests lie (or should lie) in making education more effective. Their practical concern is to identify the factors which contribute to school effectiveness and which are within their power to change. In the longer term, at least, they might be able to change the organisation and the physical fabric of a school; other factors, including the history and local context of a school, are likely to remain beyond administrative manipulation and should be statistically controlled in studies of school effectiveness which aim at longer-term improvement.

Supporters of the policy for publishing school examination results, together with policies for extending parental choice of schools, tend to make (or imply) these claims: that the policy is fair between schools, since it identifies the most effective schools; that it enables parents to choose the most effective schools; and that it thereby encourages good practice. We have already questioned these claims on the grounds that examination results tend to be poor measures of a school's effectiveness. Even the use of difference scores (or something similar) to measure effectiveness would involve a conflict between these aims. The definition of effectiveness that was fair to teachers would differ from the definition that best helped parents, and neither definition would best promote good practice in the long run.

These comments are not intended to discourage the serious study of school effectiveness. Rather, they are intended to point out that the study of school effects is closely interwoven with interests in the real world, and with ethical and political considerations that arise out of them. These considerations could easily lead to excessive caution and defensiveness; but such attitudes rarely breed innovation and change. We reserve further discussion of these points for our final chapter.

Conclusion

We have used data on intakes and outcomes in order to model the variation between schools in their effectiveness at influencing certain outcomes. Our approach has been illustrative and exploratory; we have illustrated a way of asking questions about schools and we have explored some of the consequences of asking these questions. We do not pretend that we have reached final and definitive answers.

In particular, we have recognised two limitations. The first is a matter of theory. Any attempt to model data rests upon explicit or implicit assumptions about the relationships within the data. Our modelling in this chapter is no exception; we made provisional assumptions, detailed above, about the interpretation of difference scores as school effects and especially about the partitioning of variance between intake and school effects. These assumptions were not wholly grounded in the data; as in all research, we made *a priori* assumptions, albeit tentative and provisional ones, in order to interpret the empirical evidence.

Social research is a social process; it involves dialogue and the exchange of ideas among researchers. If research is to inform practice, and to learn from it, similar dialogue must take place between researchers and practitioners. But how are these processes of dialogue possible, when research knowledge depends upon *a priori* assumptions which cannot be tested through rational discussion about evidence? How can agreement on these assumptions be reached? This question has political as well as epistemological implications. For example, if schools are being judged in terms of their effectiveness, who decides which assumptions are admissible in the modelling of school effects? And if a school believes that the assumptions that are used bias the estimate of effectiveness against it, how can it challenge them and gain acceptance for an alternative approach?

The second limitation in our approach in this chapter is a lack of some appropriate data on both intakes and schools. We have pointed out how our analysis could have been improved, if we had possessed additional data on some intake characteristics, especially on the ability and attainment of pupils when they entered secondary school. Moreover, unlike Rutter *et al.* (1979), we have lacked direct measures of school practice. We also argued that the study of schools and school effects must be grounded in a knowledge of the history, organisation and context of each school; knowledge of this kind is often possessed only by the teachers or others who are most directly involved with the school.

Although our analysis has therefore been restricted by a lack of some forms of data, this does not mean that information on these things does not exist. The administrative records of many schools and education authorities contain considerable information on the characteristics of intakes to secondary schools; and, as we have suggested, teachers and others with direct experience of schools have considerable knowledge of their local circumstances. The problem is how to harness this disparate knowledge to the study of school effects and to the informed development of more effective schools.

We have already commented that the confidentiality rule which restricted our own discussion of school effects in the section above about organisation, context and the effectiveness of schools is itself an important sociological datum. The use of the information contained in administrative records is governed by similar restrictions. We do not deny that there are sound ethical reasons for such restrictions. Nor indeed do we deny that there are equally compelling but more human reasons for restricting the flow of information. For example, at a time when rolls are falling and many schools and teachers feel vulnerable, it is not surprising that schools should be nervous about any proposal to publish comparative data on the performance of schools. This nervousness is even more understandable when it is acknowledged that any judgments about schools' effectiveness, whether based on simple comparisons of examination results or upon the types of modelling procedures outlined in this chapter, rest upon assumptions which cannot be tested by the data alone. All the judgments of social science are provisional and tentative; but this fact will be little consolation for those who lose their reputations or their jobs as a result of such judgments.

Yet, at a time when ethical and social pressures resist openness and the disclosure of information, the need to learn from such information remains. The need to discover what it is that makes one school more effective than another is as pressing as ever, and the pressures have wider implications. The publication of examination results is partly an attempt to make more accountable an education system that appears not to respond to public expectation. 'Do schools make a difference?' is not just a question about statistical methods. It is a question about the whole expansionist perspective that has informed much of post-war policy for secondary education; and, on a yet wider front, it leads to further questions about whether people can in fact construct and maintain institutions that can improve the human condition and that are capable of knowledge-based change from within. We believe that such knowledge (and such change) is possible, using the kinds of procedures exemplified in this chapter, if only the two main limitations, described above, can be overcome.

However, it may by now be evident that we do not believe that these two limitations can be overcome merely through improvements of a technical kind. We also need social, even political, changes in the organisation of research; changes that will reduce current divisions between research and practice and that will encourage wider participation and greater accountability in social research. For the reasons given at the end of the section about organisation, context and the effectiveness of schools, we envisage that such changes may also make practice more effective. Thus the question of the potency of education is inseparable from considerations of the quality of our understanding of the social world. Chapter 17 discusses the reconstruction of the relationship between research and practice that this view implies.

Chapter 16

Summary: Myth and Practice in Scottish Education

Educational expansion and its limits

We have said in chapter 1 that the expansionist perspective that sustained the first two decades of post-war thinking and practice in education was made up of two strands: an evaluative or moral strand, concerning the values that should be realised in a reconstructed society; and an explanatory strand that offered an account of how these values might be realised in practice. Both strands led to a programme aimed, among other things, at the extension and the equalisation of the opportunity to profit from education. Whatever the conceptual difficulties with the ideas of equality and opportunity, and however varied the reasons for pursuing them, doubts about these objectives were outweighed by the way in which they expressed people's hopes for the post-war world, and thereby mobilised political will. People who emphasised the right of access to education as a universal entitlement of citizenship found themselves in agreement with others who emphasised the benefits for economic growth or for political and social order. Conflicts of purpose remained latent, because expansion seemed to offer an explanation of how several purposes might simultaneously be achieved.

Within this general perspective, there was a continuing attempt to mobilise talent by encouraging larger proportions of pupils to volunteer for post-compulsory secondary education. The policy for certification, described in chapter 4, was based on the assumption that, whatever the intrinsic attractions, pupils would value particular types or levels of secondary-school course for the extrinsic rewards that certification would subsequently bring. We have argued that any such policy for certification must strike a balance between a variety of considerations: the standard of difficulty of the certificate examinations; the proportion of pupils selected for certificate courses; the stage at which selection is made; the degree of dependence on pupil voluntarism, motivated by the prospect of examination success, rather than on compulsion; the coverage of the curriculum and the extent of a common curriculum; and, finally, considerations of fairness. Fairness itself has to do with several of these aspects: with the content, phasing and finality of the selection procedures determining admission to favoured courses; with the relative difficulty of courses and examinations in different subjects; and also with the relative standards of examiners themselves.

The pull and push of these interdependent factors constituted structural constraints upon the actions of schools. In using certificates to motivate pupils during the compulsory years of schooling, and to encourage them to stay on afterwards, schools have had to make choices within the limits set by these constraints. How they have chosen has often depended upon prevailing values, explanations and perceptions. Not least, it has depended upon the degree of awareness of the interdependencies we have listed, and relatedly, upon the extent to which there has been an attempt to develop and refine such awareness as a basis for practical decisions. Where public awareness did not exist, was not sought, or could not be risked, practice and understanding have tended to be more anthropologically grounded in habit and history; and any difficulties in maintaining a coherence between values, explanations and practice in the changing post-war situation have tended to be explained away in an *ad hoc* fashion, or else ignored. This situation has not been conducive to the accumulation of what is sometimes called 'a convincing body of experience', for it has been marked by a recourse to secrecy and by a growing divide between what the schools have actually had to do, and the terms that have been available to them to discuss, and to justify or criticise, their own activities. It is in this context that myth has become important as an arbiter of purpose and as an explanation of reality; and it is in this context, too, that there has been a growing demand for better accounts of the education system and for more accountability in it.

Our own description of the reality of Scottish education since the war differs, however, from that offered by the prevailing account that we have termed the Scottish myth. After summarising the arguments and findings of our empirical chapters in the next section, we return, in the section 'The nature of the Scottish myth', to a discussion of the status of myth and of the relationship between social science and politics more generally. Then, in our final chapter, we indicate how a collaborative approach to social inquiry might handle more adequately some of the problems of this relationship.

Overview

We have argued that universal voluntary participation in education cannot be achieved solely by the universal award of certificates, because certification cannot create extrinsic value. Like any currency, the value of certificates inflates with an increase in their issue that is unrelated to an increase in wealth; and, in this instance, 'wealth' is fixed. Where the issue of certificates is less than universal, two options are open to a secondary-school system. A universal opportunity to compete for a restricted number of like-valued certificates may be maintained by postponing formal selection. A system which chooses this option attempts to promote pupils' compliance by prolonging the formal possibility of success for a large number of pupils. As we have indicated, however, various informal differentiations then arise, for example, in the number and difficulty of the courses taken; or else too many pupils find the courses too difficult for too long. The scope for variations in curriculum is restricted and the relationship of secondary education to employment is largely extrinsic, mediated by certification.

The second option, if the issue of certificates is to be restricted, is to restrict also the competition for them. Alternative strategies must then be found for mobilising the voluntary participation of pupils both during and after the period of compulsory schooling. At the same time there is increased scope for making intrinsic connections between education and employment via the curriculum of pupils who have failed the academic selection. Prior differentiation of the levels and type of certification to be awarded (for example, O-level/CSE or the Credit, General and Foundation levels proposed by the Dunning Committee) is analogous to this second option.

Scottish policy until the mid-1960s attempted to implement a combination of these two options, securing the boundary between them with two arguments. The first was the received understanding of intelligence and related techniques of selection. The second was the relative generosity with which opportunities to embark on academic secondary courses were provided. What breached this boundary was not the abolition of selective transfer at 12 years, for, as chapter 10 has argued, other forms of selection could be, and have been, substituted for it during the period of compulsory secondary education. The breach came with the introduction of the O-grade to be offered in fourth year and at a lower level than the Higher. The O-grade was intended both as an intermediate incentive and also as a legitimate outcome in its own right. If the standard of 'fairness' that applied to selection for Highers courses were also applied to selection for O-grade courses, a majority of the age-group could reasonably expect to embark on certificate work, and more especially so when the period of compulsory education was extended to include the fourth year. But if the value of the Higher and the O-grade were to be preserved, by maintaining their difficulty and by keeping success in them relatively scarce, increased participation could only be accompanied by an increasing incidence of eventual failure in certificate examinations. Moreover, there would still be some limit to the proportion of pupils who could participate with a reasonable initial prospect of success.

In practice there has remained a group of some 20 per cent of pupils who have never embarked on any certificate courses, and a further group of some 10 per cent who at some point in their third or fourth year have abandoned all hopes of presentation. Chapters 10 and 11 have shown how exclusion from work for certification has proved to be tantamount to exclusion from the moral community of the school. This, in its turn, has restricted the development of alternative curricula for such pupils. School-leavers' judgments of whether their schooling was worthwhile were heavily conditioned by their involvement in certificate courses. Both teachers and pupils have found it difficult to locate reasons for continued schooling where the prospect of certification has been remote or altogether absent. The high incidence of truancy is largely to be explained in this way.

Our discussion of the implications for the courses of Highers and O-grade leavers of prevailing standards for the acquisition of certification has rested partly on inference. Nevertheless, it is clear from chapters 5 and 6 that inherited ideas of breadth in the curriculum have only been realised for a small minority of pupils; and inflationary 'over-examination' has largely displaced even attempts to secure only marginal changes in content and in methods of teaching and learning. The standard of the O-grade examination was such that, in the late 1970s, half the 'O-grade leavers' (roughly the 'middle 40 per cent' of the age-group) attempted fewer than five subjects in certificate examinations and over half achieved fewer than two 'passes' (awards in bands A, B or C). This cannot, we infer, be a framework within which breadth of study over a range of subjects can combine with viable levels of motivation prompted by reasonable prospects of success. Among Highers leavers (roughly 30 per cent of the age-group) the large majority attempted five or more O-grade subjects and passed five or more. But a year later, at Higher grade, well under a half of Highers leavers attempted five or more subjects at Highers; and after a further, sixth, year the proportion had still only climbed to two-thirds. Again, we conjecture that, in such a framework, pupils' experience of breadth of study cannot correspond to the aspirations or assertions of the Scottish myth. More concretely we can assert that the Scottish Highers course has not generally been a five-subject course that completes an education for 17-year-old (fifth-year) school-leavers, though this is how it has commonly been described.

The examinable curriculum has developed incrementally over the years, 'from the top downwards', and it has thereby distributed to the majority of secondary-school children the experience of failure in an attenuated academic curriculum. This generalisation of failure has provided a basis for securing the participation of many pupils, but only at a high cost: it has reflected an indifference to the consequent de-moralisation of pupils, both in school and also at the point at which some might otherwise volunteer for non-academic forms of post-compulsory education; it has ignored the consequent fragmentation of the curriculum during the compulsory years; it has led to over-examination and it has restricted the scope available for the develop-ment of curricula based on alternative values and alternative methods.

The policy of an incremental extension of an academic curriculum has largely relied upon the extrinsic value of the certificates awarded in order to motivate pupils. We have seen in chapter 7 that even the most marginal of the new certificate levels has had a real value in entry to the labour market. The bond between education and employment has been extended in the last two decades to a point where educational certificates influence initial occupational success for the majority of labour-market entrants from school. However, the significance of this fact for the motivation of pupils has been limited by the workings of the labour market, which operate to obscure the value of certificates. Moreover, the influence of employers over the school curriculum does not seem to have increased commensurately with the 'tightening bond', largely because they have been less concerned with job-specific skills than with mastery of the basics and with general academic performance as indicated by the overall number of awards, especially in academic subjects. In assessing general academic level, employers have relied upon the academic values which are incorporated in educational assess-ment. If anything, therefore, employers' preferences for the certificated products of 'downward incrementalism' have further established the sway of the attenuated academic curriculum.

However, the early years of the Youth Opportunities Programme showed that employers *would* use other opportunities and criteria for judging applicants, where they were available (chapter 9). Furthermore, because leavers could only enter YOP following unemployment, and because school-leaver unemployment was concentrated so heavily among non-certificate leavers, YOP redistributed opportunity pro-gressively (if marginally) with respect to the initial overall distribution of opportunity by schools. In its early years, YOP had only a small and widely criticised educational component, though its educational potential was large and would increase as the transition from school to work became longer and was punctuated more often by periods of unemployment or of undesired employment. Nevertheless, it is evident that YOP reflected interests and objectives that were outside the usual range of educational debate. By 1981 it had yet to be determined whether, if YOP were to introduce a new dimension into post-compulsory provision, this new dimension would nevertheless be of value in terms of accepted notions of 'education'. Also, to the extent that YOP itself selected school-leavers for employment, it promised to deprive the secondary-school system of the extrinsic rewards through which it had come to motivate the majority of its pupils.

The need for YOP was, of course, an indication of the failure of one of the expectations of the expansionist perspective; for expansion had both promised, and required, economic growth. Its failure to fulfil this promise was presaged by the deceleration of economic growth in the 1960s and by the rise in youth unemployment in the 1970s. Expansion had required and promised not only growth but also the redistribution of success between the social classes. The assumption was that the equalisation of access to initial opportunities by the removal of gross material barriers was a precondition, and a sufficient condition, for the mobilisation of talented working-class children. The long-term effects of fairer competition for individual betterment would promote further growth, part of which could finance further provision aiming at further redistribution.

Our analysis of trends in class inequality in educational attainment since the war has shown that any conclusions about redistribution rest partly on definition. If one adopts what in chapter 12 we called a 'consumer' perspective, that emphasises the intrinsic (non-relative) value of education to individuals, one may conclude that expansion at all levels, from the university downwards, has tended slightly to reduce class inequalities in attainment. Of course, class inequalities have been altogether removed where the universal right to consume education of a particular sort has been recognised and applied. If, however, one describes the impact of expansion on class inequality in terms of the relative proportions of the social classes that reach, or surpass, various levels of attainment, then class relativities have in general remained constant since the war. This conclusion also rests on our adoption of a measure (and a related concept) of inequality that gives no special weight to inequalities either of inclusion or exclusion; different conclusions sometimes follow when different measures are used.

In chapter 12 we have also modelled the effects of expansion on the class distribution of attainment. In doing this, we made various (empirically grounded) assumptions about the degree of advantage with which middle-class pupils started their secondary education. 'Advantage' could be thought of in terms of individual academic

305

ability or, heuristically, of any 'non-school' factors that might influence secondary-school attainment. Comparison of the resultant predictions with the observed levels of class inequality of outcome has shown the inequalities of outcome to conform to prediction in pattern, but to exceed prediction in magnitude. Class inequalities in secondary attainment have uniformly exceeded class inequalities in average ability at age 11. The level of class inequalities in secondary education has, in general, been constant in Scotland since the war.

Two exceptions to these general conclusions merit a comment. First, access to the 'alternative route' of non-university full-time or part-time post-school education has become more unequal since the late 1940s. Second, it appears that, among the most successful 15 per cent of the age-group in the late 1950s, class inequalities in school attainment by 17 years were lower than they were some fifteen years later. These two exceptions appear to negate the view that class differences in educational attainment can never be affected by the way education is organised and conducted. At the same time, however, the trend in these two respects was towards greater class inequality.

Both these outcomes, access to further education and Highers attainment, will arguably affect subsequent life-chances. The same appears to be true of the levels of certification that have been newly gained in the last fifteen years by the majority of the age-group. In England and Wales over the last half-century education has grown in importance as a channel of occupational transmission and mobility. The level of fathers' occupations and the level of their children's occupations remain strongly correlated, but the correlation is increasingly mediated by educational attainment. With the data at our disposal we have not been able to test for all these trends in a Scottish context, but our evidence on class and education, and on education and employment, suggests that the same pattern of change may be true for Scotland over the last two or three decades.

Our study was conducted at a time when only the initial impact of comprehensive reorganisation could be assessed. In chapter 14, we divided the entire education authority and grant-aided school system into two exclusive and exhaustive sectors. The fully comprehensive sector consisted of 'uncreamed' non-selective schools offering the full range of certificate courses to a local catchment, and only to a local catchment. All other schools were treated as part of the selective sector. The two sectors differed only trivially with respect to three outcomes: truancy, corporal punishment and pupils' judgments of the 'worthwhileness' of their last year at school. There was a more substantial difference, however, between the profiles of examination attainment for the two sectors. More pupils in the comprehensive sector achieved at least a modest level of certification, such as obtaining

A–C awards at O-grade. Exactly a quarter of pupils in each of the two sectors achieved at least one pass in the terminal school examination (Highers), but more pupils in the selective sector achieved more than two such passes (17 as compared with 15 per cent).

Any judgment of the overall academic performance of the two sectors must therefore rest not just on the data, but also on various assumptions. One assumption concerns the relative value to be assigned to different levels of SCE attainment. The second, empirical, assumption concerns the comparability of the pupil intakes in the two sectors. The distributions of the pupils in the two sectors over our measure of parental occupation were very similar, and parental occupation is a moderately good predictor of educational achievement for individual pupils. We seemed, therefore, to have compared like with like and thereby to have isolated the differences in achievement associated with a comprehensive organisation of education, and perhaps even with the comprehensive reorganisation of 1965 and after. However, we also found that, on average, middle-class pupils tended to do better in the selective sector, whereas the working-class pupils tended to do better in the comprehensive sector. Put another way, the 'class-gap' in achievement was smaller in the comprehensive sector. This could be interpreted as an effect of reorganisation. Alternatively, it might mean that, although our measure of parental class showed virtually identical distributions in the two sectors, the educational implications of being middle class, or of being working class, were rather different in the two sectors. Many of the schools in our comprehensive sector were the carriers or descendants of the Scottish omnibus tradition and may have influenced the structure and meaning of social class in their locality over the years. Indeed, the Scottish Education Data Archive shows that, in the early 1960s, there had been no class difference in educational attainment among Highers pupils in the sector served by these schools, whereas there was already a substantial class difference in attainment among Highers pupils in schools in the selective sector. Whether reorganisation will eventually extend the omnibus legacy to all schools, it is still too early to say.

Our initial approach to the empirical analysis of comprehensive reorganisation was ahistorical and cross-sectional, but in interpreting the results we had found ourselves drawn increasingly back into the history of schools and of their continuing interaction with the communities they served. When we turned in our final empirical chapter (chapter 15) to a discussion of the effectiveness of individual schools *within* the comprehensive sector, the importance of continuing local practice became even more apparent. There was, in general, a strong relationship between the percentage of pupils from each school who achieved certification and the social background of the pupil intake.

Background statistically 'explained' 70 per cent of the variation between schools in their average levels of O-grade achievement. Part of the remaining 'unexplained' variation was clearly associated, however, with aspects of the schools' history. Schools that had developed Highers courses most recently, for example, appeared to be less effective, as did schools that had grown from an earlier junior existence in a bipartite system. Schools, however, that had grown to six-year, non-selective status from a previous existence as four-year area schools (truncated omnibus schools, in effect) appeared to be more effective, and so too did other schools that were not haunted by an earlier existence as the inferior part of the bipartite system; new-town schools, for example, appeared to be more effective.

These substantive conclusions were based on several assumptions, one of which was that measures of social background were equally valid and effective as predictors of educational success for all the comprehensive schools studied and could therefore be used as 'controls' for pupil intake, to help isolate statistically the contribution to SCE attainment of the school itself. A simplifying heuristic assumption here was that whatever was not contributed to a school's attainment by the characteristics of its entrants was, in some sense or other, contributed by the school itself and could therefore be thought of as 'the difference the school had made'. Although this assumption is too simple in several respects, our application of it to the data has indicated some of the complexities of the ways in which schools may have their effects. Part of the contribution of the school to the achievement of its pupils can be attributed to the history of its organisation and intake arrangements, of its provision of academic courses and of its relations with nearby schools in the context of earlier educational policies. The evidence also indicated that the school's history may in its turn have influenced the potential for education of local class cultures, reinforcing a similar conclusion that emerged from the comparison between sectors in chapter 14.

If schools do not, and cannot, 'make a difference', then the flickering light of the liberal love-affair with the Victorian ideal of progress will finally be extinguished in education. It will signify that there are no institutional means consistent with certain ideals of freedom of choice through which the state can intervene to change young persons' prospects; there will be nothing that public action can do. Our evidence has shown that, in the longer term, schools can and do make a measurable difference, though often in indirect ways. In chapter 15 we stopped short of estimating how far pupils' examination prospects are currently boosted by strategies that are directly and immediately under the control of teachers and others who manage individual schools. We have, however, pointed to some of the effects of history and of local class culture that may structure teachers' options and limit their scope for action. Our evidence is also consistent with the view that different schools are good at achieving different things: examination success, non-physical control, high attendance levels and positive evaluations from their leavers. It is likely that, wittingly or not, teachers have adopted different goals in the light of their understandings of the history of the school in the context of the local class culture. It is also likely that at least some teachers will also have been influenced by their own understanding of the potential of education to act independently of these constraints. There is, therefore, no easy boundary to be drawn between the school as an institution and the class culture with which it interacts, or between the legacy of history and the interpretative response of teachers and others involved in schooling.

The nature of the Scottish myth

Our summary and evaluation of our findings has indicated the importance of interpreting the data in the context of the historically rooted understandings and practices of the people whom the data describe. This brings us back to myth and, in particular, to the variant of the belief in the potency of education that we have termed, in chapter 3, the Scottish myth. The myth is an interconnected system of values and beliefs that both celebrates national identity and explains how that identity is realised in, and reproduced through, the national system of public education. The myth thereby invests with meaning the peculiar features of that system, features like the five-year secondary course, the broad curriculum, the Higher examination, the Ordinary (or general) degree, the omnibus school and the non-residential, non-collegiate university. These institutions are interpreted as the product of a historical endeavour to construct a society in which differences of rank, such as they are, derive solely from differences in merit, determined by education. The various parts of the system of values and beliefs are held to be logically related in some sense: 'We have an interest in the common man, therefore we have an interest in a broad education.' The myth, in other words, has a dual status as a statement of values and as a set of proto-scientific statements about the social world. It shapes the consciousness of the actors in the separate parts of the system, makes the world intelligible to them, and makes their actions intelligible to others. It thereby facilitates collective action, but only within certain limits. Thus to an actor who becomes aware of this network of belief, it may provide an effective, but limited, means of control or change. Until the mid-1960s, Scottish educational policy, for example, worked mainly through the myth: as the Senior Chief Inspector of schools put it (Brunton, 1977, pp. 21-2):

> The Leaving Certificate was traditionally the holy of holies of Scottish education. Teachers, and indeed the public at large, understood this examination, and changes in it were a matter of public interest and understanding and could meet with fairly ready acceptance. Consequent changes in the curriculum could also be accepted, provided they did not fundamentally alter the examination.

This book has been, among other things, an exploration of some of the proto-scientific statements of the myth. We have examined, for example, the correspondence between some of its descriptions of the world and other ways of representing that world with data. Our exploration could have been fuller, both empirically and theoretically. Had space permitted, we might, for instance, have extended our analysis of curriculum and selection to the Honours/Ordinary degree structure of the Scottish universities and to the development of further education. We have left largely unexamined the nature of the logical interconnections between institutions that are claimed in the myth's account of the world ('The Scottish ordinary-degree course represents a natural extension into university education of the secondary-school curriculum' – chapter 3). We have not provided a fully evidenced historical account of the origins and evolution of the myth, nor have we discussed its more recent sociography. No doubt we have evaded the difficult logical problems that arise when persons' beliefs and actions are claimed as 'evidence' that an explanation such as the myth underpinned them, at some lower and more inaccessible level of meaning. And, in this respect, a fuller discussion is also, no doubt, required of the extent to which the myth, whether in its fully elaborated form or in its more symbolic, fragmentary and implicit aspects, has 'merely' been invoked as a mystifying justification of actions undertaken in the light of other sectional 'interests' (say of class or power); or of whether it has functioned as the unifying belief and value system of the entire 'clan', to use Durkheim's phrase.

These are important questions that must be tackled in several ways: by philosophical analysis and social theorising; by patient empirical historical research (such as that of Withrington, 1974 and Wright, 1979); by empirical research into the nature and sociography of contemporary political and educational beliefs; by studies of government and policy-making (such as that reported by Raab, 1980 and forthcoming); and also, and perhaps less obviously, by action, perhaps of the type described in our final chapter.

Nevertheless, despite the shortcomings and unanswered questions in our own account, we must now move towards some conclusions about the adequacy of the myth as an explanation of the world; and in doing this, we may begin to make more explicit our view of some of the preconditions for the proper conduct of social research in education.

We have assessed the myth empirically not against the world, but against another account of the world, against another way of representing the world through data. This account, our account, has adopted its own descriptions, its own benchmarks of how far they correspond to the world and its own assumptions about the limits and possibilities of human nature. None of these assumptions has been completely arbitrary; all have been necessary in order that a dialogue with the proto-scientific account of the myth might continue. The logical status of our own account is, in other words, no different from that offered by the myth: both are contingent upon ways of describing the world which rest, in part, upon ultimately arbitrary definitions and assumptions. How, then, can we talk of the inadequacy of the myth and imply that our account is superior?

Our argument here is that a first, though not the only, test of the adequacy of an account is constituted by the *way* it is held. An account that aspires to adequacy aims consciously at self-improvement through an inclusiveness both of reference and of criticism. Myth, by contrast, maintains itself partly by discounting phenomena that might contradict or embarrass it.

Much of the Scottish myth, after all, has turned out to be 'true' in the sense that it has corresponded, often in unexpected ways, to the world that our data have represented. The omnibus-school culture *was* more 'democratic', for example, in the sense that, at least in the early 1960s, and probably before, there was relatively little class inequality in levels of achievement among the elite minority who achieved some certification. The certified curriculum itself *was* broader than that in England and it has tracked in less specialised ways into university. University itself *was* more accessible (than in England) and the formal opportunity to take courses leading to university *was* more generously provided. In many respects the myth's description of the world has corresponded, then, to other ways of representing that world through data; and this should perhaps not surprise us since, as we have argued, the evaluative or moral element in the myth served to define identity and to express purpose. Some of the things people wished to achieve, they did achieve, albeit partially and in their own terms.

Our argument, then, is not so much that the explanatory element of the myth is false but rather that it is, in several senses, incomplete. The first sense concerns the degree of correspondence of the myth's descriptive categories with the world. The omnibus-school culture did not, for example, extend to the more populous areas served by a bipartite organisation of schools. Over the country as a whole, the broad curriculum was only realised by a minority who embarked on it. Generous formal provision of selective courses at 12 years of age was followed, swiftly, by informal selection and high wastage, especially among pupils who anticipated that ultimate success would be too difficult. The myth, moreover, furnished teachers with a ready explanation for their pupils' failure: the pathology was individual, a product of defects of pupils' motivation and character. The explanations offered, for example, by teachers and researchers for the high level of wastage of able pupils from selective secondary courses in the 1948 transfer cohort rested heavily on individual pupils' moral failings.[1]

However, the incomplete correspondence of the myth with the world makes it false only when it is used to describe the experience of all persons and not just the experience of the (retrospectively identified) moral elect. We argue that it is reasonable to apply the myth to all persons, if only because no other meaning can be attached to terms like 'common man' or 'democratic'. To the extent that political movements, like that for comprehensive education, have insisted upon the principle of inclusiveness, the myth's descriptions and explanations of the world have become less adequate.

Two questions therefore arise. The first question concerns the status of the myth as a kind of explanatory science: how great must the lack of correspondence become before we abandon the myth's descriptions as inadequate? This question, of course, is pressing, if one acknowledges, for example, our logical argument that the present system can only achieve a common standard of breadth for the 'uncommon' (unusually able) man. The second question affects practice: under what circumstances can a myth that is inadequate on scientific grounds cease to be the basis for practice? The only possible answer is: under circumstances in which all persons have the opportunity to set prevailing explanations against their own experience. This means that the accounts that teachers and pupils give of their own experience and understanding must be taken seriously, alongside the accounts offered by government, professional researchers or whomever. This means, in turn, that different explanations of the world may come into conflict with each other; and it entails that procedures must be found for resolving such conflicts.

Second, the explanatory elements of the myth are also incomplete in that they interpret or operationalise the evaluative elements in selected ways only. The categories through which the world is (incompletely) described are themselves incomplete. A broad or general education, for example, is conceived only in terms of the sampling, through the study of subjects, of each area of a rather vague map of knowledge. Other ways of talking about breadth are discounted. In other words, the explanatory categories of the myth limit conceptions of what it is to be educated and, ultimately, of what it is to be a person and a member of the moral community. These limitations have been sorely felt in recent attempts to think, using traditional concepts derived from elite education, about what a 'balanced' education for all might be. Again, a procedural question arises: if different, and possibly competing, descriptions of the world may be derived from ideas of value and identity, how is such diversity to be respected and reconciled?

The description of the world that is possible through the terms of the myth entails further difficulties. It leads, third, to a denial of history. Instead, myth is mapped on to the past so as to make of it a continuous present. Consider the type of statement that one commonly encounters in discussions of Scottish education: 'Scottish education has traditionally done x...'. There are several possible readings, for example, (i) 'x was, and x continues today'; (ii) 'y was yesterday's attempt to realise x and z is today's attempt to realise x'; and (iii) 'tradition has it that there was (and is) x, but...'. The language of myth is closest to the first meaning. So, for example, many Scots take the present five-subject Ordinary degree to be the broad university education that was historically valued, whereas another reading of the past tells us that the nineteenth-century conception and realisation of breadth was in many ways antithetical to what the Ordinary degree presently offers. When the category of the Ordinary degree is mapped on to the past, therefore, the possibility of history as a critical activity is diminished. By contrast, readings (ii) and (iii) leave scope both for history and also for alternative actions and descriptions; the third allows, in addition, the need for a demythologising *critical* history (itself sorely needed in relation to the nineteenth-century Scottish universities). From all this, two further procedural questions arise. How can we use stable elements to describe a changing world? How can we talk about new elements that aim to change the world through redescribing it? If these questions seem obscure, their practical relevance is illustrated respectively in our discussion of trends in inequality (in chapter 12, especially 'Measuring inequality') and of politicians' attempts to redescribe and change the curriculum (in chapter 13, 'Circular 600').

At this point in our argument the prognosis for both social science and for politics might seem rather gloomy. Accounts that aspire to the status of social science have been acknowledged to depend upon ultimately arbitrary procedural solutions to epistemological difficulties; the accounts offered by myth have been acknowledged to be unacceptably incomplete; and yet myth has also been acknowledged to play an important part in sustaining identity and expressing political will. What sort of politics become possible, if action is always to be based on inadequate accounts of the world? What sort of action is possible, if better accounts of the world emerge only when people become conscious and sceptical of the myths that mobilise political consent? Must a society's adherence to values, to identity and to political purpose make one the permanent prisoner of myth, of the misleading descriptions, explanations and expectations that attach to its values? Or is it possible to see both the evaluative and the explanatory strands clearly in relation to one another; and, if so, how? Our final chapter offers analytical answers to these questions. But, to sound a note of optimism, we first bring this chapter to a conclusion with two illustrations of persons who were attempting to think through myth and beyond.

First, it would, perhaps, be difficult to find a more self-confident and explicit celebration of the Scottish myth than that offered by Macdonald, and quoted in chapter 4. However, 'very gratified' though he was at the degree to which the myth was realised in the north-east, he was also aware that it was less fully realised elsewhere in Scotland. Nor was this (simply) the product of a local chauvinism, for he then went on, in a passage we have not quoted, to discuss in some detail the extent to which talent was being mobilised in each locality for which he was responsible as Inspector, observing that 'in certain areas . . . the class of farm servants is little affected with educational ambition. The fishing community, too . . . make but a small contribution to the Secondary school enrolment.' And he concluded: 'Again in the slum areas of the large cities capacity gets but scant opportunity of emerging' (His Majesty's Chief Inspectors of Schools in Scotland 1922, p. 80). There was still in the 1920s, in other words, an awareness both that the myth was incompletely realised in the rural areas from which it sprang and also that it had yet to be extended to the 'lower' areas of the towns and to the great centres of population. It was possible, in other words, both to celebrate the values of the myth and, at the same time, to hold it critically as a description of the world. Indeed, celebration could entail criticism. This point has implications for our discussion of the culture of politics and social science in chapter 17.

Some two decades after Macdonald wrote, the Scottish Advisory Council addressed the same underlying question: how were the democratic forms of the smaller community to be realised in the more differentiated context of the larger towns and cities? The omnibus school was part of its answer. Indeed, we have described the Council's 1947 report, *Secondary Education*, as a heroic attempt to adapt the Scottish inheritance of forms and ideas to the requirements of mass secondary education. And the report was precisely that: an attempt to adapt and realise old values in new contexts. The Council's support for these values was unmistakable; it solemnly reproduced in both its primary and secondary reports an appendix that listed 'Scottish traditions'. These included various 'typically Scottish characteristics', among which were 'democratic patriotism' and 'freedom from class-consciousness' (Scottish

Education Department, 1947, pp. 178-9). But, the Council felt, new arrangements were required, and new explanations. For example, the link between university entrance requirements and certification at the age of 16 was to be broken; value, it was explained, would emerge, instead, from the quality of the relationships between teachers, pupils and knowledge in a new inquiry-based curriculum. But there was at the time no existing body of experience to lend conviction to such proposals.

The policy that the Advisory Council envisaged was therefore to have been open-ended and to have involved collective public learning both about what might be achieved within the broad guidelines set by the Council, and also about how it might be achieved. Consistent with this, the Council had also stressed that an element of learning was always present in good teaching (Scottish Education Department, 1947, p. 191):

> All educational experiments are a form of research. . . . While in the scientific sense the majority of teachers may not be researchers, all must be experimenters. The relationship of a teacher with a class and with the individuals composing it, her methods of class organisation and her presentation of subject matter are not static facts that can be completely predetermined, but are subject to experimental trial and error to such a degree that the good teacher never ceases to experiment to the end of her teaching days.

We have argued in chapter 13 that the policy for comprehensive re-organisation similarly required collective public learning in order that political goals might be more precisely stated, along with the means for their achievement. In other words, whatever the level of discourse, whether it be in the classroom or at the level of the entire education system, action and understanding require to be related to each other in a way that challenges the conventional division of roles and functions between politicians, administrators, teachers, pupils and researchers. How far do such divisions facilitate and hamper social inquiry? Can its organisation be improved, and how would any improvement be recognised in the quality of the actions and explanations that resulted?

Chapter 17

Politics, Education and the Reconstruction of Research[1]

Introduction

We prefaced our book by asking how the whole enterprise of secondary education was to be understood, and we have mostly dealt with this as a substantive question to which we have tried to give empirical answers. In conclusion, however, we must now treat this as a question about methods of inquiry and discuss some of the epistemological and political difficulties that we have had to acknowledge in the course of our substantive analyses. We enumerate these difficulties in the next section of this chapter. Following that, in the third section ('Political account-ability and social-scientific accounts'), we argue that these difficulties might, in principle, be solved through the further development of a form of a political and social discourse that is implicit in the ideas of democracy and of science. In particular, we argue that improvements in the production and evaluation of social explanations, or accounts, entail the further development of forms of political accountability; and vice versa. Much in our argument at this point rests on the idea that the concept of accountability has reference simultaneously in both an epistemological and a political domain; political accountability both requires and facilitates the production of adequate scientific (descriptive and explanatory) accounts. Following that, in the fourth section ('The current dilemma of government and academe'), we suggest that the solution which we pursue through the idea of accountability cannot be fully achieved, given the present organisation of social research by academics and others, and given also the present ambivalence of the government's attitudes towards the implications of knowledge for its own legitimacy. This dilemma leads us to consider some of the ways in which the production of better social accounts might be pursued through attempts to change the current organisation of social research and attempts to change the way in which knowledge is currently used

316

to legitimate or undermine the exercise of authority. We conclude in the final section ('Education and reconstruction') with a brief discussion of some of the problems arising from our argument and with an indication of some of its further possibilities. These possibilities include a reconceptualisation of the ideas of education and of research that have been taken for granted in much of this book. In brief, we believe that these can only be adequately realised in the context of a political community in which the concept of citizenship is expanded to include the right to be knowledgeable. Our argument is that epistemological and methodological difficulties in the production and evaluation of social knowledge derive from, and contribute to, difficulties in the political culture. Consequently, any attempt to answer substantive questions concerning the effectiveness of public systems such as the education system must acknowledge that the possibility, and also the nature or content, of any answer are limited by attitudes to knowledge that prevail within such a system. It is also appropriate, therefore, to indicate how change, and improvement, may be possible.

A second reason for concluding with what some readers may find a rather formal and abstract discussion is that we think that our arguments, methods and findings, and those of the related action programme of collaborative research of which this book is a part (chapter 2), may contribute to a solution to some of the chronic difficulties that have beset educational and sociological research, at least in the academic sphere, in the last ten or fifteen years. During this period, the drift of much academic thinking has been to doubt the possibility of producing and evaluating social explanations except on the most arbitrary, and therefore relativistic, of grounds. The use of quantitative methods has been regarded as dubious, and collaboration with authority, and especially with government, in producing such quantitative accounts has been treated as more dubious still. We, of course, have done both of these things. In making the argument that social accounts can be produced and improved, we have preferred, however, to work by example rather than by exhortation. This is in contrast with much recent British sociological writing in the educational area, where the emphasis has often been the reverse. The formal arguments of this chapter are also, then, an attempt to indicate, with unavoidable brevity, how the arguments and examples of the empirical parts of this book spring from an approach that might contribute to solutions to some of the dilemmas that currently trouble sociological and educational research.

Some unresolved epistemological and political problems

In this section we briefly identify some of the unresolved epistemological, political and organisational problems that we have acknowledged in the course of our empirical chapters. They do not, of course, exhaust all of the problems that must be solved in the production of better social science; nor do we even deal with all of the difficulties to which we have alluded in earlier chapters. Nevertheless, they do represent some of the major problems that must be solved and solved, in our view, in relation to each other, if social science is to progress.

First, we have indicated at a number of points that the choice between different social explanations, whether or not they are empirically grounded, is always under-determined by facts. Social explanations cannot avoid using definitions, assumptions and procedures that are ultimately arbitrary, in the sense that their justification lies, not in logic, but in individual choice or in conventions that are a product of a particular culture, society or group. This naturally poses a problem for our own empirical account. How can we justify our belief that our description and explanation of some aspects of Scottish education is superior to the account to be found in the Scottish myth? More generally, how, in the face of the arbitrariness of social explanation, can we assert that explanations of social phenomena may be improved through conceptual clarification and empirical observation? What, in short, does it mean for one explanation to be better than another?

In thinking about procedures for making and recognising such improvements, there is, second, a political dimension that must be considered. One must recognise that the definitions, assumptions and procedures that are embodied in social explanations may have powerful, and sometimes adverse, consequences for people's lives. Moreover, the people at risk may also be disenfranchised by the very procedures or assumptions used in such explanations. We have shown in part 2 that the explanation of Scottish education that is offered by the Scottish myth can only be maintained as satisfactory, if one disregards its lack of correspondence to the experience of the majority of pupils. Moreover, the arguments involved in the myth have sustained forms of educational provision and practice that many pupils have found deeply demoralising; they have been vulnerable to injurious consequences which they could not easily dispute. Thus many of them were not only (educationally) unqualified, but also (politically) disqualified in that their experience was accorded no standing and was treated as being 'of no account' (part 4). Schools that are closed as a consequence of data-based arguments about their effectiveness may sometimes be in a similar position (chapter 15).

There is, however, more to this political dimension than the injuries that may result from particular assumptions, definitions and procedures in social explanation. What is at issue here is, third, the very possibility of data themselves, in the sense of 'facts' that can be wholly separated from history and from the political and epistemological context through which they emerge. In chapter 13, for example, we have characterised the programme of comprehensive reorganisation partly as an assertion of value and will. But it was an assertion that was both polyvalent and disputed. Moreover, despite the missed opportunities for learning, it was predicated on the belief that the education system could learn, from a mixture of action and reflection, how to improve itself; that a social knowledge was both possible and desired. Inevitably, therefore, when social explanation tries to recast human history in the mould of facts about the effectiveness of programmes, as we do in chapters 12, 14 and 15, those 'facts' are partly a commentary on the state of human values, will and ingenuity at a particular point in history. What they might indicate about the possibilities for education at a subsequent point in history is problematic. We concluded chapter 15 by arguing that apparently factual or substantive questions about the effectiveness of school practice are inseparable from questions about the quality of social (and educational) knowledge related to those practices; the knowledge not just of the professional social scientist or of the politician, but of each and every actor in the situation. Questions like 'do schools make a difference?' and 'can public intervention improve the human condition?' can only be answered empirically in the context of a discussion of how well one has provided, and may in future provide, for the quality of knowing in all members of society. The analysis of the role of myth at a systemic level in part 2 indicates the need for such a discussion by showing how inadequate actions may be predicated upon incomplete understandings. At the level of the classroom, the pupils' accounts of their schooling in chapter 10 indicate how the values and explanations of the myth structure interpersonal relations, reduce the effectiveness of schooling, yet lead to patterns of behaviour that ultimately confirm and reproduce the myth.

If, then, we question the infallibility of the fact, we find that we must rethink some of the powerful and pervasive distinctions through which the social world is currently managed. For example, questions about the historical quality and future possibilities of action must also be treated as questions about the quality and possibility of knowledge preceding and arising from such actions. If one follows this line of thought a little way, one may loosen the concept of education from its present institutional realisation in which it is largely restricted to the motivation and grading of new members of an unequal society (part 3), and one may rethink it in relation to all ages and contexts, including the political. And, also following this line, one finds that the equation of social knowledge with the beliefs and expertise of citizens who call themselves social scientists becomes problematic. Are sociologists themselves immune from the factors that they say constrain the knowledge of others? How might one release and make public the social knowledge that accompanies practice throughout a social system? In what conceivable world could this happen and what would be the consequences for the quality of subsequent practice?

Our third difficulty, then, concerns the status of the fact as a datum that is independent of the knowledge, beliefs, values and interests of the persons who invoke facts or from whose actions facts are inferred. Our fourth difficulty arises from the political difficulties posed by these epistemological uncertainties. We have said that the choice between explanations is always under-determined by the facts (difficulty 1); we have said that the idea of facts as independent data that may arbitrate between explanations is problematic (difficulty 3); and we have acknowledged that people may be hurt as a consequence of the attempt to proceed with public discussion of social events in spite of these problems (difficulty 2). One superficially attractive remedy to these three difficulties might therefore be to close down the apparently futile and dangerous attempt to produce a social science. But, even if this course of action could be made intelligible (what would it mean to stop people reflecting on, and disputing, their various understandings of the world?), it simply does not follow that difficult problems are necessarily insoluble problems. More important, and this is our fourth difficulty, any view that one takes on the epistemological issue of the possibility of producing or of improving social explanations is a view that is simultaneously political. If the social world can be fully known, or better known, there is opened to people the possibility of power to achieve social ends that have been chosen in the light of explanations of good standing. To deny the possibility of social knowledge is to deny the possibility of social change based on knowledge and agreement. How, then, should the social scientist proceed in the light of the political implications of current epistemological uncertainties?

If we pose this as a practical question concerning the day-to-day activities of doing research, it gives us our fifth unresolved difficulty. How, in the light of the above, can the social scientist possibly lay claim to the resources of society to conduct research? How can he or she possibly claim the right of access to privileged or confidential situations which people might otherwise wish to keep secret in order to protect their own interests or those of others? These are not just contingent problems to do with the politics of the next research grant or, say, of the next classroom observation study. If it is reasonable for people to withhold public accounts of their activity, and reasonable also for them to deny the resources that social science requires to become established in the world, then these become facts about the world that must figure centrally in any attempt to develop a strategy for producing and improving social explanations. Our own account in chapter 15, of the 'difference' that individual schools made, itself stopped well short of addressing the problem of confidentiality, and government itself has been ambivalent about both the resources and the openness that are necessary for the practice of social science (chapter 13).

The collaborative research programme, which has furnished many of the data for this study, has been a practical attempt to address these problems by decentralising the process of research and by making researchers themselves more accountable (chapter 2). Among other things, this book offers to practitioners (who now have, through the programme, a further technical means to engage in the production of educational accounts) an alternative interpretation or construction which they may employ or dispute in achieving their own understanding. Thus, the theoretical arguments of the following sections are part of a wider attempt to elaborate, both by argument and by practice, a form of social inquiry that meets a number of requirements. Evidently it must cope with the epistemological and political problems that we have just outlined. It must recognise, moreover, that the history that funishes data to the social sciences will, like the movement for comprehensive reorganisation, always flow as a muddied stream of coercion and persuasion; persuasion through political programmes that combine a variety of goals, some mutually incompatible and some more explicitly stated than others; goals that may themselves be variously interpreted and implemented according to local circumstance and understanding, and that may be pursued with various degrees of vigour, wit and support; goals that will rarely be monitored, criticised or adjusted as the stream of action progresses. This is the sort of experience that supplies data to the social scientists and from which they must try to learn; a history that can neither be wholly disregarded (for there is no other), nor generalised in any unequivocal way. Any learning must, moreover, acknowledge the voluntaristic and human character of the learning enterprise. It must acknowledge that action at all levels is predicated upon people's descriptions and beliefs and that these must be taken seriously both as phenomena to be explained and as explanations of phenomena. It must, nevertheless, try to indicate some external criterion for arbitrating between conflicting descriptions and explanations. Finally, this form of social inquiry must provide some account of how it can expect to become established in the world; that is, the recommendations for a particular form of collaborative social inquiry must explain how that form of inquiry is itself to command resources and assent. This is a crucial test, for if it were inconceivable that people would ever wish to use procedures that were claimed to improve social knowledge, or inconceivable that they would ever prove capable of using them, then limits to the possibilities of social explanation would have to be incorporated both in the political theory of our society and in the epistemology of social science.

Political accountability and social-scientific accounts

The epistemological and political problems we have listed above stem from our initial observation that all social explanations are under-determined by facts and rest to some extent either upon social convention or upon apparently arbitrary individual choice. However, this observation does not dictate a total relativism; there are criteria for preferring one account to another. For, although there is an element of arbitrariness in all accounts, this element is variable. It is possible to devise procedures which reduce the arbitrary element in accounts, and to define criteria for preferring one account to another.

The criteria are of two kinds, logical and empirical. The logical criteria include that of consistency. One may not, for example, seek to eliminate the public category of 'non-certificate' pupils, whilst maintaining 'certificate pupils' as a category in good standing (chapter 13). Again, an empirical discussion of inequality can only fruitfully proceed on the basis of a clear and consistent definition which has resolved such issues as whether one is considering inequalities of exclusion or of inclusion (see chapter 12). Such inconsistencies tend to remain undetected where there is ambiguity or lack of clarity concerning the terminology in which an account is expressed, the group to which it is believed to refer, or even the logical status of the account itself (for example, as descriptive or prescriptive). We have several times commented in parts 2 and 4 how the Scottish myth has managed to survive as a result of its vagueness concerning which young people it claimed to describe; because its accounts were sometimes valid for the minority, people tended not to notice, or perhaps not to mind, that they did not hold for the majority. Consistency, and the clarity and explicitness which enable inconsistencies to be detected, presuppose a context of dialogue and critical examination of accounts, one in which participation is broadened to include those for whom the account may not hold true. Our logical criteria therefore presuppose further criteria for the ways in which accounts are constructed and held.

The empirical criteria are that an account should not only be consistent with the available evidence, but that it should also be actively tested against evidence that might disconfirm it. The quality of an account is therefore related to the way it is held, and to the degree of effort that goes into collecting appropriate evidence to test it. When an account is used to justify government policy or other collective action, two further criteria for a good account are implied. The first is that the experience of the policy or action, its successes and failures, should be observed systematically and used as evidence to test the account on which it is based. An important test of an account is therefore its ability to sustain successful action. Second, where collective action is premised upon an account, the action can only truly test the account, if those who act understand the account sufficiently to know how to act upon it. Otherwise the success or failure of collective action may merely reflect the rules of thumb adopted to guide the action, rather than the account itself. It therefore follows that a criterion for a good account which attempts to sustain collective action is that it should be capable of being understood by those who implement that action and of being tested by them against their own experience. Failing this, we may reject such an account not just on the procedural grounds that it cannot be subjected to the fullest possible discussion, but also on the external grounds that it denies the idea of consciousness and self-awareness as defining characteristics of membership of a human community. In doing this, the account could not possibly claim to offer 'social knowledge'. In short, what we are saying is that the epistemology of social science is more than a guide to knowing; it is also a guide to living. It is ultimately through their ability to sustain certain qualities of social life that solutions to the methodological problems are to be judged.

Both the logical and the empirical criteria for scientific advance therefore indicate further procedural criteria which should govern the construction, testing and choosing of accounts. These criteria include: openness and wide participation in the construction of accounts and in their testing through dialogue and criticism; the ability to test accounts against data and, in particular, open access to data generated through collective action; and the exercise of scepticism, that is, the active canvassing of alternative ways of observing and explaining. To this we would add a further procedural requirement: there must be procedures for reaching provisional agreements on accounts, since a measure of agreement is necessary, if data are to be used in dialogue and if the terms of debate are themselves to be agreed. Agreements, however, must always be open to subsequent revision, and the reaching of agreements for their own sake must never become the overriding purpose of debate.

To summarise our argument so far, there are criteria for preferring one account to another; these criteria ultimately depend not upon the content of an account, but upon the way in which it is held. The quality of accounts therefore depends upon the procedures which exist for constructing, testing and choosing between them. We have outlined the kinds of procedures which are indicated.

323

Our argument now is that the same kinds of procedures are required for the normative concept of accountability, in the political sense. This reflects the kinship of the political concept of accountability with the idea of 'accounting' in the sense of producing an account, a story or an explanation. The procedures we have described may therefore make it possible to provide *against* the injuriousness of the arbitrary elements of social descriptions and explanations at the same time as providing *for* tests to improve those explanations.

We make our argument here in terms of 'government'. Although this usually refers to central or local government, we believe that the argument applies (and would fail if it could not be applied) to other kinds of social relationships in which accountable authority is claimed and exercised: to the classroom, for example, as well as to the council chamber. Often the accountability of this authority is mediated; the accountability of teachers to parents, for instance, is at present largely mediated by central and local government, and the accountability of central and local government to electors is itself mediated through the various layers of representative democracy.

Our argument, however, is restricted to government which is accountable in terms of what we shall call rational democracy: this means that the basis of government's legitimacy is its claim to be acting rationally. This does not mean that government's actions are rational; merely that, if required to defend its legitimacy, government could, in principle, be forced to do so in terms of the criterion of rationality.

In representative democracy, for example, the authority of central government is ultimately controlled by the right of the electors to protect themselves from injury and to impose sanctions by voting a government out of office. But the concept of accountability can also be expressed in terms of knowledge and its communication. It is about the telling of stories, or the rendering of accounts. Electors may withdraw their support from a government, and ultimately from the entire political system, if they do not like what it is doing; but also, and related to this, if the accounts that are given are so unsatisfactory as to raise doubts about a government's comprehension of what it is doing; that is, about the authoritativeness with which it exercises its authority. However, in order to judge the quality and accuracy of an account, electors must have some means for evaluating it that is independent of government. Moreover, they must be able to force government to give an account of its actions that is honest and full. A full account must include the following: government's objectives, its perception of the situation on which it acts, and a 'theory', which explains how the action is to achieve its objectives.

Now it will be rightly objected that government actions themselves are rarely based on such rational and coherent grounds. Also, government rarely, if ever, produces accounts of its actions with such a degree of explicitness. Moreover, the responses or initiatives of citizens are rarely grounded in the sort of intellectual processes that theories of rational decision-making misleadingly presuppose. However, our argument is based on our condition of rational democracy, that the basis for the legitimacy of government's authority is its claim to be acting rationally. Any government that makes this claim can, in principle, be pressed, under pain of losing legitimacy, to give explicit and rational accounts or explanations of its actions. If it gives dishonest, incomplete or inconsistent accounts, the force of rational criticism and the testing of accounts can, in principle, expose inconsistencies, incompleteness and lack of correspondence. The main consequence of the claim to authority is that, for any action by a government that makes this claim, there is, at least potentially, a corresponding account which the government may be pressed to make explicit. This account may then be made the focus of debates about public actions. Whether, and in what circumstances, such accounts are, or can be, made public is a separate issue to which we shall come. At this point, we only stress that the concept of rational democracy concerns the basis of government's legitimacy, rather than its actions. If government attempts to justify its right to govern in terms of the criteria of democracy and rationality, then energetic critics may, in principle, press government to live up to these criteria on pain of losing legitimacy.

Governments must be able to elaborate accounts; citizens must be able to evaluate the accounts and provide other ones. The effectiveness of such pressure and sanctions must figure in a normative definition of accountability. In an accountable democracy, the actions or inactions of government can be corrected, if the members of the democracy can agree to, and implement, an alternative course of action. Here we stress both elements in the prescription; the ability to implement the alternative and also the agreement on which it is based. Neither element alone is sufficient. Government actions may be modified by others in circumstances that have nothing to do with accountability. Equally, accountability is not involved when members agree to a modified course of action but cannot effect it. 'Agreement', of course, must be defined according to various procedural conventions: for example, one man one vote, a simple majority wins, or any other set of legitimated rules. Like the action it replaces, the agreed modified action must also be based on an account. This, too, must specify its objectives, and contain a 'theory' which describes the context of the action and explains how it is to achieve these ends. An important aspect of accountability is the process for reaching agreement on an account which will serve as the basis for the modifications to action. Accountability therefore requires procedures whereby members can provisionally agree on one among several competing accounts, and for these procedures to operate, they must command assent, partly arbitrary though they may be.

This, in turn, requires that accounts be framed in terms that are public, universal and intelligible, and hence able to sustain public debate and so serve as the basis for agreed modifications of action. Moreover, there must be alternative sources for producing a variety of competing accounts, corresponding to the diverse interests, experience and perspectives of the members of the democracy. No special legitimacy should attach to accounts simply because they have been produced by government; members must practise reasoned scepticism with regard to all accounts, whatever their source. Members of the democracy must therefore have access not only to the accounts themselves, but also to the data and procedures through which the accounts have been constructed. They must have the means to re-define the concepts in terms of which the accounts have been expressed, to articulate alternative perspectives, and to supply these with evidence which may itself be new. In other words, they must have the means, not merely to challenge the accounts of government, but to produce alternative ones. They must be fully involved in the process of the production of accounts. This, we argue, is part of the meaning of citizenship in such a political system.

By way of summarising the preceding argument, the political concept of accountability requires a set of institutionalised procedures for generating, and for choosing between, alternative accounts. These procedures should be characterised by intersubjectivity, openness, scepticism and universality of participation; and they should be able to generate agreement, albeit provisional and defined in procedural terms. The procedure for recognising provisional agreement will itself be arbitrary, but must command assent. The agreed alternative must be translated into action. These procedures are the same as those for which we have already argued on scientific grounds.

In sum, the normative world implied by social science is the same as that implied by an accountable democracy. In saying this, however, we emphasise that we are not describing an illusory world of consensus from which political conflict can be progressively eliminated through the application of social science. Disputes between alternative proposals for further action will never be resolved on scientific grounds alone. Choices will always have to be made between the different values and objectives involved in different proposals. Nevertheless, any proposed policy should be based on an account or a theory of the area concerned; and a minimal condition for rational democracy is that competing accounts be subjected to the fullest possible scrutiny on scientific grounds. Nor are we claiming that the scientific and the political aspects of choices between competing accounts (or policy proposals) are easily separable. They are not. (See, for example our discussion, 'The publication of schools' examination results', in chapter 15.) The same set of procedural rules will often have to do double service, simultaneously containing the political and the scientific criteria by which choices are made between competing accounts. Indeed, this is likely always to be the case, if our argument in chapter 13 is correct in claiming that the goals of a political programme for change can never be fully specified in advance; that values and explanations are always in dialogue with each other when goals are stated, disputed or changed. It is no mere coincidence that the sorts of procedural rules which we would welcome on political grounds tend also to be those which we would justify scientifically.

The current dilemma of government and academe

Having described the normative requirements of political account-ability and of social science, and having established the affinity between these, we may now say briefly why neither government nor (academic) social science can unilaterally meet these requirements in practice.

With regard to government, once again we are not conjecturing some bloodless and dour world in which men of affairs are never motivated by considerations of power-seeking and power-holding. The world of politics is inhabited by few such self-denying saints, wracked by self-doubts that are candidly expressed in public. We may repeat the points that were argued at greater length in our discussion in chapter 13 of the movement for comprehensive reorganisation. First, vagueness about objectives may be a political asset in maintaining coalitions. Second, and more important, there is the dilemma that scepticism poses for authority. Government must sustain its legitimacy partly by appearing to know how to act and partly by appearing to act effectively in the light of that knowledge. Confidence is intrinsic to the general notion of authority. The needs (albeit not always the practice) of science, however, are that all accounts, including those of government, be treated with scepticism, and should be challenged and engaged in constructive dialogue. So, paradoxically, government in an account-able democracy would appeal for public confidence by claiming to observe procedures of scientific inquiry which themselves enshrine scepticism as a reigning principle. This contradiction provides the context for government's production of accounts, and renders that production highly problematic under current arrangements.

In the longer term, it is in the interest of government that confidence in it has at least some basis in its willingness to practise, promote

327

or tolerate a reasoned scepticism. If this happens, government can more easily acknowledge that there are gaps in its accounts: gaps between problems and available explanations, and gaps between the intended and actual outcomes of action. Any public learning that draws on the methods of social science must learn to recognise such gaps; but only government has the resources and continuity to do this routinely. Moreover, if government does not do this, gaps will tend to emerge only when they are deliberately exposed by those wishing to discredit government. Such exposure may be especially embarrassing for governments whose public self-presentation emphasises their knowledgeability.

In the shorter term, of course, government tends not to welcome such openness. Its opponents can usually argue that there were insufficient grounds for a particular action or that there is insufficient evidence of its success. Government consistently tries to pre-empt such challenges. For example, before acting, it might be deliberately vague about its intentions and it might refuse to publish information on the context of its action (say, a description of the problems it is seeking to solve). After acting, and in the light of the outcomes, it might only selectively release information about circumstances and results. In these ways, government 'gives a good account of itself' by retrospectively narrowing the gap between the expected and observed outcomes, in order to maintain public confidence and to renew the possibility of subsequent action (see chapter 6). Nevertheless, the political process is debilitated through its inability to sustain the public learning that must occur if sense is to be made of programmes for change (see chapters 13 and 15).

There are further reasons why government is inadequate as a producer of scientific accounts; we will simply list them here. First, the exigencies of government require short-term or immediate choices which are often incompatible with the lengthier processes of scientific inquiry. Second, information collected for purposes of control may be distorted by those who supply it. Third, information routinely collected in the execution of government policy tends to embody the concepts and theories underlying that policy, and may be ill-suited to inform a radical critique of it; and finally, government accounts are currently issued as 'products' and cannot be revised or reinterpreted to accommodate the knowledge acquired through experience by those to whom the accounts are addressed.

Despite all these weaknesses of government, however, it is quite fruitless to attempt to solve the problem by divorcing the production of social-scientific accounts from governmental authority. This is because the practice of social science requires authority of a kind that only government can possess or should possess. To be sure, the institutional divorce of academics from direct responsibility for public action helps to protect the principle and practice of scepticism, but often only at the cost of distancing them unacceptably from the theatre of action. To the extent that academics attempt to ease back towards the centre of action they put scepticism at risk and are exposed to the very problems that are faced by government in its management of authority and knowledge.

The academic dilemma has several aspects to it. We will consider one major aspect here, which arises from the fact that research requires resources. Social science must have the means for the repeated observation of consistently and exhaustively defined categories. Without those means, it could not express its accounts in terms that were general, intersubjective (that is, permitting debate and testing through replications) and capable of development over time. Arguably, only an accountable government has, or should have, the resources that would permit these activities, for there is no separate authority to command resources to be found within social science itself. Its claims to attention rest on the procedures it uses to discuss the world and not upon its command of a knowledge that would give its initiates predictive control over the world. From time to time, of course, social scientists have claimed to command such knowledge and therefore to deserve power and influence; but such claims have never remained convincing for long.

In some instances it can only be the state that ultimately disposes of the resources that social science requires. The idea of regularly sampling a population, for example, is only practicable in the context of political systems in which membership confers rights and imposes obligations, such that members have to identify themselves periodically to the state in order to exercise these rights; and the state, in its turn, must identify members to ensure that they discharge their obligations. Without the complex web of interlocking rights and obligations entailed in the notion of citizenship, there could be no electoral registers, school rolls, or other descriptions of populations that pretended towards completeness. Social science is parasitic upon these records of rational bureaucracy as practical resources for research. Moreover, this practical dependence reflects a deeper conceptual dependence on normative ideas of citizenship and membership in terms of which discussions about inclusion, exclusion, incompleteness and lack of correspondence become possible. All forms of social research ultimately share in this dependence.

Education and reconstruction

We argued in the section 'Political accountability and social-scientific accounts' that it is possible to state procedures to cope with the epistemological problem of arbitrariness and with the political problem of injuriousness. But in the following section, 'The current dilemma of government and academe', we argued that it is not possible to imagine either a government or an academic 'estate' that could unilaterally implement such procedures. If the possibility of improving social explanations is to be retained, a new form of organisation for social research is required. This would be based upon the principles of accountability and would seek to combine the authority of government with the procedures of science. It would seek to provide for universal public disputation over social explanations in which all disputants enjoyed equal opportunities to construct their own accounts and to dispute those of others. This would be the surest imaginable way of providing against arbitrariness, error and injury and of providing for the authority that is necessary to conduct social inquiry, an authority that must always seek universal and voluntary recognition.

But is such a reconstruction possible? Moreover, do the proposals not fail logically? Do they not presuppose an existing human capacity for the very practices they are trying to establish? What answer could we give to the objection that government could never be persuaded voluntarily to abandon its own short-term interest in the control of knowledge production; that it would need to be forced to do this, and even then in the most uncontrolled of circumstances? And how do we deal with the objection that people have neither the wish nor the wit to engage in the public discourse through which social explanations might emerge and be evaluated?

A practical answer is that the experience of the collaborative research programme in Scotland since 1975 has shown that, under certain circumstances, government can be persuaded to accept the decentralisation of the control of the production of part of the social account of education. Of course, a single programme of limited duration cannot expect to achieve the radical transformation of social research that is implied by our argument; nor does a programme such as ours by any means exhaust the repertoire of possible approaches to collaborative research. Indeed, we would stress that the principles and practices that we are advocating may be applied and, indeed, have already been applied elsewhere, in a variety of circumstances, and with and without the data-collection methods we ourselves have used. In the medium term one may envisage a variety of tactics in which the spread of a collaborative model, and an accompanying transformation of social relations to the means of knowledge production, might be achieved; tactics which allow full rein to conflict, self-interest and partiality in the approach to social knowledge of individuals and groups.

However, neither the practical examples nor the medium-term

possibilities dispose of the fact that the essentially liberal argument which we are offering here comes close to circularity. In suggesting, as we are, that the methodology of the social sciences prescribes a way of living towards which one may work, we are presupposing that the nature of human individuals and of human society is such as to make possible the social knowledge that is envisaged by the methodology. But what is the alternative? To reject the possibility of adding to the legal, political and social rights that citizens enjoy the further right of becoming a full participant in the discourse of the community? To reject the possibility of collective agreements to programmes and to actions undertaken in the light of provisionally-held explanations? To reject the possibility of learning by public evaluations of such experience? To discount the possibility of a knowledgeable society of equals? Following our argument in the section above about political accountability and social-scientific accounts, we suggest that the denial of the possibility of social knowledge is a denial of the possibility of citizenship, in the sense of a community in which all members are becoming more knowledgeable. It is also, therefore, a denial of the possibility of education. When such denials are built directly into research practice and educational practice, informing both the way that people act (or are allowed to act) in the world and also the way in which they claim to know (or are allowed to know) the world, then any generalisation from empirical observations of this practice must clearly be severely circumscribed. In other words, all assumptions about the nature of mankind, society and government, whether 'optimistic' or 'pessimistic', may tend towards circularity. Ultimately, the choice of assumptions must be, in part, a matter of value; a matter, so to speak, of whether or not one wishes to continue the affair with the idea of progress.

We have, then, offered two sorts of answers to the question of whether human institutions, such as the education system, are potent. The first has been historical and has commented on the way in which variations in educational practice have, or have not, been associated with variations in educational effects. Knowing little, however, about the assumptions and knowledge that have guided historical practice, we have been guarded in our generalisations. Nevertheless, our generalisations and speculations may, perhaps, contribute to a clarification of some of these matters in the future, if and when they are absorbed into wider public debate. Our second answer has been that knowledge of these matters is to be gained through practice, and that this practice includes the attempt to make better provision for the knowing citizen. We suggest that the *ways* in which schools and others attempt in the future to understand the effectiveness of educational institutions will have just as much bearing on the future potency of those institutions as will any particular practices that are found to have been historically associated with variations in educational effects. One cannot know an education system that does not want to know itself; and an education system that does not want to know itself cannot be fully effective.

Notes

Chapter 2

1 Further details of the 1962–3 survey were given partly in Killcross (1969) but mainly in Powell (1973). We are grateful to the SCRE for allowing us to incorporate the 1962–3 data into the archive, and also to John Powell for the help he gave us in this matter.
2 Further details of the 1971 survey are given in Jones and McPherson (1972). Details of the 1971, 1973 and 1977 surveys are given in Raffe, Lamb *et al.* (1978).
3 The construction of the first SEDA data-set was funded by the SSRC under grant HR 3187 and is reported in McPherson (1977). The data are documented in Armstrong and McPherson (1975).
4 The data from the SEDA surveys of 1977 and 1979 are documented in Raffe *et al.* (1978 and 1981); those from 1981 will be documented in Burnhill, Lamb and Weston (in preparation). The collaborative research programme was funded from 1975 to 1982 by the SSRC (HR 3262 and HR 6251). This funding covered much of the cost of the 1977 and 1981 surveys. The Manpower Services Commission funded part of the 1979 and 1981 surveys. Contributions to survey costs have also been made by Grampian Region, the Department of Health and Social Security, and the Sports Council. The Scottish Education Department entirely funded the surveys of 1971 and 1973 (see note 2), partly funded the surveys of 1977 and 1981, and largely funded that of 1979. The support of all these sponsors is gratefully acknowledged.
5 For accounts of collaborative research, see Cope *et al.* (1976), Cope and Gray (1977 and 1979), Gray, McPherson and Raffe (1979), McIntyre (1979), Weston (1979) and McPherson (1981). For some of the ideas underlying collaborative research see McPherson, Raab and Raffe (1978). A fuller bibliography is available from the Centre. The *Collaborative Research Newsletter* (1977–) is published periodically by the Centre.

6 Between 1966 and 1974 these figured in the annual SED publication *Scottish Educational Statistics*, which was discontinued after 1974. Since then periodic *Bulletins*, some relating to school-leavers, have been issued instead by the SED. The suggestion that the sample members of the SED's biennial survey of 'qualified' leavers might also furnish a sample for research purposes (see account of sampling in the section entitled 'The 1977 survey' in this chapter) came originally from the SED itself. The SED discontinued its own biennial leavers' survey in 1981, but provided sampling facilities for the CES survey of that year. The SED will be among the users of the 1981 survey. Further surveys are planned for 1983, 1985 and 1987.

7 For the reasons given in chapter 15, the public availability of data is restricted in relation to some of the questions discussed in that chapter.

8 We are grateful to the Scottish Education Department for providing us with the population figures on which the weighting coefficients were based, and also for assistance at several stages in the collection of the sample and design of the survey. Details of the weighting are given in Raffe *et al.* (1978, appendix E).

9 We are grateful to the teachers, careers officers and officials of Fife, Lothian, Tayside and Strathclyde Regions for their work and support in connection with the 1977 survey of non-certificate leavers.

10 We are grateful to the teachers, careers officers and officials of all the Scottish regions for their work and support in connection with the surveys of certificate leavers in 1977, and with the 1979 and 1981 surveys.

11 Thanks are due to the Scottish Council for Research in Education for permission to reanalyse the data, and to Keith Hope for his help in the reanalyses.

12 We are grateful to James Douglas, to Liz Atkins and to others at the MRC Unit for their help.

13 We are grateful to the National Children's Bureau and to Dougal Hutchison for advice and help.

Introduction to part 2

1 In places in part 2 we draw upon information gained in the course of a hitherto largely unpublished study of post-war policy-making in Scottish education that is being conducted in the Centre (Raab, 1980 and forthcoming). This part of the book owes a considerable debt to Charles Raab's contribution to that study.

Chapter 3

1 The main differences in this respect were, first, that the Scottish school system, unlike the English, has made full provision for Catholic denominational education within the state system since 1918; and that considerably smaller proportions of Scottish pupils have been educated privately or semi-privately.

2 This chapter was written before we had the opportunity to benefit from McCrone, Bechhofer and Kendrick (forthcoming), which argues, with extensive historical illustration, and in relation to Scottish culture generally, that 'no myth is more prevalent and persistent than that asserting Scotland is a "more equal" society than England'. McPherson (1982) develops the argument of the present chapter.

3 One obvious starting-point for an analogous exploration of beliefs in relation to English education would be Clarke (1940, 1948).

Chapter 4

1 From the National Survey of Health and Development (see chapter 2), Douglas *et al.* (1966, p. 151) estimated: 'In 1958, when the Survey children were twelve, 38 per cent of the Scottish members were in selective courses or schools as compared with 30 per cent of the English and Welsh children in the Survey.' These figures included children at private and independent schools. It should be noted, however, that the Scottish figures refer to pupils who were at the point of starting a secondary course. There was considerable subsequent net movement from selective courses with the effect that, by the age of 15 years (but before the minimum school-leaving age), only 24 per cent were classified as being on five-year selective courses (chapter 12). There is also evidence of a net downward movement of a similar magnitude in the 1948 transfer cohort from the 1947 Scottish Mental Survey (chapter 2) reported on by Macpherson (1958, chapter 4) and Maxwell (1969).

2 *Education in Scotland in 1951* (Scottish Education Department, 1952, p. 11) stated that these changes were made after 'careful consideration' of the Advisory Council's report on *Secondary Education* (Scottish Education Department, 1947). It is likely, however, that this was little more than a cosmetic reference by the SED to the Advisory Council's report. The Council had recommended individual subject awards in the context of other radical proposals for change in the examination system. It was aware of a problem of wastage (ibid., para. 235), but addressed it mainly through the proposal for an examination at 16 years that was subsequently opposed by the SED. It is possible that the SED was unable to quantify the phenomenon of wastage on a national basis

until after 1951, since *Education in Scotland in 1951* mentions only local statistics on the matter (p. 31) or leaves blank various table entries that were to have related to national figures (tables 2 and 5, pp. 92 and 95).

3 See the statement issued by the SCEEB (21 November 1972, para. 2): 'The invitation by the Secretary of State to consider the substitution of a system of grades in place of the present pass/fail system was accepted by the Board: the possible merits of such a development were recognised as were the countervailing problems it could create. After taking all known considerations into account the Board came to the conclusion that the balance of advantage lay with this new proposal.' See also the evidence of Dewar (1977) and Clark (1980).

4 On class and sex stratification within the Scottish universities, see Kelly (1976a) and McPherson (1972, 1973a).

Chapter 5

1 See Scottish Education Department (1963, para. 10).

2 From *Scottish Schools Today*, a pamphlet issued by the Scottish Information Office for SED in the 1970s (no date given).

3 *'Breadth of Courses.* It has been traditional in Scotland to avoid too early specialisation in any field. At the beginning of the third year the courses take a more definite direction, but this does not imply that they become narrow or one-sided. In a fully satisfactory course the different aspects of an all-round education should continue to be represented, though in varying degrees and not always for examination purposes. A review of the present position shows. . . [There follows a largely unquantified review of courses taken in years one to six, mainly by certificate pupils, which concludes] 'over-all there need be no fear of excessive specialisation. It is evident that, apart from some weakness on the aesthetic side and for relatively few pupils in physical education, the schools are providing courses which are sufficiently wide and well balanced.' (Scottish Education Department, 1965b, pp. 40–1.)

4 This uncertainty was reflected in the administrative arrangements for the provision and oversight of the curriculum. Founded in 1965, the Consultative Committee on the Curriculum quickly, if privately, acknowledged that, *de facto*, the Highers curriculum was largely determined by the Examination Board. An informal division of labour developed in which the CCC has concerned itself mainly with aspects of provision for the 70 per cent or so of non-Highers pupils and with courses for the earlier years of secondary education.

5 Burnhill and Redpath (1981) provide a fuller analysis of Scottish trends between 1962 and 1978.

6 '[I]t is becoming fairly clear that some pupils will tend to take

the examination in two stages, part of it in the fifth year and part in the sixth' (Scottish Education Department, 1952, p. 23).

7 'Since the Scottish Leaving Certificate has been awarded on a subject instead of on a group basis, there has been a tendency for many pupils who would formerly have attempted a group of subjects in their fifth year to take only some of these in the fifth year and the remainder in the sixth year. Thus, the sixth year, which was formerly regarded mainly as a 'post-certificate year' in which pupils pursued selected studies at a higher level, has come to serve the double purpose of enabling some pupils to add to the number of their higher [*sic*] grade passes and of providing for others the more advanced studies *traditionally appropriate* to the sixth year' (Cmnd 603, 1958, para. 15, our emphasis).

8 Expressing this trend in percentage form and basing it on sixth-year Highers pupils (that is, excluding fifth-year Highers leavers), we can say that the percentage that resat in the sixth year two or more of the subjects they had already presented at H-grade in the fifth year increased from 8 per cent in 1962–3 to 38 per cent in 1975–6 (not shown). In 1975–6 61 per cent of sixth-year pupils resat at least one SCE H-grade subject.

9 These are estimates from the SEDA for O-grade, H-grade and A-level attempts. They exclude repeat attempts. Presentations for the Certificate of Sixth Year Studies (see chapter 6, section entitled 'Concepts, actions and learning') are also excluded.

10 Among O-grade leavers in 1975–6 who had studied languages in their third year, over two-thirds of the boys and over half the girls did not present a language at O-grade. Comparable proportions for science subjects were a third and almost a half, respectively. The proportions achieving an A, B or C grade in sciences or languages at the SCE O-grade among O-grade pupils who had started on such courses were less than a third (calculated from Dickson, 1979, table 7). In mathematics, Bibby and Weston (1980, table 1) found that half the O-grade boy school-leavers had started on an O-grade mathematics course in S3; 35 per cent (of all O-grade boys) presented, and 11 per cent (of all) achieved an A–C pass. The comparable final figure for O-grade girls was 6 per cent. Amongst H-grade pupils the rates of attrition have been much lower both from O-grade courses and from fifth-year H-grade courses. The lower rate of attrition in fifth year is as one would expect in a situation in which the O-grade, a good predictor of H-grade performance, has been used to guide pupils towards the subjects they will present at Highers.

Chapter 6

1 The link between the age of a subject and its status may be strengthened in other ways. One of the reasons for the reluctance

of the Scottish Education Department to implement the Advisory Council's recommendations of 1947 was that they would reduce the schools' emphasis on the very classical languages in which the administrative and professional heads of the SED had themselves been trained. The Advisory Council itself, however, was fairly clear about the link between the status of subjects and their selective function: 'The immense prestige of these ancient disciplines has continued to draw to them a very large proportion of the nation's best brains, and it is fairly obvious that the admitted success of these men . . . may well be attributable not to any esoteric virtues inhering in classical and mathematical training alone, but to their unusually fine natural endowment' (Scottish Education Department, 1947, para. 102).

2 For the variety of post-war selective courses in Scotland and the place of languages in them, see, for example, Maxwell (1969, p. 24).

3 Dickson (1979) provides more details.

4 Details for this section may be found in McPherson and Neave (1976).

5 The 1972 White Paper said the following, and only the following, about the intentions behind the CSYS: 'it is designed to provide a stimulus for independent study in depth and so prepare pupils for the transition to higher education' (Cmnd 5175, para. 26). The introduction of the CSYS, however, was initially intended to cater for 'pupils of a fairly wide range of ability . . . and . . . for more practical as well as for more academic interests' (McPherson and Neave, 1976, pp. 26–7).

6 Among pupils who went on to attempt Highers, and using the 'narrow' assumptions (see text), the third- and fourth-year courses of 29 per cent were 'fully balanced' and only a further 29 per cent lacked two or more of the seven Munn elements. As we have seen, by contrast, only 17 per cent of the O-grade leavers had followed 'fully balanced' courses by this definition and 45 per cent lacked two or more elements.

7 This book went to press before the publication of Ryrie (1981), which throws further light on selection in Scottish comprehensive schools.

Introduction to part 3

1 For evidence on the effects of university entrance requirements on Highers courses and also on applications to university in Scotland in the early 1970s, see McPherson and Neave (1976, chapter 3).

Chapter 7

1 For a discussion of the trends in the bond revealed by the English and Scottish mobility studies, see Raffe (1981b).

2 In contrasting the situations respectively before and after the most recent expansion in SCE certification, we are leaving out of account other forms of educational differentiation which may previously have existed. In the first place, it is probable that course placement, or attendance at particular schools, had some influence on occupational success, even among the majority who had no formal qualifications (see, for example, Heath, 1981). Second, our account does not mention the use of local school-leaving certificates in some areas. As far as we are aware, there is no evidence on the link, if any, between such certificates and success in the labour market.

3 Since our analysis excludes those school-leavers who proceeded to further full-time education, any conclusions about the tightening bond drawn from our analysis assume that the association between certification and occupation among this group did not weaken. Our analysis also does not take account of the various certificates gained in part-time education as well as in post-school full-time education. Our exclusion of grant-aided and independent schools should be noted in comparisons with data from other sources.

4 The occupational categories are based on the socio-economic groups (Office of Population Censuses and Surveys, 1970) as follows:

Boys White collar: groups: 1–6, 8, 12–14 apart from shop assistants
   Skilled manual: skilled engineering, electrical, paper and printing workers in group 9
   Less skilled: other workers in group 9, shop assistants, *plus* groups 7, 10, 11, 15
   Other employed: groups 16, 17
Girls White collar: (as for boys)
   Services: group 7 *plus* shop assistants
   Manual: groups 9–11, 15
   Other employed: groups 16, 17

Note that for boys the skilled manual category is defined more narrowly than the 'skilled manual' socio-economic group; it includes only the more highly valued of the (nominally) skilled jobs (see, for example, Weir and Nolan, 1977).

5 For adults, Jencks *et al.* (1973) estimated the correlation between education and occupation among white, non-farm males in America to be about 0.65; Halsey (1977) reported a correlation among adult males in England and Wales of 0.555. Had they excluded persons with full-time post-school education, as we have done, both of these estimates would have been considerably lower. A further reason why our estimates are not comparable with estimates such as these is that we have used a very different occupational scale. Most (existing) occupational scales designed for adult males are not appropriate either for male school-leavers or for females of any age.

6 Some 16 per cent of boys and 19 per cent of girls were given some other kind of test, with or without a written test. The use of these tests was less consistently related to SCE attainment than the use of written tests.

7 These arguments must be distinguished from those of 'conflict theorists', such as Collins (1971) and Bowles and Gintis (1976), who also argue that employers have sought applicants with such qualities as the 'right' social background and attitudes. However, these writers do not argue that employers have selected on these criteria instead of on qualifications; rather, they suggest that employers have regarded qualifications (or other information on educational experience) as a measure of these personal qualities. We return to these arguments later in this chapter.

8 An *ad hoc* way of making such an allowance is to divide each percentage by the mean number of A–C awards shown at the bottom of the same column. This method of standardisation is arbitrary, incorporating as it does assumptions about the link between the number of subjects and their spread.

9 The relatively aggregated analysis presented in table 7.6 could conceal more specific associations between particular jobs and particular subjects. We have produced a more detailed version of table 7.6 based on individual subjects and more detailed job categories, although for reasons of space we do not reproduce it here. With a few exceptions (notably the connection between accounting and secretarial studies and clerical work for girls, and that between engineering drawing, applied mechanics and metal-work and a range of occupations for boys), there was no strong tendency for the more detailed job categories to be associated with particular subjects. There were a few smaller-scale exceptions, such as woodwork, and no doubt a yet finer disaggregation of jobs would yield more of these. Other expected associations were absent: girls entering nursing or ancillary medical occupations were not especially likely to have biology, although a few had O-grades in anatomy, physiology and health. Overall, the associations between particular subjects and particular jobs were infrequent and small. This conclusion is open to the objection that another, and more appropriate, categorisation of jobs would show much stronger associations with particular subjects. Since the number of alternative categorisations which could be realised on the sample data is extremely large, it is difficult to refute this objection.

Chapter 8

1 We apply this model of consumer power to the data purely as an explanatory device that helps us organise our exposition; and we emphasise that the terminology of the model should be understood

in that light. There are, for example, many contexts in which it is not appropriate to refer to pupils as 'products' of a 'system', but it may sometimes be useful for the sort of restricted purpose we have set ourselves here.

2 This proportion is smaller than the 8 per cent of 1977 leavers reported as entering university in chapter 12, table 12.1. The difference, which is exaggerated by the rounding of fractions to whole percentage points, is due to the inclusion of leavers from grant-aided schools in the analyses in chapter 12. Both proportions would be higher still if leavers from independent schools and leavers who delayed their entrance to university for a year or two were included.

3 There are, however, indications that, in recent years, a growing proportion of pupils has remained voluntarily for a fifth year but with no intention, or with no real prospect, of presenting for any Higher-grade examination (see Scottish Certificate of Education Examination Board, forthcoming). This trend has been encouraged by the high level of unemployment among school-leavers.

Chapter 9

1 Even figures for a given month, such as July, are not precisely comparable from year to year, owing to changes in the school-leaving regulations in 1976.

2 Some 60 per cent of YOP entrants in 1979–80 had not been employed since leaving school. This proportion is likely to have increased since then, if the Christmas undertaking, together with the worsening unemployment situation, meant that more school-leavers would find places on schemes before finding their first job.

3 At the time of writing, the programme of Unified Vocational Preparation, for young people in jobs which typically carried no further education or training, was represented by only fourteen experimental schemes in Scotland (Manpower Services Commission, 1980b, p. 18). However, plans being considered by the government would, if successful, greatly extend such provision.

4 The exact practice varies. In the 1972 Nuffield mobility study (see chapter 7), unemployed respondents were asked to state their last occupation. However, cohort comparisons which tested the tightening bond were typically based on respondents' occupations ten years after starting work. Respondents who were unemployed at that time were not asked to state their previous occupation. Of course, the proportion of unemployed in the Nuffield sample was much smaller than in our 1977 sample of school-leavers.

5 As workers get older, the problem of unemployment becomes more serious in that it lasts longer; but (at least up to middle age) unemployment becomes concentrated among smaller and smaller proportions of the age-group.

6 These are provisional figures, based on 1,534 sample members with no Highers passes and with no A–C awards at O-grade.

7 However, an unpublished comparison with the 1977 survey data suggests that YOP has at least been more successful in providing for unqualified young people than the programmes (such as the Work Experience Programme and the Job Creation Programme) which preceded it.

Chapter 10

1 All the quotations from school-leavers' comments in this chapter are drawn from Gow and McPherson (1980). This gives details of the procedures by which the comments were elicited and selected. The quotations used in this chapter have not been chosen in a way that guarantees that they are representative. The original spelling and punctuation have been retained in almost all instances.

2 See chapter 4, 'Controlled incrementalism: changes in national certification before the mid-1960s'. McIntosh and Walker (1970) discusses two statistical operationalisations of 'a reasonable prospect of success' in relation to the SCE O-grade.

3 Within the three SCE presentation levels, responses to this item were uncorrelated with being employed or unemployed at the time of the survey.

Chapter 11

1 This reconciliation of the estimates made from the two sources is consistent with an independent validation of the 1977 survey data against those collected by one regional authority. It concludes that the data were 'in this respect compatible with the evidence obtained from other sources' (Hill, 1978, p. 31).

2 To investigate the extent to which the apparent effect of family background on truancy could be explained by SCE-presentation level we conducted a regression analysis on all leavers. This attempted to predict truancy from four variables: the leavers' sex, size of family, social class and level of certificate presentation. Of the four, by far the most important was the level of presentation; alone it explained 12 per cent of the overall variation in truancy; the other three variables (of which sex was the most important) added only another 1 per cent to the total proportion of variation explained. The regression analysis confirms our conclusion from table 11.2, that family background variables add little to the explanation of truancy over and above the effects of presentation level. At the same time, however, we do not wish to make too much of our regression analysis as an explanation of truancy. Overall, the four variables only explained some 13 per cent of

the variation in truancy, and our own data in the area of family circumstances could reasonably attract the same kind of criticism that we ourselves have levelled at other research on this topic, namely that variables explicitly testing alternative hypotheses (to do with other aspects of family circumstances and individual pathology) were not built into the research. It is interesting, none the less, that these four variables should explain such modest proportions of the total variation amongst individuals. It is also interesting that three variables which have figured with considerable frequency in previous research (sex, size of family and social class) should explain only a negligible proportion of the variance over and above that explained by level of certification.

3 From Gow and McPherson (1980). See chapter 10, note 1.

Chapter 12

1 The sources of data are as follows: *1948 transfer cohort*: data were taken from the six-day sample from the 1947 Scottish Mental Survey, recalculated from tables 9, 10 and 11 of Maxwell (1969) ($n = 1,188$). (See chapter 2, 'Other sources of survey data'.) Estimates on school-leaving dates have been obtained from analyses of a data-set held by Dr Keith Hope of Nuffield College, Oxford, and refer to boys only ($n = 590$). The sample is representative of 11-year-olds in Scotland in 1947, and includes independent-school pupils (who only accounted for seven out of the 590 boys in the sample). *1957–8 transfer cohort: estimates labelled NS* in table 12.1 were obtained from reanalyses of a Scottish subset of the National Survey sample born in March 1946. (See chapter 2, 'Other sources of survey data'.) The subset included only those in Scotland both at birth and at age 15, and excluded those who had died before the age of 20, or who were not contacted after 1946; illegitimate children were not sampled; independent-school pupils have been excluded ($n = 505$, including respondents with missing information). *1957–8 transfer cohort: estimates labelled SEDA* in table 12.1 were obtained from the survey of all pupils who attempted Highers for the first time in 1962, stored in the Scottish Education Data Archive. (See chapter 2, 'The Scottish Education Data Archive and collaborative research'.) Independent-school pupils have been excluded. This survey covers leavers with Highers passes only. To estimate levels of inequality in relation to the whole age-group we have added estimates of the numbers of middle and working class respectively with no Highers. These estimates are based on two assumptions: (i) that 14.85 per cent of the age-group passed at least one Higher; this figure is obtained from the Scottish subset of the National Survey, and is supported by the SED's annual report for the year 1968, which gives a figure of 14.9 per cent for leavers in 1963–4 (Scottish Education

Department, 1969, p. 24; similar information is not available for earlier years); (ii) that 23.68 per cent of the classifiable age-group were middle-class. This estimate is also obtained from the Scottish subset of the National Survey; its use is subject both to sampling error and to possible differences between the procedures for coding social class employed by the National Survey and SEDA. (A substantial number of the National Survey members were not classified by social class at all.) However, a 1 per cent random sample of the Scottish 1945 birth cohort, drawn from public records and held at the Centre for Educational Sociology, has found that 18.2 per cent were born to fathers whose civilian occupations were recorded as non-manual on the certificate of birth. Since net upward intragenerational mobility will have increased the non-manual proportion among these fathers, this is at least consistent with the figure of 23.68 per cent for fathers of 15-year-olds in the early 1960s. Confidence intervals have not been reported for the 1962 SEDA estimates in table 12.1; because they are based on a 100 per cent sample, any errors result from the failure of these two assumptions rather than from predictable sampling error. *1970-2 transfer cohort*: data from the 1977 survey of 1975-6 school-leavers in the Scottish Education Data Archive, restricted to pupils from the four regions ($n = 14,275$, excluding leavers with unclassified fathers). (Pupils from independent schools were excluded.) For further details on all these sources, see chapter 2. The National Survey sampled all the middle class, but only one in four of the working class, in its original target group (see Douglas, Ross and Simpson, 1968) and working-class members of the sample have been weighted with a coefficient of 4. The 1977 SEDA data incorporate weights designed to compensate for observable sampling and response bias (see chapter 2, 'The 1977 survey'.) Wherever weights have been used, confidence limits for Yule's Q (table 12.1) have been based on the estimate of the Q derived from weighted data and estimates of the standard error of Q derived from unweighted data. All values in table 12.1 are subject to rounding; each estimate has been calculated from the original data to avoid compound rounding errors.

2 Middle and working class are defined in terms of father's occupation during or at the end of the child's secondary education. Sample members with no information on father's occupation, or whose fathers could not be classified, are excluded from the analysis. The classification of the 1948 transfer cohort is based on a reaggregation of the nine categories employed by Maxwell (1969): middle class comprises categories 1, 2, 3, 4 and 8; working class comprises categories 5, 6, 7 and 9. The 1957-8 and 1970-2 cohorts are classified in terms of the reaggregation of the Registrar-General's classification used elsewhere in this book and described in chapter 2, 'Some definitions'. See 'Addenhum' to chapter 12 for a discussion of the comparability of these two classifications.

3   As a result, we have had to make one or two rather arbitrary decisions about who has surpassed a given level. There is no problem in deciding that a person with six Highers has surpassed a person with one Higher; but has the person with one Higher, but only two O-grades surpassed the person with no Highers, but six O-grades? In this chapter we will assume that he or she has; but this assumption is somewhat arbitrary. We have assumed that anyone entering full-time post-school education surpassed the level indicated by part-time education; for the 1970–2 cohort, therefore, we have a sequence of criteria for post-school education running from 'any (full-time or part-time) post-school education' to 'any full-time post-school education' to 'advanced or degree-level course' to 'degree-level course' and culminating in 'university course'.

4   The cross ratio is sometimes referred to as the 'odds ratio'. For an example (and sociological justification) of the use of cross ratios and log-linear techniques in the analysis of social mobility see Goldthorpe, Llewellyn and Payne (1980, chapter 4, especially p. 77). For a more general account see Davis (1974).

5   For a full account of Q and its properties, see Kendall and Stuart (1973, pp. 556–81). We are indebted to our colleague Peter Burnhill for discussions of the measurement problems encountered in this chapter, for suggesting Yule's Q to us, and for producing a computer program which was used for all the calculations in table 12.1.

6   Except the 1957–8 transfer cohort, which is based on two samples. See the discussion 'The level of inequality'.

7   The alert reader will have noted that we have estimates from each source of the inequality in relation to one or more Highers and two or more Highers respectively. In each case the SEDA estimate is significantly lower; and for one or more Highers it falls just outside the confidence limits for the National Survey estimate. Much of this discrepancy may result from a sampling error affecting the National Survey; at least in part, however, it may be due either to bias in the National Survey sample or to mistaken assumptions used in the adjustment of the SEDA data, or both.

8   In our estimates we have assumed that VRQ is normally distributed within each class (as in figure 12.4) with a standard deviation of 16 points; the difference between the class means is 10 points.

9   On the possible effects of trends in the class composition of the population see the discussion in Halsey, Heath and Ridge (1980, pp. 64ff). They argue that the likely effect of an increase in the middle-class proportion of the population is for the gap between the average IQs of the classes to narrow. In terms of our diagram this would push the prediction line downwards, towards slightly greater equality. Since our estimates have not allowed for this effect, we may have underestimated the difference between actual inequality in our later cohorts and the inequality that would be predicted from class differences in VRQ scores at age 11.

10 It is relevant to note that the National Survey found evidence in Scotland of class divergence in performance on tests of reading and of arithmetic and mathematics between 11 years and 15 years, but no evidence of class divergence in tests on non-verbal and verbal intelligence between these two ages (Douglas, Ross and Simpson, 1968, statistical supplement, table 111.3).

11 The concept of 'meritocracy' was satirised by Michael Young (1958), although our present discussion is more directly related to that of Halsey, Heath and Ridge (1980).

12 Whether a meritocracy would produce equality of educational opportunity therefore depends on how this is defined. Some operational definitions of equality such as Coleman's (1968) 'results' concept, implicitly assume either that influences on success such as ability are equally distributed between classes, or that their influence is inconsistent with equality of opportunity. According to this definition, any inequality between groups in educational attainment is indicative of inequality of educational opportunity.

13 The slope of the prediction line is much less steep than it would be if inequality were measured by the disparity ratio rather than by Yule's Q.

14 Once again, these differences were much greater when measured by a disparity ratio than when measured by Yule's Q (the disparity ratios are reported in column (iv) of table 12.1). An incidental advantage of using Q as a measure is that it is less sensitive than other measures to an increase in the proportion of the age-group reaching the criterion.

15 The distinction between contest and sponsored mobility is a matter of degree; as one of us has argued elsewhere, sponsorship norms have been consistently weaker in Scotland than in England (McPherson, 1973a).

16 See especially the discussion of table 14.5, part of which is based on the same data as are discussed here.

17 See chapters 4, 5 and 6 for a discussion of the SLC or SCE Higher grade. The 1970–2 B course requirements were less exacting. Like the A course, it refers to subjects in which a pupil *started* an SCE course: an A course includes mathematics, English, a language and a science; a B course includes English, mathematics *or* arithmetic, and a language *or* a science.

18 There is an intriguing possibility, but only a possibility, that inequality in placement on an academic course at 15 years diminished for a while in the years between the late 1940s and the early 1970s, during the heyday of the bipartite selective system. Table 12.1 shows that, of the 1957–8 cohort, 24 per cent were on a selective course at age 15 years, but that the level of inequality associated with this figure was slightly lower than in the earlier or later cohorts (0.58 as compared to 0.68 and 0.63) and lay closer to the prediction line. Possibly this feature reflects improvements

in the transfer procedure in the 1950s; possibly it is only a function of factors internal to the sample survey itself (the confidence interval for the estimate, for example, is very wide). However it may be, internal comparisons within the 1957–8 sample data indicate that between the ages of 15 and 16 any lingering effects of a relatively meritocratic transfer system were dissipated.

19 Expansion is likely to produce a rather steeper decline in inequality as measured by the disparity ratio. Our conclusions here are broadly consistent with those for England and Wales of Little and Westergaard (1964), but not with those of Halsey, Heath and Ridge (1980), who find little evidence of a decline in inequality even as measured by the disparity ratio.

Chapter 13

1 We are grateful to Lesley Gow for help with the preparation of this chapter. It also draws on research, most of which is currently unpublished, being conducted at the Centre for Educational Sociology into policy-making in Scottish education (Raab, 1980 and forthcoming). Charles Raab has contributed to this chapter through his role in that research.

2 Critics of the 1947 report of the Advisory Council have pointed to its apparent inconsistency in recommending both that the omnibus school should be adopted and also that 'there are adequate reasons why the system of senior and junior secondary schools should be given a longer trial under more favourable conditions, wherever an education authority considers that the adoption of the omnibus school system is not in the best interests of its area' (Scottish Education Department, 1947, para. 161). Contrast also the trenchant critique of social-class-based educational provision in the main report (ibid., paras. 154–5) with the conclusion in the Appendix that 'parents may desire that their children should be enrolled at a particular secondary school not merely for the intrinsic value of the education given but also for the standing and prestige of the school, which may be regarded as giving an advantage in personal contacts of future employment. It may, however, be said that on the whole Scottish secondary education is democratic and sturdy enough to resist any widespread growth of this tendency, that while this may give a temporary advantage to a few mediocre people, real talent is discovered and developed pretty evenly in all Scottish secondary schools, large and small, rural and urban; and that the real remedy, though a slow one, is to be found not in depressing the status of schools with ancient prestige and traditions but in encouraging others to develop their own prestige and standards along lines of their own natural development.'

Reports are often the product of compromise, and more research (now possible with the release of the official papers under the thirty-year rule) is required into the Advisory Council proceedings of 1942–7.

3 See Mackenzie (1967), who also comments that 'in 1954 the only motion on the subject submitted to the Scottish Council Conference suggested that the National Policy on comprehensive schools should not apply to Scotland. Most of the pressure on the Labour leadership towards the comprehensive system came from England' (ibid., p. 30). Our own evidence from sources such as Clark (1980) indicates that, in a number of Labour-controlled authorities in Scotland, changes in the membership of the education committees in the early 1960s had the effect of reducing the influence over the committee of the Director of Education and of increasing that of the national party organisation.

4 These guidelines were elaborated in Circular 614 (Scottish Education Department, 1966b). It also confirmed that selection within secondary education was to be in terms of certificate courses and that provision was to accommodate pupils of 'middling' ability who might be capable of attaining a number of O-grade passes that would earlier have been regarded as 'marginal': 'While allocation to either certificate or non-certificate courses may be educationally justifiable in the case of the minority of pupils whose attainments are clearly well above or well below the average, it does not take adequate account of the very large number of pupils whose achievements at the primary stage cannot be categorised with any accuracy . . . there should be no rigid division of the pupils into two separate "sides" – those who are in classes following entirely certificate courses in their major subjects and those who are not working towards the certificate in any subjects at all. Such pupils will, of course, be found in all schools but between them, if the evidence about the distribution of abilities, apititudes and interests is to be recognised frankly, there must be a number who will do certificate work in a few subjects, and non-certificate work in other subjects.' (ibid., paras. 3 and 12.)

5 For example: 'In these experiments organisation int the initial stage normally takes one of two forms: mixed-ability classes based on random classification or a balance of ability within each class, or division into broad bands of ability with subdivision into mixed-ability groupings within the bands. Thereafter most pupils follow a common course of subjects, usually for at least the whole of the first year. Since most of these experiments are still only in their first or second year of operation, it is too early to attempt any definitive assessment. . . . Teachers vary in their reactions to these developments. While some have commented favourably on the good social effects of the new types of organisation, others are concerned that able pupils, unless special provision can be made for them early, may lose impetus and interest. This fear is probably

exaggerated; the experience of some schools suggests that the use of group and individual methods, the establishment of setting where necessary and the provision of optional additions to the curriculum in the second year can ensure that interest and progress are maintained.' (Scottish Education Department, 1969, pp. 14–15.) The annual reports are published by HMSO in Edinburgh and are entitled *Education in Scotland in 19–*.

6 'HM Inspectors also report that secondary schools, and in particular their boards of studies, have a number of important problems to resolve. An increasing number of them are beginning to question the length of the "common course" at present generally two years particularly as it affects abler pupils.' (Scottish Education Department, 1980b, para. 38.)

Chapter 15

1 Six of these schools were excluded because there were no non-certificate pupils from these schools in our sample. This may well have been a legitimate result of the sampling process, but it may have reflected sampling bias and the schools were therefore excluded as a precaution.

2 The effect of excluding the fifteen schools was to increase, very slightly, the association between intake and outcomes among schools.

3 Another intake variable available in the archive, which helps to predict outcomes, is the average number of siblings of pupils in a school. However, the strength of the association between the variable and outcomes varies according to the denominational status of schools. Since our 69 schools include both Catholic and non-denominational schools we have not used the siblings measure in this analysis. A discussion of the associations among individual leavers between SCE attainment and number of siblings in denominational and non-denominational schools respectively may be found in Cruickshank (1979).

4 In particular it assumes that this relation is linear, and that it can best be represented by a straight line, as in figure 15.1. It therefore assumes that there are no threshold or ceiling effects whereby the relation between intake and outcome changes according to whether schools are above or below certain levels of the intake measure. Readers may wish to make their own judgments about the validity of this assumption by inspecting figure 15.1. For a discussion of some further limitations of regression analysis and of some other techniques, see Burnhill, Raffe and Weston (1981).

5 Once again we must note a technical reservation. With data such as those in figure 15.1, we would normally expect schools to be more widely scattered above or below the regression line, the

nearer they are to the average level of the intake measure. Standardising the difference scores would control for this tendency; it would reduce the relative size (plus or minus) of difference scores of schools with nearer-to-average intakes, and it would give more weight to schools (such as school B) with atypical intakes which score above or below the prediction. Once again, however, we feel that in this exploratory and illustrative chapter the technical arguments for this procedure do not outweigh the need to keep the conceptual argument as simple as possible.

6 Part of the reason for these low correlations is the attenuation resulting from unreliability. Residuals (difference scores) contain a higher proportion of error than actual outcome scores; the correlations between residuals are thereby further attenuated. However, this does not invalidate our general point, that part of the correlation between actual outcome scores reflects intake rather than school effectiveness.

7 Among the 69 schools the standard deviation of O-grade difference scores was 8.8 per cent.

8 Indeed, there is some evidence to suggest that these schools were doing rather better in examinations than their intakes would predict. Several of these schools, unlike nearly all other Scottish schools, presented pupils for CSE examinations; since our O-grade outcome measure does not reflect CSE performance, it underestimates these schools' average performance in all examinations, including CSE. Since these schools were achieving up to prediction on an outcome measured based on O-grade alone, it is possible that a measure which combined CSE and O-grade results would reveal them to be achieving better than prediction. Unfortunately we do not have the data with which to test this precisely.

9 One caution must be given about this conclusion. Although all 69 schools were formally comprehensive by 1970, it is possible that informal kinds of selective transfer at 12 years persisted. For example, some children were able to enter schools outside their catchment areas, if they had elder brothers or sisters there; and, in authorities which did not practise strict zoning, it is possible that the 'better' children tended to gravitate towards the 'better' schools. Such processes are likely to have favoured the schools with good reputations and the former senior secondaries, giving them more promising intakes than they would otherwise have had. To the extent that our difference scores are not based on all the relevant aspects of intake, they will not control for all the effects of these informal selection processes. Consequently, if our difference scores are biased, they are likely to be biased in favour of former senior secondaries and against former junior secondaries. We have no means of estimating the extent of this bias, although we have noted that, where two or more comprehensive schools served a single burgh, the difference scores of the two (or more) schools were usually more than 5 percentage points apart, and the

former senior secondary usually had the better score. This may, of course, be a genuine school effect; former senior secondaries may have had 'better' teaching staff, in some sense, and often better material resources, as well as probable advantages with respect to the less tangible factors of ethos and morale. Less probably, it may be the effect of informal selection processes, with the 'better' school continuing to attract the 'better' pupils, the effects of this being inadequately controlled for by our intake measures.

10 This is calculated from a gamma statistic, correlating difference scores with actual outcomes. The figure is probably an under-estimate of the reversal that would take place, since additional intake variables would probably reduce further the correlation between outcomes and difference scores.

Chapter 16

1 See Macpherson (1958, especially pp. 42, 74 and 77): '[The conclusion was] inescapable that character plays a most important role in determining whether a pupil stays on course or drops out. Perseverance, conscientiousness, and the will to do well are factors which count. . . . Unless we are prepared to take measures to improve pupils' characters and attitudes, a most difficult task, it would seem that not all of the potential ability in an age-group could be realised in practice.' By contrast, the 'reformist' view, associated with Brunton (chapter 4), was that the task was not all that 'difficult'. The inadequacy of the Highers course and un-resolved systemic problems of difficulty and motivation were held to be responsible for failures of individual motivation (Scottish Education Department, 1959a, para. 27–8): 'Once real interest has been aroused, the pupils themselves will lead the way.' The Macpherson study actually reduced its quantified estimates of the size of wastage on the grounds that pupils with motivational deficiencies who left school at 15 years had only limited prospects of success in the Highers examination (Macpherson, 1958, pp. 64ff).

Chapter 17

1 This chapter was written jointly with Charles Raab and draws on McPherson, Raab and Raffe (1978) in which some of the present arguments have been elaborated.

References

Items marked CES are available from the Centre for Educational Sociology, University of Edinburgh.

Acland, H. (1973), 'The social determinants of educational achievement: an evaluation and criticism of research', unpublished D.Phil. thesis, Oxford University.

Armstrong, C. and McPherson, A. F. (1975), *Dictionary of Variables for the SCE 'H' Grade Qualified School Leavers in 1962, 1970 and 1972*, CES.

Ashton, D. N. and Maguire, M. J. (1980), 'The function of academic and non-academic criteria in employers' selection strategies', *British Journal of Guidance and Counselling*, vol. 8, no. 2, pp.146–57.

Ballantyne, W. and Taylor, D. (1979), 'The CSE experience: a first look', *Collaborative Research Newsletter*, no. 6, pp. 45–57, CES.

Baxter, J. L. (1975), 'The chronic job-changer: a study of youth unemployment', *Social and Economic Administration*, vol. 9, no. 3, pp. 184–206.

Belson, W. A. (1975), *Juvenile Theft: The Causal Factors*, London, Harper & Row.

Bibby, J. and Weston, P. B. (1980), 'Sex differentials in maths enrolements: sudden death or gradual decline?', *Collaborative Research Newsletter*, no. 7, pp. 3–10, CES.

Bland, R. (1979), 'Measuring social class: a discussion of the Registrar-General's classification', *Sociology*, vol. 13, no. 2, pp. 283–91.

Bowles, S. and Gintis, H. (1976), *Schooling in Capitalist America*, London, Routledge & Kegan Paul.

Brimer, A., Madaus, G. F., Chapman, B., Kellaghan, T. and Wood, R. (1978), *Sources of Difference in School Achievement*, Slough, NFER.

Brunton, J. S. (1977), Transcript of interview of J. S. Brunton with A. F. McPherson and C. D. Raab, 12 August 1976 with amendments, 31 March 1977.

Burnhill, P., Lamb, J. M. and Weston, P. B. (in preparation), *Collaborative Research Dictionary and Questionnaires 1981*, CES.

Burnhill, P., Raffe, D. and Weston, P. B. (1981), 'How good is my school? School-based evaluation and public accountability', paper given at the Annual Conference of the British Educational Research Association, Alsager, September, CES.

Burnhill, P. and Redpath, A. (1981), 'Higher education in Scotland: the re-emergence of pre-war patterns', paper given at the Fifth International Conference on Higher Education, Lancaster University, September, CES.

Byrne, D., Williamson, W. and Fletcher, B. (1975), *The Poverty of Education: a Study in the Politics of Opportunity*, Oxford, Martin Robertson.

Carroll, H. C. M. (1977), 'The problem of absenteeism: research studies, past and present', in H. C. M. Carroll (ed.), *Absenteeism in South Wales*, Faculty of Education, University College of Swansea.

Carter, M. P. (1962), *Home, School and Work*, Oxford, Pergamon Press.

Central Advisory Council for Education (England) (1954), *Early Leaving*, London, HMSO.

Central Advisory Council for Education (England) (1967), *Children and their Primary Schools: a Report*, London, HMSO (the Plowden Report).

Central Policy Review Staff (1980), *Education, Training and Industrial Performance*, London, HMSO.

Centre for Educational Sociology (1979), 'A code of practice for collaborative research', *Collaborative Research Newsletter*, no. 6, pp. 84–6, CES.

Clark, J. R. (1980), Transcript of interview of J. R. Clark with A. F. McPherson and C. D. Raab, 25 May 1977 and 6 June 1977 with amendments, 18 May 1980.

Clarke, F. (1940), *Education and Social Change: An English Interpretation*, London, Sheldon Press.

Clarke, F. (1948), *Freedom in the Educative Society*, London, University of London Press.

Cochran, M. (1980), 'The special programmes in Scotland', in Scottish Education Department, *All The Time in the World: Education in a Changing Society*, Edinburgh, HMSO.

Coleman, J. S. (1968), 'The concept of equality of educational opportunity', *Harvard Educational Review*, vol. 38, no. 1, pp. 7–22.

Coleman, J. S., Campbell, E. Q., Hobson, C. J., McPartland, J., Mood, A. M., Weinfeld, F. and York, R. L. (1966), *Equality of Educational Opportunity*, Washington, US Government Printing Office.

Collaborative Research Working Party (1978), 'How far to Munn? A provisional assessment of the extent of curriculum balance among Scottish O-grade leavers', *Collaborative Research Newsletter*, no. 2, pp. 17–30, CES.

Collins, R. (1971), 'Functional and conflict themes of educational stratification', *American Sociological Review*, vol. 36, no. 6, pp. 1002–18.

Cmnd 603 (1958), *Education in Scotland: The Next Step*, Edinburgh, HMSO.

Cmnd 5175 (1972), *Education in Scotland: A Statement of Policy*, Edinburgh, HMSO.

Cope, E. and Gray, J. (1977), 'Research as in-service education', *British Journal of In-Service Education*, vol. 4, no. 1, pp. 13–17.

Cope, E. and Gray, J. (1978), 'Figures and perspectives on the national problem of truancy: an opening discussion', *Collaborative Research Newletter*, no. 3, pp. 16–25, CES.

Cope, E. and Gray, J. (1979), 'Teachers as researchers: some experience of an alternative paradigm', *British Educational Research Journal*, vol. 5, no. 2, pp. 237–51.

Cope, E., Gray, J., McPherson, A. F. and Raffe, D. (1976), 'Dissemination as dialogue', *Social Science Research Council Newsletter*, October, pp. 4–7.

Cotgrove, S. F. (1958), *Technical Education and Social Change*, London, George Allen & Unwin.

Council for Scientific Policy (1968), *Enquiry into the Flow of Candidates in Science and Technology into Higher Education*, London, HMSO, Cmnd 3541 (the Dainton Report).

Cruickshank, H. (1979), 'Is Catholic secular education second rate?', *Collaborative Research Newletter*, no. 6, pp. 71–83, CES.

Davie, G. (1961), *The Democratic Intellect: Scotland and Her Universities in the Nineteenth Century*, Edinburgh, Edinburgh University Press.

Davie, R., Butler, N. and Goldstein, H. (1972), *From Birth to Seven*, London, Longman.

Davis, J. A. (1974), 'Hierarchical models for significance tests in multivariate contingency tables: an exegesis of Goodman's recent papers', in H. L. Costner (ed.), *Sociological Methodology 1973–4*, San Francisco, Jossey-Bass, pp. 189–231.

Department of Education and Science (1965), *The Organisation of Secondary Education*, London, HMSO (Circular 10/65).

Department of Education and Science (1974), *Statistics of Education, Vol. 1, Schools: England and Wales*, London, HMSO.

Department of Education and Science (1978) *Statistics of Education, Vol. 2, Leavers CSE and GCE: England and Wales*, London, HMSO.

Dewar, W. McL. (1977), Transcript of interview of W. McL. Dewar with A. F. McPherson and C. D. Raab, 22 June 1976 with amendments, 13 May 1977.

Dickson, C. (1979), 'The state of modern languages', *Collaborative Research Newsletter*, no. 5, pp. 3–22, CES.

Douglas, J. W. B. (1964), *The Home and The School*, London, MacGibbon & Kee.

Douglas, J. W. B., Ross, J. M., Maxwell, S. M. M. and Walker, D. A. (1966), 'Differences in test score and in the gaining of selective places for Scottish children and those in England and Wales', *British Journal of Educational Psychology*, vol. 36, no. 2, pp. 150–7.

Douglas, J. W. B., Ross, J. M. and Simpson, H. R. (1968), *All Our*

Future, London, Peter Davies. (A copy of the Statistical Supplement to this volume is held at the National Library of Scotland, Edinburgh.)

Durkheim, E. (1915), *The Elementary Forms of the Religious Life*, London, George Allen & Unwin (5th impression, 1964).

Education Commission (Scotland) (1868), *Third Report of Her Majesty's Commissioners*, Edinburgh, HMSO.

Fogelman, K. (1976), *Britain's Sixteen Year-Olds*, London, National Children's Bureau.

General Register Office (1966), *Classification of Occupations 1966*, London, HMSO.

Goldthorpe, J., Llewellyn, C. and Payne, C. (1980), *Social Mobility and Class Structure in Modern Britain*, Oxford, Clarendon Press.

Gow, L. and McPherson, A. F. (1980), *Tell Them From Me: Scottish School Leavers Write about School and Life Afterwards*, Aberdeen, Aberdeen University Press.

Gray, J. (1981), 'Towards effective schools', *British Educational Research Journal*, vol. 7, no. 1, pp. 59–69.

Gray, J. and McPherson, A. F. (1978), 'Piecemeal exam reform: some lessons from Sixth Year Studies', *Collaborative Research Newsletter*, no. 3, pp. 70–82, CES.

Gray, J. and McPherson, A. F. (1979), *Figuring It Out: a course of self-instruction on the Scottish Education Data Archive*, CES.

Gray, J., McPherson, A. F. and Raffe, D. (1979), 'Collaborative research in Scotland: a new departure', *Educational Research*, vol. 21, no. 3, pp. 178–85.

Halsey, A. H. (1975), 'Education and social mobility in Britain since World War II', in Organisation for Economic Cooperation and Development (ed.), *Education Inequality and Life Chances*, vol. 1, Paris, OECD.

Halsey, A. H. (1977), 'Towards meritocracy? The case of Britain', in J. Karabel and A. H. Halsey (eds), *Power and Ideology in Education*, New York, Oxford University Press.

Halsey, A. H., Heath, A. F. and Ridge, J. M. (1980), *Origins and Destinations: Family, Class and Education in Modern Britain*, Oxford, Clarendon Press.

Heath, A. (1981), 'What difference does the old school tie make now?', *New Society*, vol. 56, no. 970, 18 June, pp. 472–4.

Hill, D. (1978), 'The Pack and SEDA statistics on truancy: a reconciliation', *Collaborative Research Newsletter*, no. 4, pp. 30–1, CES.

His Majesty's Chief Inspectors of Schools in Scotland (1922), *General Reports For The Year 1921*, London, HMSO.

Hodgson, G. (1973), 'Inequality: do schools make a difference?', in H. Silver (ed.), *Equal Opportunity in Education*, London, Methuen.

House of Commons Debates (1966), Standing Committee, session 66–7, 'Scottish Grand Committee: Scottish Estimates, First Sitting, 24th May', *Hansard*, vol. 12, cols. 1–112.

House of Commons Debates (1967), Standing Committee, session 66–7,

'Scottish Grand Committee: Scottish Estimates, Third Sitting, 4th July', *Hansard*, vol. 12, cols. 107–58.

Hutchison, D., Jones, C. L., Littlejohn, G. M. and McPherson, A. F. (1974), 'The influence of the university on school curricula: the context of subject choice', unpublished paper, CES.

Hutchison, D. and Littlejohn, G. M. (1975), 'The impact of social science on flows from school to university', *Research in Education*, no. 13, May, pp. 1–26.

Inner London Education Authority (1980), *School Examination Results in the ILEA 1978*, London, Inner London Education Authority.

Jencks, C. S., Smith, M., Acland, H., Bane, M. J., Cohen, D., Gintis, H., Heyns, B. and Michelson, S. (1973), *Inequality: A Reassessment of the Effects of Family and Schooling in America*, London, Allen Lane.

Jones, C. L., Littlejohn, G. M. and McPherson, A. F. (1974), 'Predicting science-based study at university', *Journal of the Royal Statistical Society, Series A*, vol. 1, pp. 48–59.

Jones, C. L. and McPherson, A. F. (1972), 'Implications of non-response to postal surveys for the development of nationally-based data on flows out of educational systems', *Scottish Educational Studies*, vol. 4, no. 1, pp. 28–38.

Kelly, A. (1975), 'The relative standards of subject examinations', paper given at the Annual Conference of the British Educational Research Association, Stirling University, September, CES.

Kelly, A. (1976a), 'Family background, subject specialisation and occupational recruitment of Scottish university students: some patterns and trends', *Higher Education*, vol. 5, pp. 177–88.

Kelly, A. (1976b), *The Comparability of Examining Standards in Scottish Certificate of Education Ordinary and Higher Grade Examinations*, Dalkeith, Scottish Certificate of Education Examination Board.

Kelly, A. (1976c), 'A study of the comparability of external examinations in different subjects', *Research in Education*, vol. 16, pp. 37–63.

Kendall, M. G. and Stuart, A. (1973), *The Advanced Theory of Statistics*, vol. 2, 3rd edn, London, Griffin.

Killcross, M. C. (1969), 'Assessment for Higher Education', unpublished paper, CES.

Knox, H. M. (1953), *Two Hundred and Fifty Years of Scottish Education 1696–1946*, Edinburgh, Oliver & Boyd.

Kogan, M. (1978), *The Politics of Educational Change*, Manchester, Manchester University Press.

Lee, G. and Wrench, J. (1981), 'Inequality in the skilled labour market: the case of black youths in Birmingham', paper given at the Annual Conference of the British Sociological Association, Aberystwyth, April.

Little, A. and Westergaard, J. (1964), 'Trends of class differentials in educational opportunity in England and Wales', *British Journal of Sociology*, vol. 15, pp. 301–16.

McClelland, W. (1935), 'Distinctive features of Scottish education', *The New Era in Home and School*, vol. 16, no. 7, pp. 172–4.

McClelland, W. (1942), *Selection for Secondary Education*, London, University of London Press.

McCrone, D., Bechhofer, F. and Kendrick, S. (forthcoming), 'Egalitarianism and social inequality in Scotland', paper given at the Annual Conference of the British Sociological Association, Aberystwyth, April 1981 (to be published).

McEwan, J. S. (1965), 'The nature and organisation of secondary education: a review of current and possible developments', Appendix 1 to the *Minute of Meeting of the Education Committee of the County Council of Lanarkshire*, 7 July 1965, pp. 1664–86.

McIntosh, D. M. and Walker, D. A. (1970), 'The O-grade of the Scottish Certificate of Education', *British Journal of Educational Psychology*, vol. 40, no. 2, pp. 179–99.

McIntyre, D. (1979), 'Collaborative research from the outside', *Collaborative Research Newsletter*, no. 6, pp. 3–6, CES.

McKechin, W. (1976), 'Consultation in Renfrewshire', *Times Educational Supplement (Scotland)*, 21 May, p. 19.

Mackenzie, M. (1967), 'The road to the circulars: a study of the evolution of Labour Party policy with regard to the comprehensive school', *Scottish Educational Studies*, vol. 1, no. 1, pp. 25–33.

Macpherson, J. S. (1958), *Eleven-Year-Olds Grow Up*, London, University of London Press.

McPherson, A. F. (1971), *Survey of Education and Occupations*, final report to the SSRC on grant HR 459, CES.

McPherson, A. F. (1972), 'The generally educated Scot: an old ideal in a changing university structure', in A. F. McPherson, D. Swift and B. Bernstein, *Eighteen Plus – The Final Selection*, unit 15, Bletchley, The Open University.

McPherson, A. F. (1973a), 'Selections and survivals: a sociology of the ancient Scottish universities', in R. Brown (ed.), *Knowledge, Education and Cultural Change: Papers In The Sociology Of Education*, London, Tavistock.

McPherson, A. F. (1973b), 'Some methodological and substantive conclusions from a longitudinal study of the educational and occupational behaviour of Scots entering tertiary education', *Sociological Microjournal*, vol. 7, pp. 1–32.

McPherson, A. F. (1976), 'The examination problem: some unresolved consequences of deferred selection', in Convention of Scottish Local Authorities, *Signposts for Education*, Edinburgh. (A longer version, with tables included, is available from the author.)

McPherson, A. F. (1977), *An Archive on Flows from Secondary Education in Scotland since 1962*, final report to the SSRC on grant HR 3187, CES.

McPherson, A. F. (1981), Participatory Research in Secondary and Tertiary Education, final report to the SSRC on grant HR 3262, CES.

357

McPherson, A. F. (1982, in press), 'An angle on the Geist: persistence and change in the Scottish educational tradition', in W. Humes and H. Paterson (eds), *Scottish Culture and Scottish Education*, Edinburgh, John Donald.

McPherson, A. F. and Neave, G. R. (1976), *The Scottish Sixth: A Sociological Evaluation of Sixth Year Studies and the Changing Relationship between School and University in Scotland*, Slough, NFER.

McPherson, A. F., Raab, C. D. and Raffe, D. (1978), 'Social explanation and political accountability: two related problems with a single solution', paper given at the Annual Conference of the British Educational Research Association, Leeds University, September, CES.

McPherson, A. F. and Raffe, D. (1978), 'Some political and social influences on a national education survey', paper given at the Edinburgh local group of the Royal Statistical Society, November, CES.

Madaus, G. F., Kellaghan, T., Rakow, E. A. and King, D. (1979), 'The sensitivity of measures of school effectiveness', *Harvard Educational Review*, vol. 49, no. 2, pp. 207–30.

Maizels, J. (1970), *Adolescent Needs and the Transition from School to Work*, London, Athlone Press.

Makeham, P. (1980), *Youth Unemployment: An Examination of Evidence on Youth Unemployment using National Statistics*, Research Paper no. 10, London, Department of Employment.

Manpower Services Commission (1977), *Young People and Work*, London, Manpower Services Commission (the Holland Report).

Manpower Services Commission (1978), *Young People and Work: Manpower Studies No. 19781*, London, HMSO.

Manpower Services Commission (1979), *Review of the First Year of Special Programmes*, London, Manpower Services Commission.

Manpower Services Commission (1980a), *Review of the Second Year of Special Programmes*, London, Manpower Services Commission.

Manpower Services Commission (1980b), *MSC Plan for Scotland 1980–1984*, Edinburgh, Manpower Services Commission.

Marshall, T. H. (1963), 'Citizenship and social class', in *Sociology at the Crossroads and Other Essays*, London, Heinemann Educational Books, pp. 67–127.

Maxwell, J. (1969), *Sixteen Years On: A Follow-up of the 1947 Scottish Survey*, London, University of London Press for the Scottish Council for Research in Education.

May, D. (1975), 'Truancy, school absenteeism and delinquency', *Scottish Educational Studies*, vol. 7, no. 2, pp. 97–107.

National Youth Employment Council (1974), *Unqualified, Untrained and Unemployed*, London, HMSO.

Office of Population Censuses and Surveys (1970), *Classification of Occupations 1970*, London, HMSO.

Payne, G. and Ford, G. (1977), 'Religion, class and educational policy',

Scottish Educational Studies, vol. 9, no. 2, pp. 83–99.

Payne, G., Ford, G. and Ulas, M. (1979), 'Education and social mobility: some social and theoretical developments', *Sociologists in Polytechnics*, paper no. 8, Edinburgh, Moray House College.

Phillips, D. (1973), 'Young and unemployed in a northern city', in D. Weir (ed.), *Men and Work in Modern Britain*, Glasgow, Fontana.

Powell, J. L. (1973), *Selection for University in Scotland*, Edinburgh, Scottish Council for Research in Education.

Raab, C. D. (1980), 'The changing machinery of Scottish educational policy-making', *Scottish Educational Review*, vol. 12, no. 2, pp. 88–98.

Raab, C. D. (forthcoming), 'The quasi-government of Scottish education', in A. Barker (ed.), *Quangos in Britain: Government and the Networks of Public Policy-Making*, London, Macmillan.

Raffe, D. (1977), 'Social class and entry to further education', *Scottish Educational Studies*, vol. 9, no. 2, pp. 100–11.

Raffe, D. (1981a), 'Special programmes in Scotland: the first year of YOP', *Policy and Politics*, vol. 9, no. 4, pp. 471–87.

Raffe, D. (1981b), 'Education, the "tightening bond" and social mobility', paper given at the Annual Conference of the British Sociological Association, Aberystwyth, CES.

Raffe, D. (1981c), 'Education, employment and the Youth Opportunities Programme: some sociological perspectives', *Oxford Review of Education*, vol. 7, no. 3, pp. 211–22.

Raffe, D., Lamb, J., Cassels, F., Cope, E., Gray, J., McPherson, A. and Wylie, L. (1978), *Collaborative Research Dictionary 1977 and Collaborative Research Questionnaires 1977*, CES.

Raffe, D., Lamb, J. Garner, C., Hughes, J., MacDougall, M. and Pike, D. (1981), *Collaborative Research Dictionary and Questionnaires 1979*, CES.

Reeder, D. (1979), 'A recurring debate: education and industry', in G. Bernbaum (ed.), *Schooling in Decline*, London, Macmillan.

Reynolds, D. (1976), 'The delinquent school', in M. Hammersley and P. Woods (eds), *The Process of Schooling*, London, Routledge & Kegan Paul.

Roberts, K., Armstrong, J. and Noble, M. (1980), 'The sociology of school-leaving and work entry', paper given at the Sociology of Education Conference, Westhill College, Birmingham.

Royal Commission on the Constitution 1969–1973 (1973–4), *Minute of Evidence II: Scotland 29th–30th September 1969*, London, HMSO, Cmnd 5460 (the Kilbrandon Commission).

Rutter, M., Maughan, B., Mortimore, P. and Ouston, J. with Smith, A. (1979), *Fifteen Thousand Hours: Secondary Schools and their Effects on Children*, London, Open Books.

Ryrie, A. C. (1981), *Routes and Results*, London, Hodder & Stoughton.

Ryrie, A. C., Furst, A. and Lauder, M. (1979), *Choices and Chances: a Study of Pupils' Subject Choices and Future Career Intentions*, London, Hodder & Stoughton.

Scottish Certificate of Education Examination Board (annual 1965–)
Report, Edinburgh (1965–75) and Dalkeith (1976–), Scottish
Certificate of Education Examination Board.

Scottish Certificate of Education Examination Board (1970), *Report
of Conference on Examinations March 1970*, Edinburgh, Scottish
Certificate of Education Examination Board.

Scottish Certificate of Education Examination Board (1979), *Report
of Conference on the Post-Fourth Year Examination Structure in
Scottish Schools, 23rd November 1979*, Dalkeith, Scottish Certificate
of Education Examination Board.

Scottish Certificate of Education Examination Board (forthcoming),
Full-Time Education after S4: A Statistical Study, Dalkeith, Scottish
Certificate of Education Examination Board.

Scottish Council for Research in Education (1953), *Social Implications
of the 1947 Scottish Mental Survey*, London, University of London
Press.

Scottish Education Department (1921), *Circular 44* (no title), London,
HMSO.

Scottish Education Department (1947), *Secondary Education: A
Report of the Advisory Council on Education in Scotland*, Edinburgh,
HMSO, Cmnd 7005.

Scottish Education Department (1951), *Secondary Education: The
Report of the Advisory Council*, Edinburgh, HMSO (Circular 206).

Scottish Education Department (1952), *Education in Scotland in 1951*,
Edinburgh, HMSO, Cmnd 8515.

Scottish Education Department (1953), *Education in Scotland in 1952*,
Edinburgh, HMSO, Cmnd 8813.

Scottish Education Department (1955), *Junior Secondary Education*,
Edinburgh, HMSO.

Scottish Education Department (1959a), *Report of the Working Party
on the Curriculum of the Senior Secondary School: Introduction of
the Ordinary Grade of the Scottish Leaving Certificate*, Edinburgh,
HMSO.

Scottish Education Department (1959b), *Report of the Working Party
on the Curriculum of the Senior Secondary School*, Edinburgh,
HMSO (Circular 412).

Scottish Education Department (1960), *The Post-Fourth Year Examination Structure in Scotland: A Report of a Special Committee of
the Advisory Council on Education in Scotland*, Edinburgh, HMSO,
Cmnd 1068.

Scottish Education Department (1961), *Transfer from Primary to
Secondary Education: A Report of a Special Committee of the
Advisory Council on Education in Scotland*, Edinburgh, HMSO,
Cmnd 1538.

Scottish Education Department (1962), *Transfer of Pupils from
Primary to Secondary Education*, Edinburgh, HMSO (Circular 501).

Scottish Education Department (1963), *From School to Further
Education*, Edinburgh, HMSO (the Brunton Report).

Scottish Education Department (1965a), *Reorganisation of Secondary Education on Comprehensive Lines*, Edinburgh, HMSO (Circular 600).

Scottish Education Department (1965b), *Education in Scotland in 1964*, Edinburgh, HMSO, Cmnd 2600.

Scottish Education Department (1966a), *Education in Scotland in 1965*, Edinburgh, HMSO, Cmnd 2914.

Scottish Education Department (1966b), *Transfer of Pupils from Primary to Secondary Education*, Edinburgh, HMSO (Circular 614).

Scottish Education Department (1969), *Education in Scotland in 1968*, Edinburgh, HMSO, Cmnd 3949.

Scottish Education Department (1972a), *Second Report of the Consultative Committee on the Curriculum 1968–71*, Edinburgh, HMSO.

Scottish Education Department (1972b), *Scottish Educational Statistics 1971*, Edinburgh, HMSO.

Scottish Education Department (1973a), *Education in Fife: a Report by HM Inspector of Schools*, Edinburgh, HMSO.

Scottish Education Department (1973b), *Education in Renfrewshire: a Report by HM Inspector of Schools*, Edinburgh, HMSO.

Scottish Education Department (1975), *Education in Scotland in 1974*, Edinburgh, HMSO, Cmnd 5908.

Scottish Education Department (1977a), *Assessment for All: Report of the Committee to Review Assessment in the Third and Fourth Years of Secondary Education in Scotland*, Edinburgh, HMSO (the Dunning Report).

Scottish Education Department (1977b), *The Structure of the Curriculum in the Third and Fourth Years of the Scottish Secondary School*, Edinburgh, HMSO (the Munn Report).

Scottish Education Department (1977c), *Truancy and Indiscipline in Schools in Scotland*, Edinburgh, HMSO (the Pack Report).

Scottish Education Department (1977d), *Education in Lanarkshire: a Report by HM Inspector of Schools*, Edinburgh, HMSO.

Scottish Education Department (1977e), *Scottish Educational Statistics 1974–5 (Special Edition): Schools, Pupils, Teachers*, Edinburgh, HMSO.

Scottish Education Department (1978), *School Leavers*, Statistical Bulletin no. 4/E2/1978, Edinburgh, Scottish Education Department.

Scottish Education Department (no date, 1979), *Curriculum and Assessment in the Third and Fourth Years of Secondary Education in Scotland: Proposals for Action*, Edinburgh, HMSO.

Scottish Education Department (1980a), *Young People Leaving School*, Statistical Bulletin no. 10/E3/1980, Edinburgh, Scottish Education Department.

Scottish Education Department (1980b), *Education in Scotland in 1979*, Edinburgh, HMSO, Cmnd 7892.

Scottish Education Department (no date, 1980), *The Munn and Dunning Reports: the Government's Development Programme*, Edinburgh, Scottish Education Department.

361

Scottish Information Office (no date, 1970s), *Scottish Schools Today*, Edinburgh HMSO.

Scottish Mobility Study (1976), *Scottish Education Fact Sheet No. 1: Social Class and Success in Secondary Education*, Department of Sociology, Aberdeen University.

Scottish Office (1954), 'Early school leaving in Scotland', Press Release, 30 December 1954, DE 13788/1, Edinburgh.

Steedman, J. (1980), *Progress in Secondary Schools: Findings From the National Child Development Study*, London, National Children's Bureau.

Thomas, R. and Wetherall, D. (1974), *Looking Forward to Work*, London, HMSO.

Thurow, L. and Lucas, R. (1972), *The American Distribution of Income: A Structural Problem*, a study prepared for the use of the Joint Economic Committee, Congress of the United States, Washington, US Government Printing Office.

Tibbenham, A. (1977), 'Housing and truancy', *New Society*, vol. 39, no. 753, pp. 501-2.

Turner, R. H. (1960), 'Sponsored and contest mobility and the school system', *American Sociological Review*, vol. 25, no. 5, pp. 855-67.

Tyler, W. (1977), *The Sociology of Educational Inequality*, London, Methuen.

Weir, D. and Nolan, F. (1977), *Glad To Be Out: A Study of School-Leavers*, Edinburgh, Scottish Council for Research in Education.

Weston, P. B. (1979), 'Four years of collaborative research: some regional reflections', *Collaborative Research Newsletter*, no. 6, pp. 7-11, CES.

Weston, P. B. (1980), 'Questions for the pilot: an interim report on the 1981 survey', *Collaborative Research Newsletter*, no. 7, pp. 35-7, CES.

Williams, R. (1978), 'Help wanted . . . returns guaranteed', *Collaborative Research Newsletter*, no. 4, pp. 3-8, CES.

Wishart, D. (1980), 'Scotland's schools', *Social Trends*, no. 10, pp. 52-60.

Withrington, D. (1974), 'The Scottish Universities Commission of 1826-1830', paper given at a meeting of the History of Scottish Education Society, Stirling University, March.

Wright, C. J. (1979), 'Academics and their aims: English and Scottish approaches to university education in the nineteenth century', *History of Education*, vol. 8, no. 2, pp. 91-7.

Young, A. L. (1967), 'Comprehensive education in Aberdeenshire', *Education in the North*, vol. 3, no. 3, pp. 57-61.

Young, A. (1971), 'Comprehensive reorganisation in Renfrewshire: a case study', unpublished M.Ed. thesis, Glasgow University.

Young, M. (1958), *The Rise of the Meritocracy*, London, Thames & Hudson.

Index

363